THE
INTERNATIONAL
APPETIZER
COOKBOOK

THE INTERNATIONAL APPETIZER COOKBOOK

BY SONIA UVEZIAN

◇

FAWCETT COLUMBINE • NEW YORK

To my husband David Kaiserman, who
shared equally in the task of writing this book.

A Fawcett Columbine Book
Published by Ballantine Books
Copyright © 1984 by Sonia Uvezian

Illustrations copyright © 1984 by Jeanne Fisher

Interior Design By Michaelis/Carpelis
Design Assoc. Inc.

All rights reserved under International and Pan-
American Copyright Conventions. Published in the
United States by Ballantine Books, a division of
Random House, Inc., New York, and simultaneously
in Canada by Random House of Canada Limited,
Toronto.

Library of Congress Catalog Card Number: 83-91179
ISBN: 0-449-90115-7

Manufactured in the United States of America
First Ballantine Books Edition: July 1984
10 9 8 7 6 5 4 3 2 1

CONTENTS

INTRODUCTION

It has long been a matter of general agreement that appetizers are fun to serve, a joy to behold, and a delight to taste. Agreement on the meaning of the word itself has not been so general. A distinction between appetizers and hors d'oeuvre has frequently been made in American culinary language. "Hors d'oeuvre," a French term, translates as "outside the work," or, in a gastronomic sense, "outside the meal." In France, hors d'oeuvre consist of a selection of piquant foods served hot or cold at table, while in America they have often been thought of as the finger foods that accompany cocktails. The word appetizer, however, has had a more inclusive meaning, embracing any beverage or savory food served before a meal.

Present-day styles of entertaining in America have progressed beyond the rather limited concept of hors d'oeuvre being strictly cocktail fare, with the old patterns giving way to more creative and informal ones where the food shares center stage alongside the drinks. With this evolution has come the interchangeability of the two terms, and nowadays both "appetizer" and "hors d'oeuvre" (along with other terms such as "starters") can readily be used to describe this vast family of premeal palate stimulators.

Appetizers have always played an important role in culinary history, having existed in considerable diversity during the great civilizations of antiquity. Some food historians postulate that they may have entered the cuisines of modern Europe from the East: from China into Russia and Scandinavia, then to France and central Europe; or perhaps they came by way of a more southerly route, through Persia to the eastern Mediterranean, Italy, and Spain. It is certain, however, that they enjoyed a golden age in prerevolutionary Russia. There the aristocracy partook of a lavish array of appetizers, called *zakuski* ("small bites"), set out on a table in a room separate from that where the actual meal was to be served. This custom survives in present-day Russia, though on a more proletarian scale. *Smörgåsbord*, with its impressive spread of appetizers, is the Swedish relative of the *zakuska* table. Elsewhere in Europe and Asia national cuisines proudly feature resplendent collections of appetizers, among them *mezzeh* in the Middle East, *antipasti* in Italy, *hors d'oeuvre variés* in France, *Vorspeisen* in Germany, *tapas* in Spain, and *zensai* in Japan.

Although appetizers are an institution in American social life, the custom of serving them has been imported from abroad. What with our melting pot of cultures, the selection available for entertaining in this country is incredibly wide-ranging and imaginative. Latin America, which has assimilated many of our cocktail appetizers, possesses its own rich heritage of traditional dishes that have been adapted to function superbly in a preprandial role. And a cosmopolitan panorama of appetizers is enjoyed in the Pacific Islands, as exemplified by the Hawaiian *pupu* tray.

Deprive a Russian of his zakuski, a Spaniard of his tapas, or a Middle Easterner of his mezzeh and he will bemoan the fact that a large measure of excitement has gone out of his ongoing love affair with food. Whatever the occasion in whatever corner of the globe, the savoring of appetizers can be among the greatest pleasures of eating and socializing.

The recipes in this book encompass a wide geographic diversity and are suitable for both casual and formal gatherings. Some require a little time and effort, but none is particularly difficult either to prepare or serve, and a great many are quite uncomplicated. Although numerous classics and old favorites are represented, you will not be disappointed if your taste leans more toward the unusual than the familiar. On the following pages you will find a collection that richly illustrates one glorious category of mankind's culinary ingenuity.

BEFORE YOU BEGIN

Appetizers can be divided into two main categories: those served cold and those served hot or warm. Cold appetizers are a more convenient choice since most can be made ahead and, once served, require little or no further attention. They range from simple, easily prepared, and readily available items such as cold shellfish accompanied with a flavored mayonnaise or other complementary sauce, hard-cooked eggs in various guises, and assorted cold cuts to rarer and more luxurious fare, for example Beluga caviar and pâté de foie gras from Strasbourg. When preparing cold appetizers, season them more liberally than you would hot ones because chilling tends to dull flavors. Present cold appetizers on chilled platters or on platters set over cracked ice.

Hot appetizers, although they may in some cases require more attention than cold ones, are always a welcome treat. Some can be completely cooked in advance and reheated just before serving, while all or part of the preparation of others must be done at the last moment, an inconvenience amply rewarded by the results. Unless you have someone assisting you in the kitchen, you should probably not attempt to offer more than two hot appetizers. Be sure to serve them piping hot (warn your guests when necessary), or warm if the recipe so specifies. Use heated platters or, when appropriate, such aids as electric serving trays, fondue pots, and chafing dishes. When entertaining outdoors, your barbecue or hibachi can function as both cooker and server for succulent, sizzling grilled hors d'oeuvre.

Appetizers should delight the eye and stimulate the palate. They should awaken, not satiate, the appetite; therefore emphasize salted or piquant foods rather than sweet ones, which have a cloying effect. In their usual role appetizers should be an introduction to a meal, not a small repast that is followed by a somewhat larger one. You can, however, make a whole meal out of appetizers (see page xi and chapter 21).

Your choice of appetizers will be determined by several factors, among them the occasion and its duration, the number of guests and their food preferences, and your budget. Some appetizers make ideal finger food; others are best suited for serving at table as a first course. Estimating the quantity of food per person will depend in part on the type of gathering, for instance whether you are offering an assortment of predinner hors d'oeuvre or are giving a full-fledged cocktail party.

Both cold and hot appetizers should provide contrasting flavors and textures. When planning your menu, try to achieve as much variety as possible. For a large get-together include at least one appetizer from each of the following categories: cheese, seafood, meat, vegetables, and fruit. Offer a balanced selection for a smaller group, but in a more limited quantity.

THE PRESENTATION OF APPETIZERS

Visual appeal contributes significantly to one's enjoyment of appetizers. Even the most unpretentious of them can be glamorized by the addition of colorful garnishes. In your efforts to present appetizers attractively, however, guard against overdecoration. Use edible garnishes and keep them simple. Sprigs of dark green parsley or watercress, bright red cherry tomatoes, shiny black or light green olives, and attractively cut vegetables such as radish roses and carrot curls are just some of the garnishes that can impart an ornamental touch. Elegant trays, stylish platters, compartmentalized dishes, and handsome chafing dishes all lend interest to appetizers.

For the presentation of hors d'oeuvre impaled on cocktail picks, use serving trays or a centerpiece into which the picks can be inserted at intervals. A pineapple, melon, or grapefruit half can be placed cut side down on a plate and surrounded with a garnish. One can also use a honeydew melon half cut side up and fill it with pitted black olives, inserting the pierced hors d'oeuvre around the edge. Another possibility is to stud the sides of a filled Edam or Gouda cheese (page 55) with pierced hors d'oeuvre and border it with crackers or slices of cocktail bread.

APPETIZERS AS A FIRST COURSE AT DINNER

Since appetizers set the stage for the courses that follow, it pays to give careful thought to their selection. They should complement and contrast with the rest of the meal, neither duplicating nor displacing it. Your choice will depend on the kind of dinner that is to come. Provide light hors d'oeuvre before a rich meal and a more substantial offering before a modest repast. For a menu featuring poultry, ham, or veal a fruit cocktail would be a refreshing opener, while a shellfish appetizer would make a fitting introduction to one highlighting roast beef or steak. A seafood entrée can be preceded by a cheese or vegetable appetizer. It is best not to serve meat or poultry before a main dish consisting of seafood, just as it is better not to incorporate meat or poultry among the appetizers if they are to play a leading role in the principal course. It is always interesting to plan an ethnic dinner, choosing foods, including hors d'oeuvre, from a particular cuisine. There is also excitement, however, in putting together a mix-and-match menu of dishes from around the world. What is more, innumerable ethnic appetizers can provide excellent preludes to American meals.

Many people prefer to offer appetizers along with cocktails before seating guests at the dinner table. This helps everyone to relax and gives the host or hostess time to make final preparations for the meal. In addition, the dinner will not be disrupted should some latecomers arrive during these preliminaries. Even when planning to serve hors d'oeuvre at table, a little something to munch on, such as nuts, olives, cheese straws, or pretzels, is still often expected to accompany the apéritif.

Since appetizers preceding a meal are meant to arouse the palate, not satisfy it, two or three should suffice. Even one well-chosen selection, served either at table or away from it, can ensure a memorable beginning and earn an ovation from your audience.

APPETIZERS FOR A COCKTAIL PARTY

Most Europeans, along with many other peoples of the world, consider hors d'oeuvre a prelude to a meal and tend to present them to guests seated at table. Many Americans, on the other hand, think of hors d'oeuvre as an accompaniment to drinks. Usually we offer an assortment in the living room or family room, or on the patio, as an enticement to thirst that simultaneously moderates the effects of alcohol. This mating of hors d'oeuvre with drinks has given rise to the typically American social institution known as the cocktail party and its offshoot, the cocktail hour (or the so-called happy hour, as it is known in bars and cocktail lounges).

There are basically two kinds of cocktail parties. The first, often planned with large groups in mind, is meant to last only two or three hours, with guests going on to dinner elsewhere. Since at this type of affair people usually remain standing throughout, you should offer finger foods, that is, small sturdy morsels that can be eaten with two fingers without a fork or plate and without their falling apart or dripping. To simplify serving, set out on tables around the room bowls of nibbles, such as nuts and olives, along with dips and raw vegetables or chips for scooping so that guests can help themselves. Have some appetizers such as canapés and miniature pastries passed on trays. You can augment your selections with a buffet table holding a variety of cheeses and thinly sliced cocktail breads as well as a pâté or something hot, such as tiny meatballs in sauce, served from a chafing dish with food picks alongside. Have plenty of cocktail napkins available, and be sure that there are ashtrays or other containers for discarded food picks.

The second kind of cocktail party, more suitable for smaller groups, is meant to last the whole evening; the food should therefore be substantial enough to substitute for a full meal. In addition to nibbles and dips, present a hearty spread of hot and cold appetizers arranged on a buffet table with small plates, forks, and napkins and invite guests to serve themselves at their own pace. Even a baked ham or roast turkey can make its appearance. Such an evening can draw to a close with coffee and, perhaps, cookies or little cakes.

For a discussion of some international appetizer buffets, please see page 401.

THE
INTERNATIONAL
APPETIZER
COOKBOOK

NUTS, SEEDS, AND CHIPS

With their delightful flavors and textures that complement so many wines and spirits, it is little wonder that nuts, seeds, and chips rank among the most widely appreciated of hors d'oeuvre. Homemade cocktail tidbits can be quickly and easily prepared and possess the further merit of being considerably more economical than practically any that are store-bought. Best of all, most of the snacks listed in this chapter are not only unusual but are unavailable commercially at any price, making them all the more appealing.

◇

MEDITERRANEAN FRIED ALMONDS

Very simple and very good.

Cover the bottom of a heavy skillet with olive oil and heat over moderate heat. Add whole blanched almonds and sauté, stirring constantly, until golden brown. Transfer the nuts to paper towels to drain. Sprinkle them with salt to taste, tossing them about to season them evenly. Serve warm or at room temperature.

VARIATION:

The almonds are also delicious sautéed in butter (preferably Clarified Butter, page 288) instead of olive oil.

ALMONDS WITH APRICOTS

This combination was for me a childhood passion representing the quintessence of gastronomic pleasure, one that I have not entirely overcome.

 1 cup Mediterranean Fried Almonds
   (page 1)
 ½ cup julienne-cut dried apricots

In a medium bowl toss the almonds with the apricots and serve. Makes 1½ cups.

ROMAN ALMONDS

1 egg white
2 cups shelled whole almonds, blanched or
   unblanched
2 teaspoons coarse salt or to taste

In a medium bowl beat the egg white until frothy. Add the almonds and the salt and stir until the almonds are thoroughly coated with the egg white and salt. Spread the coated nuts in a single layer on a buttered rimmed baking sheet. Bake in a preheated 325°F oven about 20 minutes or until the almonds are shiny, crisp, and golden. Allow to cool to room temperature before serving. Makes 2 cups.

VARIATIONS:

Substitute 2 tablespoons freshly grated imported Parmesan or Romano cheese for the coarse salt, or for a south-of-the-border flavor substitute 2 to 3 teaspoons Mexican seasoning.

SPANISH TOASTED HAZELNUTS

Spread shelled unblanched hazelnuts in a single layer on a rimmed baking sheet. Toast in a preheated 275°F oven about 25 minutes or until the nuts taste roasted and the skins come off easily. Place the nuts in a kitchen towel and rub to remove the skins. Season with salt to taste and serve warm or at room temperature.

MOORISH PINE NUTS

Although they are rarely encountered as an hors d'oeuvre on their own, pine nuts served in this manner are too good to be ignored. Sautéing enhances their flavor, which is somewhat bland but far from boring.

Follow the recipe for Mediterranean Fried Almonds (page 1), substituting pine nuts for the almonds.

INDIAN CASHEWS

These take only minutes to make and are delicious.

1 teaspoon curry powder
¾ teaspoon cumin
1 teaspoon salt or to taste
3 tablespoons Clarified Butter (page 288)
2 cups raw cashew nuts (available at natural food stores)

In a small bowl combine the curry powder, cumin, and salt. Set aside. In a heavy skillet melt the Clarified Butter over moderate heat. Add the nuts and sauté, stirring constantly, until they are a pale gold. Sprinkle evenly with the seasonings and cook, stirring, until the nuts are lightly browned. Transfer them to paper towels to drain. Serve warm or at room temperature. Makes 2 cups.

ROQUEFORT WALNUTS OR PECANS

Unusual enough to be a nice surprise.

Spread 1½ cups walnut or pecan halves in a single layer on a rimmed baking sheet. Toast them in a preheated 350°F oven, stirring occasionally, 10 to 15 minutes or until very lightly browned. Let cool. Spread a thick layer of Roquefort Cheese Spread (page 27) on the flat sides of half the nuts. Top with the remaining nuts, flat sides down, pressing together gently but firmly. Cover and chill before serving. Makes about 36.

CANTONESE FRIED WALNUTS

1½ cups walnut halves
2 cups boiling water
½ cup sugar
1 cup peanut oil or flavorless vegetable oil

Place the walnuts in a bowl, pour the boiling water over them, and set aside about 3 minutes. Drain the walnuts thoroughly and transfer them to a rimmed baking sheet. Sprinkle with the sugar, tossing the nuts about to coat them evenly. Spread them in a single layer and let stand overnight to dry.

In a wok or skillet heat the oil over moderate heat until very hot. Add the walnuts in small batches and fry until lightly browned, watching closely to prevent burning. With a slotted spoon transfer them to paper towels to drain and cool. Makes 1½ cups.

VARIATION:

Substitute raw cashew nuts (available at natural food stores) for the walnuts.

SALTED MIXED NUTS

1⅓ cups macadamia nuts
1⅓ cups shelled and skinned raw peanuts
    (available at natural food stores)
1⅓ cups pecan halves
¼ cup unsalted butter, melted
1 tablespoon coarse salt or to taste

In a medium bowl toss the nuts with the melted butter. Spread them in a single layer on a rimmed baking sheet and toast in a preheated 325°F oven, stirring occasionally, about 25 minutes or until they are golden. Sprinkle the nuts with the salt, tossing them about to season them evenly. Serve warm or at room temperature. Makes 4 cups.

TOASTED NUTS TERIYAKI

This hors d'oeuvre seems to bridge the gulf between Eastern and Western tastes.

　2 cups walnut halves or unsalted mixed
　　nuts *
　2 tablespoons butter
　2 teaspoons imported soy sauce
　1½ teaspoons freshly squeezed and strained
　　lemon juice
　1 small garlic clove, crushed and finely
　　chopped, or ¼ teaspoon garlic powder
　½ teaspoon ginger
　¼ teaspoon salt or to taste

Spread the nuts in a single layer on a rimmed baking sheet. Toast them in a pre-heated 350°F oven 8 minutes. In a small skillet melt the butter over moderately high heat. Stir in the remaining ingredients. Spoon evenly over the nuts and stir to coat them thoroughly with the mixture. Return the nuts to the oven and toast them, stirring twice, about 7 minutes or until crisp and lightly browned. Serve warm or at room temperature. Makes 2 cups.

*Use pecan or walnut halves, shelled and skinned Brazil nuts and hazelnuts, and shelled unblanched almonds.

BOMBAY COCKTAIL MIX

Wildly differing flavors and textures blend in fascinating fashion in this spicy Indian mix.

　¼ cup lentils
　¼ cup split peas
　¼ cup long-grain white rice
　3 cups water
　2 tablespoons peanut oil or corn oil
　2 tablespoons sesame seed
　1 teaspoon cumin
　1 teaspoon coriander
　¼ teaspoon turmeric
　½ cup roasted salted peanuts
　½ cup roasted salted cashew nuts
　⅓ cup seedless dark raisins
　¼ teaspoon cloves
　⅛ teaspoon cayenne pepper or to taste
　1 teaspoon salt or to taste
　　Tortilla chips or potato chips

Rinse the lentils, peas, and rice in a sieve under cold running water. Place them in a saucepan and add the 3 cups water. Bring to a boil and boil 1 minute. Remove from the heat, cover, and let stand 10 minutes. Drain and rinse with cold water. Spread on paper towels and pat dry.

In a large, heavy skillet heat the oil over

moderate heat. Add the lentils, peas, rice, sesame seed, cumin, coriander, and turmeric. Cook, stirring constantly, about 15 minutes or until the ingredients are toasted. Remove from the heat and add the nuts, raisins, cloves, cayenne pepper, and salt. Toss to mix. Transfer to a serving bowl and surround with the chips for scooping up the mixture. Makes about 2 cups.

TOASTED PUMPKIN SEEDS

What to do with the seeds from your Hallowe'en pumpkin.

2 cups pumpkin seeds (from a medium-sized pumpkin)
1½ teaspoons salt or to taste

Place the pumpkin seeds in a colander and rinse thoroughly under cold running water, removing the fibers from the seeds. Drain well and blot the excess water with paper towels. Spread the seeds in a single layer on a rimmed baking sheet. Sprinkle with the salt, tossing the seeds about to season them evenly. Toast in a preheated 300°F oven, stirring frequently, about 25 minutes or until golden and crisp. Serve at room temperature. To eat, gently crack a seed open between your teeth and eat the center portion, discarding the shell. Makes 2 cups.

VARIATION:

Moisten the seeds with 2 tablespoons melted butter before spreading them on the baking sheet. Season them with coarse salt, or regular salt as above.

PHILIPPINE SWEET POTATO CHIPS

A tempting alternative to the usual potato chips.

3 long, narrow sweet potatoes
Peanut oil or corn oil for deep-frying
Confectioners' sugar or salt

With a vegetable parer peel the sweet potatoes, then cut them crosswise into paper-thin slices. Soak the slices in cold water 20 minutes. Drain and dry thoroughly with paper towels.

In a deep-fryer or heavy saucepan heat 3 inches oil to 375°F. Put the potato slices, one third at a time, in a frying basket and slowly immerse them into the hot oil. Fry 2 to 3 minutes, turning the slices once or twice until golden on both sides. Drain on paper towels.

Serve warm or at room temperature, sprinkled lightly with confectioners' sugar in the Philippine manner or with salt, Western style. Makes 6 servings.

HOMEMADE POTATO CHIPS

Follow the recipe for Philippine Sweet Potato Chips (page 6), substituting Idaho potatoes for the sweet potatoes. Sprinkle the potato chips with salt rather than with confectioners' sugar. Makes 6 servings.

HOMEMADE TORTILLA CHIPS

See page 298.

PUERTO RICAN PLANTAIN CHIPS

Serve this version of a Latin American favorite with rum punch and watch it disappear.

1 large green plantain (about 1 pound)
Flavorless vegetable oil for deep-frying
Salt to taste

Peel the plantain and slice it crosswise as thinly as possible. Drop into a bowl of ice water and let stand 30 minutes. Drain and dry with paper towels.

In a deep-fryer or large, heavy saucepan heat 2 inches oil to 375°F. Add the plantain slices, a dozen or so at a time, and fry about 3 minutes, turning them with a slotted spoon until they are golden brown on both sides. Transfer them to paper towels to drain. Sprinkle with the salt and serve warm or at room temperature. Makes about 2 cups.

Note: Plantain is a member of the banana family, but larger and less sweet. It must be cooked before eating.

CARIBBEAN BANANA CHIPS

Follow the recipe for Puerto Rican Plantain Chips (above), substituting 1 pound green bananas for the plantain. Makes about 2 cups.

HAWAIIAN COCONUT CHIPS

No collection of chip recipes would be complete without this one.

1 medium coconut
½ teaspoon salt

Choose a coconut without any cracks that is full of liquid. With an ice pick or a skewer puncture the eyes of the coconut. Drain the liquid and reserve it for another use. Bake the coconut in a preheated 375°F oven 15 minutes. Lightly tap the entire surface of the coconut shell with a hammer, then crack the shell with a sharp blow of the hammer. Remove the meat in large pieces from the shell, prying it out carefully with the point of a small, strong knife. Peel the brown outer skin of the coconut meat with a vegetable parer. Using a small, sharp knife, slice the meat into paper-thin chips about 2 inches long. Spread the chips in a single layer on a rimmed baking sheet and sprinkle evenly with the salt. Toast in a preheated 325°F oven, stirring occasionally, about 15 minutes or until the chips are golden and crisp. Serve warm or at room temperature. Makes about 2½ cups.

VARIATIONS:

Toss the coconut chips with melted unsalted butter before spreading them on the sheet.

Instead of plain salt, use a mixture of ½ teaspoon each salt and ginger.

CRÊPE CHIPS

An unusual and innovative use of crêpes.

Prepare ¼ recipe Crêpes (page 310), stirring 2 teaspoons each minced fresh chives and parsley into the crêpe batter, if desired. Cut each crêpe into quarters. Cut each quarter into 3 equal wedges. In a deep-fryer or large, heavy saucepan heat 2 inches flavorless vegetable oil to 375°F. Add the crêpe wedges in batches and fry, turning them with a slotted spoon until they are golden brown and crisp. Transfer them to paper towels to drain. Serve with Crab Fondue (page 24) or other light dips. Makes about 72.

VARIATION:

Brush the crêpes with melted butter and sprinkle them evenly with freshly grated imported Parmesan cheese. Cut into wedges as above. Arrange the wedges, cheese sides up, on ungreased baking sheets. Bake in a preheated 325°F oven 6 to 8 minutes or until crisp. Serve as above.

OLIVES

Olives are among the first fruits to have been cultivated by man. The semitropical evergreen tree that bears this fruit is native to the eastern Mediterranean, where it has been known for well over four millennia. Mature trees, which may range from 10 to 40 feet in height, can attain great age; some specimens are believed to be at least a thousand years old.

Even when fully tree-ripened so that they have turned black, olives are extremely bitter-tasting unless subjected to a curing process. How that process was discovered is lost in the mists of antiquity, but even before the time of the Romans the nibbling of palate-pleasing green and ripe olives had become a popular pastime and the fruit itself a standby of daily existence, particularly as a source of oil. Today in many parts of the world the extensive use of olive oil for cooking, as well as for cosmetic purposes as a lubricant and as an ingredient in soap, is proof of its continuing importance, while the olive itself is justly celebrated as a favorite food.

Olives are now grown not only throughout the Mediterranean area but in a number of other warm-weather regions of the globe. They were introduced into Mexico and California by Jesuit missionaries in the seventeenth century. Olives are also grown in Arizona and New Mexico, while the California olive industry has become one of world's largest. Another great producer of olives is Spain, in the area around the city of Seville. Some 60% of the olives exported from Spain are sent to the United States; they and the California crop account for the vast majority of all the olives found in American markets.

Olives are available in various shapes and colors, from small black ones that seem to be mostly pit to pulpy, purplish giants the size of walnuts. Methods of pickling are diverse, ranging from simply storing the olives in water with the addition of a little olive oil and vinegar to slitting them so they absorb flavors more readily and covering them with a marinade containing a variety of seasonings, including herbs, spices, garlic, citrus rind and juice, and wine.

The olives found in most markets are generally green, green ripe, or black. Green olives, which are firm and unripe, come almost entirely from Spain, where they are picked early to avoid damage from the dacus fly, which poses a serious threat to Mediterranean olives. After curing, the olives are pickled in a lactic acid fermentation to give them a tart taste. You will find them packed in jars, covered with a salt brine. The term "green ripe" refers to partially ripe California olives that are protected from the air while being cured. They can also be cured while exposed to the air and turn the same black color as tree-ripened olives; such olives are called "ripe." California ripe or green ripe olives are preserved by canning and are not pickled, a process that gives them a milder taste than the tree-ripened Greek and Sicilian olives which are found in delicatessens or specialty food markets. Often these stores also carry Sicilian green olives (somewhat similar to Spanish olives but prepared with vinegar and spices) and Italian and French dried ripe olives. Use the Greek, Italian, or French types in Mediterranean recipes calling for olives.

When buying olives, take advantage of the wide assortment offered in sizes, colors, flavorings, seasoned brines and marinades, and, if pitted, in stuffings such as pimentos, anchovies, onions, almonds, and lemon rind. It is no wonder that olives, savored by rich and poor alike through the ages, have been so consistently and enthusiastically prized.

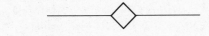

STUFFED GREEN OLIVES

Fill the cavities of large, pitted green olives with any one of the following mixtures, piping it through a pastry bag fitted with a decorative tip or using either a ¼-teaspoon measuring spoon or a small knife. Serve the stuffed olives chilled.

FILLINGS FOR GREEN OLIVES

Shrimp Paste (page 29)
Portuguese Tuna Pâté (page 30)
Curried Chicken and Almond Filling (page 43)
Liverwurst Pâté with Bacon (page 34)
Cream Cheese and Bacon Filling (page 37)
Gorgonzola Cheese and Prosciutto Spread (page 27)
Ham Filling (page 44)
Prosciutto Filling (page 44)

STUFFED BLACK OLIVES

Stuff large, pitted black olives (preferably oil-cured) in one of the following ways and serve them chilled.

Fill the cavities of the olives with Chicken Liver Pâté (page 31), omitting the parsley sprigs. Close the opening of each stuffed olive with a shelled unsalted pistachio nut.

Fill the cavities of the olives with Serbian Herb Cheese Spread (page 28), Herb Cheese (page 51), or Herb Yogurt Cheese (page 57).

Fill the cavities of the olives with Taramosalata (page 22), Shrimp Paste (page 29), Curried Crabmeat Filling (page 39), Smoked Salmon Spread (page 30), Anchovy and Cream Cheese Filling (page 42), or Portuguese Tuna Pâté (page 30).

MEXICAN ANCHOVY-STUFFED OLIVES:

Stuff the olives with minced anchovy fillets and marinate them for several hours in a mixture of Sauce Vinaigrette (page 387) and chopped pimento. About 30 minutes before serving, stir in minced parsley to taste.

ITALIAN BLACK OLIVES WITH ANCHOVIES

Once you team black olives with anchovies, they'll go steady in your kitchen.

1 pound Italian or Greek black olives
⅔ cup olive oil
1 medium onion, finely chopped
1 medium garlic clove, finely chopped
4 anchovy fillets, finely chopped
½ teaspoon crushed dried oregano or to taste
   Lemon wedges
   Parsley sprigs

If possible, use an olive pitter to remove the pits from the olives. Place the olives in a serving bowl and set aside. In a small, heavy saucepan combine the oil, onion, garlic, and anchovy fillets. Sprinkle with the oregano, cover, and cook over medium-low heat, stirring occasionally, until the onion is soft. Force the mixture through a fine sieve over the olives. Toss gently but thoroughly and let the olives stand at room temperature 2 hours. Garnish with the lemon wedges and parsley sprigs and serve with cocktail picks. Makes about 1 pound.

OLIVE, CHEESE, AND NUT HORS D'OEUVRE

A surprise awaits in each bite.
Pat 24 small, pitted green or black olives dry with paper towels. Coat the olives with Roquefort Cheese Spread (page 27) and roll them in 1 cup finely chopped toasted pecans. Arrange the coated olives on a platter, cover, and chill 1 hour before serving. Makes 24.

WINE-MARINATED SPANISH OLIVES

2 jars (about 7 ounces each) large, pitted green Spanish olives
   Shredded fresh lemon rind
2 small red chili peppers
¼ teaspoon crushed dried thyme
1 cup water
1 cup dry Sherry or dry white wine
1 tablespoon olive oil

Drain the olives and fill the cavities with the shredded lemon rind. Combine the stuffed olives and chili peppers in a large, wide-mouthed glass jar with a tight-fitting lid. Sprinkle evenly with the thyme. Combine the water and Sherry or white wine and pour over the ingredients in the jar. Sprinkle the olive oil over the top. Cover tightly and let the olives marinate in the refrigerator, stirring occasionally, for 2 days. Drain well, discarding the chili peppers. Serve the olives in a shallow bowl, speared with cocktail picks. Makes about 1 pound.

MARINATED GREEK OLIVES

1 jar (11 ounces) black, purple, or brown
  Greek olives, undrained
4 medium garlic cloves, lightly crushed
2 dried hot red peppers, broken
5 whole cloves
1 cup olive oil
  Rind and juice of 1 large orange
3 tablespoons wine vinegar
  Thin orange twists

Combine all the ingredients except the orange twists in a large, wide-mouthed glass jar with a tight-fitting lid. Cover tightly and refrigerate at least 4 days, shaking and inverting the jar several times daily. Drain well, discarding the garlic, peppers, cloves, and orange rind. Transfer the olives to a shallow serving bowl and garnish them with the orange twists. Set out a separate small container of cocktail picks for spearing the olives. Makes about ¾ pound.

DIPS, SPREADS AND FILLINGS

No repertoire of appetizers would be complete without a choice selection of dips and spreads which, along with nuts, far surpass all other hors d'oeuvre in popularity. A dip has the consistency of a thick sauce, while a spread is somewhat denser. The two are frequently interchangeable; thus the same mixture that can be scooped up with a raw vegetable stick can often be spread on a cracker as well. A general rule to remember when preparing either is that a dip should be soft enough not to cause the dipping object to break yet be thick enough not to drip, while a spread should be soft enough for bread or crackers to remain intact yet not be too thin.

Dips and spreads hold an important place in many of the world's cuisines. They are easy enough for family snacking while still being special enough for company. Most can be prepared ahead and, once served, require no further attention. Being self-help items, they offer a relaxed way to entertain.

Given the wealth of dips and spreads from which to choose, there is no reason to remain in an uninspired rut of clam and onion soup dips. Nor is there any need to limit yourself to the ubiquitous store-bought potato chips or crackers for dipping or spreading. An interesting variety of alternatives is suggested on the following pages.

I have also included in this chapter a selection of all-purpose savory fillings that are called for in recipes throughout this book. For additional fillings that are used in conjunction with particular recipes, please consult the Index.

◇

DIPS

SWISS CHEESE FONDUE

Famous the world over.

1 garlic clove, cut in half
1½ cups dry white wine such as Swiss
   Neuchâtel or Fendant
1 pound imported Swiss Emmenthaler
   cheese, or ½ pound each Emmenthaler
   and imported Swiss Gruyère cheese,
   coarsely grated
2 teaspoons cornstarch
2 tablespoons kirsch
   Freshly grated nutmeg to taste
   Salt and freshly ground pepper to taste
1 large loaf French or Italian bread with
   the crust left on, cut into 1-inch cubes

Rub the bottom and sides of a fondue pot or chafing dish with the garlic. Pour in the wine and bring to a boil over moderate heat. Reduce the heat to low and add the cheese, a handful at a time, stirring constantly with a wooden fork or spoon until the cheese is melted. Blend the cornstarch with the kirsch and stir into the fondue until the mixture bubbles. Season with the nutmeg, salt, and pepper.

To serve, place the fondue over an alcohol or gas table burner, regulating the heat so that the fondue barely simmers. Serve with a basketful of the bread cubes. Invite each diner to spear a cube of bread on a fondue fork, swirl it about in the fondue until it is thoroughly coated, and then eat it at once. Makes 6 servings.

VARIATIONS:

FONDUE WITH MUSHROOMS

Sauté 6 ounces mushrooms, chopped, and ¼ cup minced onion in butter until lightly browned. Stir into the fondue just before serving.

FONDUE WITH HAM

Sauté 4 slices cooked ham, diced, in butter. Stir into the fondue just before serving. Or cut cooked ham into 1-inch cubes and use them for dunking in the fondue instead of the bread.

FONDUE WITH CHAMPAGNE

Substitute dry Champagne for the wine.

FONDUE WITH TRUFFLES

Add 2 to 4 ounces canned white truffles, very thinly sliced, to the fondue just before serving.

CHILE CON QUESO
Mexican Cheese and Green Chili Dip

A treat on a cold winter day, and just as appropriate for an outdoor barbecue.

    2 tablespoons butter
    2 tablespoons flour
    1 cup half-and-half
    2 large tomatoes, peeled, seeded, and
        coarsely chopped
    1 large garlic clove, finely chopped
    ½ teaspoon salt
    1 can (4 ounces) peeled green chilies,
        drained, seeded, and finely chopped
    2 cups (½ pound) freshly grated Monterey
        Jack cheese or Muenster cheese

In a small, heavy saucepan melt the butter over moderate heat. Add the flour and mix well. Gradually add the half-and-half, whisking constantly until the sauce comes to a boil, thickens, and is smooth. Reduce the heat to low and simmer 2 minutes. Remove from the heat and set aside.

In a large, heavy skillet combine the tomatoes, garlic, and salt. Cook, uncovered, over medium-high heat, stirring frequently, until the tomato juice is evaporated and the mixture is very much thickened. Reduce the heat to low and stir in the cream sauce and chilies. Gradually add the grated cheese, stirring until melted.

Ladle the *chile con queso* into a fondue pot or chafing dish and serve immediately, accompanied with tortilla chips. Makes about 2½ cups.

BLUE CHEESE DIP

See page 28.

MUSHROOM DIP

If pressed for a favorite yogurt-based dip, I might single out this one.

    1 tablespoon butter
    ¼ pound mushrooms, finely chopped
    4 scallions, finely chopped, including 2
       inches of the green tops
    3 ounces cream cheese or Neufchâtel
       cheese, at room temperature
    ½ cup unflavored yogurt
    1 small garlic clove, crushed
       Salt to taste
    1½ tablespoons finely chopped fresh dill

In a heavy skillet melt the butter over moderate heat. Add the mushrooms and scallions and sauté until golden brown, stirring frequently. Remove from the heat and let cool to room temperature.

In a bowl mash the cream cheese with a fork. Add the yogurt and garlic and blend until smooth. Add the sautéed mushrooms and scallions, salt, and 1 tablespoon of the dill. Mix thoroughly. Taste and adjust the seasoning, cover, and chill. Garnish with the remaining ½ tablespoon dill. Serve with *lavash* (Armenian cracker bread), lightly toasted pita bread, or crackers. Makes about 1½ cups.

EGGPLANT CAVIAR

Justifiably esteemed not only in its native Caucasus but throughout much of the Soviet Union, this appetizer, also known as "Poor Man's Caviar," is coveted at all levels of society.

    1 large eggplant (about 2 pounds)
    6 tablespoons olive oil
    1 large onion, finely chopped
    ½ cup finely chopped green pepper
    1 medium garlic clove, finely chopped
    2 medium tomatoes, peeled, seeded, and
       finely chopped
       Salt and freshly ground pepper to taste
    2 tablespoons freshly squeezed and
       strained lemon juice or to taste

Cut the stem and green top from the eggplant and discard. Place the eggplant on a baking sheet and bake in a preheated 425°F oven about 1 hour, turning occasionally, until the flesh is very soft and juicy and the skin charred.

Meanwhile, in a small skillet heat 4 tablespoons of the oil over moderate heat. Add the onion and sauté until soft but not browned, stirring frequently. Add the green pepper and garlic and cook, stirring, 5 minutes. Remove from the heat and set aside.

When the eggplant is cool enough to handle, gently squeeze it to remove the bitter juices. Peel off the skin, remove the badly charred spots, and slit the eggplant open. Scoop out the seeds and discard.

Place the eggplant pulp in a bowl and mash it. Stir in the contents of the skillet, the tomatoes, and the salt and pepper and mix well. Place the remaining 2 tablespoons oil in the skillet and heat over moderate heat. Add the eggplant mixture and bring to a boil, stirring constantly, then reduce the heat, cover, and simmer 45 minutes. Uncover and cook 30 minutes longer, stirring from time to time, until all the moisture in the pan has evaporated and the mixture has thickened. Remove from the heat and stir in the lemon juice. Taste and adjust the seasoning. Pour into a serving bowl, cover, and chill. Serve with *lavash* (Armenian cracker bread), toasted pita bread, or sesame seed crackers. Makes about 3 cups.

BABA GHANNOUJ
Eggplant Dip

Deservedly one of the most popular Middle Eastern dips, this rich, earthy cream tastes best when the eggplant has been broiled over an open fire.

1 eggplant (1 to 1½ pounds)
¼ cup freshly squeezed and strained lemon juice
¼ cup tahini (sesame seed paste, available at Middle Eastern groceries and specialty shops)
1 medium garlic clove, crushed
1 teaspoon salt or to taste
Pomegranate seeds
1 tablespoon chopped parsley

Cut the stem and green top from the eggplant and discard. Using a long-handled fork, prick the skin of the eggplant in several places, then insert the fork tines into it and broil over charcoal or a gas flame, turning it frequently until the flesh is very soft and the skin charred. (The eggplant may instead be broiled in an electric oven. Place it on a baking sheet and broil 4 inches from the heat about 25 minutes, turning it to char evenly on all sides.) It is important that the eggplant be thoroughly cooked inside; otherwise it will have a bitter taste, rendering the dish inedible. When the eggplant is cool enough to handle, gently squeeze it to remove the bitter juices. Peel off the skin, remove the badly charred spots, and slit the eggplant open. Scoop out the seeds and discard.

Place the eggplant flesh, lemon juice, *tahini*, garlic, and salt in the container of an electric blender. Cover and blend until smooth and creamy. (Alternatively, place the eggplant flesh in a bowl and mash it thoroughly with a fork. Gradually beat in the lemon juice, tahini, garlic, and salt until the mixture is smooth and creamy.) Taste and adjust the seasoning. Transfer the dip to a serving dish, cover, and chill. Just before serving, garnish the top with the pomegranate seeds and parsley. Accompany with warmed pita bread. Makes about 2 cups.

HUMMUS BI TAHINI
Chickpea Dip

Undoubtedly the best known of all Middle Eastern dips, and certainly among the best liked.

  1 can (15 ounces) chickpeas
¼ cup freshly squeezed and strained lemon
      juice or to taste
      Up to 3 tablespoons chickpea liquid from
      the can or cold water
¼ cup tahini (sesame seed paste, available
      at Middle Eastern groceries and specialty
      shops)
  1 medium garlic clove, crushed
¾ teaspoon salt or to taste
      Paprika

Drain the chickpeas, reserving 3 tablespoons of the liquid from the can unless you are using cold water. Remove the transparent shells from the chickpeas, if desired. Put the lemon juice, chickpea liquid or water, tahini, garlic, salt, and chickpeas in the container of an electric blender. Cover and blend until smooth and creamy. (Alternatively, force the chickpeas through a sieve or food mill or pound them in a mortar. Add the crushed garlic and mash together until well mixed. Gradually beat in the lemon juice, chickpea liquid or water, tahini, and salt until the mixture is smooth and creamy.) Taste and adjust the seasoning. Just before serving, sprinkle lightly with the paprika. Accompany with warmed pita bread. Makes about 1½ cups.

Note: If upon opening the can or jar of tahini you find that the paste has separated with the oil having risen to the top, transfer the entire contents to the container of an electric blender and whirl until it is recombined. Then measure the amount called for in the recipe.

VARIATION:

Add ¼ teaspoon cumin or to taste with the garlic.

MEXICAN-STYLE BEAN DIP

Relatively inexpensive ingredients unite to produce a decidedly rustic and flavorful dip.

¼ cup butter
1 medium-sized yellow onion
1 medium garlic clove, crushed and finely chopped
2 cups cooked pinto or kidney beans, mashed
1 cup (¼ pound) freshly grated Monterey Jack or Cheddar cheese
Salt and cayenne pepper to taste

In a medium-sized, heavy skillet melt the butter over moderate heat. Add the onion and garlic and sauté until golden brown, stirring frequently. Add the beans, reduce the heat to low, and cook, stirring, until heated. Add the cheese, salt, and cayenne pepper and cook, stirring, until the cheese is melted. Transfer to a fondue pot or chafing dish. Serve hot with tortilla chips. Makes about 2 cups.

GUACAMOLE

A standard Mexican dish that has been enthusiastically adopted by Americans.

2 large, ripe avocados
2 tablespoons freshly squeezed and strained lemon or lime juice
2 tablespoons very finely chopped mild white onion
1 small garlic clove, crushed to a smooth purée
1 teaspoon chili powder or to taste
Dash Tabasco sauce
1 teaspoon salt or to taste
2 teaspoons olive oil (optional)
1 large tomato, peeled, seeded, and finely chopped

Halve the avocado lengthwise, remove the pit, and with a large spoon scoop out the flesh into a mixing bowl. Mash the avocado flesh with a fork. Add the lemon or lime juice, onion, garlic, chili powder, Tabasco sauce, salt, and olive oil (if used) and blend well. Fold in the tomato gently but thoroughly. Taste and adjust the seasoning. Transfer the guacamole to an attractive bowl and serve at once with tortilla chips, or cover the bowl tightly with plastic wrap and refrigerate until ready to use. Makes about 2½ cups.

VARIATION:

Omit the lemon or lime juice, garlic, chili powder, Tabasco sauce, and olive oil. Chop the tomato into coarse pieces. Put the onion, 4 large sprigs fresh coriander (leaves only), 1 or 2 fresh green *serrano* chilies, seeded and finely chopped, and the salt in a mortar and pound them to a thick paste. Transfer the paste to a bowl. Add the avocado flesh and mash it coarsely with a fork, mixing it into the paste. When the ingredients are thoroughly blended, fold in the tomato. Taste and adjust the seasoning. Serve at once with tortilla chips.

Note: Serrano chilies are small (about 1½ inches long), tapering, smooth-skinned, and medium green in color. Although they are hot they possess a distinctive flavor. Remove the seeds and veins carefully to avoid being burned by the volatile oils. Do not touch your face, wear rubber gloves if possible, and wash your hands immediately afterward. Serrano chilies are very commonly used in Mexican cooking and are found both fresh and canned in Latin American groceries. If fresh serranos are unavailable, canned ones may be substituted. If a milder taste is desired, green chilies may be used although their flavor is quite different.

AVOCADO DIP WITH BACON

Prepare Guacamole (page 21), omitting the olive oil and adding 4 slices bacon, cooked crisp and crumbled, with the tomato. Sprinkle the dip with 1 hard-cooked egg, sieved, and serve with tortilla chips.

AVOCADO DIP WITH CAVIAR

There is potential romance between avocado and caviar.

  1 large, ripe avocado
  ¼ cup sour cream
  2 tablespoons freshly squeezed and
    strained lime or lemon juice
  1 teaspoon grated mild white onion
    (optional)
  Salt to taste
  2 tablespoons red or black caviar

Halve the avocado lengthwise, remove the pit, and with a large spoon scoop out the flesh into a mixing bowl. Mash with a fork to a smooth purée. Add the sour cream, lime or lemon juice, onion (if used), and salt. Mix until thoroughly blended. Taste and adjust the seasoning. Transfer to a serv-

ing bowl, cover, and chill. With the back of a spoon, make a cavity in the center of the dip. Fill the hollow with the caviar. Serve with thin slices of toast or crackers. Makes about 1½ cups.

TARAMOSALATA
Salted Fish Roe Dip

A Greek classic whose fame has traveled far beyond the Balkans.

  3 slices white bread, trimmed of crusts
  ¼ cup tarama* or red caviar
  2 tablespoons freshly squeezed and
    strained lemon juice or to taste
  2 tablespoons grated mild onion
  ⅓ to ½ cup olive oil

Dip the bread in water and squeeze dry. Place it and the tarama or red caviar in the container of an electric blender and blend until smooth. With the motor running, add the lemon juice and onion; pour in olive oil in a slow, steady stream, using enough to make a rich, smooth texture. (Alternatively, dip the bread in water and squeeze dry. Place it in a shallow bowl. Add the tarama or red caviar, a little at a time, mashing and mixing it with a spoon. Beat in the lemon

*Salted fish roe (gray mullet, carp, or cod), available at Middle Eastern groceries and specialty food shops.

juice, onion, and enough oil to achieve a thick, creamy mixture.) Taste and adjust the seasoning. Transfer to a serving bowl, cover, and chill. Serve with thin toast or crackers. Makes about 1 cup.

NORWEGIAN RED CAVIAR DIP

Fancy enough for company, but easy on the cook.

6 ounces cream cheese, at room
 temperature
2 to 3 tablespoons sour cream
2 tablespoons finely chopped·chives or
 scallions (includes 2 inches of the green
 tops of the scallions), or 1 tablespoon
 each chives and scallions
1 jar (4 ounces) salmon roe caviar

In a medium bowl beat together the cream cheese, sour cream, and chives and/or scallions until well blended and fluffy. Fold in the caviar until thoroughly mixed. Transfer to a serving bowl, cover, and chill. Serve with crackers, Melba toast, or crisp raw vegetables. Makes about 1½ cups.

VARIATION:

SOUR CREAM AND RED CAVIAR DIP
 Combine 1 cup sour cream, the caviar, and 2 teaspoons grated mild white onion. Mix well, cover, and chill. Serve as above. Makes about 1½ cups.

LOBSTER DIP

For an attractive presentation, pile this dip into an empty lobster shell or tail.

1 ounce Roquefort or other blue cheese
8 ounces cream cheese or Neufchâtel
 cheese, at room temperature
½ cup sour cream or unflavored yogurt
1 tablespoon freshly squeezed and strained
 lemon juice
2 tablespoons finely chopped scallions,
 including 2 inches of the green tops
1 tiny garlic clove, crushed and finely
 chopped
1 cup finely diced cooked lobster meat
 Finely chopped parsley or chives

In a medium bowl mash the Roquefort or other blue cheese with a fork. Add the cream cheese and beat until well blended and smooth. Add the sour cream or yogurt, lemon juice, scallions, and garlic and mix thoroughly. Stir in the lobster meat. Taste and adjust the seasoning. Transfer to a serving bowl, cover, and chill. Sprinkle with the parsley or chives and serve with raw vegetables, crackers, or potato chips. Makes about 2 cups.

CRAB FONDUE

Everything a dip lover could ask for.

  2 tablespoons butter
  ¼ cup finely chopped onion or scallions
     (include 2 inches of the green tops of
     the scallions)
  2 tablespoons all-purpose flour
  1¼ cups half-and-half
  1 tablespoon dry Sherry
  1 cup (¼ pound) grated Gruyère cheese
     Salt and cayenne pepper to taste
  ½ pound cooked crabmeat, flaked
     Paprika

In a heavy saucepan melt the butter over moderate heat. Add the onion and sauté until soft but not browned, stirring frequently. Add the flour and cook, stirring constantly, 2 to 3 minutes. Gradually add the half-and-half and cook, stirring, until the mixture is thickened and smooth. Reduce the heat to low. Add the Sherry, cheese, salt, and cayenne pepper and cook, stirring, until the cheese is melted. Stir in the crabmeat.

Transfer the dip to a fondue pot over heat. Adjust the heat so that the mixture remains hot but does not boil. Sprinkle with the paprika. Serve with French bread cubes or Crêpe Chips (page 8) and crudités. Makes about 2 cups.

CLAM AND CREAM CHEESE DIP

See page 41.

SMOKED SALMON AND AVOCADO DIP

An innovative blend.

  ½ pound smoked salmon, shredded
  3 ounces cream cheese, at room
     temperature
  ⅓ cup mashed ripe avocado
  2 tablespoons heavy cream or as needed
  1 tablespoon freshly squeezed and strained
     lemon juice
  ¼ teaspoon crushed drained green
     peppercorns
     Salt and freshly ground pepper to taste
     Whole green peppercorns

Place the salmon and cream cheese in the container of an electric blender and blend until smooth. Transfer to a bowl. Add the avocado, heavy cream, lemon juice, crushed peppercorns, salt, and pepper and mix well. Taste and adjust the seasoning. Transfer to a serving bowl, cover, and chill. Garnish with the whole peppercorns. Serve with slices of apple and pear and crackers. Makes about 1½ cups.

SALMON REMOULADE DIP

Once tasted, this may well become a favorite.

    1 cup sour cream
    1 medium garlic clove, crushed to a
      smooth purée
    ¼ teaspoon anchovy paste
    1 teaspoon Dijon-style mustard
    1½ teaspoons finely chopped fresh tarragon
      or ½ teaspoon crushed dried tarragon
    1 tablespoon finely chopped parsley
    2 teaspoons freshly squeezed and strained
      lemon juice
      Salt to taste
    1 can (7¾ ounces) salmon, drained, any
      bones and skin removed, and flaked
    1 hard-cooked egg, finely chopped

In a medium bowl combine the sour cream, garlic, anchovy paste, mustard, tarragon, parsley, lemon juice, and salt. Blend well. Add the salmon and egg and mix gently but thoroughly. Taste and adjust the seasoning. Transfer to a serving bowl, cover, and chill. Serve with raw vegetables, potato chips, or crackers. Makes about 1¾ cups.

TAPÉNADE

Conceived by a late 19th-century Marseilles chef, this zesty Provençal appetizer is based on olives, anchovies, and capers, with the addition of other ingredients being a matter of personal taste.

    ½ cup dry oil-cured Mediterranean or
      Greek black olives, pitted
    2 salt anchovies, soaked in water 30
      minutes, filleted, patted dry, and
      coarsely chopped
    1 to 2 tablespoons capers, rinsed and
      drained
    ¼ cup olive oil or as needed
    1 tablespoon freshly squeezed and strained
      lemon juice or to taste
      Freshly ground pepper to taste
    1 teaspoon dry mustard (optional)

In a large mortar pound together the olives, anchovies, and capers until they form a paste. Gradually stir in enough olive oil to obtain a thick sauce. Add the lemon juice, pepper, and mustard, if used. (Alternatively, put the olives, anchovies, capers, lemon juice, pepper, and mustard, if used, in the container of an electric blender. Whirl until smooth. Add the olive oil in a slow, steady stream until the mixture is thick and creamy.) Taste and adjust the seasoning. Transfer to a serving bowl, cover, and chill. Serve as a dip with crudités such as cherry tomatoes, red and green pepper strips, zucchini rounds, Belgian endive sliced in half lengthwise, and/or thin asparagus spears. Makes about 1 cup.

Note: 4 to 6 oil-packed anchovy fillets, drained, can be substituted for the salt anchovies.

VARIATION:

You can pound one or more of the following ingredients into the *tapénade:* 1 small garlic clove, crushed; 1 tablespoon finely chopped fresh basil; 3 tablespoons finely chopped parsley; ¼ teaspoon ground bay leaf; ¼ teaspoon thyme; 3 tablespoons or more drained tuna; 1 hard-cooked egg, sieved; 1 teaspoon Cognac or to taste.

BAGNA CAUDA
Italian Hot Anchovy and Garlic Dip

A peasant specialty of the Piedmont region that provides an assertive foil for bread and raw vegetables.

½ cup butter
¼ cup olive oil
3 medium garlic cloves, finely chopped
1 can (2 ounces) flat anchovy fillets, drained on paper towels and finely chopped
Italian breadsticks or thin slices of Italian or French bread
Raw vegetables

In an earthenware crock or heatproof container heat the butter and oil over low heat, stirring until the butter melts. Add the garlic and anchovies and cook gently, stirring, until the anchovies dissolve into a paste and the mixture bubbles.

Place the container over a candle warmer or an alcohol table burner. Serve as a dip, accompanied with the breadsticks or bread slices and raw vegetables such as sticks of cucumber, carrot, green or red bell pepper, celery, scallions, cherry tomatoes, radishes, small whole mushrooms (or quartered large mushrooms), cauliflower or broccoli florets, and zucchini or fennel slices.

To eat, dip a breadstick or piece of vegetable into the hot sauce. If using bread slices, hold a slice under the vegetable to catch drips as you lift it. Eat the bread itself when it has soaked up enough drippings. Makes about 1 cup.

SPREADS

ROQUEFORT CHEESE SPREAD

2 ounces Roquefort cheese
¼ pound cream cheese, at room temperature
1 tablespoon butter, at room temperature
1 tablespoon finely chopped chives or scallion tops (optional)
1 tablespoon dry Sherry

Combine all the ingredients in a bowl and beat until the mixture is well blended and smooth. Cover and chill. Serve with crackers or thinly sliced pumpernickel bread. Makes about 1 cup.

VARIATIONS:

ROQUEFORT CHEESE AND WALNUT SPREAD

Substitute tawny Port or amaretto liqueur for the Sherry, if desired. Add 3 tablespoons finely chopped toasted walnuts and mix well.

GORGONZOLA CHEESE AND PROSCIUTTO SPREAD

Follow the recipe for Roquefort Cheese Spread (above), substituting Gorgonzola cheese for the Roquefort and adding 1 ounce prosciutto, finely chopped. Serve with small slices of Italian bread.

SWEDISH CHEESE SPREAD

2 to 3 ounces Roquefort, Gorgonzola, or
  other blue cheese
6 ounces cream cheese, at room
  temperature
¼ cup heavy cream, whipped
2 teaspoons finely chopped chives or
  scallion tops or to taste (optional)
¼ cup finely chopped salted pistachio nuts

In a bowl mash together the cheeses and beat until well blended and smooth. Fold in the whipped cream and chives or scallion tops, if used. Transfer to a serving bowl. Sprinkle with the nuts. Serve with thinly sliced pumpernickel bread, crackers, or un-peeled pear slices. Makes about 1½ cups.

VARIATION:

BLUE CHEESE DIP

Substitute ½ cup unflavored yogurt or sour cream for the whipped cream. Serve with crackers, crudités, or pineapple sticks.

SERBIAN CHEESE SPREAD

6 ounces cream cheese, at room
  temperature
½ cup finely crumbled or grated feta cheese
¼ cup butter, at room temperature
1 tablespoon heavy cream (optional)

Combine all the ingredients in a bowl and beat until the mixture is well blended and fluffy, or mix in an electric blender or food processor. Cover and chill. Serve with pumpernickel or pita bread. Makes about 1½ cups.

VARIATION:

SERBIAN HERB CHEESE SPREAD

Add 1 tablespoon each minced fresh dill, chives, and parsley or mint, and, if desired, 1 tiny garlic clove, crushed to a smooth purée. Mix well.

SHRIMP PASTE

*A popular accompaniment to drinks in
Charleston, South Carolina.*

¾ *pound shrimp, shelled and deveined*
¼ *cup butter, at room temperature*
1 *tablespoon dry Sherry*
2 *teaspoons freshly squeezed and strained
   lemon juice*
2 *teaspoons finely grated mild onion*
¼ *teaspoon mace*
¼ *teaspoon dry mustard*
⅛ *teaspoon cayenne pepper or to taste*
Salt and freshly ground pepper to taste

Drop the shrimp into enough boiling water to cover them and boil briskly, uncovered, about 3 minutes or until they are firm and pink. Drain the shrimp and pat them dry with paper towels. Put the shrimp through the finest blade of a food grinder, or chop them finely and pound them to a smooth paste with a mortar and pestle.

In a medium bowl cream the butter until it is light and fluffy. Beat in the Sherry, lemon juice, onion, mace, mustard, cayenne pepper, salt, and pepper until thoroughly blended. Add the shrimp and beat until the mixture is smooth. Taste and adjust the seasoning. Transfer the shrimp paste to a 1½-cup serving bowl or mold, spreading it and smoothing the top with a spatula. Cover with aluminum foil or plastic wrap and chill 6 hours or overnight.

The paste can be served directly from the bowl or it can be unmolded. To unmold, insert a thin knife around the edge of the mold to loosen it and dip the bottom in hot water for a few seconds. Invert a serving plate over the bowl, and holding both together securely, turn them over. Rap the plate on the counter to allow the shrimp paste to slide out. Serve with crackers, Melba toast, or crisp raw vegetables such as cauliflower florets, cucumber or zucchini slices, or green pepper strips. Makes about 1½ cups.

Note: Shrimp paste can be made in an electric blender. Put the cooked shrimp and all other ingredients except the butter in the container of the blender and blend to a smooth paste. Cream the butter as above. Add the shrimp mixture and mix thoroughly. Proceed as directed.

VARIATIONS:

Substitute ½ teaspoon Dijon-style mustard for the dry mustard and add ¼ teaspoon crushed dried tarragon.

Substitute ½ teaspoon Dijon-style mustard for the dry mustard and 1 tablespoon Pernod for the Sherry.

Substitute 1 small garlic clove, crushed to a smooth purée, for the onion, and add 1 teaspoon finely chopped fresh dill. Omit the Sherry, if you like.

SMOKED SALMON SPREAD

½ pound smoked salmon, chopped
6 ounces cream cheese, at room
   temperature
1 tablespoon grated onion
1 tablespoon freshly squeezed and strained
   lemon juice or to taste
   Salt and freshly ground pepper to taste
2 tablespoons finely chopped fresh dill

Place all the ingredients except the dill in the container of an electric blender and blend until smooth. Add the dill and blend until well mixed. Transfer to a serving bowl, cover, and chill. Serve with dark rye or pumpernickel bread or Scandinavian crispbread. Makes about 1 cup.

PORTUGUESE TUNA PÂTÉ

1 can (7 ounces) Italian tuna packed in
   olive oil, drained
½ cup butter, cut into small pieces
2 tablespoons heavy cream
½ teaspoon dry mustard
   Pinch cayenne pepper or to taste
   Salt and freshly ground pepper to taste
2 tablespoons Madeira

Place all the ingredients except the Madeira in the container of an electric blender and blend until smooth. With the motor running, add the Madeira and blend until the ingredients are well mixed. Taste and adjust the seasoning. Transfer the pâté to a serving bowl or crock. Smooth the top, cover, and refrigerate about 2 hours or until firm. Serve with French bread or crackers. Makes about 1¼ cups.

CHICKEN AND ALMOND PÂTÉ

2 cups ground cooked chicken
¼ cup butter, at room temperature
3 tablespoons dry Sherry
¼ cup very finely chopped mild onion, or 1 small garlic clove, crushed to a smooth purée
1 teaspoon freshly squeezed and strained lemon juice
Dash Tabasco sauce
Salt to taste
¼ cup chopped toasted blanched almonds

Combine the chicken and butter in a medium mixing bowl and mix until well blended. Add the Sherry, onion or garlic, lemon juice, Tabasco sauce, and salt and blend thoroughly. Taste and adjust the seasoning. Transfer to a serving bowl or crock. Cover and refrigerate. Sprinkle with the almonds and serve with French bread, Melba toast, or crackers. Makes about 2 cups.

CHICKEN LIVER PÂTÉ

1 pound chicken livers
2 tablespoons butter
2 tablespoons chopped shallots or scallions (use only the white parts of the scallions)
⅓ cup Madeira or Cognac
¼ cup heavy cream
⅛ teaspoon allspice
⅛ teaspoon crushed dried thyme
½ teaspoon salt or to taste
⅛ teaspoon freshly ground pepper
½ cup butter, melted
Parsley sprigs

Clean the chicken livers, removing any dark or green spots. Dry them with paper towels and cut into ½-inch pieces.

In a heavy skillet melt the 2 tablespoons butter over medium-high heat. Add the chicken livers and shallots or scallions and sauté, stirring frequently, about 3 minutes or until the chicken livers are lightly browned outside but still pink inside. Scrape the mixture into the container of an electric blender.

Pour the Madeira or Cognac into the skillet and boil it down quickly until it has reduced to 3 tablespoons. Pour it into the blender container. Add the heavy cream, allspice, thyme, salt, and pepper. Cover and blend until smooth. Add the melted butter and blend a few seconds more. Taste and adjust the seasoning. Pack the pâté into an attractive serving bowl. Cover with aluminum foil or plastic wrap and chill about 4 hours. Garnish with the parsley sprigs and serve with Melba toast or crackers. Makes 1 pound.

VARIATION:

CHICKEN LIVER PÂTÉ IN ASPIC

Prepare the pâté as above. Transfer it to a bowl, cover, and chill. Meanwhile, in a small saucepan sprinkle 1 envelope unflavored gelatin over ½ cup beef broth. Let stand 5 minutes to soften. Heat the mixture over low heat, stirring, until the gelatin is dissolved. Remove from the heat and stir in 1 cup beef broth and 1 tablespoon Madeira or Cognac. Spoon half of the gelatin mixture into a lightly oiled 4½-cup mold and chill until set. Spread the pâté over the gelatin layer and chill until firm. Spoon the remaining gelatin mixture over the pâté. Cover with aluminum foil or plastic wrap and chill at least 6 hours or overnight.

Unmold as directed on page 29. Garnish and serve as above.

RUSSIAN LIVER PÂTÉ

¼ cup flavorless vegetable oil
1 pound calf's liver, trimmed and cut into
  ½-inch dice
10 tablespoons unsalted butter
1 carrot, coarsely chopped
1 medium onion, coarsely chopped
1 tablespoon finely chopped parsley
1½ teaspoons salt
⅛ teaspoon freshly ground pepper
⅛ teaspoon freshly grated nutmeg
4 hard-cooked eggs, halved

In a large, heavy skillet heat the oil over high heat. Add the liver and sauté, stirring constantly, until lightly browned. Transfer the liver to a bowl and set aside.

In the same skillet melt 2 tablespoons of the butter over moderate heat. Add the carrot and onion and sauté, stirring frequently, until the vegetables are soft but not browned. Add them to the liver in the bowl. Stir in the parsley and put the contents of the bowl through the finest blade of a meat grinder. Using a large spoon, beat in the salt, pepper, and nutmeg, then beat in the remaining 8 tablespoons butter, a tablespoon or so at a time. Purée the mixture through the finest blade of a food mill. Taste and adjust the seasoning. Pack the pâté into a 1- to 1½-quart mold and smooth the top. Cover with plastic wrap and chill at least 8 hours or until firm.

Serve the pâté directly from the mold, or unmold it as follows: Run a thin knife around the inside of the mold. Invert a serving platter over the top and, holding both the plate and mold securely together, turn them over. The pâté should slide out. Carefully lift off the mold. Surround the pâté with the hard-cooked egg halves and serve as a first course or as part of a *zakuska* table (page 413). Makes 8 servings.

VARIATION:

Omit the carrot. Beat 2 tablespoons Madeira or Cognac into the mixture along with the seasonings and butter.

LIVERWURST PÂTÉ

*½ pound good quality Braunschweiger-style
  liver sausage
2 tablespoons butter, at room temperature
2 teaspoons grated mild white onion
1 tiny garlic clove, crushed to a smooth
  purée
1 teaspoon Düsseldorf or Dijon-style
  mustard
1 tablespoon Cognac
¾ teaspoon Worcestershire sauce
¼ teaspoon crushed dried tarragon
  Salt and cayenne pepper to taste
  Finely chopped unsalted shelled
  pistachio nuts or parsley*

Combine all the ingredients except the pistachio nuts or parsley in the container of an electric blender. Cover and blend until thoroughly mixed. Taste and adjust the seasoning. Transfer to a serving bowl or crock. Cover and chill at least 4 hours or overnight. Garnish with the nuts or parsley. Serve with French bread or crackers. Makes about 1 cup.

VARIATIONS:

LIVERWURST PÂTÉ WITH MUSHROOMS

In a small, heavy skillet melt 2 tablespoons butter over moderate heat. Add ¼ pound mushrooms, chopped, and 1 shallot, finely chopped, and sauté until golden brown, stirring frequently. Scrape the mixture into the container of an electric blender. Add ¼ pound Braunschweiger-style liver sausage, ¼ pound cream cheese, at room temperature, 1 tiny garlic clove, crushed to a smooth purée, ½ tablespoon finely chopped parsley, ⅛ teaspoon crushed dried tarragon, and salt and freshly ground pepper to taste. Cover and blend until thoroughly mixed. Taste and adjust the seasoning. Transfer to a serving bowl or crock. Chill and serve as above. Makes about 2 cups.

LIVERWURST PÂTÉ WITH BACON

In the container of an electric blender combine ½ pound Braunschweiger-style liver sausage, 2 tablespoons butter, at room temperature, 2 tablespoons very thinly sliced scallions, including 2 inches of the green tops, and 1 tablespoon dry Sherry. Cover and blend until thoroughly mixed. Add 6 slices bacon, cooked crisp and crumbled, and blend just until mixed. Transfer to a serving bowl or crock. Chill and serve as above. Makes about 1 cup.

FLAVORED BUTTERS

Canapés and sandwiches can often be enhanced by flavored or "compound" butters—butter creamed with herbs, spices, meat or seafood, vegetables, hard-cooked eggs, nuts, or other flavorings.

To make flavored butters, start with fresh, good butter (preferably unsalted for best taste) and cream it so that it will be soft enough for the flavorings to be blended into it. This can be done with an electric beater, blender, or food processor or by hand in a two-step operation: first pound it, either with a rolling pin or in a bowl with a pestle, or mash it, a little at a time, with the back of a wooden spoon; then aerate it by beating it vigorously with a spoon until it is light and smooth. Next, cream the butter and flavoring together and chill until firm enough to spread. When chilled but still malleable, flavored butters can be piped through a pastry bag fitted with a small fancy tip to decorate canapés and other open-faced appetizer sandwiches. Some make excellent spreads for bland sliced vegetables such as zucchini, or fillings for celery hearts, cucumber cups, and hard-cooked egg whites. Thoroughly chilled flavored butters can be cut into attractive shapes for garnishes.

Flavored butters can be shaped into logs,

wrapped tightly in aluminum foil, and frozen up to 2 weeks. Simply open the frozen packages and slice off what you need. They can also be refrigerated up to 24 hours.

HERB BUTTER

Blanch 1 cup mixed fresh herbs (parsley, chervil, chives, and watercress) by plunging them into boiling water for 1 minute. Drain the herbs well, dry them on paper towels, and chop them very fine. Cream ½ cup unsalted butter. Beat the herbs into the butter, then force the mixture through a fine-meshed sieve into a bowl, using a pestle or wooden spoon. Season to taste with salt and freshly ground pepper.

VARIATIONS:

Add ½ teaspoon freshly squeezed and strained lemon juice with the salt and pepper.

Instead of the above herbs, you may substitute a combination of parsley, chervil, watercress, and tarragon and/or savory; parsley, basil or dill, and chives; parsley, basil or tarragon, and chives; or a complementary mixture of your own choice.

PARSLEY AND CREAM CHEESE BUTTER

Cream ½ cup unsalted butter. Gradually beat in ¼ pound cream cheese, at room temperature, and ½ teaspoon anchovy paste, then add ½ cup finely chopped parsley, and 1 tablespoon finely chopped chives.

MUSTARD BUTTER

Cream ½ cup unsalted butter. Gradually beat in 2 tablespoons Dijon-style mustard and 1 teaspoon freshly squeezed and strained lemon juice, then beat in 1 tablespoon finely chopped parsley. Season to taste with salt and freshly ground pepper.

AVOCADO BUTTER

Mash 1 small peeled and pitted ripe avocado with 1 tablespoon freshly squeezed and strained lemon or lime juice. Cream ½ cup butter. Gradually beat in the mashed avocado, then beat in 2 ounces cream cheese, at room temperature, and 2 teaspoons finely chopped chives. Season to taste with salt and Tabasco sauce.

CHEESE BUTTER

Cream ½ cup unsalted butter. Beat in ¼ pound cream cheese, at room temperature, 1½ ounces Roquefort cheese, crumbled, 1 tablespoon dry vermouth, and 1 teaspoon grated mild onion until well blended. Force the mixture through a fine-meshed sieve. Season to taste with salt and freshly ground pepper.

HERB CHEESE BUTTER

Cream ½ cup unsalted butter. Beat in ¼ pound cream cheese, at room temperature, 2 ounces goat cheese, crumbled, ½ cup very finely chopped parsley, and ½ cup very finely chopped mixed fresh herbs (basil, chives, and thyme or rosemary) until well blended. Force the mixture through a fine-meshed sieve. Season to taste with salt and freshly ground pepper.

ANCHOVY BUTTER

Drain 4 oil-packed flat anchovy fillets and pound them in a mortar with a pestle until they are reduced to a paste. Cream ½ cup unsalted butter. Press the anchovy paste, a little at a time, through a fine-meshed sieve into the creamed butter, blending the mixture well and tasting after each addition. Use only as much paste as desired. The butter should have a well-defined but not overly strong anchovy flavor. Season to taste with freshly ground pepper.

ANCHOVY AND CREAM CHEESE BUTTER

Cream ½ cup unsalted butter. Gradually beat in ¼ pound cream cheese, at room temperature, ½ teaspoon or more anchovy paste, 2 teaspoons freshly squeezed and strained lemon juice, and 1 tablespoon finely chopped fresh dill.

SHRIMP BUTTER

Poach ¼ pound unpeeled shrimp in lightly salted water 3 to 4 minutes or until they are pink and firm. Drain the shrimp, chop coarsely, and pound with their shells in a mortar to a rough paste. Cream ½ cup unsalted butter. Add the creamed butter, a spoonful at a time, to the shrimp and pound until a fairly smooth paste forms. Force the mixture through a fine-meshed sieve into a bowl. Stir in 1 teaspoon freshly squeezed and strained lemon juice and season to taste with salt and freshly ground pepper.

LOBSTER BUTTER

In a mortar pound ½ cup chopped cooked lobster meat to a paste. Cream ½ cup unsalted butter. Gradually beat in the lobster paste. Add ½ teaspoon each freshly squeezed and strained lemon juice and very finely chopped fresh tarragon. Season to taste with salt and freshly ground pepper and blend well.

SMOKED OYSTER BUTTER

Drain 1 jar (4 ounces) smoked oysters and dry the oysters on paper towels. Force them through a fine-meshed sieve. Cream ¼ cup unsalted butter. Beat in the sieved oysters, ½ teaspoon freshly squeezed and strained lemon juice, and ¼ teaspoon finely grated lemon rind.

FILLINGS

CREAM CHEESE AND BACON FILLING

6 ounces cream cheese, at room temperature
2 tablespoons cream or milk
½ cup cooked crisp, drained, and crumbled bacon

In a small bowl beat the cream cheese with the cream or milk until light and fluffy. Add the bacon and mix well. Cover and refrigerate. Makes about 1 cup.

CREAM CHEESE AND MUSHROOM FILLING

Follow the recipe for Mushroom Dip (page 17), but use only 1 to 2 tablespoons yogurt. Makes about 1 cup.

PARSLEY-CHEESE FILLING

1½ cups firmly packed parsley, preferably
    Italian flat-leaf
1 cup (¼ pound) freshly grated imported
    Parmesan cheese
½ cup olive oil
3 tablespoons freshly squeezed and
    strained lemon juice
    Salt to taste

Combine the parsley, cheese, oil, and lemon juice in an electric blender or food processor. Whirl until the parsley is finely chopped and the ingredients are thoroughly blended. Season with the salt. Use at once or cover and chill as long as overnight. Makes about 1½ cups.

EGG FILLING

4 hard-cooked eggs, sieved
1 tablespoon very finely chopped mild
    onion or scallions (include 2 inches of the
    green tops of the scallions)
3 tablespoons Mayonnaise (page 387)
1 tablespoon Dijon-style mustard
    Salt and freshly ground pepper to taste

Combine all the ingredients in a bowl and blend thoroughly. Taste and adjust the sea-soning. Cover and refrigerate. Makes about 1 cup.

VARIATIONS:

CURRIED EGG FILLING

Substitute ½ teaspoon curry powder or to taste for the mustard and, if desired, butter (at room temperature) for the Mayonnaise.

EGG AND OLIVE FILLING

Add 3 tablespoons each minced pimento-stuffed olives and celery and 2 tablespoons minced parsley. Substitute butter (at room temperature) for the Mayonnaise, if desired.

HERB EGG FILLING

Add minced fresh parsley, chives, and tarragon, basil, or dill to taste.

BACON AND EGG FILLING

Add 2 slices bacon, cooked crisp and crumbled.

SHRIMP AND AVOCADO FILLING

1 large, ripe avocado, peeled, pitted, and cubed
¼ pound cream cheese, at room temperature
½ teaspoon freshly squeezed and strained lemon juice
  Salt, freshly ground pepper, and Tabasco sauce to taste
6 medium shrimp, cooked, shelled, deveined, and finely chopped
2 tablespoons finely chopped fresh chives
1 tablespoon finely chopped fresh dill or tarragon

In a mixing bowl combine the avocado, cream cheese, lemon juice, salt, pepper, and Tabasco sauce. Mash together with a fork until smooth. Stir in the remaining ingredients. Taste and adjust the seasoning. Cover and refrigerate. Makes about 1½ cups.

CRABMEAT FILLING

¼ pound cream cheese, at room temperature
1 tablespoon freshly squeezed and strained lemon juice or to taste
1 tablespoon finely chopped fresh chives
1 tablespoon finely chopped scallions, including 2 inches of the green tops
1 teaspoon finely chopped fresh tarragon, or ¼ teaspoon crushed dried tarragon
¼ teaspoon Worcestershire sauce or to taste
  Salt and Tabasco sauce to taste
1 cup picked over and flaked cooked crabmeat

In a bowl beat the cream cheese with the lemon juice until light and fluffy. Add the chives, scallions, tarragon, Worcestershire sauce, salt, and Tabasco sauce and mix thoroughly. Add the crabmeat and blend well. Taste and adjust the seasoning. Cover and refrigerate. Makes about 1½ cups.

VARIATIONS:

CURRIED CRABMEAT FILLING

Use 2 cups crabmeat or 1 cup each crabmeat and shrimp. Add ¼ cup sour cream or 2 tablespoons each sour cream and Mayonnaise (page 387) with the cream cheese. Substitute ½ teaspoon curry powder for the tarragon. Stir in 2 tablespoons finely chopped macadamia nuts or toasted blanched almonds. Makes about 3 cups.

CRABMEAT AND AVOCADO FILLING

Use 1½ to 2 cups crabmeat. Substitute ½ large, ripe avocado, peeled, pitted, and mashed, and 2 tablespoons sour cream or unflavored yogurt or 1 tablespoon each sour cream and Mayonnaise (page 387) for the cream cheese. Omit the Worcestershire sauce and, if desired, substitute ⅛ teaspoon chili powder for the tarragon.

SHRIMP FILLING

Substitute cooked, shelled, deveined, and finely chopped shrimp for the crabmeat and finely chopped fresh dill to taste for the tarragon.

SEAFOOD SALAD FILLING

1½ cups finely chopped cooked shrimp, lobster meat, crabmeat, cold flaked poached salmon, or drained and flaked canned salmon or tuna
1 hard-cooked egg, finely chopped
⅓ cup finely chopped celery
1 tablespoon finely chopped scallions, including 2 inches of the green tops
¼ cup Mayonnaise (page 387)
1 teaspoon freshly squeezed and strained lemon juice
½ teaspoon Dijon-style mustard or to taste
Finely chopped fresh tarragon, parsley, or dill to taste
Salt and freshly ground pepper to taste

Combine all the ingredients in a bowl and mix well. Taste and adjust the seasoning. Cover and refrigerate. Makes about 2½ cups.

SHELLFISH AND AVOCADO FILLING

1 cup finely diced cooked shrimp or
  crabmeat
1 cup finely chopped avocado
2 hard-cooked eggs, finely chopped
3 tablespoons finely chopped scallions,
  including 2 inches of the green tops
¼ teaspoon crushed dried tarragon
⅓ to ½ cup Mayonnaise (page 387)
2 tablespoons freshly squeezed and
  strained lemon or lime juice
  Salt, freshly ground pepper, and Tabasco
  sauce to taste

Combine all the ingredients in a bowl and toss gently but thoroughly. Taste and adjust the seasoning. Cover and refrigerate. Makes about 2½ cups.

CLAM AND CREAM CHEESE FILLING

1 can (6½ ounces) minced clams, drained
6 ounces cream cheese, at room
  temperature
1 tablespoon finely chopped fresh chives
2 teaspoons finely chopped parsley
2 teaspoons grated onion
1 small garlic clove or to taste, crushed and
  finely chopped
2 teaspoons freshly squeezed and strained
  lemon juice
1 teaspoon Worcestershire sauce
  Salt and Tabasco sauce to taste

Combine all the ingredients in a bowl and beat until well blended. Taste and adjust the seasoning. Cover and refrigerate. Makes about 1½ cups.

Note: For a thinner consistency beat in about 2 tablespoons sour cream.

VARIATION:

CLAM AND CREAM CHEESE DIP

Use 2 tablespoons lemon juice and add 1 tablespoon Mayonnaise (page 387). Serve with crudités or potato chips.

ANCHOVY AND CREAM CHEESE FILLING

6 anchovy fillets
¼ pound cream cheese, at room
   temperature
1 tablespoon sour cream
2 teaspoons finely chopped fresh dill
1 teaspoon finely chopped fresh chives
   Freshly ground pepper to taste

In a small bowl mash the anchovies. Add the remaining ingredients and mix until thoroughly blended and fluffy. Taste and adjust the seasoning. Cover and refrigerate. Makes about ⅔ cup.

CAVIAR AND CREAM CHEESE FILLING

6 ounces cream cheese, at room
   temperature
2 tablespoons sour cream
1 tablespoon freshly squeezed and strained
   lemon juice
2 to 4 tablespoons finely chopped fresh
   chives or scallions (include 2 inches of
   the green tops of the scallions), or 1 to 2
   tablespoons each chives and scallions
¼ cup heavy cream, whipped
2 ounces red or black caviar

In a medium mixing bowl mash the cream cheese with a fork. Add the sour cream and lemon juice and whisk until the mixture is well blended and smooth. Stir in the chives and/or scallions. Fold in the whipped cream gently but thoroughly, then fold in the caviar. Cover and refrigerate. Makes about 1½ cups.

CURRIED CHICKEN FILLING

2 cups ground or very finely chopped
    cooked chicken breast
½ cup very finely chopped watercress
    leaves
½ cup Curry Mayonnaise (page 388)
1 teaspoon freshly squeezed and strained
    lemon juice
    Salt, freshly ground pepper, and cayenne
    pepper to taste

Combine all the ingredients in a bowl and mix well. Taste and adjust the seasoning. Cover and refrigerate. Makes about 2½ cups.

VARIATION:

CURRIED CHICKEN AND ALMOND FILLING

Substitute ⅓ cup finely chopped toasted blanched almonds for the watercress and add 1½ tablespoons finely chopped mild onion or scallions (include 2 inches of the scallion tops).

CHICKEN LIVER AND MUSHROOM FILLING

4 tablespoons butter
½ pound chicken livers, trimmed and dried
    with paper towels
    Salt and freshly ground pepper to taste
½ pound mushrooms, finely chopped
3 tablespoons finely chopped shallots or
    scallions (include 2 inches of the green
    tops of the scallions)
6 ounces cream cheese, at room
    temperature
¼ cup sour cream
1 large garlic clove, crushed and finely
    chopped
1 tablespoon very finely chopped parsley

In a medium-sized, heavy skillet melt 2 tablespoons of the butter over medium-high heat. Add the chicken livers and sauté, turning to brown on all sides. Season with salt and pepper. Scrape into a bowl and reserve.

Add the remaining 2 tablespoons butter to the skillet and melt over medium-high heat. Add the mushrooms and shallots or scallions and cook, stirring, until all the moisture in the skillet is evaporated. Season with salt and pepper. Finely chop the reserved chicken livers and add them to the mushroom mixture. Set aside.

In a large mixing bowl mash the cream cheese with a fork, gradually adding the sour cream until the mixture is well blended and smooth. Add the garlic, parsley, and chicken liver and mushroom mixture and blend thoroughly. Taste and adjust the seasoning. Cover and refrigerate. Makes about 2½ cups.

VARIATION:

Add 1 tablespoon minced fresh dill or tarragon with the parsley.

HAM FILLING

1 cup ground lean cooked ham
½ cup sour cream
2 tablespoons finely chopped chives or scallions (include 2 inches of the green tops of the scallions)
¼ teaspoon Dijon-style mustard or to taste
  Salt and freshly ground pepper to taste

Combine all the ingredients in a bowl and mix until thoroughly blended. Taste and adjust the seasoning. Cover and refrigerate. Makes about 1½ cups.

VARIATION:

PROSCIUTTO FILLING

Substitute ½ pound prosciutto, minced, for the ham. Instead of the sour cream, use ¼ pound cream cheese or Neufchâtel cheese, at room temperature, beaten with 2 to 4 tablespoons sour cream until light and fluffy. Substitute 2 tablespoons minced Italian flat-leaf parsley and 1 tablespoon minced chives for the chives or scallions. Omit the mustard.

SPINACH, MUSHROOM, AND HAM FILLING

1 pound fresh spinach
⅓ cup cold water
2 tablespoons butter
4 shallots, finely chopped
1 cup finely chopped mushrooms
¼ pound lean cooked ham, finely chopped
¼ teaspoon freshly grated nutmeg
  Salt and freshly ground pepper to taste
6 ounces cream cheese, at room temperature
¼ cup sour cream
2 teaspoons Dijon-style mustard or to taste

Wash the spinach thoroughly under cold running water, discarding the stems and bruised leaves. Drain. Chop the spinach and combine with the water in a large saucepan. Bring to a boil over high heat. Reduce the heat to low, cover, and simmer 5 minutes or until the spinach is wilted. Transfer the spinach to a colander and allow to drain and cool. Squeeze it dry, chop it finely, and set aside.

In a medium-sized, heavy skillet melt the butter over moderate heat. Add the shallots and sauté until soft but not browned, stirring frequently. Add the mushrooms and sauté over medium-high heat, stirring, until lightly browned. Add the reserved spinach, ham, nutmeg, salt, and pepper and mix well. Remove from the heat and let cool to room temperature.

In a large mixing bowl beat the cream cheese with the sour cream and mustard until light and fluffy. Add the spinach mixture and blend thoroughly. Taste and adjust the seasoning, cover, and refrigerate. Makes about 3½ cups.

VARIATION:

Omit the nutmeg and mustard. Substitute 4 scallions, including 2 inches of the green tops, for the shallots. Stir 1 large garlic clove, crushed and finely chopped, 1 tablespoon finely chopped fresh dill, and, if desired, 2 tablespoons freshly grated imported Parmesan cheese into the cream cheese and sour cream mixture before adding the spinach mixture.

HOT CREAM FILLINGS

CREAM FILLING WITH HAM AND CHEESE

5 tablespoons butter
3 ounces lean cooked ham (about ¾ cup),
    finely chopped
3 tablespoons all-purpose flour
1 cup hot milk or hot heavy cream
    Pinch freshly grated nutmeg
    Pinch cayenne pepper
    Salt and freshly ground pepper to taste
1 egg yolk
½ cup grated Swiss cheese, or ¼ cup each
    freshly grated Swiss and imported
    Parmesan cheese

In a small skillet melt ½ tablespoon of the butter over moderate heat. Add the ham and sauté until lightly browned, stirring frequently. Remove from the heat and reserve.

In a heavy saucepan melt 2½ tablespoons of the remaining butter over low heat. Add the flour and cook 1 to 2 minutes, whisking constantly. Add the hot milk or cream, nutmeg, cayenne pepper, salt, and pepper and cook, stirring, about 1 minute, or until the mixture comes to a boil and is thick and smooth. Taste and adjust the seasoning. Remove from the heat. Place the egg yolk in the center of the sauce and beat it vigorously with a wire whisk, then beat in the cheese, reserved ham, and, finally, the remaining 2 tablespoons butter. Taste again for seasoning. Makes about 2 cups.

VARIATION:

CREAM FILLING WITH MUSHROOMS AND CHEESE

Use 5½ tablespoons butter and omit the ham. Sauté ¼ pound diced mushrooms in 1 tablespoon of the butter over medium-high heat until lightly browned, stirring frequently. Add the mushrooms to the sauce along with the cheese.

CREAM FILLING WITH SHELLFISH

4 tablespoons butter
2 tablespoons chopped shallots or scallions (include 2 inches of the green tops of the scallions)
10 ounces diced or flaked cooked shellfish
¼ cup dry white wine, Madeira, or Sherry
1 tablespoon finely chopped fresh tarragon, or 1 teaspoon crushed dried tarragon
Salt and freshly ground pepper to taste
3 tablespoons all-purpose flour
1 cup hot milk, or ½ cup each hot milk and concentrated fish stock or clam broth
1 egg yolk
¼ cup heavy cream
¼ cup grated Swiss cheese

In a heavy skillet melt 2 tablespoons of the butter over low heat. Add the shallots or scallions and sauté about ½ minute, stirring frequently. Add the shellfish and sauté 2 minutes, stirring frequently. Add the wine, cover, and simmer 1 minute. Uncover, increase the heat to high, and cook until most of the liquid in the skillet has evaporated. Stir in the tarragon and salt and pepper. Remove from the heat and set aside.

In a heavy saucepan melt the remaining 2

tablespoons butter over low heat. Add the flour and cook 1 to 2 minutes, whisking constantly. Add the hot milk or hot milk mixture, salt, and pepper and cook, stirring, about 1 minute, or until the mixture comes to a boil and is thick and smooth. Remove from the heat and keep warm.

In a mixing bowl beat the egg yolk with the cream, then beat in the sauce, 1 tablespoon at a time. Return to the saucepan and boil, stirring, 1 minute or until very thick. Fold in the shellfish mixture and cheese. Taste and adjust the seasoning. Makes about 2 cups.

VARIATIONS:

Substitute 1 tablespoon minced fresh chervil or 1 teaspoon crushed dried oregano for the tarragon.

Substitute 2 tablespoons minced fresh dill or to taste for the tarragon and omit the wine and cheese. Stir in 2 teaspoons freshly squeezed and strained lemon juice at the end.

CREAM FILLING WITH CHICKEN

2 tablespoons butter
3 tablespoons all-purpose flour
1 cup hot milk
1 ¼ teaspoons curry powder or to taste, or ¼ teaspoon freshly grated nutmeg or to taste
Salt and freshly ground pepper to taste
1 egg
1 ½ cups finely chopped cooked chicken

In a saucepan melt the butter over low heat. Add the flour and cook 1 to 2 minutes, whisking constantly. Gradually add the milk, stirring until the mixture is very thick and smooth. Add the curry powder or nutmeg, salt, and pepper and simmer gently a few minutes. Remove from the heat, add the egg, and beat thoroughly. Add the chicken and mix well. Taste and adjust the seasoning. Makes about 2 cups.

VARIATION:

Turkey, shrimp, lobster meat, or crabmeat may be substituted for the chicken.

CREAM FILLING WITH CHICKEN LIVERS AND MUSHROOMS

4½ tablespoons butter
1 tablespoon all-purpose flour
⅔ cup half-and-half
⅛ teaspoon freshly grated nutmeg
 Salt, freshly ground pepper, and
 cayenne pepper to taste
⅓ cup freshly grated imported Parmesan
 or Romano cheese
1 egg yolk
4 shallots, finely chopped
1 medium garlic clove, very finely
 chopped
8 medium mushroom caps, chopped
¾ pound chicken livers, cleaned and dried
 with paper towels
2 tablespoons Cognac
2 tablespoons finely chopped parsley

In a small saucepan melt ½ tablespoon of the butter. Add the flour and cook over low heat about 1 minute, stirring constantly. Gradually stir in the half-and-half, then add the nutmeg, salt, pepper, and cayenne pepper. Bring to a boil, stirring. Add the cheese, mix well, and remove from the heat.

In a small bowl beat the egg yolk lightly. Beat a small quantity of the hot sauce into the egg yolk and return the mixture to the saucepan.

In a small, heavy skillet melt 2 tablespoons of the remaining butter over moderate heat. Add the shallots and garlic and sauté until tender but not browned, stirring frequently. Add the mushrooms and cook 2 minutes. Increase the heat and add the remaining 2 tablespoons butter. When the butter is melted add the chicken livers and cook, turning to brown on all sides. Transfer the mixture to a chopping board and chop finely. Add the Cognac, parsley, and salt and pepper to taste. Stir into the cheese sauce. Makes about 2½ cups.

CHEESE

Although cheese has earned a reputation as one of the most accommodating and versatile of edibles when used in combination with other foods, it can shine simply when served alone with good crusty bread or crackers. Cheese forms the basis of innumerable dips and spreads. It can be shaped into attractive balls or logs as well as into interesting molds. In addition, it can be served as a hot appetizer in a host of delightful ways.

If you intend to serve cheese as hors d'oeuvre, choose types that are rich or strongly flavored (but avoid those such as Liederkranz or Limburger, which are overly strong); otherwise guests may be tempted to overindulge themselves on bland-tasting cheeses and thus lose their appetites. For a small gathering two kinds are usually sufficient, each served with its own knife and, preferably, with unsalted, unseasoned crackers offered on a separate plate. If, however, you are planning a rather large cocktail party and wish to include a selection of cheeses, you might choose as many as four different kinds: one soft, one semi-firm, one firm, and one bleu. Be sure to serve all ripened cheese (that is, cheese fermented through the action of rennet or various bacteria cultures) at room temperature.

Try to shop for cheese at a store that specializes in it, where you are apt to find a wider selection and where you can usually sample it before buying in order to determine its freshness and flavor. When cooking with cheese, avoid overheating since high temperatures cause it to become tough and stringy.

There are some people who caution against serving cheese as an appetizer, finding it more suited to the end of a meal since it is said to close the stomach. If you are of a similar opinion, please feel free to proceed to the next chapter. For those whose stomachs, despite this injunction, remain open after ingesting cheese at the beginning of a meal, this section offers some palate-provoking starters in which cheese assumes a feature role.

In addition to the recipes in this chapter, you will find many others that make use of cheese throughout this book.

COLD CHEESE APPETIZERS

HOMEMADE CREAMY CHEESE

Making your own fresh cheese is simple and economical, and you will be amply rewarded by its clean, delicate taste and creamy texture. It can be used as a substitute in recipes calling for cream cheese and will keep under refrigeration for about one week.

  2 quarts whole milk
  2 cups cultured buttermilk
½ teaspoon salt or to taste

In a large, heavy kettle combine the milk and buttermilk. Attach a candy or deep-fat thermometer to the side of the kettle and place the kettle over moderate heat. Cook, stirring gently every 5 to 10 minutes to prevent scorching. When the temperature reaches 170°F, reduce the heat to low if necessary to keep it between 170° and 175°F. (If the temperature exceeds 175°F, remove the kettle from the heat until it returns to 170° to 175°F.)

Meanwhile, line a colander with a few

West African Filled Papaya Halves (p. 173)

Mexican Shrimp Cocktail (p. 179).

Cheese-Stuffed Pepper Rings (p. 141)

Tiropetes
(Greek Phyllo Pastry
Triangles) (p. 347)

Crudites with Clam and Cream Cheese Dip (p. 24);
Upper right:
Miniature Biscuits with Ham (p. 293)

Left to Right:
Liptauer Log (p. 52);
Goat Cheese Marinated in Oil and Herbs (p. 56);
Norwegian Red Caviar Dip (p. 23)

Quick Antipasto Platter (p. 404)
*including Tuscan White Bean
and Tuna Salad* (p. 108)

*Green Fettucine with
Mushrooms,
Prosciutto, and Peas* (p. 382)

*Left to Right:
Caviar; Hard-Cooked
Egg Yolks
and Chives*

Clockwise from Top:
Herring Platter
(p. 189); *New Boiled*
Potatoes with Dill;
Herring Salad
(p. 120); *Köttbullar*
(Swedish Meatballs)
(p. 259); *Basket of*
Swedish Breads and
Crackers; Cheeses:
Fontina, Blue Saga
and Havarti with Dill;
Deviled and Salmon-
Stuffed Eggs *(p. 64)*
surrounding Gravlax
(Swedish Dill-Cured
Salmon) *(p. 188);*
Assorted Meats Platter
(Ham, Head Cheese
and Tongue); Butter
(middle).

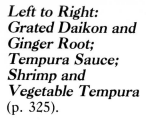

Left to Right:
Grated Daikon and
Ginger Root;
Tempura Sauce;
Shrimp and
Vegetable Tempura
(p. 325).

Clockwise from Top Left: Baltic-
Russian Cucumber and Sour Cream
Salad (p. 104); *Roasted Pepper Salad*
with Tomato and Onion (p. 106);
Tabbouli (Cracked Wheat Salad)
(p. 114); *Spanish Chick Pea Salad* (p. 109).

Left to Right: **Apricot-Glazed Chicken Wings with Scallion Brushes** (p. 220); **Chinese Shrimp Toast** (p. 285); **Chinese Barbecued Spare Ribs with Hot Mustard and Plum Sauce** (p. 247).

layers of dampened cheesecloth. Place the colander inside a bowl alongside the kettle of milk. When thick white curds separate from the whey, with a slotted spoon transfer the curds into the colander. When most of the curds have been transferred, place the colander in the kitchen sink and pour in the remaining curds and whey from the kettle. Discard the whey remaining in the bowl. Let the curd drain about 3 hours.

Turn the cheese into a bowl and mix in salt to taste. Cover and refrigerate. Makes about 2 cups.

HERB CHEESE

8 ounces cream cheese or Neufchâtel
cheese, at room temperature
2 teaspoons dry white wine or heavy cream
1 small garlic clove or to taste, crushed and
finely chopped
¼ teaspoon crushed dried basil
¼ teaspoon finely chopped chives
⅛ teaspoon crushed dried tarragon
⅛ teaspoon crushed dried thyme
Salt to taste

Combine all the ingredients in a bowl and beat until well blended and smooth. Taste and adjust the seasoning. Line a ramekin or other small, round mold with plastic wrap, waxed paper, or aluminum foil, leaving enough overlap to cover the top. Fill the ramekin or mold with the cheese mixture, packing it firmly. Cover the top with the extra plastic wrap, waxed paper, or foil and chill 4 hours or until the cheese is firm. Unwrap the herb cheese and serve with crackers or raw vegetables. Makes about 1 cup.

LIPTAUER

Liptauer, *or more correctly,* Liptauer garniert, *originally referred to a spread made in Austria that used as its base a soft white cheese. Today the name Liptauer commonly applies to cheeses spiced with paprika and other zesty seasonings.*

    8 ounces cream cheese, at room
        temperature
    ¼ cup unsalted butter
    ¼ cup creamed cottage cheese
    1 tablespoon heavy cream or sour cream
    1½ teaspoons anisette
    1 teaspoon caraway seed
    1½ teaspoons sweet Hungarian paprika
        (available in specialty shops and many
        supermarkets)
    ½ cup finely chopped mild white or red
        onions
    6 oil-packed flat anchovy fillets, chopped
    ⅓ cup capers, rinsed and drained
        thoroughly
    ½ cup chopped chives
    1 bunch white radishes, trimmed

In a medium mixing bowl beat the cream cheese and butter with an electric mixer until light and creamy. Add the cottage cheese and beat until fluffy. Add the cream, anisette, and caraway seed and blend thoroughly. Cover and chill. Transfer the Liptauer to a crock, or mound it on a serving plate. Sprinkle with the paprika. Fill small bowls with the onions, anchovies, capers, and chives. Serve them as condiments for the Liptauer. Accompany with the radishes and thinly sliced rye or pumpernickel bread. Makes 4 servings.

VARIATION:

LIPTAUER LOG

Omit the paprika, onions, anchovies, capers, chives, and radishes. On a long strip of waxed paper form the cheese into a log. Wrap securely in the waxed paper and chill several hours. Unroll the cheese and smooth out any uneven spots with a spatula. Using a fine-meshed sieve, sift sweet Hungarian paprika along the log, rolling it gently until it is evenly coated. Dust off any excess paprika with a pastry brush. Serve with rye or pumpernickel bread.

COEUR À LA CRÈME WITH CAVIAR

Almost too beautiful to eat.

1 pound cottage cheese
1 pound cream cheese, at room
  temperature
2 cups heavy cream
  Salt to taste
  Black caviar
  Red caviar

Put the cottage cheese and cream cheese in the container of an electric blender. Cover and blend until smooth. Or place them in a large bowl and beat with an electric mixer until smooth. Gradually beat in the cream. Season with the salt and blend well.

Line 6 individual heart-shaped *coeur à la crème* baskets or molds with perforated bottoms with several layers of dampened cheesecloth and fill with the cheese mixture. Set them on a rack over a plate and refrigerate overnight to drain and set. Unmold the hearts onto chilled appetizer plates. Surround each heart with a border of black caviar and garnish the center with a small spoonful of red caviar. Serve with thin toast or crisp crackers and lemon wedges. Makes 6.

QUARK OR WEISSKÄSE
German Whipped Cottage Cheese

Here is a morale-booster for the calorie-conscious.

Put 1 pint large curd cottage cheese in the container of an electric blender. Blend until smooth and creamy. Mound the whipped cheese on a serving plate. Surround with small dishes of thinly sliced scallions (including 2 inches of the green tops), thinly sliced radishes, chopped cucumber, sliced black olives, crumbled crisp bacon, chopped parsley, chives, or dill, caraway seed, and chopped toasted hazelnuts or blanched almonds. Serve with toasted thinly sliced whole wheat or French bread. To eat, spread toast with the cheese and top with the condiments of your choice. Makes 4 servings.

CAMEMBERT AMANDINE

½ pound Camembert cheese
¾ cup white wine, or enough to cover the cheese
½ cup butter, at room temperature
2 teaspoons Cognac
 Salt and cayenne pepper to taste
½ cup coarsely chopped toasted blanched almonds

Cut the rind from the Camembert. Quarter the cheese and place the pieces in a glass or ceramic bowl. Cover the cheese with the wine, cover the bowl, and let soak at room temperature 8 hours or overnight. Transfer the cheese quarters to paper towels to drain. Pat them dry and place in a mixing bowl. Add the butter and mash with a wooden spoon, adding a little of the wine to the mixture if necessary. Add the Cognac, salt, and cayenne pepper and beat until thoroughly blended. Taste and adjust the seasoning.

Line a small, round mold or the container in which the Camembert was packed with plastic wrap, waxed paper, or aluminum foil, leaving enough overlap to cover the top. Fill the mold with the cheese mixture, packing it firmly. Cover the top with the extra plastic wrap, waxed paper, or foil and chill 4 hours or until the cheese is firm. Unwrap the cheese and sprinkle the entire surface with the chopped almonds. Makes 6 servings.

VARIATIONS:

Fold ¼ cup finely chopped toasted blanched almonds into the cheese mixture before molding it. After unwrapping the cheese, garnish the top with halves of toasted almonds.

Spoon half of the cheese mixture into the lined mold and top with ½ cup coarsely chopped unsalted pistachio nuts. Add the remaining cheese, spreading it and smoothing the top with a spatula. Cover and chill as above. Spread ½ cup finely chopped unsalted pistachio nuts on a plate. On another plate spread 1 cup crumbs made from bread cubes toasted in a 400°F oven about 5 minutes. After unwrapping the cheese, roll the edges in the nuts. Coat the bottom and top with the breadcrumbs. Walnuts or hazelnuts can be substituted for the pistachio nuts.

FILLED EDAM OR GOUDA CHEESE

A common enough hors d'oeuvre, but uncommonly good.

    1 Edam or Gouda cheese (about 1 pound)
    ¼ cup butter, at room temperature
    ⅓ cup dry Sherry
    2 tablespoons brandy
    ½ teaspoon dry mustard
      Salt and Tabasco sauce to taste

Cut a 2½-inch circle from the top of the cheese and reserve. Carefully scoop out the cheese inside, leaving a ¼-inch shell. Use a small, curved knife, such as a grapefruit knife, to remove most of the cheese at first, then use a teaspoon to remove the remaining cheese, working carefully to avoid puncturing the shell. Set the shell aside.

Grate the cheese and mix it in a large bowl with the butter. Gradually stir in the Sherry and brandy. Add the mustard, salt, and Tabasco sauce and stir vigorously until the mixture is well blended and smooth. Alternatively, cut the larger pieces of the scooped-out cheese into small cubes. Put all the ingredients in an electric blender or in a food processor fitted with the steel blade and blend until smooth. Taste and adjust the seasoning.

Fill the cheese shell with the cheese mixture. Cover and refrigerate any remaining cheese mixture and use to refill the shell as needed. Replace the reserved top of the cheese. Wrap the filled cheese in aluminum foil or plastic wrap and refrigerate overnight. To serve, remove the filled cheese from the refrigerator and allow it to come to room temperature. Surround with pumpernickel squares or triangles, cocktail rye bread, or crackers. Makes about 1½ cups.

VARIATION:

Add ½ teaspoon caraway seed or 2 teaspoons finely chopped chives. If desired, substitute ⅓ to ½ cup beer for the Sherry and brandy and 2 teaspoons Düsseldorf or Dijon-style mustard for the dry mustard.

GOAT CHEESE MARINATED IN OIL AND HERBS

If you enjoy goat cheese, this robustly flavorful appetizer is for you.

2 tablespoons finely chopped parsley
2 tablespoons finely chopped fresh chives
1 tablespoon finely chopped fresh basil, or
   ½ teaspoon crushed dried basil
1 tablespoon finely chopped fresh thyme,
   or ½ teaspoon crushed dried thyme
1 bay leaf
1 medium garlic clove, sliced
½ teaspoon freshly ground pepper
1 cup hot olive oil
½ pound French goat cheese, such as
   Bucheron, Crottin, or Chabichou, rind
   removed

In a small, heatproof bowl combine the parsley, chives, basil, thyme, bay leaf, garlic, and pepper. Pour the hot olive oil over the mixture and allow it to cool to room temperature. Add the cheese and make certain that it is thoroughly coated with the oil. Cover and store in a cool, dry place (not the refrigerator) 3 or 4 days. With a slotted spoon, transfer the cheese to a plate. Serve with slices of French bread. Makes 4 servings as a first course.

COCKTAIL CHEESE BALLS

CAMEMBERT-ALMOND BALLS

Follow the directions for Camembert Amandine (page 54), but instead of packing the cheese mixture into a mold, shape it into 1-inch balls. Roll the balls in the chopped almonds. Makes about 18.

ROQUEFORT-HAZELNUT BALLS

In a medium mixing bowl combine ¼ pound each Roquefort cheese and cream cheese, both at room temperature, 1 tablespoon finely chopped chives, and 1 tablespoon Cognac, dry Sherry, or tawny Port. Beat until the mixture is well blended and smooth. Form into 1-inch balls and roll in finely chopped toasted skinned hazelnuts. Makes about 12.

VARIATIONS:
Substitute toasted blanched almonds, walnuts, or pistachio nuts for the hazelnuts.

Use Sherry and substitute finely chopped prosciutto for the hazelnuts and, if desired, Gorgonzola cheese for the Roquefort.

LABNEH
Lebanese Yogurt Cheese Balls

Prepare Yogurt Cheese (below) and form it into 1-inch balls. Place the balls in a serving dish and spoon a thin coating of olive oil over them. Sprinkle lightly with paprika. Serve with pita bread, *lavash* (Armenian cracker bread), or sesame crackers. Makes about 12.

YOGURT CHEESE
Dieters can easily justify this tangy and refreshing low-calorie alternative to cream cheese.

2 cups unflavored whole milk (not lowfat) additive-free yogurt
Salt to taste (optional)

Line a colander or strainer with a clean muslin cloth wrung out in cold water or with a few layers of dampened cheesecloth. Pour the yogurt into the cloth. Tie opposite corners of the cloth together securely to form a bag. Suspend the bag from the neck of your kitchen sink faucet several hours or overnight. The whey will drain away, leaving a soft, creamy white cheese. When the yogurt has become firm enough to spread, remove it from the bag and place it in a bowl. Salt to taste if desired. Cover and refrigerate. Makes about 1 cup.

VARIATIONS:
For a richer cheese, combine the yogurt with 1 cup heavy cream and proceed as directed. Makes about 1½ cups.

HERB YOGURT CHEESE
In a bowl combine Yogurt Cheese with 1 tablespoon mixed minced fresh herbs such as chives, parsley, and basil; chives, parsley or mint, and dill; or chives, parsley, and mint.

HAWAIIAN CREAM CHEESE BALLS WITH GINGER AND COCONUT

In a bowl mix 3 ounces cream cheese, at room temperature, with 1 teaspoon peeled and grated fresh ginger root and ½ teaspoon each imported soy sauce and superfine sugar until well blended and smooth. Cover and chill 2 hours or until firm. Form the cheese mixture into ½-inch balls and roll the balls in freshly grated coconut. Serve on cocktail picks. Makes about 12.

RUSSIAN CAVIAR CHEESE BALL

A simple but arresting appetizer worthy of any zakuska table (page 413) or holiday buffet.

>   8 ounces cream cheese, at room
>   temperature
> ¼ cup cottage cheese
> 2 tablespoons sour cream
> 1 jar (4 ounces) red caviar, drained

In a bowl beat together the cream cheese and cottage cheese until well blended and smooth. Cover and chill 2 hours or until firm. Form the cheese mixture into a ball and place it on a chilled round serving plate. Coat the cheese ball with the sour cream and press the caviar onto the surface of the ball, being careful not to break the caviar eggs. Serve with thinly sliced rye or pumpernickel bread. Makes 12 to 16 servings.

CHEESE TORTE WITH DILL

This recipe is so simple that you will be amused in the face of effusive compliments.

> 1½ cups stale breadcrumbs
>   1 cup ground almonds
>   ½ cup unsalted butter, at room
>   temperature
>   ¾ pound cream cheese, cut into small
>   pieces, at room temperature
>   1 cup ricotta cheese
>   2 large eggs
>   ⅓ cup finely chopped fresh dill
>   2 tablespoons heavy cream
>   1 teaspoon grated lemon rind
>   1 teaspoon salt
>   ½ teaspoon freshly grated nutmeg
>   Dill sprigs

In a medium mixing bowl combine the breadcrumbs, almonds, and butter and mix well. Press the mixture onto the bottom and 1 inch up the sides of a buttered 9-inch springform pan.

In the container of an electric blender combine the cream cheese, ricotta cheese, eggs, dill, heavy cream, lemon rind, salt, and nutmeg. Cover and blend until smooth. Turn the cheese mixture into the prepared springform pan. Bake the torte in a preheated 350°F oven 45 minutes or until a knife inserted in the center comes out clean.

Remove the torte from the oven and place it on a wire rack. Allow it to cool to room temperature. Carefully remove the sides of the pan and transfer the torte to a serving plate. Garnish the torte with the dill sprigs. Serve at room temperature, or cover and chill before serving. Makes about 12 servings.

HOT CHEESE APPETIZERS

MILAN-STYLED FRIED CHEESE

Cut mozzarella or Bel Paese cheese into slices about 3 inches long, 1½ inches wide, and ⅛ to ¼ inch thick. Dredge the slices in flour, dip them in beaten egg, and coat them with fine breadcrumbs. In a heavy skillet heat enough olive oil or butter to coat the bottom generously. Add the cheese slices and fry in the hot oil or butter until golden and crisp on both sides. Drain on paper towels and serve at once.

VARIATION:

Cut the cheese into 2½ by ¼ by ¼-inch strips. Fry as above. Sprinkle with freshly grated imported Parmesan or Romano cheese and serve with Tomato Sauce (page 398) for dipping.

SAUTÉED CAMEMBERT OR BRIE

Select the freshest cheese possible for this and the following recipe. If the cheese has a shelf life date, choose one that has at least 4 to 6 weeks remaining on it. Use a baguette or other thin loaf of French bread for this particular appetizer.

1 whole, firm Camembert or Brie cheese
   (7 to 8 ounces)
⅓ cup fine dry breadcrumbs
½ teaspoon fines herbes *
1 egg, beaten
3 tablespoons butter
2 tablespoons very thinly sliced scallions,
   including 2 inches of the green tops
   Toasted baguette slices

Allow the cheese to stand at room temperature 15 minutes. On a sheet of waxed paper combine the bread crumbs with the fines herbes. Coat the cheese with the beaten egg, then with the bread-crumb mixture. In a 7- to 8-inch heavy skillet melt the butter over moderate heat. When the skillet is hot, add the cheese and cook about 1½ minutes or until lightly browned on the underside. (If the cheese starts to leak out on the edges, turn it over at once.) Cook the other side about 1 minute or until golden brown. Transfer to a platter and garnish the top with the scallions. Serve at once with the toasted baguette slices. To eat, break through the crisp coating of the sautéed Camembert or Brie and spread the cheese on the baguette slices. Makes 6 to 8 servings.

Fines herbes consists of an equal mixture of fresh parsley, tarragon, chives, and chervil.

EGGS

Virtually every culture has appreciated the economy and versatility of the nutritious egg. Few other foods can compare with it in convenience and adaptability. While eggs have been a favorite breakfast staple in this country, it is only within recent times that we have begun to tap their wide-ranging culinary potential.

Eggs as hors d'oeuvre play an important role in the cuisines of many lands.

Served unadorned save for a sprinkling of coarse salt, hard-cooked eggs make a simple but satisfying appetizer. And what would the hors d'oeuvre tray be without the presence of stuffed eggs, which entice and delight in any of their artful guises? Also popular as starters in international cookery are omelets such as the Italian frittata, Spanish tortilla, Arab ijjah, and Persian kuku. Cut into small pieces, these make fine accompaniments to cocktails; in larger portions they can be served as first courses. An elegant egg appetizer is the souffléed omelet, which is spread with a creamy filling, rolled into a cylinder, and sliced.

The following recipes illustrate some of the imaginative ways in which eggs can be savored as appetizers.

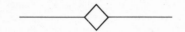

STUFFED EGGS

Stuffed eggs have long ranked high on many people's lists of preferred hors d'oeuvre.

    6 hard-cooked eggs*
    3 tablespoons Mayonnaise (page 387)
    ½ teaspoon Dijon-style mustard
    2 teaspoons white wine vinegar or fresh
        lemon juice
        Salt and cayenne pepper to taste
        Parsley sprigs or slices of pimento-
        stuffed olives

Halve the eggs lengthwise. Remove the yolks, reserving the egg whites. Force the yolks through a fine sieve into a mixing bowl. Add the Mayonnaise, mustard, vin-

*To hard-cook the eggs, place them, at room temperature, in a medium saucepan with cold water to cover. Bring to a boil over moderate heat, reduce the heat to low, and simmer, uncovered, 12 minutes. Drain quickly and cool under cold running water before peeling.

egar or lemon juice, salt, and cayenne pepper. Blend thoroughly. Taste and adjust the seasoning. Using a pastry bag fitted with a fluted tip, pipe the mixture into the egg whites, mounding it, or use a spoon to fill the egg whites.

Arrange the eggs in a single layer in a large, deep dish. Cover and chill. Remove the eggs from the refrigerator half an hour before serving and arrange them on a platter. Garnish the centers of the eggs with the parsley sprigs or olive slices. Makes 12 servings.

VARIATIONS:

ANCHOVY- AND HERB-STUFFED EGGS

Use 8 hard-cooked eggs. Force the yolks through a fine sieve into a mixing bowl. Add ⅓ cup sour cream, 2 tablespoons finely chopped fresh dill, 2 teaspoons each finely chopped chives and parsley, 2 teaspoons mashed anchovy fillets, ½ teaspoon freshly squeezed and strained lemon juice, and salt and freshly ground pepper to taste. Blend thoroughly. Taste and adjust the seasoning. Fill 12 of the reserved egg whites with the mixture as above. Finely chop the remaining 4 egg whites and use to garnish the centers of the eggs. Or save them for another use and garnish the center of each stuffed egg half with a rolled anchovy fillet. Makes 12 servings.

STUFFED EGGS WITH ASPARAGUS

Combine the sieved egg yolks with ¼ cup sour cream or unflavored yogurt, 1 tablespoon each finely chopped chives, parsley, and freshly squeezed and strained lemon juice, ½ teaspoon curry powder, and salt, freshly ground pepper, and cayenne pepper to taste. Blend thoroughly. Taste and adjust the seasoning. Fill the egg whites with the mixture as above. Top each stuffed egg half with 2 cooked asparagus tips and a strip of pimento. Makes 12 servings.

TUNA-STUFFED EGGS

Force the egg yolks and ¼ cup drained canned tuna through a fine sieve into a mixing bowl. Add 2 tablespoons butter, at room temperature, 1 teaspoon Düsseldorf or Dijon-style mustard, 1 tablespoon each Mayonnaise (page 387) and finely chopped parsley, 1 tiny garlic clove, crushed and finely chopped, 2 teaspoons freshly squeezed and strained lemon juice or to taste, and salt, freshly ground pepper, and Tabasco sauce to taste. Blend thoroughly. Taste and adjust the seasoning. Fill the egg whites with the mixture as above. Garnish the center of each stuffed egg half with a caper. Makes 12 servings.

CAVIAR-STUFFED EGGS

Combine the sieved egg yolks with 3 tablespoons Mayonnaise (page 387) or sour cream, 1 teaspoon freshly squeezed and strained lemon juice, 1 teaspoon grated mild onion, and salt and cayenne pepper to taste. Blend thoroughly. Taste and adjust the seasoning. Fill the egg whites with the mixture as above. Garnish the center of each stuffed egg half with ¼ teaspoon red or black caviar. Makes 12 servings.

STUFFED EGGS WITH LOBSTER AND AVOCADO

Combine the sieved yolks with ⅓ cup mashed cooked lobster meat, 2 tablespoons butter, at room temperature, 1 teaspoon grated mild onion, ½ teaspoon Worcestershire sauce, and salt and cayenne pepper to taste. Blend thoroughly. Taste and adjust the seasoning. Fill the egg whites with the mixture as above. Top each stuffed egg half with a small slice of avocado. Place 1 tiny piece of cooked lobster claw on each side of the avocado slice. Makes 12 servings.

CRAB-STUFFED EGGS

Combine the sieved yolks with ½ cup mashed cooked crabmeat, 3 tablespoons Mayonnaise (page 387), 1 teaspoon each Dijon-style mustard, grated mild onion, and finely chopped parsley, dash Worcestershire sauce, and salt and freshly ground pepper to taste. Blend thoroughly. Taste and adjust the seasoning. Fill the egg whites with the mixture as above and garnish with strips of pimento. Makes 12 servings.

SALMON-STUFFED EGGS

In the container of an electric blender blend the yolks with ¼ pound smoked salmon, finely chopped, ⅓ cup sour cream, 2 tablespoons freshly squeezed and strained lemon juice, and salt and freshly ground pepper to taste. Taste and adjust the seasoning. Fill the egg whites with the mixture as above. Garnish the center of each stuffed egg half with a sprig of dill. Makes 12 servings.

STUFFED EGGS WITH SALMON AND CAVIAR

Use 8 hard-cooked eggs. Reserve the whites of 2 eggs for another use. Combine the sieved yolks with 2 tablespoons freshly squeezed and strained lemon juice, 1 teaspoon grated mild onion, and salt and cayenne pepper to taste. Blend thoroughly. Taste and adjust the seasoning. Fill the egg whites with the mixture as above. Top each stuffed egg half with a tiny cornucopia of smoked salmon filled with black caviar. Makes 12 servings.

CHICKEN-STUFFED EGGS

Combine the sieved yolks with ¼ cup ground cooked chicken, 2 tablespoons Mayonnaise (page 387), ½ teaspoon curry powder or to taste, 1 teaspoon very finely chopped chives or scallion tops, ½ teaspoon freshly squeezed and strained lemon juice, and salt and cayenne pepper to taste. Blend thoroughly. Taste and adjust the seasoning. Fill the egg whites with the mixture as above. Garnish the center of each stuffed egg half with a sliver of toasted blanched almond. Makes 12 servings.

HAM-STUFFED EGGS

Combine the sieved yolks with ¼ cup ground cooked ham, 2 tablespoons Mayonnaise (page 387), 2 tablespoons butter, at room temperature, 1 teaspoon each Düsseldorf or Dijon-style mustard and grated mild onion, ¼ teaspoon Worcestershire sauce, and salt and Tabasco sauce to taste. Blend thoroughly. Taste and adjust the seasoning. Fill the egg whites with the mixture as above. Garnish the center of each stuffed egg half with a sprig of parsley or a slice of pimento-stuffed olive. Makes 12 servings.

SPINACH-STUFFED EGGS

Combine the sieved yolks with 3 ounces cream cheese or Neufchâtel cheese, at room temperature, 3 tablespoons each cooked spinach and freshly grated Parmesan cheese, and salt, freshly ground pepper, and freshly grated nutmeg to taste. Blend thoroughly, adding 2 tablespoons heavy cream or as needed to give the mixture a creamy consistency. Taste and adjust the seasoning. Fill the egg whites with the mixture as above. Makes 12 servings.

MUSHROOM-STUFFED EGGS

Finely chop 6 medium mushrooms and toss them with 1 tablespoon freshly squeezed and strained lemon juice. In a small, heavy skillet melt 1 tablespoon butter over medium-high heat. Add the mushrooms and sauté, stirring frequently, until almost all the liquid in the pan has evaporated. Remove from the heat and cool. Combine the sieved yolks with 2 tablespoons butter, at room temperature, the cooked mushroom mixture, 1 tablespoon finely chopped fresh dill, and salt and freshly ground pepper to taste. Blend thoroughly. Taste and adjust the seasoning. Fill the egg whites with the mixture as above. Makes 12 servings.

EGG CROUSTADES WITH PESTO MAYONNAISE

Trim the crusts from 6 thick slices of white bread and carefully hollow out the centers. Lightly brush all the surfaces except the undersides with melted butter and arrange the croustades on an ungreased baking sheet. Bake in a preheated 400°F oven about 10 minutes or until golden brown. Place each croustade on a small plate and put 1 halved or quartered hard-cooked egg in the center. Spoon Pesto Mayonnaise (page 388) over the eggs and garnish with thin strips of pimento. Makes 6 servings.

VARIATION:

EGG CROUSTADES WITH TAPÉNADE

Substitute Tapénade (page 25) for the Pesto Mayonnaise.

EGG AND SMOKED SALMON APPETIZER

Easy to make and impressive to serve.

   4 hard-cooked eggs
   6 tablespoons Mayonnaise (page 387)
     Salt and freshly ground pepper to taste
   8 toast rounds, each 2 inches in diameter,
     buttered
   8 rounds smoked salmon, each 2 inches
     in diameter
   ¼ cup sour cream
 1½ teaspoons freshly squeezed and strained
     lemon juice
   1 ounce caviar
     Watercress sprigs

Halve the eggs crosswise. Remove the yolks, reserving the egg whites. Force the yolks through a fine sieve into a mixing bowl. Add 2 tablespoons of the Mayonnaise, salt, and pepper and mix well. Taste and adjust the seasoning. Fill the reserved egg whites with the mixture.

Arrange the toast rounds on a serving platter. Top each with a round of salmon. Place a stuffed egg half, cut side down, on each salmon round. In a small bowl mix together the remaining 4 tablespoons Mayonnaise, sour cream, and lemon juice. Fold in the caviar. Spoon the sauce over the eggs, coating them completely, and garnish with the watercress. Makes 8 servings.

CHINESE RED-COOKED EGGS

Excellent as appetizers or snacks, these conversation-makers also provide tempting fare for a buffet or picnic.

   8 eggs, at room temperature
   ½ cup imported dark soy sauce
   ½ cup imported light soy sauce
   ½ cup dry Sherry
   3 tablespoons sugar
   3 thin slices ginger root
   2 sticks cinnamon, each 2 inches long
   2 teaspoons whole cloves
   2 teaspoons grated orange rind

In a medium saucepan cover the eggs with cold water and bring the water to a boil over moderate heat. Reduce the heat to low and simmer, uncovered, about 15 minutes. Remove the saucepan from the heat and run cold water into the pan until the water in the pan is no longer hot. Allow the eggs to cool in the cold water. Drain them when they are cool enough to handle.

Tap the shells of the eggs lightly all over with the back of a spoon, being careful not to crack them so hard that they come loose. Return the eggs to the saucepan and add the remaining ingredients. Add enough cold water to cover the eggs and bring to a boil over moderate heat. Reduce the heat to low, cover, and simmer about 1½ hours. Remove from the heat and allow the eggs to cool to room temperature in the cooking liquid. Refrigerate the eggs in the cooking liquid several hours or up to several days. (The longer the eggs soak, the better flavor they will develop.) Just before serving, drain the eggs, discarding the cooking liquid. Shell the eggs, cut them in half lengthwise, and arrange them on a serving platter. Makes 8 servings.

APPETIZER FRITTATAS

These frittatas *incorporate some everyday ingredients with remarkably delicious results. When made in miniature (see Variation), they will not only charm your palate but steal your heart as well.*

½ pound fresh spinach
5 tablespoons butter
4 scallions, thinly sliced, including 2
    inches of the green tops
¼ pound mushrooms, chopped
2 medium garlic cloves, finely chopped
3 tablespoons finely chopped parsley
5 eggs
½ cup freshly grated imported Parmesan or
    Romano cheese
    Salt and freshly ground pepper to taste
    Garlic Yogurt Sauce (page 392)

Wash the spinach thoroughly under cold running water, discarding the tough stems and bruised leaves. Drain thoroughly, chop finely, and set aside.

In a large, heavy skillet melt 2 tablespoons of the butter over medium-high heat. Add the scallions and mushrooms and sauté until golden, stirring frequently. Stir in the spinach, garlic, and parsley. Cook, stirring constantly, until almost all of the liquid in the skillet has evaporated. Remove from the heat.

In a medium bowl beat the eggs until frothy. Stir in the contents of the skillet, ¼ cup of the cheese, salt, and pepper.

Brush the bottoms and sides of 18 2½-inch muffin cups with the remaining 3 tablespoons butter. Heat the cups in a preheated 425°F oven until the butter sizzles. Spoon about 2 tablespoons of the egg mixture into each muffin cup. Sprinkle the tops evenly with the remaining ¼ cup cheese. Bake 8 to 10 minutes or until puffed and golden brown. Transfer to a wire rack and cool 1 minute. Run a small spatula around the edges of the muffin cups and remove the frittatas. Serve at once, accompanied with the Garlic Yogurt Sauce. Makes 18.

VARIATION:

MINIATURE FRITTATAS

Use 24 1¾-inch muffin cups. Spoon about 1 heaping tablespoon of the egg mixture into each cup. Bake 6 to 8 minutes. If desired, top each frittata with a small spoonful of the Garlic Yogurt Sauce and garnish with finely chopped parsley. Serve immediately. Makes 24.

TORTILLA DE PATATA A LA ESPAÑOLA
Spanish Potato Omelet

This most Spanish of omelets is almost always found among a selection of tapas *(page 405).*

> 1 cup olive oil
> 3 large boiling potatoes, peeled and sliced
>   into ⅛-inch-thick rounds
> 1 large onion, thinly sliced
>   Salt
> 4 eggs

In a large, heavy skillet heat all but 2 tablespoons of the oil over medium-high heat. Add the potato and onion slices, sprinkle them lightly with salt, and turn them about in the pan until they are well coated with the oil. Reduce the heat to moderate and fry the vegetables slowly, turning the slices over occasionally, until they are tender but not brown. Transfer the contents of the skillet to a large sieve or colander and drain the potatoes and onions of all their excess oil. Pat the vegetables dry with paper towels.

Using a fork or whisk, in a large bowl beat the eggs with salt to taste until frothy. Gently stir in the potatoes and onion, making certain that the vegetables are completely covered with the eggs. Let stand at room temperature 10 to 15 minutes.

In a medium-sized, heavy skillet heat the remaining 2 tablespoons oil over high heat until very hot. Add the omelet mixture, spreading it evenly with a spatula. Reduce the heat to moderate and cook, shaking the pan from time to time to prevent the eggs from sticking, until the bottom of the omelet is lightly browned. Invert a large, flat plate over the top of the skillet and, with one hand on the plate and the other gripping the skillet handle, quickly invert the pan and turn the omelet out onto the plate. Carefully slide the omelet back into the skillet and cook until it is lightly browned on the second side. Turn the omelet out onto a large, round serving plate. With a sharp knife, cut the omelet into concentric rings, each about 1 inch wide, then cut the rings into 1-inch pieces. Serve hot, warm, or at room temperature with cocktail picks for spearing. Makes about 60 pieces.

VARIATION:

Add fried chopped Spanish *chorizo* or other garlic-seasoned smoked pork sausage to the beaten eggs along with the fried vegetables.

AUSTRIAN EGGS WITH HAM AND HAZELNUTS

A clever way of finishing up leftover ham without noticing the fact.

 6 eggs
⅔ cup sour cream
¾ cup finely chopped lean cooked ham
½ cup grated Swiss or Gruyère cheese
 2 tablespoons finely chopped scallions,
    including 2 inches of the green tops
 3 tablespoons finely chopped parsley
 1 tablespoon finely chopped fresh dill
    (optional)
 2 tablespoons butter, melted
½ teaspoon salt
¼ cup finely chopped hazelnuts
    Paprika

In a large mixing bowl beat the eggs until blended, then beat in the sour cream. Add the ham, cheese, scallions, parsley, dill (if used), butter, salt, and 2 tablespoons of the hazelnuts and mix well. Pour into a well-buttered 9-inch-square baking dish. Sprinkle evenly with the remaining hazelnuts and the paprika. Bake in a preheated 350°F oven about 25 minutes or until set and lightly browned. Cut into small squares. Serve hot. Makes about 24 squares.

MEXICAN EGGS WITH GREEN CHILIES AND BACON

This is just one of Mexico's numerous culinary contributions to egg cookery.

> 6 slices bacon, diced
> 8 scallions, thinly sliced, including 2
>   inches of the green tops
> 8 eggs
> 1 cup half-and-half or milk
> 1 can (4 ounces) peeled and diced green
>   chilies
> 1½ cups (6 ounces) shredded Monterey
>   Jack cheese
> 1 cup (4 ounces) shredded sharp Cheddar
>   cheese
> ¼ teaspoon cumin
> ½ teaspoon salt
> ¼ teaspoon freshly ground pepper or to
>   taste
> 1 tablespoon butter, melted

In a medium-sized, heavy skillet fry the bacon over moderate heat, stirring frequently, until crisp. Transfer with a slotted spoon to paper towels to drain. Pour off all but 1 tablespoon of the bacon fat from the skillet. Add the scallions and sauté, stirring, until soft and golden. Remove from the heat.

In a medium mixing bowl beat the eggs until blended, then slowly beat in the half-and-half or milk. Add the bacon, scallions, green chilies, cheeses, cumin, salt, and pepper and mix well. Pour the mixture into a well-buttered 9-inch-square baking dish. Drizzle the top with the melted butter. Bake in a preheated 325°F oven about 40 minutes or until set and lightly browned. Cut into small squares. Serve hot. Makes about 24 squares.

OMELET WITH HERBS, WALNUTS, AND CURRANTS

Intriguing flavors and textures blend harmoniously in this Middle Eastern omelet.

> 4 eggs
> ¼ cup finely chopped parsley
> ⅓ cup finely chopped mixed fresh herbs
>   (chives, dill, and coriander)
> 2 tablespoons chopped walnuts
> 2 tablespoons dried currants
>   Pinch saffron or turmeric
>   Salt and freshly ground pepper to taste
> 1 tablespoon butter
>   Unflavored yogurt (optional)

Place the eggs in a mixing bowl and beat until frothy. Add the parsley, mixed fresh herbs, walnuts, currants, saffron or turmeric, salt, and pepper and mix well.

Melt the butter in a shallow ovenproof baking dish about 9 inches in diameter and pour in the egg mixture. Bake in a preheated 350°F oven about 30 minutes or until the eggs are firm. Cut into wedges and serve hot or cold, accompanied with a bowl of unflavored yogurt, if you like. Makes 2 servings.

CRUSTLESS SWISS CHARD QUICHE

Here is a good way to use a vegetable that remains relatively unappreciated in this country.

> 2 pounds Swiss chard
> ¼ cup butter
> 1 large onion, finely chopped
> 2 medium garlic cloves, finely chopped
> ½ teaspoon crushed dried basil
> ½ teaspoon crushed dried oregano
> ½ teaspoon crushed dried thyme
> 12 eggs
> ½ teaspoon salt
> ¼ teaspoon freshly ground pepper
> ½ cup heavy cream or sour cream
> 2 cups (½ pound) shredded Swiss cheese
> 1 cup (¼ pound) freshly grated imported
>   Parmesan cheese

Wash the chard thoroughly under cold running water. Trim off the stem ends and discard. Cut off and reserve the stems. With a food processor or knife, finely chop the leaves and stems separately; set aside.

In a large, heavy skillet melt the butter over moderate heat. Add the chard stems, onion, and garlic and sauté, stirring almost constantly, until the onion is soft but not browned. Add the chard leaves and cook, stirring, about 3 minutes or until they are just limp and heated through. Remove from the heat and stir in the basil, oregano, and thyme.

In a large bowl lightly beat the eggs with the salt, pepper, heavy cream or sour cream, 1½ cups of the Swiss cheese, ½ cup of the Parmesan cheese, and the cooked vegetable mixture. Pour into a well-buttered 10 by 15-inch rimmed baking pan. Sprinkle evenly with the remaining ½ cup Parmesan cheese. Bake in a preheated 350°F oven about 20 minutes or until a knife inserted in the center comes out clean. Sprinkle the remaining ½ cup Swiss cheese evenly on top and bake about 1 minute more or until the cheese melts. Transfer to a wire rack and let stand 10 minutes at room temperature. Cut into 1¼-inch squares and serve. Makes 96 squares.

VARIATION:

CRUSTLESS SPINACH QUICHE

Substitute 2 pounds fresh spinach for the chard. Cut off the spinach roots and discard, then proceed as directed above.

APPETIZER SOUFFLÉ ROLL

To skip this recipe would be to miss one of the glories of this chapter.

> *Butter*
> *All-purpose flour*
> *2 cups warm milk*
> *Salt and freshly ground pepper to taste*
> *4 eggs, separated*
> *2 tablespoons freshly grated imported Parmesan cheese*
> *Fine dry breadcrumbs*
> *Spinach, Mushroom, and Ham Filling (page 44)*
> *Watercress*
> *1 cup sour cream*
> *2 to 3 tablespoons heavy cream*
> *1 tablespoon finely chopped chives (optional)*

Butter a 10 by 15-inch jelly roll pan and line it with waxed paper. Butter the paper and sprinkle with flour, shaking off the excess. Set aside.

In a medium-sized, heavy saucepan melt ¼ cup butter over low heat. Whisk in 6 tablespoons flour and cook, whisking constantly, 2 minutes or until the mixture is foamy. Gradually whisk in the milk until the mixture is smooth. Season with the salt and pepper and simmer about 2 minutes, stirring constantly, until the sauce is thickened to the consistency of heavy cream. Remove from the heat and whisk the egg yolks thoroughly into the white sauce, one at a time, until all of the yolks are incorporated into the sauce. Using a clean whisk, beat the egg whites until they are stiff but not dry. Gently fold them into the yolk-sauce mixture. Spread the omelet mixture evenly into the prepared jelly roll pan. Sprinkle evenly with the cheese. Bake in a preheated 325°F oven about 40 minutes or until lightly browned.

Quickly turn the souffléed omelet out on a towel that has been sprinkled with fine breadcrumbs to prevent it from sticking to the omelet. Peel off the waxed paper and trim off any dry or irregular edges. Fold the edge of the towel over one of the long sides of the omelet. Carefully roll up the omelet lengthwise with the towel. Let cool to room temperature. Unroll the cooled omelet and spread it with the Spinach, Mushroom, and Ham Filling. Roll up the filled omelet lengthwise like a jelly roll. Using 2 large spatulas, transfer the roll to a long, narrow serving platter. Garnish with the watercress.

Thin the sour cream with the heavy cream and season lightly with salt. Sprinkle with the chives, if desired. Accompany the roll with a bowl of the thinned sour cream.

To serve, cut the roll crosswise into slices about 1 inch thick and top each slice with a spoonful of the thinned sour cream. Makes 10 to 12 servings.

VARIATIONS:

Substitute 2 recipes Ham Filling (page 44) for the Spinach, Mushroom, and Ham Filling.

Omit the Parmesan cheese, sour cream, heavy cream, and optional chives. Substitute Chicken Liver and Mushroom Filling (page 43) for the Spinach, Mushroom, and Ham Filling.

Omit the Parmesan cheese. Prepare 2 recipes Smoked Salmon Spread (page 30) and fold in ¼ cup heavy cream, whipped. Substitute this spread for the Spinach, Mushroom, and Ham Filling.

Omit the Parmesan cheese, heavy cream, and optional chives. Substitute Caviar and Cream Cheese Filling (page 42) for the Spinach, Mushroom, and Ham Filling. Use ¾ cup sour cream and blend it with 2 ounces red or black caviar. Serve with the roll. Alternatively, top each slice with a dollop of sour cream and garnish with 1 teaspoon caviar.

ITALIAN SPINACH TIMBALES WITH FONDUTA

Glamorous enough to be company fare.

½ pound Italian Fontina cheese, diced
½ cup milk or half-and-half
  Butter
  Fine breadcrumbs
3 large bunches spinach
1 medium shallot or scallion, finely
  chopped (include 2 inches of the green
  top of the scallion)
½ cup heavy cream
1 ounce Italian Fontina cheese, finely
  diced
3 eggs
1 large egg yolk plus 2 small egg yolks
1 tablespoon freshly squeezed and strained
  lemon juice
⅛ teaspoon freshly grated nutmeg
¼ teaspoon salt or to taste
⅛ teaspoon freshly ground black pepper
⅛ teaspoon freshly ground white pepper

In a medium bowl combine the ½ pound cheese and milk or half-and-half. Cover and refrigerate 8 hours or overnight. Brush a 6-cup muffin pan generously with butter and sprinkle it with breadcrumbs.

Wash the spinach thoroughly under cold running water, discarding the tough stems and bruised leaves. Drain well on paper towels. In a large, heavy skillet melt 1 tablespoon butter over medium-high heat. Gradually add the spinach, stirring almost constantly. Cover and cook over moderate heat, stirring from time to time, about 5 minutes or until the spinach is wilted. Transfer to a colander and let the spinach drain and cool. Squeeze it dry, chop it finely, and reserve.

Add ½ tablespoon butter to the skillet and melt over moderate heat. Add the shallot or scallion and reduce the heat to low. Cover and cook, stirring occasionally, until it is soft but not browned. Add the reserved spinach and gradually stir in the cream until it is absorbed. Transfer the mixture to a large mixing bowl, stir in the 1 ounce cheese, and cool. Add the eggs, 1 large egg yolk, lemon juice, nutmeg, salt, and black pepper and mix well. Taste and adjust the seasoning. Spoon the mixture into the prepared muffin pan. Cover the pan with buttered waxed paper. Place the muffin pan in a large baking pan and pour enough hot water into the baking pan to reach three-fourths of the way up the sides of the muffin pan. Bake in a preheated 325°F oven about 25 minutes or until the timbales are puffed and a tester inserted in the center comes out clean. Remove the timbales from the oven and keep them warm in the water bath.

Prepare the *fonduta:* In a medium-sized, heavy saucepan beat the remaining 2 small egg yolks over low heat until thickened. Add the cheese and milk or half-and-half mixture and beat until thoroughly blended. Stir in 1½ tablespoons butter ½ tablespoon at a time until blended. Season with the white pepper and remove from the heat.

Run a thin, sharp knife around each timbale and invert onto a heated platter. Spoon the fonduta over the timbales and serve. Makes 6.

PÂTÉS, TERRINES, AND MOLDED MOUSSES

A succulent, richly, flavored pâté can be a rare taste experience, yet for all their seeming mystique pâtés are not really difficult to prepare. They make splendid first courses and are ideal for appetizer buffets. Pâtés can be prepared well ahead of serving time, and some will keep up to a week if refrigerated, actually improving in taste as the flavors blend together for a few days.

Although the term pâté originally applied only to a dish enclosed in pastry (pâté en croute) and that of terrine, its close relative, to one baked without a crust in a special earthenware container (also called terrine) lined with strips of pork fat, these definitions have grown less rigid nowadays, with the word pâté often being more loosely used to include both types of dishes plus others that contain neither pastry nor pork fat.

Molded mousses, like pâtés, make excellent first courses. Molds are available in an assortment of attractive designs and shapes. Small decorative ones work beautifully for individual servings, while a large mold is particularly suitable for a buffet. Food often looks more dramatic when presented in molded form, and even the simplest of molded appetizers has an air of elegance about it. A mousse is a perfect way to glamorize almost any leftovers. It is also a convenient choice since it can be prepared a day in advance and refrigerated until ready to unmold and garnish.

For additional pâtés please see the Spreads section of Chapter 4.

MUSHROOM, SPINACH, AND WALNUT PÂTÉ

This uncommonly savory production will delight vegetarians and nonvegetarians alike.

    ¼ cup butter
    1 medium-sized yellow onion, finely
        chopped
    1 pound mushrooms, finely chopped
    1 medium garlic clove, finely chopped
    3 tablespoons medium-dry Sherry
    ¾ teaspoon crushed dried rosemary
        Salt and freshly ground pepper to taste
    2 cups finely chopped spinach leaves
 1⅓ cups ground walnuts
    1 cup pot cheese
    2 eggs, lightly beaten
    ⅓ cup finely chopped parsley
    ¼ teaspoon freshly grated nutmeg

In a large, heavy skillet melt the butter over medium-high heat. Add the onion and sauté until it is soft but not browned, stirring frequently. Add the mushrooms and garlic and sauté, stirring, 5 minutes. Add the Sherry, rosemary, salt, and pepper and cook over low heat, stirring occasionally, about 8 minutes or until the liquid is evaporated.

Transfer the contents of the skillet to a large bowl. Stir in the spinach and walnuts and let the mixture cool. Force the pot cheese through a sieve into the bowl. Add the eggs, parsley, and nutmeg and mix thoroughly.

Line a buttered 1-quart loaf pan with parchment paper, allowing enough overhang to fold over the top, and butter the paper. Spoon the mixture into the pan, tap the pan on the counter several times to expel any air pockets, and smooth the top with a spatula. Fold the overhanging paper over the pâté and cover the pan with a double layer of aluminum foil. Place the loaf pan in a large baking pan and pour enough hot water into the baking pan to reach halfway up the sides of the loaf pan. Bake the pâté in a preheated 375°F oven 1½ hours. Transfer the loaf pan to a rack and let stand 30 minutes. Weight the pâté with a 2-pound weight (such as 2 unopened 1-pound cans) for 1 hour. Remove the weight and foil, place an inverted serving platter over the pan, and invert onto the platter. Remove the parchment paper, slice the pâté, and serve at room temperature. Or wrap the pâté in foil and chill several hours before serving.

Makes 8 to 10 servings as a first course, 20 as an hors d'oeuvre.

Note: Parchment paper can be purchased in the housewares sections of department stores and at specialty kitchenware stores, cake decorating shops, and some supermarkets.

SWEDISH SEAFOOD PÂTÉ

As glorious a seafood pâté as is likely to be found this side of paradise.

¾ *pound uncooked medium or large shrimp, shelled and deveined*
¼ *pound haddock fillet, skinned*
⅓ *cup dry white wine*
2 *tablespoons Cognac*
1 *cup heavy cream*
1 *egg*
2 *teaspoons salt*
⅛ *teaspoon cayenne pepper or to taste*
⅔ *cup finely chopped fresh dill*
¼ *pound medium or large shrimp, shelled, deveined, cooked, and chopped*
¼ *pound cooked crabmeat, picked over and flaked*
2 *ounces cooked lobster meat, chopped*
2 *teaspoons freshly squeezed and strained lemon juice or to taste*
  Mayonnaise (page 387) (optional)

In a food processor fitted with the steel blade purée the uncooked shrimp, haddock, wine, Cognac, ⅓ cup of the cream, egg, salt, and cayenne pepper. Transfer the mixture to a bowl, add the dill, chopped cooked shrimp, crabmeat, lobster meat, and lemon juice and mix well.

In a chilled bowl beat the remaining ⅔ cup cream until it stands in stiff peaks. Fold it into the seafood mixture. Spoon the mixture into a buttered 8 by 4 by 2-inch glass loaf pan, packing it gently. Tap the pan on the counter several times to expel any air pockets and smooth the top with a spatula. Cover the loaf pan with buttered waxed paper and alunimum foil. Set it in a shallow baking pan and pour enough hot water into the baking pan to reach halfway up the sides of the loaf pan. Bake the pâté in a preheated 200°F oven about 1 hour and 15 minutes or until a skewer inserted in the center comes out clean. Transfer the loaf pan to a rack and let the pâté stand 10 minutes, then chill it, covered, 1 hour. Remove the foil and waxed paper, place an inverted serving platter over the pan, and invert the pâté onto the platter. Remove any liquid from the platter with a paper towel. Serve the pâté at room temperature with Mayonnaise, if you like. Makes 10 servings as a first course.

TERRINE OF PORK AND VEAL WITH HAM

One bite will convince you that the effort involved is more than justified.

½ pound boneless veal from the round or
    fillet, cut into ¼-inch-thick strips
3 tablespoons Cognac
1 tablespoon finely chopped shallots
¾ teaspoon crushed dried thyme
½ teaspoon allspice
1¾ teaspoons salt
¼ teaspoon freshly ground pepper
2 tablespoons butter
½ cup very finely chopped onion
⅓ cup Port or Madeira
¾ pound lean ground pork
¾ pound lean ground veal
½ pound ground fresh pork fatback
2 eggs, lightly beaten
1 garlic clove, crushed to a smooth purée
    Thinly sliced strips of fresh pork
    fatback
½ pound lean boiled ham, cut into
    ¼-inch-wide strips
1 bay leaf

In a bowl combine the veal strips with the Cognac, shallots, ½ teaspoon of the thyme, ¼ teaspoon of the allspice, ¼ teaspoon of the salt, and ⅛ teaspoon of the pepper. Mix well and set aside to marinate.

Meanwhile, in a small, heavy skillet melt the butter over moderate heat. Add the onion and sauté until soft but not browned, stirring frequently. Scrape the onion into a large mixing bowl. Pour the Port or Madeira into the skillet and boil it down until reduced by half. Pour it into the mixing bowl. Add the ground pork, ground veal, ground pork fatback, eggs, garlic, and remaining ¼ teaspoon thyme, ¼ teaspoon allspice, 1½ teaspoons salt, and ⅛ teaspoon pepper. Beat vigorously with a wooden spoon until the mixture has become light in texture and well blended. In a small skillet sauté a spoonful of the mixture until cooked through, taste it, and add additional seasoning to the remaining mixture if needed. Drain the veal strips and beat the marinade into the ground meat mixture. Divide the ground meat mixture into 3 equal parts.

Line an 8-cup rectangular terrine with the strips of pork fatback, letting the ends extend over the sides. Press one third of the meat mixture in the bottom of the terrine.

Cover with half the strips of marinated veal, alternating with half the strips of ham. Top with the second third of the meat mixture and a final layer of veal and ham strips. Spread the remaining third of meat mixture over the veal and ham. Place the bay leaf on top and fold the overhanging strips of fatback over the meat mixture.

Enclose the top of the terrine with aluminum foil and cover with the lid. Set the terrine in a shallow baking pan and pour enough boiling water into the pan to reach halfway up the sides of the terrine; add boiling water during cooking as necessary. Bake in a preheated 350°F oven about 1½ hours or until the pâté pulls away slightly from the sides of the terrine and the juices are clear yellow, with no traces of pink.

Remove the terrine from the oven, then remove it from the pan. Pour out the water and return the terrine to the pan. Remove the lid but leave the foil covering intact. Put a piece of heavy cardboard that is cut slightly smaller than the terrine on top of the foil and place a 3- to 4-pound weight on it, such as a brick or heavy unopened cans. Or place a pan that is slightly smaller than the terrine on top of the foil and fill it with the heavy objects. Let stand at room temperature 4 hours, then refrigerate, still weighted, 8 hours or overnight.

Remove the weights, cardboard or pan, and the foil. Serve the pâté directly from the terrine, slicing down through it with a knife. Or loosen the pâté with a thin knife and unmold it onto a platter. Remove excess fat before serving. Makes about 24 servings.

COUNTRY TERRINE

A many-splendored creation whose profound satisfactions are not even hinted at in its title.

  1 pound diced lean pork
  1 pound diced lean veal
  ½ pound diced fresh pork fatback
  1 small whole chicken breast (8 to 10
    ounces), skinned, boned, and diced
  3 chicken livers
  3 tablespoons butter
  ½ cup finely chopped onion
  ¼ cup finely chopped shallots
  1 large garlic clove, very finely chopped
  ½ cup Port or Madeira
  ¼ cup Cognac
  3 eggs, lightly beaten
  ¾ teaspoon crushed dried thyme
1½ teaspoons Épices Fines (page 83)
1½ teaspoons salt
  ½ teaspoon freshly ground pepper
  ½ cup unsalted shelled and skinned
    pistachio nuts
    Thinly sliced strips of fresh pork
    fatback

Coarsely grind the pork, veal, diced pork fatback, chicken breast, and chicken livers together in a meat grinder or food processor. Transfer to a large mixing bowl.

In a small, heavy skillet melt the butter over moderate heat. Add the onion, shallots, and garlic and sauté until soft but not browned, stirring frequently. Scrape into the mixing bowl. Add the Port or Madeira and Cognac to the skillet and boil it down until reduced by half. Pour into the mixing bowl. Add the eggs, thyme, Épices Fines, salt, pepper, and nuts and mix thoroughly. In a small skillet sauté a spoonful of the mixture until cooked through, taste it, and add additional seasoning to the remaining mixture if needed.

Line an 8-cup rectangular terrine with the strips of pork fatback, letting the ends extend over the sides. Spread the meat mixture on top and press firmly. Fold the overhanging strips of fatback over the meat mixture. Cover the terrine with a double layer of aluminum foil. Set it in a shallow baking pan and pour enough boiling water into the pan to reach halfway up the sides of the terrine; add boiling water during cooking as necessary. Bake in a preheated 350°F oven about 1½ hours or until the pâté pulls away slightly from the sides of the pan and the juices are clear yellow, with no traces of pink.

Remove the terrine from the oven, then remove it from the pan. Pour out the water and return the terrine, still with its foil covering, to the pan. Put a piece of heavy cardboard that is cut slightly smaller than the terrine on top of the foil and place a 3- to 4-pound weight on it, such as a brick or heavy unopened cans. Or place a pan that is slightly smaller than the terrine on top of the foil and fill it with the heavy objects. Let stand at room temperature 2 hours, then refrigerate, still weighted, 8 hours or overnight.

Remove the weights, cardboard or pan, and the foil. Serve the pâté directly from the terrine, slicing down through it with a knife. Or loosen the pâté with a thin knife and unmold it onto a platter. Remove excess fat before serving. Makes about 24 servings.

ÉPICES FINES

1 tablespoon each whole cloves, ground cinnamon, grated nutmeg, paprika, dried thyme, and crumbled bay leaves
1½ teaspoons each ground allspice, ground ginger, dried basil, dried oregano, dried marjoram, dried savory, and dried sage
1 teaspoon each whole white and black peppercorns

Place all the ingredients in the container of an electric blender. Cover and blend at high speed until finely ground. Store in an airtight container. Makes 1 cup.

PÂTÉ MAISON WITH CUMBERLAND SAUCE

This will remain a haunting memory for some weeks after the fact.

1 pound sliced bacon
1½ pounds chicken livers, trimmed and ground
1 pound lean ground beef
1 pound lean ground veal
1 cup heavy cream
6 eggs
1 cup unsalted shelled and skinned pistachio nuts
2 teaspoons salt
½ teaspoon freshly ground pepper or to taste
¾ teaspoon freshly grated nutmeg
Pinch allspice
½ cup brandy
6 whole chicken livers
6 slices uncooked bacon
6 slices boiled ham, cut into ¼-inch-wide strips
Cumberland Sauce (page 84)

In a saucepan cover the 1 pound bacon with water. Bring to a boil and simmer 10 minutes. Drain. Line a 12 by 3 by 3-inch loaf pan with overlapping slices of the bacon. Refrigerate. Reserve the remaining slices of cooked bacon.

Put the ground chicken livers, beef, and veal through the fine blade of a meat grinder, or grind them in a food processor. Transfer to a large mixing bowl. Add the cream, eggs, nuts, salt, pepper, nutmeg, and allspice. Warm the brandy, ignite, and add to the mixing bowl. Mix thoroughly. In a small skillet sauté a spoonful of the mixture until cooked through, taste it, and add additional seasoning to the remaining mixture if needed.

Press half of the meat mixture in the bottom of the loaf pan. Wrap each whole chicken liver in a slice of uncooked bacon and arrange down the middle of the pan. Fill the spaces between the bacon-wrapped chicken livers with the ham strips. Spread the remaining meat mixture evenly over the top. Cover with overlapping slices of the reserved cooked bacon.

Enclose the top of the loaf pan with a double layer of aluminum foil. Set it in a shallow baking pan and pour boiling water into the pan to reach halfway up the sides of the loaf pan; add boiling water during cooking as necessary. Bake in a preheated 350°F oven 2 hours. Remove the loaf pan from the water, uncover, and bake about 30 minutes longer or until the pâté pulls away slightly from the sides of the pan and the juices are clear yellow, with no traces of pink.

Remove the loaf pan from the oven, pour off the excess liquid, and let cool to room temperature. Set it in a shallow pan that will fit in the refrigerator. Cut a piece of heavy cardboard to fit inside the top of the loaf pan. Wrap it with aluminum foil and place it over the pâté. Put a 3- to 4-pound weight on it, such as a brick or heavy unopened cans. Or place a pan that is slightly smaller than the terrine on top of the foil and fill it with the heavy objects. Refrigerate, weighted, 8 hours or overnight.

Remove the weights and foil-wrapped cardboard. Loosen the pâté with a thin knife and unmold it onto a platter. Remove excess fat. Serve with the Cumberland Sauce. Makes about 10 servings.

CUMBERLAND SAUCE

Rind and juice of 1 orange, rind cut into julienne strips
Rind and juice of 1 lemon, rind cut into julienne strips
4 shallots, finely chopped
½ cup tawny Port
½ cup red currant jelly
1 teaspoon Düsseldorf or Dijon-style mustard
Pinch ginger
Pinch cayenne pepper

Combine the citrus rind and juice and shallots in a small saucepan. Simmer over low heat, uncovered, 10 minutes, stirring occasionally. Add the remaining ingredients and simmer 10 minutes, stirring frequently. Serve at room temperature or chilled. Makes about 1⅓ cups.

CARIBBEAN DUCK PÂTÉ WITH ORANGE AND PISTACHIOS

To say that this pâté is a rare and wondrous pleasure is not to overstate the case.

> 1 4½-pound duck
> ½ pound lean pork shoulder, cubed
> ⅓ pound chicken livers
> 1¼ cups heavy cream
> ½ cup finely chopped onion
> ⅓ cup orange Curaçao or other orange-
> flavored liqueur
> ⅓ cup unsalted shelled and skinned
> pistachio nuts
> 2 eggs, lightly beaten
> 3 tablespoons dry white wine
> ¾ teaspoon crushed dried marjoram
> ¾ teaspoon crushed dried thyme
> 1 tablespoon salt
> 1½ teaspoons freshly ground pepper
> Thinly sliced strips of fresh pork
> fatback
> Thin wedges of orange, peeled (remove
> the seeds and white membrane)
> 1 tablespoon minced truffle (optional)

Ask the butcher to skin and bone the duck, reserving the fat and liver. Put the duck meat, pork shoulder, chicken livers, ¼ pound of the reserved duck fat, and the reserved duck liver through the medium blade of a food grinder into a large mixing bowl. Add the cream, onion, liqueur, nuts, eggs, wine, marjoram, thyme, salt, and pepper. Mix well. In a small skillet sauté a spoonful of the mixture until it is cooked through, taste it, and add additional seasoning to the remaining mixture if needed.

Line a 1½-quart mold with the strips of pork fatback, letting the ends extend over the sides. Spread half of the duck mixture in the mold. Arrange a row of the orange wedges and a row of the minced truffle (if used) over it. Spread the remaining duck mixture evenly on top. Fold the overhanging strips of pork fatback over the pâté.

Cover the mold with a double layer of aluminum foil. Set the mold in a shallow baking pan and pour enough boiling water into the pan to reach halfway up the sides of the mold; add boiling water during cooking as necessary. Bake in a preheated 325°F oven about 2 hours or until the pâté pulls away slightly from the sides of the mold and the juices are clear yellow, with no traces of pink.

Remove the mold from the pan, pour out the water, and return the mold, still with its foil covering, to the pan. Let the pâté stand 15 minutes. Put a piece of heavy cardboard that is cut slightly smaller than the mold on top of the foil and place a 3- to 4-pound weight on it, such as a brick or heavy unopened cans. Or place a pan that is slightly smaller than the mold on top of the foil and fill it with the heavy objects. Let stand at room temperature 4 hours, then refrigerate, still weighted, 8 hours or overnight.

Remove the weights, cardboard or pan, and the foil. Loosen the pâté with a thin knife and unmold it onto a platter. Remove excess fat before serving. Makes about 8 servings.

SCANDINAVIAN LIVER PASTE

No smörgåsbord *would be complete without this Nordic classic.*

2 tablespoons butter
2 tablespoons all-purpose flour
1 cup milk
1 cup heavy cream
1 pound fresh calf's or pork liver, diced
¾ pound fresh pork fatback, diced
1 medium onion, coarsely chopped
3 flat anchovy fillets, drained (optional)
2 eggs
1½ teaspoons salt
¾ teaspoon freshly ground white pepper
½ teaspoon allspice
¼ teaspoon cloves
¾ pound thinly sliced strips of fresh pork fatback

In a heavy saucepan melt the butter over low heat. Add the flour and cook 2 minutes, whisking constantly. Gradually add the milk and cream and cook, stirring, until the mixture is thick and smooth. Remove from the heat and allow to cool.

Put the liver, diced pork fatback, onion, and anchovy fillets (if used) through the fine blade of a meat grinder 3 times. Transfer to a large bowl, add the cooled cream sauce, and beat thoroughly. In a small bowl beat the eggs well with the salt, pepper, allspice, and cloves. Add to the liver mixture and beat vigorously until the ingredients are thoroughly blended.

Line a 1-quart loaf pan with the strips of pork fatback, letting the ends extend over the sides. Spread the liver mixture evenly on top and fold the overhanging strips of fatback over it. Cover the loaf pan with a double layer of aluminum foil. Set it in a shallow baking pan and pour enough boiling water into the pan to reach halfway up the sides of the loaf pan; add boiling water during cooking as necessary. Bake in a preheated 350°F oven about 1½ hours or until the liver paste pulls away slightly from the sides of the pan and the juices are clear yellow, with no traces of pink.

Remove from the oven, lift off the foil, and let the liver paste cool to room temperature. Recover with foil and refrigerate several hours until thoroughly chilled. To serve, loosen the liver paste with a thin knife and unmold it onto a platter. Remove excess fat and cut into ½-inch-thick slices. Makes about 12 servings.

GALANTINE OF TURKEY BREAST

A relative of pâtés and terrines, a galantine is a dish of boned poultry or, less commonly, meat or fish, stuffed, formed into a symmetrical shape, and then cooked, chilled, and coated with aspic. Although its preparation takes time and care, it is not particularly arduous, and one's effort is richly rewarded by the end result—a resplendent cold buffet piece or party dinner first course.

1 whole turkey breast (about 6 pounds)
½ pound lean boneless veal, cut up
½ pound lean boneless pork, cut up
½ pound fresh pork fatback, sliced
½ cup Cognac or Madeira
4 eggs, lightly beaten
¼ cup finely chopped parsley, preferably Italian flat-leaf parsley
2 teaspoons Worcestershire sauce
1 teaspoon crushed dried thyme
½ teaspoon freshly grated nutmeg
2 teaspoons salt
⅛ teaspoon freshly ground pepper
1 pound lean boiled ham, sliced ½ inch thick and cut into ½-inch wide strips
14 pitted black olives

14 unsalted shelled and skinned pistachio nuts
2 cans (10½ ounces each) chicken broth
1½ cups dry white wine
2 cups water
1 large onion, quartered
2 stalks celery, coarsely chopped
3 medium carrots, peeled and coarsely chopped
2 teaspoons salt
6 whole black peppercorns
1 bay leaf

GLAZE

2 envelopes unflavored gelatin
3½ cups of reserved broth from galantine recipe
1 cup heavy cream

GARNISH

1 unwaxed cucumber
Chives
Pitted black olives, cut in half
1 carrot, peeled and cut crosswise in thin slices
Capers
Watercress

Rinse the turkey breast under cold running water. Dry thoroughly with paper towels. Place the breast, skin side up, on a cutting board. Using your fingers and a sharp knife, carefully remove the skin by pulling it away from the flesh so that it comes off in one piece. Cut the membrane and remove the fat with the knife, taking care not to pierce the turkey skin. Cover the skin with damp paper towels.

With a sharp knife, remove the breastbone from the meat. Cut half of the turkey breast into ½-inch-thick slices, then cut the slices into ½-inch-wide lengthwise strips. Reserve. Cut up the remaining half of the turkey breast and put it through a food processor or the finest blade of a food chopper, along with the cut-up veal, pork, and half of the sliced fatback.

In a large bowl combine the meat mixture, ¼ cup of the Cognac or Madeira, beaten eggs, parsley, Worcestershire sauce, thyme, nutmeg, salt, and pepper. Mix thoroughly. In a shallow dish combine the reserved turkey strips and the ham strips with the remaining ¼ cup Cognac or Madeira. Cover and let marinate 1 hour in the refrigerator. Drain and add the Cognac or Madeira to the meat mixture. Divide the meat mixture into 3 equal parts.

Spread a large piece of cheesecloth on your work surface. Lay the turkey skin, outer side down, in the center. Spread one third of the meat mixture in an even layer, 4 inches wide and 14 inches long, in the center of the skin. Cover with half of the turkey strips, alternating with half of the ham strips in lengthwise rows. Spread the second third of the meat mixture evenly over the strips. Stuff each black olive with a pistachio nut. Arrange the olives in a row down the center. Cover with the remaining turkey and ham strips. Spread the remaining third of the meat mixture evenly over the strips. Bring up the 2 sides of the skin over the center to cover the filling. Since the skin will not completely enclose the filling, use the remaining fatback slices for this purpose. Roll the filled turkey skin securely in cheesecloth. Tie the ends with strong thread.

In a large, oval Dutch oven combine the chicken broth, wine, water, onion, celery, carrots, salt, peppercorns, and bay leaf. Bring the mixture to a boil over moderate heat. Add the turkey roll, seam side down, and return the mixture to a boil. Reduce the heat to low, cover, and simmer about 2 hours or until the roll is just firm to the touch. Remove from the heat, cool to room temperature, and refrigerate in the broth overnight. Transfer the turkey roll to a tray. Skim off the fat from the broth. Bring the broth to a boil, then strain it through a sieve lined with several thicknesses of cheesecloth and reserve.

Carefully remove the cheesecloth from the turkey roll. Place the galantine, seam side down, on a rack set on a tray and refrigerate. Meanwhile, prepare the glaze: In a small saucepan sprinkle the gelatin over ½ cup of the reserved broth. Let stand 5 minutes to soften. Add 3 cups of the remaining broth. Heat over low heat, stirring, to dissolve the gelatin. In a medium bowl combine 1½ cups of the gelatin mixture and the cream. Place the bowl in a larger bowl of ice water. Let the mixture stand about 15 minutes, stirring occasionally, or until it is chilled and attains the consistency of unbeaten egg white. Remove the bowl from the ice water. Remove the galantine, still on its rack and tray, from the refrigerator. Spoon the glaze over the galantine. Return the galantine to the refrigerator and chill about 30 minutes or until the glaze sets. Remove the galantine from the refrigerator. Scrape the glaze from the tray and reheat. Chill again in a bowl set in ice water, then spoon the glaze over the galantine. Refrigerate the galantine.

Peel the skin from the cucumber (reserve the flesh for another use). Cut the skin into leaf shapes. Decorate the surface of the galantine to simulate flowers, using the chives for stems, cucumber skin for leaves, olive halves placed cut sides down for petals, and carrot slices topped with a caper each for centers. Gently press the flowers into the surface of the galantine. Refrigerate the galantine.

Chill the remaining clear glaze in a bowl set in ice water, stirring until it is thickened. Reglaze the galantine, covering the surface completely. Transfer the galantine to a serving platter and refrigerate. Just before serving, decorate the platter with the watercress. With a sharp knife, cut the galantine into ¼-inch-thick slices. Makes about 20 servings.

ROQUEFORT MOUSSE

Roquefort enthusiasts are invariably delighted with this appetizer.

1 envelope unflavored gelatin
¼ cup cold water
½ cup heavy cream
2 teaspoons brandy or dry Sherry
¼ teaspoon Worcestershire sauce
　Dash Tabasco sauce
　Salt and freshly ground pepper to taste
¼ pound Roquefort cheese, cut in chunks
8 ounces cream cheese, at room
　temperature
2 tablespoons finely chopped chives
　Watercress

In a small, heatproof bowl sprinkle the gelatin over the water. Let stand about 5 minutes to soften. Place the bowl in a small skillet containing 1 inch of simmering water and stir the mixture until the gelatin is dissolved.

Place the dissolved gelatin, cream, brandy or Sherry, Worcestershire sauce, Tabasco sauce, salt, and pepper in the container of an electric blender. Cover and blend a few seconds. Add half of the Roquefort cheese, cover, and blend. Repeat with the other half. Add the cream cheese in two parts, blending after each addition. Stir in the chives. Turn into a rinsed and chilled 3-cup mold. Cover with aluminum foil and chill at least 3 hours or until set.

To unmold, run a thin knife around the inside of the mold. Carefully dip the bottom of the mold in a pan of hot water for just a few seconds. Quickly wipe it dry. Invert a chilled serving platter over the mold and, holding the plate and mold firmly together, turn them over. Rap the platter on the counter to dislodge the mousse from the mold. Carefully lift off the mold. Alternatively, after inverting the mold onto the chilled platter, cover it with a cloth that has been dipped in very hot water and wrung out. As soon as the mousse slides out, lift off the mold. Garnish the mousse with the watercress and serve with crackers. Makes 16 servings.

VARIATION:

Use 6 ounces each Roquefort cheese and cream cheese.

CAVIAR MOUSSE

Your only problem will be proper modesty.

1 envelope unflavored gelatin
¼ cup cold water
2 egg yolks
2 tablespoons heavy cream
¼ pound cream cheese, pressed through a sieve
1½ teaspoons finely grated lemon rind
2 tablespoons freshly squeezed and strained lemon juice
4 shallots, puréed
Salt and freshly ground white pepper to taste
¾ cup heavy cream, whipped
3 egg whites, stiffly beaten
1 jar (2 ounces) red or black caviar
2 tablespoons finely chopped chives
1 slice lemon
1 sprig parsley

In a small, heatproof bowl sprinkle the gelatin over the water. Let stand about 5 minutes to soften. Place the bowl in a small skillet containing 1 inch of simmering water and stir the mixture until the gelatin is dissolved.

In a heavy enameled or stainless steel saucepan combine the egg yolks and the 2 tablespoons heavy cream and beat with a wire whisk over low heat until the mixture thickens. Pour into a large mixing bowl. Add the dissolved gelatin and slowly stir in the cream cheese. Add the lemon rind, lemon juice, shallots, salt, and white pepper and mix well. Fold in the whipping cream and egg whites. Taste and adjust the seasoning. Turn the mixture into a lightly oiled 2½-cup mold or soufflé dish. Smooth the top with a spatula. Cover and chill at least 3 hours or until set.

Unmold the mousse as directed on page 91. Spoon the caviar in a ring around the rim of the top. Spoon the chives in a ring inside the caviar. Cut the lemon slice into 6 wedges. Arrange 3 of the wedges, points touching, in the center of the mousse (reserve the other 3 for another use). Top the lemon wedges with the parsley sprig. Serve with thin toast. Makes about 12 servings.

GREEK TARAMA MOUSSES

Both this contemporary Greek original and the following one are poetic efforts of the first order.

½ envelope unflavored gelatin
1½ tablespoons medium dry Sherry
2½ tablespoons tarama (page 22) (available at Middle Eastern groceries and specialty food shops)
5 ounces cream cheese, at room temperature
⅓ cup plus ¼ cup unflavored yogurt
⅓ cup sour cream
2 tablespoons finely chopped fresh dill
1 tablespoon freshly squeezed and strained lemon juice
⅓ cup heavy cream, whipped
¼ cup half-and-half
Red caviar

In a small, heatproof bowl sprinkle the gelatin over the Sherry. Let stand 5 minutes to soften. Place the bowl in a small skillet containing 1 inch of simmering water and stir the mixture until the gelatin is dissolved.

In a medium bowl beat the *tarama* with an electric mixer 1 minute. Add the cream cheese and beat until the mixture is light and fluffy. Add the ⅓ cup yogurt, the sour cream, the dissolved gelatin, 1 tablespoon of the dill, and the lemon juice and continue to beat until the mixture is thoroughly blended. In a chilled small bowl beat the heavy cream until it stands in stiff peaks. Fold it gently but thoroughly into the tarama mixture. Taste and adjust the seasoning. Divide the mixture among 6 rinsed and chilled ⅓-cup ramekins. Smooth the tops with a spatula. Cover and chill about 2 hours or until set.

To unmold, run a thin knife around the inside of each ramekin. Dip the ramekins up to the rims in a bowl of hot water for just a few seconds, and invert the mousses onto chilled appetizer plates. In a small bowl combine the remaining ¼ cup yogurt, remaining 1 tablespoon dill, and the half-and-half. Mix until well blended. Spoon the sauce around the mousses and sprinkle a small amount across each one. Decorate the mousses with the red caviar and serve with thin toast. Makes 6 servings.

ATHENIAN SHRIMP, AVOCADO, AND CAVIAR MOUSSES

6 ounces small shrimp
5 teaspoons unflavored gelatin
¼ cup cold water
2 medium-sized, ripe avocados
6½ tablespoons freshly squeezed and strained lemon juice
1 tablespoon brandy
3 tablespoons plus 4 teaspoons red caviar, lightly rinsed and thoroughly drained
Salt and freshly ground white pepper to taste
1 cup plus 2 tablespoons heavy cream
1 large tomato, peeled, seeded, and chopped
1½ tablespoons tomato paste
½ cup olive oil

Drop the shrimp into a saucepan of boiling salted water and return the water to a boil. Cook the shrimp, uncovered, 1 to 2 minutes or until they turn pink. Drain them in a colander or sieve and rinse under cold running water. Shell and devein the shrimp. Reserve 4 of the shrimp and finely chop the remainder.

In a small saucepan sprinkle the gelatin over the water. Let stand about 5 minutes to soften. Heat the mixture over low heat, stirring, until the gelatin is dissolved. Remove from the heat.

Peel, pit, and quarter the avocados. Force the avocado flesh through a fine sieve into a bowl. Whisk in 4 tablespoons of the lemon juice and the brandy until the mixture is smooth. Stir in the finely chopped shrimp, 3 tablespoons of the caviar, the gelatin mixture, salt, and white pepper and mix well. In a chilled bowl beat 1 cup of the cream until it stands in stiff peaks. Fold it gently but thoroughly into the avocado mixture. Taste and adjust the seasoning. Divide the mousse among 4 rinsed and chilled ½-cup ramekins. Smooth the tops with a spatula. Cover and chill about 2 hours or until set.

In a food processor fitted with the steel blade or in a blender purée the tomato with the remaining 2½ tablespoons lemon juice, remaining 2 tablespoons cream, tomato paste, salt, and pepper. With the motor running, slowly add the olive oil in a thin, steady stream and blend the mixture thoroughly. Transfer the sauce to a ceramic or glass bowl. Cover and chill at least 1 hour.

To unmold, run a thin knife around the inside of each ramekin. Dip the ramekins up to the rims in a bowl of hot water for just a few seconds, and invert the mousses onto chilled appetizer plates. Spoon the tomato sauce around the mousses. Garnish each mousse with 1 of the reserved shrimp and sprinkle it with 1 teaspoon of the remaining caviar. Makes 4 servings.

SALMON MOUSSE

The attractive appearance of this flavorsome mousse belies the ease with which it can be prepared.

1 envelope unflavored gelatin
¼ cup cold water
⅓ cup boiling water
½ cup Mayonnaise (page 387)
2 tablespoons grated mild white onion
2 tablespoons freshly squeezed and
   strained lemon juice
¾ teaspoon salt or to taste
¼ teaspoon paprika
⅛ teaspoon Tabasco sauce or to taste
1 can (16 ounces) salmon, drained, picked
   over, and finely chopped
1 tablespoon finely chopped fresh dill
½ cup heavy cream, whipped
   Watercress sprigs or cucumber slices
   Sour Cream and Avocado Sauce (page
   391) (optional)

In a large bowl sprinkle the gelatin over the cold water. Let stand 5 minutes to soften. Add the boiling water and stir to dissolve the gelatin. Add the Mayonnaise, onion, lemon juice, salt, paprika, and Tabasco sauce and mix well. Cover and chill until partially set. Add the salmon and dill and beat until thoroughly blended and smooth (this can be done very quickly and easily in an electric blender; in fact, the result will be smoother than beating by hand). Fold in the whipped cream. Taste and adjust the seasoning. Turn into a lightly oiled 4-cup fish mold or other mold. Cover with aluminum foil and chill until set, at least 4 hours or overnight.

Unmold the Salmon Mousse as directed on page 91. Garnish with the watercress sprigs or cucumber slices. Serve with the Sour Cream and Avocado Sauce, if desired. Makes 8 servings.

AUSTRIAN SALMON MOUSSE

Admittedly more demanding to execute than the previous mousse, but a rewarding choice for those who insist on a little more effort on the part of the cook.

> 1 pound fresh salmon, sliced
> 2 cups dry white wine
> 1 tablespoon butter
> 1 tablespoon finely chopped onion
> 1 tablespoon all-purpose flour
> ½ cup milk
> ½ teaspoon anchovy paste
>   Pinch cayenne pepper
>   Salt and freshly ground pepper to taste
> ¼ cup finely chopped unsalted pistachio nuts
> 1 tablespoon finely chopped fresh dill
> 1 envelope unflavored gelatin
> ½ cup cold water
> ½ cup chicken broth
> ⅓ cup dry Sherry
>   Truffle slices or black olive slices
> 1 cup heavy cream
>   Sliced hard-cooked eggs
>   Watercress
>   Cold cooked shrimp
>   Herb Mayonnaise (page 388)

Place the salmon in a heavy enameled or stainless steel saucepan. Add the wine, cover, and simmer about 12 minutes or until the salmon flakes easily. Drain the salmon thoroughly. Pound it in a mortar to a fine paste, or put it through the finest blade of a food chopper twice. Set aside.

In a small saucepan melt the butter over moderate heat. Add the onion and sauté until soft but not browned, stirring frequently. Add the flour and cook, stirring constantly, 2 or 3 minutes. Gradually add the milk, stirring until the sauce is smooth and thickened. Add the anchovy paste and cayenne pepper and stir the sauce into the salmon paste. Season with the salt and pepper. Add the pistachio nuts and dill and chill the mixture in the refrigerator.

In a small saucepan sprinkle the gelatin over the water. Let stand 5 minutes to soften. Heat the mixture over low heat, stirring, until the gelatin is dissolved. Remove from the heat. Combine the chicken broth and Sherry in a small saucepan and bring to a boil. Remove from the heat, stir in the gelatin mixture, and cool the aspic.

Place a 1-quart fish mold in a bed of cracked ice. Coat the bottom and sides with a layer of cool, but still liquid, aspic and let it set. Place a slice of truffle or olive in the mold as an eye and a line of crescent-shaped truffle or olive slices to simulate the spine of the fish. Pour in additional aspic and continue to coat the sides of the mold until it has a layer at least ⅛ inch thick. Chill the remainder of the aspic in a shallow pan in the refrigerator until it sets.

Whip the cream with a pinch of salt. Fold it gently into the salmon paste, blending the mixture until it is smooth. Turn it into the mold, cover with aluminum foil, and chill at least 4 hours or overnight.

Unmold the salmon mousse as directed on page 91. Garnish with the eggs, watercress, and shrimp. Decorate the platter with the remaining aspic, chopped. Serve the Herb Mayonnaise separately. Makes 8 servings.

CHICKEN MOUSSE WITH PISTACHIOS

If chicken is your preference, here is one way to make it memorable.

1½ envelopes unflavored gelatin
¼ cup Sercial Madeira
2 cups chicken broth
½ teaspoon crushed dried tarragon
½ teaspoon crushed dried basil
2 tablespoons butter
6 ounces chicken livers, trimmed and dried with paper towels
1½ tablespoons brandy, heated
2 cups diced cooked chicken
Freshly grated nutmeg to taste
Salt, freshly ground pepper, and cayenne pepper to taste
1 egg white, stiffly beaten
⅔ cup heavy cream, whipped
⅓ cup unsalted shelled and skinned pistachio nuts, chopped
Watercress sprigs

In a medium bowl sprinkle the gelatin over the Madeira. Let stand 5 minutes to soften. In a small saucepan combine the chicken broth, tarragon, and basil. Simmer 5 minutes and add the broth to the gelatin mixture.

In a small, heavy skillet melt the butter over moderate heat. Add the chicken livers and sauté, stirring frequently, until they are lightly browned outside but still pink inside. Add the heated brandy, ignite it, and shake the skillet until the flames go out. Scrape the contents of the skillet into the container of an electric blender. Add the chicken broth mixture, the chicken, nutmeg, salt, pepper, and cayenne pepper and blend until the ingredients are puréed. Transfer the mixture to a large bowl. Taste and adjust the seasoning. Stir half the egg white into the chicken mixture and carefully fold in the remaining egg white. Fold in the whipped cream and nuts gently but thoroughly. Turn the mousse into a lightly oiled 1½-quart mold and smooth the top with a spatula. Cover and chill 8 hours or overnight.

Unmold the mousse as directed on page 91. Garnish with the watercress sprigs and serve. Makes 12 servings.

HAM MOUSSE

Should you need to use up some leftover ham, here is how to make a virtue of necessity.

4 cups lean ground cooked ham (about 1 pound)
1 teaspoon tomato paste
2 tablespoons medium dry Sherry or Madeira
2 teaspoons Dijon-style mustard
Salt and cayenne pepper to taste
2 envelopes unflavored gelatin
⅓ cup cold water
1 cup chicken broth
1 cup heavy cream, whipped
Thin slices of cucumber
Watercress sprigs

Put the ham through the finest blade of a food chopper with the tomato paste. Stir in the Sherry or Madeira, mustard, salt, and cayenne pepper.

In a small saucepan sprinkle the gelatin over the water. Let stand 5 minutes to soften. Add the chicken broth and heat over low heat, stirring, until the gelatin is dissolved. Add the dissolved gelatin to the ham, blend thoroughly, and press the mixture through a fine sieve, or purée it in an electric blender. Cool the mixture, stirring now and then, and fold in the whipped cream. Taste and adjust the seasoning. Turn into a lightly oiled 1½-quart mold. Cover with aluminum foil and chill until set, at least 4 hours or overnight.

To serve, unmold the mousse as directed on page 91. Garnish the top of the mousse with the cucumber slices and surround it with the watercress. Makes about 12 servings.

SALADS

When in doubt about your choice of starters, consider salads, whose freshness and piquancy make them eminently suited to an appetite-stimulating role. Although salads have become quite popular here in America, their potential as hors d'oeuvre still remains largely to be explored; however, they figure prominently on the appetizer tables of many other countries. The Italian antipasto, French hors d'oeuvre variés, *Middle Eastern* mezzeh, *Swedish* smörgåsbord, *Spanish* tapas, *German* Vorspeisen, *and Russian* zakuski, *for example, all conspicuously feature salads.*

In composing appetizer salads remember that the ingredients must have an affinity to one another, each element being carefully selected for a balance of contrasting but sympathetic flavors. You will find these salads appropriate not only for an hors d'oeuvre table or first course; several well-chosen ones can form the basis of a memorable and satisfying lunch or supper.

Most of the following salads are ideal

candidates for an appetizer buffet since they can be prepared in advance and kept without wilting in the refrigerator, where their flavors can mingle and mellow. Once served, they will retain their attractiveness, taste, and texture for several hours.

STUFFED ARTICHOKE SALAD

This impeccable appetizer is distinguished by simplicity and understatement.

6 medium artichokes
Juice of 1 lemon, freshly squeezed and strained
Curry Mayonnaise (page 388) or Herb Mayonnaise (page 388)
Parsley sprigs

Prepare each artichoke as follows: Remove any coarse outer leaves and cut 1 inch off the top of the remaining leaves. Separate the top leaves and pull out the thorny pinkish leaves from the center. With a spoon scrape out the fuzzy choke underneath, being careful not to puncture the meaty part. Cut off the stem and drop the artichoke into a bowl of salted water mixed with the lemon juice (this prevents discoloration).

Drain the artichokes and cook them in boiling salted water 30 to 40 minutes or until the hearts are tender when tested with a fork and a leaf can be pulled out easily. With a slotted spoon lift the artichokes from the water and place them upside down on paper towels to drain and cool. Place the artichokes on a platter, cover with plastic wrap, and chill. Shortly before serving, fill the centers of the artichokes with the Curry Mayonnaise or Herb Mayonnaise. Garnish with the parsley sprigs. Dip the artichoke leaves in the mayonnaise before eating. Makes 6 servings.

VARIATIONS:

Add ½ cup minced chilled cooked shrimp or lobster meat to either mayonnaise.

Substitute Egg Sauce (page 390) for the mayonnaise and minced fresh dill for the parsley sprigs.

ASPARAGUS WITH MUSTARD SAUCE

One of the great delights of spring is fresh asparagus, and here is a simple but splendid recipe to do it justice.

    2 pounds fresh asparagus
      Mustard Sauce (page 390)
    1 tablespoon finely chopped hard-cooked
      egg white

Snap off the tough lower parts of the asparagus stalks. Tie the asparagus in bundles of about 10 to 12 stalks and drop them into a large saucepan of rapidly boiling salted water. Boil, uncovered, about 8 minutes or until just tender. Drain. Plunge into a large bowl of cold water. Untie the bundles and drain thoroughly on paper towels. Place the asparagus on a serving platter, cover, and chill. Spoon the Mustard Sauce over the asparagus. Garnish with the egg white and serve. Makes 6 servings.

CHILEAN STUFFED AVOCADOS

The avocado is justifiably popular in Latin America, and never more so than when stuffed and served as a first course.

      Romaine lettuce leaves
    3 large, ripe avocados
      Freshly squeezed and strained lemon
      juice
      Tomato-Cognac Mayonnaise (page 388)
    ¾ pound small shrimp, cooked, shelled,
      and deveined

Line 6 individual appetizer plates with the lettuce leaves. Cut the avocados in half lengthwise. Remove and discard the pits. Carefully peel the avocados and coat the surfaces with the lemon juice to prevent discoloration. Arrange the avocado halves on the lettuce-lined plates.

Mix ½ cup of the Tomato-Cognac Mayonnaise with the shrimp. Fill the avocado halves with the mixture and serve them chilled, accompanied with a small bowl of the remaining mayonnaise. Makes 6 servings.

CRAB-STUFFED AVOCADOS

The flavors of crabmeat and avocado set each other off to perfection.

1 pound cooked crabmeat (preferably
    Dungeness), picked over to remove any
    bits of shell and cartilage and cut into
    bite-sized pieces
    Louis Dressing (page 389)
2 large, ripe avocados
    Bibb, Boston, or romaine lettuce leaves
2 medium-sized, firm, ripe tomatoes, cut
    into wedges
2 hard-cooked eggs, quartered
    Pitted black olives

Combine the crabmeat with the dressing in a bowl and toss lightly but thoroughly. Taste and adjust the seasoning. Cut the avocados in half lengthwise. Remove the pits and discard. Place each avocado half on an individual serving plate. Fill the cavities of the avocado halves with the crab mixture, dividing it equally. Surround the filled avocado halves with the lettuce leaves and garnish the leaves with the tomatoes, eggs, and olives, dividing equally. Serve at once. Makes 4 servings.

STUFFED AVOCADO PLATES

A stylish first course for easy entertaining.

½ medium bunch watercress
½ recipe Lemon Vinaigrette (page 387)
1 medium-sized ripe avocado
1 hard-cooked egg
1 teaspoon butter, at room temperature
1 teaspoon Mayonnaise (page 387)
    Salt and freshly ground pepper to taste
1 ounce red or black caviar
¼ cup heavy cream, chilled
1½ teaspoons Dijon-style mustard
½ teaspoon freshly squeezed and strained
    lemon juice
1 teaspoon finely chopped fresh chives
6 tiny artichoke hearts in olive oil,
    drained
6 cocktail mushrooms in olive oil, drained
    (available in jars in specialty food shops
    and many supermarkets)

Toss the watercress with some of the vinaigrette and arrange it on 2 individual appetizer plates, dividing it equally. Cut the avocado in half lengthwise. Remove and discard the pit. Carefully peel the avocado halves and brush them all over with the remaining vinaigrette. Place an avocado half over the watercress on each plate.

Halve the egg lengthwise. Remove the yolk, reserving the egg white. Force the yolk through a fine sieve into a small bowl. Add the butter, Mayonnaise, salt, and pepper and blend well. Fill the egg white halves with the caviar, dividing equally. Using a pastry bag fitted with a fluted tip, pipe the egg yolk mixture on top of the caviar, mounding it, or use a small spoon to pile the mixture over the caviar, spreading it to form a mound. Place a stuffed egg half in the cavity of each avocado half.

Whip the cream until it is thickened but not stiff. Add the mustard, lemon juice, and a pinch of salt and mix well. Spoon the cream mixture over each egg half and sprinkle with the chives. Arrange the artichoke hearts and mushrooms attractively around the avocado halves. Cover and chill before serving. Makes 2 servings.

BALTIC-RUSSIAN CUCUMBER AND SOUR CREAM SALAD

4 medium cucumbers, peeled, halved lengthwise, seeded, and thinly sliced
1 tablespoon coarse salt, or 2 tablespoons table salt
½ teaspoon distilled white vinegar
3 hard-cooked eggs
⅓ cup sour cream
2 teaspoons white wine vinegar
1 teaspoon Dijon-style or Düsseldorf mustard
¼ teaspoon sugar
⅛ teaspoon freshly ground white pepper
Lettuce leaves
1 tablespoon finely chopped fresh dill

In a mixing bowl toss the cucumber slices with the salt and distilled vinegar and let stand 30 minutes at room temperature. Drain the cucumbers, dry with paper towels, and place them in a large mixing bowl.

Separate the yolks from the whites of the hard-cooked eggs. Cut the whites into strips ⅛ inch wide and about 1½ inches long and add to the cucumbers. Rub the egg yolks through a fine sieve placed over a small bowl. Gradually beat in the sour cream. Add the wine vinegar, mustard, sugar, and white pepper and mix until smooth. Pour the dressing over the cucumbers and egg whites and toss gently but thoroughly. Taste and adjust the seasoning. Transfer the salad to a serving dish lined with the lettuce leaves. Sprinkle with the dill, cover, and chill 1 hour before serving. Makes 8 servings.

ROASTED PEPPER SALAD WITH TOMATO AND ONION

The pepper is one of several vegetables that can benefit from roasting. Its charred skin can be peeled off easily, while its flesh acquires a tender-crisp texture and a mellow, pungently sweet flavor that lends a distinctive character to a number of dishes. Salads incorporating roasted peppers turn up in various forms throughout the Mediterranean region.

2 large green bell peppers
2 large red bell peppers
1 small mild red onion, finely sliced
6 tablespoons olive oil
2 tablespoons red wine vinegar or freshly squeezed and strained lemon juice or to taste
1 large garlic clove, crushed and finely chopped
Salt and freshly ground pepper to taste
1 large tomato, peeled, seeded, and cut into bite-sized pieces
¼ cup finely chopped parsley

Roast the peppers over an open flame, or set them on the rack of a broiler pan and broil under a preheated broiler about 2 inches from the heat, turning the peppers frequently until the skins are evenly blistered and charred. Remove the peppers from the oven and place them in a paper bag. Close the bag tightly and let the peppers steam until they are cool enough to handle. Strip off the skins and cut the peppers lengthwise in quarters. Cut out the stems and white membranes and discard the seeds. Cut the peppers into ½-inch strips and combine them in a bowl with the onion. In a small bowl beat together the olive oil, vinegar or lemon juice, garlic, salt, and pepper and pour over the peppers and onion.

Toss gently but thoroughly. Carefully stir in the tomato. Taste and adjust the seasoning, cover, and chill 1 hour. Sprinkle with the parsley, transfer to a salad bowl, and serve. Makes 4 servings.

VARIATIONS:

You may garnish the salad with 1 can (7 ounces) tuna packed in oil, drained and broken into small chunks, 2 hard-cooked eggs, cut into wedges, 1 small cucumber, peeled and sliced, and 8 oil-cured black olives.

ROASTED PEPPER SALAD

Use 3 each green and red bell peppers and 2 tablespoons parsley. Omit the onion and tomato.

ROASTED EGGPLANT AND PEPPER SALAD

Roast 5 small Japanese eggplants over an open flame or under the broiler, turning often, until the skins are blistered and blackened. Cool, skin, and cut the eggplants into ½-inch strips. Add to the peppers in the bowl. Use lemon juice rather than vinegar and omit the onion and tomato.

BEET SALAD WITH YOGURT

A favorite Middle Eastern way of preparing beets that is delicious and unusual.

1 pound beets, cooked and peeled
½ cup unflavored yogurt
1 tablespoon freshly squeezed and strained lemon juice
2 teaspoons olive oil
1 tiny garlic clove, crushed to a purée
  Salt to taste
  Thin unpeeled slices of European cucumber, or thin slices of small cooked beets

Coarsely grate the whole beets or cut them into small dice or thin matchlike strips. Drain and place in a shallow bowl. Cover and chill.

In a small bowl combine the yogurt, lemon juice, oil, garlic, and salt and beat with a fork or whisk until well blended. Cover and chill.

Shortly before serving, add the yogurt dressing to the beets and toss gently but thoroughly. Taste and adjust the seasoning. Garnish with a border of overlapping cucumber or beet slices and serve. Makes 4 servings.

MEXICAN CAULIFLOWER SALAD

This salad is a great asset to a buffet table. Its dramatic appearance belies the ease with which it can be prepared.

1 medium head cauliflower
  Lettuce leaves
  Guacamole (page 21)
  Radish roses or tomato slices

Trim the cauliflower and cut a cross in the bottom of the stem end. Put the cauliflower, stem end down, into a large saucepan of boiling salted water. Cover and simmer about 20 minutes or until just tender. Lift out the cauliflower, drain, and cool to room temperature, then cover and chill.

To serve, transfer the cauliflower to a round platter lined with the lettuce leaves. Mask the entire surface with the Guacamole. Surround the base with the radish roses or tomato slices. Makes 4 to 6 servings.

VARIATION:

Spoon ⅓ cup Lemon Vinaigrette or Lime Vinaigrette (page 387) over the cauliflower before chilling it.

WHITE BEAN SALAD

Nourishing and economical, this salad exists in many versions throughout the Mediterranean area, Balkans, Middle East, and Caucasus. Though not particularly refined, it has an appealing honesty and elemental goodness.

2 cups dried white beans, preferably Great Northern
⅓ cup olive oil
⅓ cup freshly squeezed and strained lemon juice or to taste
  Salt and freshly ground pepper to taste
2 medium tomatoes, seeded and chopped
4 scallions, finely chopped, including 2 inches of the green tops
⅓ cup finely chopped parsley, preferably Italian flat-leaf
  Oil-cured black olives, preferably Greek

Soak the beans overnight in water to cover. Drain and rinse. Cover with fresh water and bring to a boil over high heat. Reduce the heat to low and simmer, partially covered, until the beans are tender but not mushy.

Drain the beans well and place them in a bowl. Combine the olive oil, lemon juice, salt, and pepper and pour over the beans. Toss gently but thoroughly. Taste and adjust the seasoning, cover, and chill. Just before serving, carefully mix in the tomatoes, scallions, and parsley. Taste again for seasoning. Garnish with the olives and serve. Makes 6 servings.

VARIATION:

Add 1 small green pepper, seeded, deribbed, and diced, with the tomatoes and sprinkle the salad with paprika. Minced fresh dill, basil, or mint to taste may be added with the parsley. Two hard-cooked eggs, cut in wedges, may be used to garnish the salad along with the olives.

TUSCAN WHITE BEAN AND TUNA SALAD

Tuscans have been notoriously fond of beans for centuries, featuring them in all manner of dishes except dessert. A favorite is this substantial white bean and tuna salad, famed far beyond the confines of Tuscany.

2 cups dried white beans, preferably Great Northern
⅓ cup olive oil
2 tablespoons red wine vinegar or to taste Salt and freshly ground pepper to taste
1 medium tomato, seeded and chopped
1 small green or red bell pepper, seeded, deribbed, and cut into strips
1 small mild red onion, very thinly sliced
2 tablespoons finely chopped parsley, preferably Italian flat-leaf
1 can (7 ounces) tuna, preferably Italian tuna packed in olive oil, drained and broken into chunks

Soak the beans overnight in water to cover. Drain and rinse. Cover with fresh water and bring to a boil over high heat. Reduce the heat to low and simmer, partially covered, until the beans are tender but not mushy.

Drain the beans well and place them in a bowl. Combine the olive oil, wine vinegar, salt, and pepper and pour over the beans. Toss gently but thoroughly. Taste and adjust the seasoning, cover, and chill. Just before serving, carefully mix in the tomato, green or red pepper, onion, parsley, and tuna. Taste again for seasoning. Serve as a first course or as part of an *antipasto* (page xi). Makes 6 servings.

VARIATION:

Omit the tomato and green or red pepper.

ROMAN WHITE BEAN AND CAVIAR SALAD

Sounds odd if you have never eaten it, but white beans and caviar make a most happy pair.

    2 cups dried white beans, preferably Great
        Northern
    1 small mild red onion, thinly sliced
    ½ cup Garlic Vinaigrette (page 387)
    3 tablespoons Danish lumpfish caviar
    2 tablespoons freshly squeezed and
        strained lemon juice
    2 tablespoons finely chopped parsley

Cook the beans as directed in the recipe for White Bean Salad (page 107). Drain the beans well and combine them in a bowl with the onion and Garlic Vinaigrette. Toss

gently but thoroughly, cover, and chill. Add the caviar and lemon juice. Sprinkle with the parsley and toss lightly. Taste and adjust the seasoning. Serve as a first course or as part of an *antipasto* (page xi). Makes 6 servings.

SPANISH CHICKPEA SALAD

An earthy, countrified quality characterizes chickpea salads, which are found in one form or another from end to end of the Mediterranean. Here is a robustly flavored example.

    1½ cups dried chickpeas
     1 hard-cooked egg yolk
    ¼ cup olive oil
     3 tablespoons red wine vinegar or freshly
        squeezed and strained lemon juice
     1 medium garlic clove, crushed and finely
        chopped
     3 tablespoons finely chopped mild white
        or red onion
    ¼ cup finely chopped parsley
     2 teaspoons capers, drained and rinsed
        Salt to taste

Place the chickpeas in a large bowl and add enough water to cover them by 2 inches. Let soak at room temperature 12 hours or overnight. Drain the chickpeas and place them in a small, heavy saucepan. Cover with water and bring to a boil over high heat. Reduce the heat to low and simmer, partially covered, about 1½ hours or until the chickpeas are just tender. Add boiling water to the saucepan if necessary to keep the chickpeas covered throughout the cooking period. Drain the chickpeas thoroughly, transfer them to a bowl, and let cool to room temperature. Set aside.

Sieve the egg yolk into a medium bowl. Whisk in the olive oil and vinegar or lemon juice until thoroughly blended. Stir in the chickpeas, garlic, onion, 3 tablespoons of the parsley, capers, and salt. Taste and adjust the seasoning. Cover and chill several hours or overnight, stirring occasionally. Transfer to a serving dish, sprinkle with the remaining 1 tablespoon parsley, and serve. Makes 6 servings.

FILLED TOMATO ACCORDIONS

An alluring creation that tastes as marvelous as it looks.

4 medium-sized firm, ripe tomatoes
  Salt
2 hard-cooked eggs, cut crosswise into
  ¼-inch-thick slices
  Tapénade (page 25)
  Pesto Sauce (page 393)
  Watercress
  Sauce Vinaigrette (page 387)

Blanch the tomatoes and peel them. With the stem ends down and using a sharp knife, cut each tomato vertically into 6 slices, each ½ to ¾ inch thick, cutting to, but not through, the bases. Gently spread the first 2 tomato slices apart slightly; remove the seeds with your finger and discard. Remove the seeds from the remaining slices in the same manner. Sprinkle salt between the slices and lay the tomatoes on their sides on paper towels to drain for 20 minutes. Fill the spaces between the tomato slices alternately with egg slices and spoonfuls of Tapénade and Pesto Sauce. Arrange the filled tomato accordions in an attractive pattern on a large, round platter. Cover and chill 1 hour. Toss the watercress with just enough Sauce Vinaigrette to moisten. Garnish the platter with the watercress and serve. Makes 6 servings.

PANZANELLA TOSCANA

Tuscan Bread and Vegetable Salad

Yesterday's bread need not be a faded memory of past glory.

4 cups bite-sized cubes of slightly stale or
    lightly toasted Italian or French bread
1 medium cucumber, peeled, seeded, and
    diced
2 medium-sized, firm tomatoes, peeled,
    seeded, and diced
1 small yellow, green, or red bell pepper,
    seeded, deribbed, and diced
1 small mild red onion, finely sliced
1 tablespoon chopped fresh basil or to taste
½ cup olive oil
3 tablespoons red wine vinegar or to taste
1 medium garlic clove, crushed and finely
    chopped
    Salt and freshly ground pepper to taste
2 hard-cooked eggs, cut into wedges
6 flat anchovy fillets

In a salad bowl combine the bread, cucumber, tomatoes, bell pepper, onion, and basil. In a small bowl beat together the oil, vinegar, garlic, salt, and pepper until well blended. Pour over the salad and toss gently but thoroughly. Taste and adjust the seasoning. Garnish with the wedges of hard-cooked eggs and the anchovy fillets. Cover and chill about 30 minutes. Serve as a first course or as part of an *antipasto*. Makes 8 servings.

VARIATIONS:

Instead of garnishing the salad with the anchovy fillets, mash them to a pulp along with 1½ tablespoons capers, drained, and mix them well with the dressing.

Bite-sized pieces of romaine lettuce may be added with the vegetables and the salad sprinkled with a few tablespoons of freshly grated imported Parmesan cheese.

PAELLA-STYLE SALAD

Saffron can be relied upon to impart a rich, yellow color and a delicate but compelling flavor to rice. Here it performs its magic for a luxurious salad inspired by that flamboyant Spanish triumph, paella.

2 cups water
1 teaspoon salt
1 cup long-grain white rice
⅛ teaspoon powdered saffron dissolved in
   1 tablespoon warm water
⅓ cup olive oil
3 tablespoons freshly squeezed and
   strained lemon juice
2 tablespoons white wine vinegar or
   tarragon-flavored white wine vinegar
4 scallions, finely chopped, including 2
   inches of the green tops
2 tablespoons chopped pimento
1 ounce anchovy fillets, drained and finely
   chopped (optional)
4 lobster tails, split and cooked
16 large shrimp, cooked, shelled, and
   deveined
   Shellfish Marinade (page 113)
   Leaf lettuce
1 small avocado
   Juice of ½ lemon, freshly squeezed and
   strained

2 medium tomatoes, cut into wedges
8 marinated artichoke hearts, cut
   lengthwise in half
16 pitted black olives
   Lemon wedges

In a heavy saucepan bring the water and ½ teaspoon of the salt to a boil over high heat. Stir in the rice and dissolved saffron and reduce the heat to low. Cover and simmer about 15 minutes or until the water in the pan is absorbed and the rice is tender but still firm to the bite, not mushy. Remove from the heat. Turn the rice into a mixing bowl and set aside.

In a small bowl combine the oil, lemon juice, vinegar, scallions, pimento, anchovies (if used), and the remaining ½ teaspoon salt. Mix together and pour over the rice. Toss gently but thoroughly. Taste and adjust the seasoning, cover, and chill 3 to 4 hours.

Meanwhile, with a fork loosen the lobster meat from the shells, then replace it in the shells. Place the lobster tails in a shallow dish along with the shrimp and spoon the Shellfish Marinade over both. Cover and chill 3 to 4 hours, turning from time to time.

To serve, mound the rice salad in a shallow serving bowl (or on a platter) lined with the lettuce leaves. Halve, peel, pit, and slice the avocado, then dip the slices into the lemon juice. Garnish the salad with the marinated lobster tails and shrimp, avocado slices, tomato wedges, artichoke hearts, olives, and lemon wedges. Serve at once. Makes 8 servings.

SHELLFISH MARINADE

3 tablespoons olive oil
3 tablespoons freshly squeezed and
    strained lemon juice
¼ teaspoon dry mustard
    Salt and freshly ground pepper to taste

Mix together all the ingredients until well blended.

VARIATIONS:

Crabmeat may be substituted for the lobster. Or a combination of lobster or crab, shrimp, and scallops may be used.

TOMATOES STUFFED WITH PAELLA-STYLE SALAD

Prepare Paella-Style Salad (page 112) with these changes: Substitute ¼ pound each diced cooked lobster meat and shrimp for the lobster tails and whole shrimp. Omit the lettuce, avocado, lemon juice, tomatoes, marinated artichoke hearts, olives, and lemon wedges. Have ready 8 medium-sized, ripe, firm tomatoes. With the stem ends down, cut each tomato into 6 wedges, cutting to, but not through, the bases. Gently spread the wedges apart slightly. Using a spoon, carefully scoop out the seeds and pulp (reserve them for another use), leaving a ¼-inch-thick shell. Chill the tomato shells, covered, 1 hour. Drain the marinated shellfish and add to the chilled rice. Toss gently but thoroughly. Spoon the rice and shellfish salad into the tomato shells, dividing equally. Top each stuffed tomato with a large black olive. Arrange the stuffed tomatoes on a large platter lined with watercress and serve. Makes 8 servings.

ZUCCHINI STUFFED WITH PAELLA-STYLE SALAD

Substitute 8 medium zucchini for the tomatoes. Cook the zucchini in lightly salted boiling water 8 minutes. Drain them and cut in half lengthwise. Scoop out the seeds, being careful not to damage the shells. Arrange the zucchini boats in a large, shallow dish and sprinkle with Lemon Vinaigrette (page 387). Cover and chill 2 hours. Drain the zucchini boats and fill with the rice and shellfish salad. Garnish the top of each filled zucchini boat with a row of overlapping slices of pimento-stuffed olives. Arrange the filled zucchini boats on a large platter and serve. Makes 16 servings.

TABBOULI

Bulgur, Vegetable, and Herb Salad

Despite its availability in Middle Eastern groceries, natural food and specialty stores, and some supermarkets, bulgur continues to be relatively unknown in parts of the United States. The following celebrated Lebanese classic features this nutty-flavored, chewy-textured cereal in a first-rate treatment redolent of mint and distinguished by its refreshing tang of lemon. A correlation of the senses of smell, taste, sight, and touch that is totally satisfying, this, truly, is one masterpiece you can afford.

1 cup fine bulgur
2 cups finely chopped parsley, preferably
Italian flat-leaf
⅓ cup finely chopped fresh mint leaves
½ cup seeded, deribbed, and finely
chopped green pepper
½ cup finely chopped mild onion or
scallions (include 2 inches of the green
tops of the scallions)
1 large, ripe tomato, seeded and finely
chopped
¼ cup olive oil
¼ cup freshly squeezed and strained lemon
juice or to taste

Salt and freshly ground pepper to taste
Romaine lettuce hearts
2 medium tomatoes, cut into wedges

Soak the bulgur in cold water to cover about 30 minutes. Drain and squeeze out as much moisture as possible with your hands. Combine the bulgur, parsley, mint, green pepper, onion or scallions, and finely chopped tomato in a mixing bowl. Sprinkle with the olive oil, lemon juice, salt, and pepper and mix gently but thoroughly. Taste and adjust the seasoning. If made ahead, cover and chill.

To serve, mound the *tabbouli* in the center of a serving platter. Decorate with the romaine lettuce hearts and tomato wedges. Use the romaine to scoop up the salad to eat out of hand. Makes 6 servings.

ITALIAN PASTA SALAD WITH PESTO

An ingenious way to save leftover veal or ham from oblivion.

2 cups small shell macaroni
3 cups julienne-cut cooked veal or lean
  cooked ham
  Pesto Sauce (page 393)
  Escarole or chicory leaves
  Niçoise or Italian oil-cured black olives
  Freshly grated imported Parmesan cheese

Cook the macaroni in plenty of rapidly boiling salted water until *al dente,* tender but firm to the bite. Drain well and combine it in a large bowl with the veal or ham. Add the Pesto Sauce and toss gently but thoroughly. Taste and adjust the seasoning. Transfer to a serving platter lined with the escarole or chicory leaves. Garnish with the olives and sprinkle evenly with the cheese. Serve at room temperature. Makes 10 to 12 servings.

ITALIAN MOZZARELLA AND TOMATO SALAD

Simplicity abetted by the freshest of ingredients is the essence of this traditional Italian salad.

1 pound fresh mozzarella cheese, cut into
  ¼-inch-thick slices*
4 large, firm, ripe tomatoes, cut lengthwise
  into ¼-inch-thick slices
6 tablespoons olive oil
2 tablespoons red wine vinegar or to taste
1 small garlic clove, crushed and finely
  chopped
  Salt and freshly ground pepper to taste
¼ cup finely chopped fresh basil

On a large platter arrange alternate slices of the mozzarella and tomato in rows, overlapping the slices a bit. In a small bowl beat together the oil, vinegar, garlic, salt, and pepper until well blended. Spoon the dressing over the cheese and tomatoes. Sprinkle evenly with the basil and serve. Makes 8 servings.

*The mozzarella called for in this recipe is a young, light-textured, and mild white cheese made from whole rather than skim milk. It should be purchased from a store that stocks it in bulk and regularly receives a fresh supply.

115

VARIATION:

Top the salad with 1 mild red onion, cut into paper-thin slices, and 1 can flat anchovies, well drained, arranged in an attractive pattern. Garnish the platter with parsley sprigs and Nicoise or Italian oil-cured black olives.

CAPPON MAGRO

Genoese Christmas Seafood and Vegetable Salad

This spectacular salad, which hails from the northwest coastal province of Liguria, is one of Italy's most fanciful and elaborate dishes. Although its preparation is admittedly somewhat laborious, the end result is nothing less than a chef d'oeuvre.

SAUCE

¼ slice white bread, trimmed of crust
4 tablespoons wine vinegar
2 tablespoons parsley leaves
1 tiny garlic clove, peeled
1½ teaspoons pine nuts
1 teaspoon capers
1 anchovy fillet
1 hard-cooked egg yolk
4 pitted green olives, sliced
½ cup olive oil
Salt and freshly ground pepper to taste

1½ cups olive oil
½ cup freshly squeezed and strained lemon juice
Salt and freshly ground pepper to taste
½ head cauliflower, separated into florets and cooked
4 cooked artichoke hearts, thickly sliced
1 cup sliced cooked celery
1 cup diced cooked green beans
1 cup diced cooked carrots
1 cup peeled and diced cooked beets
1 cup peeled and diced cooked firm potatoes
2 cups flaked cooked codfish, haddock, or sea bass
1 cup cooked lobster meat
24 small shrimp, cooked and peeled
3 slices dry white bread, trimmed of crusts
1 small garlic clove, halved
1 tablespoon cold water
1 tablespoon wine vinegar
12 Niçoise or Italian oil-cured black olives
4 hard-cooked eggs, quartered
8 anchovy fillets

To make the sauce, place the bread in the container of an electric blender. Add 1 tablespoon of the vinegar, the parsley, garlic, pine nuts, capers, anchovy, egg yolk, and olives. Turn on the motor and gradually add the remaining 3 tablespoons vinegar and the oil while blending. Season with salt and pepper and set aside. (If you have no blender, combine all the ingredients except the oil in a mortar and pound together, gradually adding the oil.)

Mix together the oil, lemon juice, salt, and pepper. In a large bowl marinate the cauliflower, artichoke hearts, celery, green beans, carrots, beets, and potatoes in half of the oil and lemon dressing. In another bowl marinate the fish and shellfish in the remaining dressing. Rub the bread slices with the garlic and place them on a serving platter. Combine the water and vinegar, add salt to taste, and sprinkle over the bread slices.

Remove the shrimp from the marinade and reserve. Pile alternate layers of fish and vegetables on the bread to form a pyramid, ending with the fish and lobster and spooning a little of the sauce over each layer. Spoon the remaining sauce over the pyramid. Decorate the entire surface of the salad with the reserved shrimp and the olives pierced with food picks. Garnish the base with the hard-cooked eggs and anchovies. Makes 12 servings.

SCANDINAVIAN WEST COAST SALAD

A familiar salad all over Scandinavia, where it exists in numerous variations, this standard dish is found on almost every restaurant's smörgåsbord.

½ pound fresh asparagus
¼ pound mushrooms, sliced
1 pound cooked shellfish (a combination of shrimp, clams or mussels, crayfish, crabmeat, or lobster chunks)
1 large, ripe tomato, cut into small wedges
¼ cup finely chopped fresh dill or to taste
⅓ cup olive oil
3 tablespoons freshly squeezed and strained lemon juice or white wine vinegar
Salt and freshly ground pepper to taste
Lettuce leaves
2 hard-cooked eggs, cut into wedges
Dill sprigs

Snap off the tough lower parts of the asparagus stalks. Tie the asparagus in bundles and drop into a large saucepan of rapidly boiling salted water. Boil, uncovered, about 8 minutes or until just tender. Drain. Plunge into a bowl of cold water. Untie the bundles, drain thoroughly on paper towels, and let cool. Cut the asparagus into 1-inch pieces and set aside.

Drop the mushrooms into boiling salted water and boil 3 minutes. Drain well and cool.

In a large bowl combine the shellfish, asparagus, mushrooms, tomato, and dill. In a small bowl whisk together the oil, lemon juice or vinegar, salt, and pepper until well blended and pour over the ingredients in the large bowl. Toss gently but thoroughly. Taste and adjust the seasoning. Cover and chill 1 hour. Transfer the salad to a serving bowl lined with the lettuce leaves. Garnish with the wedges of hard-cooked eggs and dill sprigs and serve. Makes 6 servings.

VARIATIONS:

One cup shredded lettuce may be added to the salad just before serving.

Instead of combining the tomato with the ingredients, you may use it along with the eggs and dill sprigs to garnish the salad.

MEXICAN SHRIMP SALAD

Here is a gastronomic treat that is not at all difficult to prepare.

1 pound small shrimp, cooked, shelled, and deveined
¼ cup olive oil
2 tablespoons freshly squeezed and strained lemon juice, or 1 tablespoon each lemon juice and red wine vinegar
¼ teaspoon crushed dried oregano
Salt, freshly ground pepper, and cayenne pepper to taste
2 firm, ripe avocados
2 large tomatoes, peeled, seeded, and diced
2 tablespoons finely chopped red onion
10 pimento-stuffed olives, sliced
Lettuce leaves
16 asparagus spears, cooked and chilled
2 hard-cooked eggs, quartered
8 pitted black olives
Pimento strips
2 lemons, quartered

Place the shrimp in a large bowl. Combine the oil, lemon juice, oregano, salt, pepper, and cayenne pepper in a small bowl. Beat with a fork or whisk until well blended. Pour over the shrimp, cover, and chill 2 hours, stirring occasionally. Halve, peel, pit, and dice the avocados. Add to the shrimp along with the tomatoes, onion, and sliced olives. Toss gently but thoroughly. Taste and adjust the seasoning. Transfer to a serving dish lined with the lettuce leaves. Garnish with the remaining ingredients and serve. Makes 8 servings.

PAPAYA AND LOBSTER SALAD

An example of how the simplest appetizer can sometimes be immensely gratifying.

2 large, ripe papayas
   Boston lettuce leaves
2 lobster tails (about ½ pound each),
   cooked
4 lime wedges
   Chutney Dressing (page 391) or South
   Seas Dressing (page 391)

Peel the papayas, using a vegetable peeler, then cut them in half lengthwise. Scoop out and discard the seeds. Line 4 salad plates with the lettuce leaves and set a papaya half on each plate. Carefully remove the lobster meat from each shell and cut it in half lengthwise. Cut each half into ½-inch-thick pieces and reassemble, placing one half of each lobster tail across each papaya half. Place a lime wedge, rind side down, in the cavity of each papaya half. Serve with a bowl of the dressing. Makes 4 servings.

SCANDINAVIAN HERRING SALAD

If you are partial to herring and potatoes, you will enjoy this great European peasant favorite. It makes a festive dish for a buffet and is a must on the smörgåsbord.

6 matjes *herring fillets, cut into bite-sized pieces*

4 *medium-sized boiling potatoes, peeled, cooked, and diced*

1 *cup diced pickled beets*

¾ *cup diced dill gherkins*

2 *medium-sized tart apples, peeled, cored, and diced*

2 *tablespoons finely chopped mild onion*

½ *cup sour cream*

Salt and freshly ground white pepper to taste

Lettuce leaves

2 *hard-cooked eggs, sliced*

Parsley sprigs

In a large bowl combine the herring, potatoes, pickled beets, dill gherkins, apples, and onion. Mix the sour cream with the salt and pepper and add to the ingredients in the bowl. Toss gently but thoroughly. Taste and adjust the seasoning, cover, and chill.

Transfer the salad to a shallow serving bowl lined with the lettuce leaves. Garnish with the sliced eggs and parsley sprigs and serve. Makes 6 to 8 servings.

VARIATIONS:

Substitute 1 salt herring for the *matjes* herring. Soak in cold water 24 hours. Drain the herring and rinse it in cold running water. Remove the head and tail. Skin and bone the fish. Dry with paper towels and fillet the herring. Cut the fillets into bite-sized pieces.

Substitute 1 jar (12 ounces) herring in wine sauce for the matjes herring. Drain, discard the onions, and dice the fish.

Toss the ingredients in the bowl with Sauce Vinaigrette (page 387), mixed, if desired, with finely chopped fresh dill, parsley, chives, or fennel to taste, then add the seasoned sour cream.

SALADE NIÇOISE

This colorful, internationally renowned salad, which lends itself to many variations, is one of the classics of Provençal cuisine.

4 large boiling potatoes
¾ cup olive oil
¼ cup red wine vinegar
¼ cup finely chopped fresh herbs (parsley, chives, tarragon, and basil)
Salt and freshly ground pepper to taste
1½ pounds green beans, trimmed and cut into 1½-inch lengths
Boston or leaf lettuce leaves
1 can (7 ounces) imported tuna packed in olive oil, drained and broken into small chunks
2 medium tomatoes, peeled and cut into wedges
2 hard-cooked eggs, quartered
8 rolled anchovy fillets stuffed with capers
8 black Greek olives, or 8 pitted black olives
2 tablespoons finely chopped chives or scallion tops

Cook the potatoes in boiling salted water about 20 minutes or until just tender. Drain and cool under cold running water to stop further cooking. Peel and slice the potatoes and place them in a mixing bowl. Combine the oil, vinegar, herbs, salt, and pepper in a small bowl. Beat with a fork or whisk until well blended. Pour just enough dressing over the potatoes to coat the slices. Mix gently, cover, and chill 2 hours.

Cook the green beans in boiling salted water about 15 minutes or until just tender. Drain and cool under cold running water. Drain again and place them in a bowl. Coat lightly with a little of the remaining dressing. Cover and chill 2 hours.

To serve, line a platter with the lettuce leaves. Place the marinated potato slices down the center and spoon the marinated green beans on each side. Arrange the tuna, tomatoes, eggs, anchovy fillets, and olives in a decorative pattern over the potatoes and beans. Sprinkle with the chives and remaining dressing. Makes 8 servings.

SALAT OLIVIER

Named after its creator, the French chef of Tsar Nicholas II, this most famous of zakuska salads is usually called salade russe *outside of Russia, with variations of it existing in many lands.*

2 cups diced cooked chicken
1 cup diced lean cooked ham
2 cups peeled and diced cooked potatoes
1 cup scraped and diced cooked carrots
½ cup peeled and diced cooked beets
½ medium cucumber, peeled, seeded, and diced
2 hard-cooked eggs, chopped
4 scallions, very thinly sliced
1 cup Mayonnaise (page 387)
½ cup sour cream
1 tablespoon Dijon-style mustard
2 dill gherkins, diced
2 tablespoons finely chopped fresh dill
Salt and freshly ground pepper to taste
Boston lettuce leaves
1 tablespoon capers
2 hard-cooked eggs, sliced
1 beet, cooked, peeled, and sliced
Pitted black olives

In a large bowl combine the chicken, ham, potatoes, carrots, diced beets, cucumber, chopped hard-cooked eggs, and scallions. In a small bowl mix together the Mayonnaise, sour cream, mustard, dill gherkins, 1 tablespoon of the dill, salt, and pepper until well blended. Add to the salad and toss gently but thoroughly. Taste and adjust the seasoning.

Transfer the salad to a serving dish lined with the lettuce leaves and form it into a mound or pyramid. Sprinkle with the capers and remaining 1 tablespoon dill. Garnish the sides with the slices of hard-cooked eggs, sliced beet, and olives. Cover and chill 1 hour. Serve as a first course or as part of a zakuska table. Makes 8 servings.

Note: If you must prepare this salad several hours in advance, fold in the diced beets and garnish with the sliced beet close to serving time since their color has a tendency to run.

ROSSOLYE
Estonian Meat, Herring, and Potato Salad

A favorite party dish, versions of which are also encountered at Latvian, Lithuanian, and Finnish gatherings, rossolye provides an excellent choice for a winter buffet and goes particularly well with vodka.

1 pound boiled beef or cooked ham or veal, trimmed of fat and cut into ½-inch dice

1 fillet matjes herring, drained and cut into ¼-inch dice

3 medium-sized boiling potatoes, cooked, peeled, and cut into ½-inch dice

1 medium carrot, cooked and cut into ½-inch dice (optional)

1 large, tart apple, peeled, cored, and cut into ½-inch dice

4 to 6 dill gherkins, diced

1 small mild red onion, finely chopped

2 hard-cooked eggs, finely chopped

1 cup sour cream

1 tablespoon Dijon-style or Düsseldorf mustard

1 tablespoon wine vinegar

1 teaspoon sugar

Salt to taste

3 medium beets, cooked, peeled, and sliced

2 hard-cooked eggs, sliced

In a large bowl combine the meat, herring, potatoes, carrot (if used), apple, gherkins, onion, and finely chopped eggs. In a small bowl mix together the sour cream, mustard, vinegar, sugar, and salt until well blended. Add to the salad and toss gently but thoroughly. Taste and adjust the seasoning. Mound the salad on a square or round serving platter. Garnish with the sliced beets and sliced hard-cooked eggs. Cover and chill 1 hour. Serve as a first course or as part of a *zakuska* table. Makes 8 servings.

VEGETABLES

Having grown up in Lebanon, where vegetables play a major role in everyday cookery, I learned to esteem them at a very young age. It has therefore been heartening for me to observe the dramatic growth of interest in vegetables that has occurred here in America, where they are at last coming to be valued not only for their nutritional importance and low calorie content but also for their relatively mod-est cost, visual attractiveness, and variety.

Since much of the world has long had a love affair with vegetables, it is only natural that they have figured prominently in the international repertoire of appetizers. The result is a seemingly endless choice of possibilities available to Americans, whether cold or hot, raw or cooked.

A host of imaginative and easily prepared appetizers can be made with raw vegetables. Crudités, small vegetables served whole and larger ones sliced into sticks or rounds or, where applicable, broken into florets, can be presented simply, accompanied with a dipping sauce or coarse salt, this last being especially welcomed by dieters. (If you are serving alcoholic beverages with hors d'oeuvre, which is almost always the case, it is advisable to include along with raw vegetables other foods containing some fat that will better soften the impact of alcohol on the system.) Some vegetables, such as celery, mushrooms, and Belgian endive, make natural containers for fillings; others, among them cucumbers, zucchini, and cherry tomatoes, can be hollowed out or shaped into containers. If you care to be more adventurous, you can slice and sculpt vegetables into other, more fanciful forms, such as cups, rings, curls, and flowers.

Cooked vegetables can be the highlight of an appetizer table, with a treasury of temptations from which to choose. However you decide to cook them, be sure to take only the briefest time needed in order to retain as much flavor, texture, and nutrients as possible.

The category of vegetables is one of the richest of all appetizers, and for anyone with a bit of enterprise it can be an area of joyful discovery and blissful satisfaction.

Other recipes featuring vegetables can be located by checking the Index.

COLD VEGETABLE APPETIZERS

VEGETABLE ANTIPASTO

A simple but effective treatment of vegetables that will impart a blaze of color and a refreshing touch to any hors d'oeuvre table.

1 small unpeeled eggplant, stem and green top removed and cut into 1-inch cubes
½ cauliflower, separated into florets
2 green bell peppers, seeded, deribbed, and sliced
1 red bell pepper, seeded, deribbed, and sliced
12 large green olives
12 black Greek olives
12 small white cocktail onions
½ bunch broccoli, separated into florets and the stems thinly sliced
½ pound small white mushrooms, stemmed
10 small French carrots, left whole
1 cup olive oil
1 cup water

1 bay leaf
2 or 3 sprigs fresh thyme
2 medium garlic cloves, peeled
    Salt and freshly ground pepper to taste
½ cup red wine vinegar

In a large enameled or stainless steel skillet combine all the ingredients except the salt, pepper, and vinegar. Bring to a boil and cook over moderate heat, stirring frequently, 5 minutes. Add the salt, pepper, and vinegar and cook, stirring, 5 minutes or until the vegetables are tender but still crisp. Remove from the heat and cool to room temperature. Transfer to a large jar or glass bowl. Cover and chill overnight before serving. Makes 12 servings.

VEGETABLES À LA GRECQUE

Despite its simplicity, this basic French method of preparing vegetables (with some help from the Greeks!) results in a superbly seasoned hors d'oeuvre that is strikingly handsome, with the contrasting colors and textures of the vegetables emphasized by their orderly arrangement. Besides the ones given below, other vegetables, such as zucchini, cucumber, celery hearts, fennel, and artichoke hearts or bottoms can be used.

1 pound carrots
½ pound green beans
1 small head cauliflower, separated into
    florets
3 baby eggplants, cut crosswise into ⅓-
    inch-thick slices
    Marinade (page 127)
½ pound small white button mushrooms
    Freshly squeezed and strained lemon
    juice to taste
    Salt to taste
1 long strip pimento
    Anchovy fillets (optional)
    Lemon slices or wedges

Peel the carrots and trim the ends. Cut them in half lengthwise, then cut each piece in half crosswise. Blanch the green beans in boiling water to cover 5 minutes and drain. In a heavy enameled or stainless steel saucepan cook the carrots, cauliflower, and eggplants separately in the marinade 6 to 8 minutes or until they are just tender, using a fresh recipe of the marinade for each vegetable. Transfer the vegetables and their marinade as they are cooked to separate bowls and allow to cool to room temperature. Meanwhile, in another, larger heavy enameled or stainless steel saucepan cook the mushrooms in 2 recipes marinade 5 minutes. Add the blanched green beans and cook 5 minutes. Transfer the mushrooms, green beans, and their marinade to a bowl and allow to cool to room temperature. Add lemon juice and salt to all the vegetables. Cover and chill several hours or overnight.

With a slotted spoon, lift the vegetables out of their marinade and arrange them attractively on a serving platter, forming the green beans into a bundle. "Tie" the beans with the pimento strip. Crisscross the anchovy fillets over the cauliflower, if desired. Moisten each vegetable with a little of its marinade. Garnish the platter with the lemon slices or wedges and serve at room temperature or chilled. Makes 10 servings.

MARINADE

½ teaspoon whole peppercorns
½ teaspoon coriander seed
4 sprigs parsley
3 sprigs fresh thyme
1 bay leaf
1 cup chicken broth
½ cup dry white wine
½ cup olive oil
2 tablespoons freshly squeezed and strained lemon juice
2 tablespoons chopped shallots
1 large garlic clove, coarsely chopped
½ stalk celery, coarsely chopped
¼ teaspoon salt

Combine the peppercorns, coriander seed, parsley, thyme, and bay leaf and tie in a cheesecloth bag. In an enameled or stainless steel saucepan combine the herb bundle, chicken broth, wine, oil, lemon juice, shallots, garlic, celery, and salt. Bring the mixture to a boil, cover, and simmer 5 minutes. Makes about 2 cups.

ARTICHOKE BOTTOMS WITH SALMON MOUSSE

An elegant, altogether exemplary appetizer.

6 large artichokes
  Juice of 1 lemon, freshly squeezed and
  strained
½ cup Lemon Vinaigrette (page 387)
1½ cups flaked Poached Salmon (page 129)
3 tablespoons Mayonnaise (page 387)
1 tablespoon heavy cream, whipped
2 teaspoons freshly squeezed and strained
  lemon juice
2 teaspoons finely chopped fresh dill
  Tabasco sauce to taste
  Salt and freshly ground white pepper to
  taste
  Paprika
6 pitted black olives

Prepare and cook the artichokes as directed in the recipe for Stuffed Artichoke Salad (page 101). When cool enough to handle, pull off all the leaves and reserve them to be eaten at another time. Place the artichoke bottoms in a bowl and spoon the Lemon Vinaigrette over them. Cover and let the bottoms marinate 2 hours.

Purée the salmon in an electric blender or in a food processor fitted with the steel blade, or put it through the finest blade of a food chopper. In a small bowl blend together the puréed salmon, Mayonnaise, whipped cream, lemon juice, dill, Tabasco sauce, salt, and white pepper. Taste and adjust the seasoning. Cover and chill 1 hour.

Drain the artichoke bottoms and dry them on paper towels. Place each one on an individual appetizer plate. Top each artichoke bottom with a mound of salmon mousse, dust with paprika, and garnish with an olive. Serve chilled. Makes 6 servings.

VARIATION:

Substitute Seafood Salad Filling (page 40) for the salmon mousse.

POACHED SALMON

3 cups water
1 cup white wine
1 small onion, sliced
1 celery stalk with leaves, sliced
1 carrot, sliced
1 bay leaf
3 sprigs parsley
A cheesecloth bag containing 1½ teaspoons finely chopped fresh thyme or ½ teaspoon dried thyme and 4 whole white or black peppercorns
1 tablespoon white wine vinegar or freshly squeezed and strained lemon juice
½ teaspoon salt
2 salmon steaks, each about 1 inch thick

In a deep enameled or stainless steel skillet just large enough to hold the salmon steaks in one layer, combine all the ingredients except the salmon. Bring to a boil over high heat. Reduce the heat to low and simmer, partially covered, 30 minutes. Add the salmon steaks, cover, and simmer gently about 12 minutes or until the fish just flakes when tested with a fork. With a slotted spatula, transfer the salmon to a board. Remove and discard the skin, dark flesh, and any bones, and let the salmon cool to room temperature. Transfer the salmon to a platter, cover with plastic wrap, and chill.

ARTICHOKE BOTTOMS WITH CAVIAR

Prepare cooked artichoke bottoms (page 101) and chill. Fill the bottoms with black caviar, sprinkle with a few drops of fresh lemon juice, and garnish with a little sieved hard-cooked egg yolk. Or fill the bottoms with Caviar and Cream Cheese Filling (page 42).

ARTICHOKE BOTTOMS WITH PÂTÉ

Prepare cooked artichoke bottoms (page 101) and chill. Fill the bottoms with Chicken Liver Pâté (page 31, omitting the parsley sprigs).

ARTICHOKE BOTTOMS WITH GORGONZOLA

Prepare cooked artichoke bottoms (page 101) and chill. Fill the bottoms with Gorgonzola Cheese and Prosciutto Spread (page 27) or Swedish Cheese Spread (page 28, omitting the nuts).

GREEK ARTICHOKES

While this Hellenic triumph will not transport you to the summit of Mount Olympus, it should certainly bring you within hailing distance of the gods.

> 6 medium artichokes
> Juice of 1 lemon
> 2 cups hot water
> ½ cup olive oil
> 12 small white boiling onions
> Salt and freshly ground white pepper to taste
> 1 teaspoon sugar
> 1½ tablespoons freshly squeezed and strained lemon juice
> 3 tablespoons finely chopped fresh dill

Prepare each artichoke as follows: Peel the tough outer skin from the stem and trim off ⅛ inch of the stem end. Remove any coarse or discolored outer leaves and cut 1 inch off the top of the remaining leaves. Cut the artichoke in half lengthwise. Remove the fuzzy choke and thorny pinkish leaves from the center. Drop the artichokes into a large bowl of salted cold water mixed with the lemon juice (this prevents discoloration).

Combine the hot water, oil, and onions in a heavy saucepan or casserole and cook over moderate heat about 10 minutes. Remove the artichokes from the salted water and arrange cut sides down in the saucepan. Sprinkle with the salt and pepper, sugar, lemon juice, and dill and baste thoroughly with the liquid in the pan. Lower the heat, cover, and simmer 20 minutes. Turn the artichokes cut sides up and place an onion in the center of each. Cover and simmer 30 minutes or until tender, basting occasionally. Remove from the heat and allow to cool in the saucepan. Serve chilled. Makes 6 servings.

ARTICHOKES, MUSHROOMS, AND OLIVES SOTT'OLIO

This is a much-admired antipasto in Florence. Sott'olio means, literally, "under oil."

    6 medium artichokes
    ½ lemon
    ½ cup olive oil
    2¼ cups water
    3 tablespoons white wine vinegar
    1 bay leaf
    3 sprigs parsley
    2 sprigs thyme
    ¾ teaspoon crushed coriander seed
    3 lemon slices
    ¼ teaspoon salt
    6 ounces medium mushrooms, trimmed
    ⅓ cup black Niçoise olives
    Salt and freshly ground pepper to taste

Prepare each artichoke as follows: Peel the tough outer skin from the stem and trim off ⅛ inch of the stem end. Remove any coarse or discolored outer leaves and cut 1 inch off the top of the remaining leaves. Quarter the artichoke and remove the fuzzy choke and thorny pinkish leaves from the center. Rub all cut surfaces of the artichoke with the lemon half to prevent discoloration. Drop the quartered artichokes into a bowl containing the olive oil and rub them all over with the oil. Drain the artichokes, reserving the oil.

Combine the water, vinegar, bay leaf, parsley, thyme, coriander seed, lemon slices, and ¼ teaspoon salt in an enameled or stainless steel saucepan. Bring to a boil, cover, and simmer 5 minutes. Add the artichokes, cover, and simmer about 20 minutes or until they are tender. With a slotted spoon, transfer the artichokes to paper towels to drain and cool. Add the mushrooms to the saucepan and cook about 4 minutes or until they are tender. Transfer them with the slotted spoon to paper towels to drain and cool. Boil the liquid in the saucepan over high heat, uncovered, until it is reduced to about 1 cup, then strain the liquid.

Combine the artichokes and mushrooms in a serving dish and scatter the olives over them. Add the reserved oil to the reduced liquid and pour the mixture over the ingredients in the dish. Season with the salt and pepper. Cover and chill. Makes 6 servings.

FILLED BEETS

Even skeptics who claim previous indifference, if not outright aversion, light up when they sample beets this way.

Wash tiny beets (about 1½ inches in diameter) in cold water. Cook the beets in lightly salted boiling water in a heavy saucepan about 30 minutes or until just tender. Drain well, peel, and let cool. Trim the stems. Cut a slice off the bottom of each beet so that it stands upright. With a melon-ball cutter, carefully hollow out each beet, leaving a ¼-inch-thick shell (reserve the scooped-out beet pulp for another use). Fill the beet cups with any of the following mixtures and arrange them on a platter. Serve at once, or cover with a domed lid or inverted bowl and chill up to 2 hours before serving.

Skordalia (page 393)
Herb Egg Filling (page 38)
Caviar and Cream Cheese Filling (page 42)
Ham Filling (page 44)

VARIATION:

In a bowl cover the beet cups with Sauce Vinaigrette (page 387) and chill, covered, about 2 hours. Invert them on paper towels to drain thoroughly and pat dry with the towels before filling. If desired, dip the rim of each cup in Sauce Vinaigrette and then in finely minced parsley to make a green border.

FILLED BRUSSELS SPROUTS

If you treat Brussels sprouts with care, they will provide wonderful eating.

Wash medium Brussels sprouts in cold water, removing any wilted leaves. Cut off the stem of each sprout so that it stands upright. Cook the Brussels sprouts in lightly salted boiling water in a heavy saucepan about 8 minutes or until just tender. Drain, plunge into cold water, drain thoroughly, and let cool. With the tip of a small, sharp paring knife or melon-ball cutter, carefully hollow out a small cavity in the top of each Brussels sprout (reserve the scooped-out centers for another use). Pat the hollowed-out sprouts dry with paper towels. Fill the cavities with any of the following mixtures and arrange them on a platter. Serve at once, or cover with a domed lid or inverted bowl and chill up to 2 hours before serving.

Skordalia (page 393)
Roquefort Cheese Spread (page 27),
   substituting 1 teaspoon minced fresh dill
   or to taste for the Sherry
Ham Filling (page 44)

VARIATION:

In a bowl cover the hollowed-out Brussels sprouts with Sauce Vinaigrette (page 387) and chill, covered, about 1 hour. Invert them on paper towels to drain thoroughly and pat dry with the towels before filling.

ARMENIAN STUFFED GRAPE LEAVES

One bite offers eloquent proof that this appetizer's global renown is more than justified.

> Rice Stuffing (page 134)
> 60 fresh, tender leaves from a grapevine, or 60 preserved grape leaves (a 1-pound jar)
> 1½ tablespoons freshly squeezed and strained lemon juice
> 1 cup water
> 1 lemon, cut into wedges

Prepare the Rice Stuffing and set aside.

If using fresh grape leaves, soak them in boiling salted water 2 minutes to soften, then rinse under cold water. Rinse preserved grape leaves in hot water to remove brine. Spread the washed leaves on paper towels to drain.

Cover the bottom of a heavy casserole with 10 of the leaves to prevent the stuffed leaves from burning during cooking. Stuff each of the remaining 50 leaves as follows: Remove the stem, if any, and spread the leaf on a plate, stem end toward you, dull side up. Place about 1 heaping teaspoon (or more for larger leaves) of the rice mixture near the stem end. Fold the stem end over the stuffing, then fold over the sides to enclose the stuffing securely. Beginning at the stem end, roll the grape leaf firmly away from you toward the tip, forming a cylinder.

Layer the stuffed leaves, seam sides down and close together, in neat rows in the casserole. Sprinkle the lemon juice over them and add the water. Gently place an inverted plate over the top to keep the stuffed leaves in place while cooking. Bring to a boil over moderate heat. Reduce the heat to low, cover, and simmer about 50 to 60 minutes or until the stuffing is very tender. If necessary, more water may be added. Remove from the heat and cool to room temperature. Remove the plate. Carefully transfer the stuffed leaves to a serving platter and arrange them attractively. Serve at room temperature or slightly chilled, garnished with the lemon wedges. Makes about 50.

RICE STUFFING

⅓ cup olive oil
2 large onions, finely chopped
2 tablespoons pine nuts
½ cup uncooked long-grain white rice
2 tablespoons dried currants
1 small tomato, peeled, seeded, and finely chopped
¼ teaspoon allspice
⅛ teaspoon cinnamon
¼ teaspoon paprika
¼ teaspoon freshly ground pepper
¾ teaspoon salt or to taste
½ cup water
1 tablespoon finely chopped parsley
1 tablespoon finely chopped fresh dill
1 tablespoon finely chopped fresh mint leaves

In a heavy skillet heat the olive oil over moderate heat. Add the onions and pine nuts and sauté, stirring frequently, until golden. Add the rice and cook, stirring, until the grains are thoroughly coated with the oil. Add the currants, tomato, allspice, cinnamon, paprika, pepper, salt, and water. Bring the mixture to a boil, stirring. Reduce the heat to low, cover, and simmer about 10 minutes or until the liquid is absorbed. Remove from the heat and stir in the parsley, dill, and mint.

STUFFED CHARD LEAVES

Some people like these even better than stuffed grape leaves.

Follow the recipe for Armenian Stuffed Grape Leaves (page 133), substituting Swiss chard leaves for the grape leaves. Remove the stems and dip the leaves, a few at a time, in boiling salted water for 1 minute or less until they soften, then proceed as directed in the recipe. Makes about 50.

FILLED BELGIAN ENDIVE SLICES

Separate the leaves of 3 heads of Belgian endive, trimmed. Beginning with the innermost leaves, spread Roquefort Cheese Spread (page 27), Serbian Herb Cheese Spread (page 28), or Anchovy and Cream Cheese Filling (page 42) on the leaves and re-form the endives as each leaf is filled. Wrap the endives securely in plastic wrap or waxed paper and chill 2 hours. With a sharp knife, cut the filled endives crosswise into ½-inch-thick slices. Arrange the slices on a chilled platter and serve. Makes about 24 slices.

FILLED ROMAINE LETTUCE SLICES

Remove the larger outer leaves from 3 hearts of romaine lettuce and reserve them for another use. Spread open the inner leaves and stuff them with Roquefort Cheese Spread (page 27) or Serbian Cheese Spread (page 28). Re-form the romaine hearts, wrap them securely in plastic wrap or waxed paper, and chill 2 hours. With a sharp knife, cut the stuffed romaine hearts crosswise into ½-inch-thick slices. Arrange the slices on a chilled platter and serve. Makes about 24 slices.

FILLED CARROT CURLS

Available all year round, carrots are still one of the few remaining bargains in the market place. Here is an original and tempting use for this appealing and nutritious vegetable.

Peel large, young carrots and cut them lengthwise into wide ⅛-inch-thick strips. Curl each strip around your finger, slip it off, and fasten it with a wooden pick. Place the carrot curls in a bowl, cover with cold water, and chill 2 hours. Drain well, pat dry with paper towels, and remove the picks. Line the carrot curls with a tiny piece of Boston or other soft lettuce, pressing the lettuce inside each one with your little finger to form a cup. Spoon any of the following mixtures into the lettuce-lined carrot curls, mounding the mixture slightly. Arrange the filled curls on a chilled platter. Serve at once, or cover with a domed lid or inverted bowl and chill up to 2 hours before serving.

Tapénade (page 25)
Chicken Liver Pâté (page 31), omitting the parsley sprigs
Liverwurst Pâté (page 33), omitting the nuts or parsley
Anchovy and Cream Cheese Filling (page 42)

STUFFED CELERY

Wash choice, inner stalks of celery under cold running water and dry with paper towels. Trim the stalks and cut into 2-inch lengths. Fill the centers of the stalks with any of the following mixtures, piping it through a pastry bag fitted with a decorative tip or using a small spoon. Arrange on a platter, cover with a domed lid or inverted bowl, and chill 1 hour before serving.

Norwegian Red Caviar Dip (page 23)
Roquefort Cheese Spread (page 27)
Serbian Herb Cheese Spread (page 28)
Shrimp Filling (page 40)
Clam and Cream Cheese Filling (page 41)
Anchovy and Cream Cheese Filling (page 42)
Curried Chicken Filling (page 43)
Ham Filling (page 44)

FILLED CUCUMBER CUPS

This and the following cucumber hors d'oeuvre are as appetizing for their crunch as they are for their refreshing taste.

Score seedless cucumbers lengthwise with the tines of a fork and cut into 1-inch pieces. With a melon-ball cutter, carefully scoop out the center of each piece, leaving a shell about ¼ inch thick to form a cup. Pat the cucumber cups dry with paper towels. Fill the cups with Taramosalata (page 22), piping it through a pastry bag fitted with a decorative tip or using a small spoon. Arrange the filled cucumber cups on a platter and garnish each with a small black Greek olive. Cover with a domed lid or inverted bowl and chill at least 1 hour before serving.

VARIATIONS:

Dip the top edge of each cucumber cup in fresh lemon juice, then dip it in minced parsley to make a green border. Instead of filling the cucumber cups with Taramosalata, fill with Caviar and Cream Cheese Filling (page 42). Omit the olives.

Substitute Anchovy and Cream Cheese Filling (page 42) for the Taramosalata and omit the olives. Garnish each filled cucumber cup with a dab of sour cream and top with a dot of caviar.

Substitute Smoked Salmon Spread (page 30) for the Taramosalata and slices of pitted black olives or minced parsley for the Greek olives.

Substitute Roquefort Cheese Spread (page 27) or Gorgonzola Cheese and Prosciutto Spread (page 27) for the Taramosalata. Instead of garnishing the filled cucumber cups with the olives, sprinkle them with minced parsley.

Substitute Serbian Herb Cheese Spread (page 28) or Herb Yogurt Cheese (page 57) for the Taramosalata and garnish the filled cucumber cups with the olives or tiny mint sprigs.

Substitute Beet Salad with Yogurt (page 106) for the Taramosalata. Prepare the salad with grated beets and omit the cucumber or beet slices. Instead of garnishing the filled cucumber cups with the olives, sprinkle the centers with minced parsley.

FILLED CUCUMBER BOATS

Peel small cucumbers (about 4 inches long) lengthwise with a lemon zester, or run the tines of a fork down unpeeled ones. Cut the cucumbers in half lengthwise. Scoop out the seeds with a grapefruit spoon and discard. Pat the cucumbers dry with paper towels. Fill the cucumber boats with Norwegian Red Caviar Dip (page 23), mounding it, and garnish each with a sprig of parsley. Arrange the filled boats on a serving platter. Cover with a domed lid or inverted bowl and chill at least 1 hour before serving.

VARIATIONS:

Substitute Swedish Cheese Spread (page 28), omitting the nuts, for the red caviar dip.

Substitute Curried Crabmeat Filling (page 39) for the red caviar dip and minced parsley for the parsley sprigs. Cut the filled cucumber boats crosswise into ¾-inch-thick slices before serving.

Substitute Seafood Salad Filling (page 40) for the red caviar dip and minced parsley or chives for the parsley sprigs.

Substitute 1 pound picked-over lump crabmeat mixed with Louis Dressing (page 389) for the red caviar dip. Garnish with parsley sprigs or minced hard-cooked egg.

Substitute Herb Cheese (page 51) or Herb Yogurt Cheese (page 57) for the red caviar dip.

STUFFED CUCUMBER SLICES

Cut ½ inch off the tips of small cucumbers. With an apple corer, remove the centers from the cucumbers, leaving a shell about ¼ inch thick. Dry the cucumber cavities with a paper towel and stuff them tightly with Roquefort Cheese Spread (page 27), substituting 1 teaspoon minced fresh dill or to taste for the Sherry. When all the cucumbers are tightly packed, wrap them separately in waxed paper or plastic wrap and chill at least 2 hours. To serve, cut the stuffed cucumbers crosswise into ½-inch-thick slices. Garnish each slice with a sprig of parsley or a tiny strip of pimento.

VARIATIONS:

Substitute Serbian Herb Cheese Spread (page 28), Shrimp Paste (page 29), Liverwurst Pâté (page 33), or Crabmeat Filling (page 39) for the Roquefort Cheese Spread.

CAPONATA
Cold Eggplant Appetizer

A celebrated Sicilian classic, easy to make and sure to delight.

    2 small eggplants (about ¾ pound each)
      Salt
    5 tablespoons olive oil, more if needed
    1 cup finely chopped celery
    ½ cup finely chopped onion
    ¼ cup best-quality red wine vinegar
    1 tablespoon sugar
    1 pound tomatoes, peeled, seeded, and
      chopped
    1 tablespoon tomato paste
    3 tablespoons coarsely chopped green
      olives
    1 tablespoon capers, rinsed and drained
    2 flat anchovy fillets, rinsed and mashed
      to a smooth paste
      Freshly ground pepper to taste
 1½ tablespoons pine nuts

Remove the stems and green tops from the eggplants but do not peel them. Cut the eggplants into ½-inch cubes. Sprinkle the cubes generously with salt and place them in a colander to drain 30 minutes. Rinse under cold running water and dry with paper towels. Set aside.

In a large, heavy skillet heat 2 tablespoons of the oil over moderate heat. Add the celery and onion and sauté, stirring frequently, about 10 minutes or until they are soft and golden. With a slotted spoon, transfer the vegetables to a bowl.

Add the remaining 3 tablespoons oil to the skillet and heat over medium-high heat. Add the eggplant cubes and sauté, stirring, 5 minutes or until golden brown, adding more oil if necessary. In a small bowl combine the vinegar with the sugar and stir until the sugar is dissolved. Add the sweetened vinegar to the skillet along with the celery and onion mixture, tomatoes, tomato paste, olives, capers, anchovies, salt, and pepper. Bring to a boil, reduce the heat, and simmer, uncovered, 15 minutes, stirring frequently. Stir in the nuts. Taste and adjust the seasoning. Remove the skillet from the heat and cool the *caponata* to room temperature. Transfer to a serving bowl, cover, and refrigerate several hours or overnight. Makes 6 servings.

STUFFED MUSHROOMS

Juice of 1 lemon, freshly squeezed and strained
1 pound medium mushrooms
  Roquefort Cheese and Walnut Spread (page 27)
  Finely chopped parsley

In a large saucepan combine boiling salted water with the lemon juice. Add the mushrooms and blanch them 3 minutes. Drain in a colander and rinse under cold running water. Remove the stems and reserve them for another use. Pat the mushroom caps dry with paper towels. Transfer them to a plate, cover, and chill 1 hour. Fill the mushroom caps with the Roquefort Cheese and Walnut Spread, piping it through a pastry bag fitted with a star tip or using a small spoon. Sprinkle with the parsley. Arrange the mushrooms on a platter. Cover with a domed lid or inverted bowl and chill 1 hour before serving. Makes about 30.

VARIATIONS:

Prepare Swedish Cheese Spread (page 28), folding the pistachio nuts into the cheese mixture. Stuff each mushroom cap with this mixture, mounding it in the center to form a cone. Dip the tips of the cheese cones into a small amount of paprika.

Stuff the mushroom caps with Cream Cheese and Mushroom Filling (page 37), Herb Cheese (page 51), or Boursin cheese. Garnish the centers with thin strips of green pepper.

Stuff the mushroom caps with Gorgonzola Cheese and Prosciutto Spread (page 27), Ham Filling (page 44), or Prosciutto Filling (page 44). Garnish the centers with thin strips of red bell pepper or pimento.

Stuff the mushroom caps with Crabmeat Filling (page 39), Clam and Cream Cheese Filling (page 41), or Anchovy and Cream Cheese Filling (page 42). Sprinkle with minced parsley.

Stuff the mushroom caps with Liverwurst Pâté (page 33) and sprinkle with minced unsalted shelled pistachio nuts.

Stuff the mushroom caps with the ratatouille mixture given in the recipe for Baby Eggplants Stuffed with Ratatouille (page 153). Sprinkle with minced parsley.

STUFFED SNOW PEAS

East and West collaborate on a felicitous interplay of crisp and creamy textures.

Trim the ends and remove the strings from ¾ pound snow peas. In a saucepan blanch the snow peas in boiling salted water to cover 1 minute. Drain the peas well and immediately plunge them into cold water. Drain again and pat them dry with paper towels. With the tip of a small, sharp knife, carefully make a cut along the curved edge of each pod. Slit open the snow peas to within ¼ inch of each end. Using a pastry bag fitted with a decorative tip, pipe Swedish Cheese Spread (page 28) or Ham Filling (page 44) into the snow peas. Arrange the snow peas on a platter and sprinkle them with finely chopped parsley. Cover with a domed lid or inverted bowl and chill 2 hours before serving. Makes about 50.

VARIATIONS:

Blanch untrimmed snow peas and dry them as directed. With a sharp knife, trim ¼ inch from the stem end of each pod and discard. Using a pastry bag fitted with a ¼- to ⅛-inch tip, pipe Cream Cheese and Bacon Filling (page 37), Shrimp Filling (page 40), or Prosciutto Filling (page 44) into the cut end of each snow pea. Chill 2 hours before serving.

CHEESE-STUFFED PEPPER RINGS

Cut about ⅜ inch off the stem ends of 4 small green or red bell peppers or 2 each green and red bell peppers. Remove the seeds and white membranes. Stuff the peppers with Serbian Herb Cheese Spread (page 28) or Herb Yogurt Cheese (page 57) mixed with ¼ cup minced pitted black Greek olives, forcing it in with a pastry tube to fill the corners or packing it down with the back of a small spoon. Wrap the stuffed peppers in aluminum foil or plastic wrap and chill at least 3 hours. To serve, place each pepper on its side and cut into ¼- to ⅜-inch-thick slices. Arrange the slices in a fan pattern on a chilled platter, alternating red peppers with green if using both kinds. Makes about 48.

VARIATIONS:

Substitute 2 recipes Roquefort Cheese Spread (page 27) mixed with 6 tablespoons finely chopped unsalted shelled pistachio nuts for the Serbian Herb Cheese Spread.

Substitute 6 long, thin green peppers or frying peppers for the green and red bell peppers.

MOORISH PIMENTOS

4 large red bell peppers
½ recipe Lemon Vinaigrette (page 387)
1 can (7 ounces) imported tuna packed in olive oil, drained
2 tablespoons butter
2 anchovy fillets
2 tablespoons finely chopped parsley
1 tablespoon freshly squeezed and strained lemon juice or to taste
Salt and freshly ground pepper to taste

Roast the peppers over an open flame, or set them on the rack of a broiler pan and broil under a preheated broiler about 2 inches from the heat, turning them frequently until the skins are evenly blistered and charred. Cool the peppers slightly, then peel off the skins. Remove and discard the stems, seeds, and ribs. Cut each pepper lengthwise into 6 strips. In a small bowl gently toss the strips with the Lemon Vinaigrette. Cover and chill.

Mash the tuna in a mortar with the butter and anchovy fillets until a smooth paste is formed, or combine the ingredients in the container of an electric blender and blend until smooth. Add the remaining ingredients and mix well. Taste and adjust the seasoning. Transfer to a small bowl, cover, and chill 2 hours. Put about 1 teaspoon of the mixture at the wide end of each pepper strip, skinned side down. Roll up each strip like a jelly roll and fasten with a cocktail pick. Arrange the stuffed rolls attractively on a platter. Cover and chill 1 hour before serving. Makes 24.

PROVENÇAL STUFFED PEPPERS

A commendable starter on all counts.

> 2 medium eggplants, peeled and cubed
> Salt
> Olive oil
> 1 medium onion, finely chopped
> 2 medium garlic cloves, finely chopped
> 3 medium tomatoes, peeled, seeded, and chopped
> ½ cup pitted black olives, finely chopped
> 3 tablespoons pine nuts
> 1 tablespoon capers, rinsed, drained, and chopped
> 2 tablespoons finely chopped parsley
> 1 teaspoon finely chopped fresh basil
> ½ cup fresh soft breadcrumbs (made from French or Italian bread)
> Freshly ground pepper to taste
> 8 medium-sized green bell peppers, or 4 each green and red bell peppers, cored and seeded
> Wine vinegar or freshly squeezed and strained lemon juice

Sprinkle the eggplant cubes generously with salt and let them drain in a colander 30 minutes. Rinse under cold running water and dry thoroughly with paper towels.

In a large, heavy skillet heat ¼ cup olive oil over medium-high heat. Add the eggplant cubes and sauté, stirring frequently, until lightly browned on all sides, adding more oil if necessary. With a slotted spoon, transfer the eggplant to a plate and set aside.

Add a little olive oil to the skillet and heat. Add the onion and garlic and sauté, stirring frequently, until the onion is soft but not browned. Stir in the tomatoes and cook until all the liquid has evaporated and the mixture has thickened. Remove from the heat and add the olives, pine nuts, capers, parsley, basil, sautéed eggplant cubes, breadcrumbs, salt, and pepper. Mix gently and taste and adjust the seasoning. Fill the peppers with the mixture, packing it fairly firmly.

Brush a shallow baking dish just large enough to hold the stuffed peppers in one layer generously with olive oil. Arrange the peppers in the dish and drizzle them with 3 tablespoons oil. Bake in a preheated 350°F oven about 1 hour or until tender. Remove from the oven and cool to room temperature. Transfer the peppers to a serving platter. Slice each pepper in half lengthwise and sprinkle with a little olive oil and wine vinegar or lemon juice. Serve at room temperature. Makes 8 servings.

VARIATION:

Add 1 can (7 ounces) Italian tuna packed in olive oil, drained and broken into small pieces, and 5 anchovy fillets, very finely chopped, with the olives.

STUFFED RADISH ROSES

These delightfully crunchy morsels will please your palate as well as your purse.

Select large, round, firm red radishes. Trim off the root of each radish and cut off the stem end so the radish sits flat. Starting from the root end, cut 4 or 5 thin petals around the radish, cutting down almost to the base (stem end), leaving a little red between the petals. Place the radishes in ice water until the petals spread open like a flower. Drain well and pat dry with paper towels. With the tip of a small, sharp knife, carefully hollow out a bit of the center of each radish to form a small cup. Fill the cup with any of the following mixtures, piping it through a pastry bag fitted with a decorative tip or using a ¼-teaspoon measuring spoon. Arrange the stuffed radish roses on a platter. Cover with a domed lid or inverted bowl and chill at least 1 hour before serving.

Roquefort Cheese Spread (page 27)
Serbian Herb Cheese Spread (page 28)
Anchovy and Cream Cheese Butter (page 36)
Herb Cheese (page 51)

VARIATION:

Instead of making radish roses, simply cut a slice from the top of each radish and remove the center to form a cup. Fill the radish cups as above.

RADISH CANAPÉS

Select large, firm red radishes. Trim the radishes, leaving each with a ¼-inch green stem. Cut the radishes in half lengthwise, making certain that each half retains its portion of stem. Using a pastry bag fitted with a decorative tip, pipe a circle of any one of the following flavored butters onto the cut surface of each radish half, using about ½ teaspoon butter for each half. Arrange the radish canapés on a platter. Cover with a domed lid or inverted bowl and chill 2 hours or until the butter is hard.

Parsley and Cream Cheese Butter (page 35)
Cheese Butter (page 36)
Herb Cheese Butter (page 36)
Anchovy and Cream Cheese Butter (page 36)

STUFFED CHERRY TOMATOES

Full-flavored, firm-textured tomatoes are essential to the success of this irresistible hors d'oeuvre.

Have ready 1 pint large, firm, ripe, cherry tomatoes. Cut a thin slice from the side away from the stem end of each tomato. With a small melon-ball cutter, carefully scoop out the seeds and pulp, leaving a shell about ¼ inch thick. Sprinkle the insides of the tomato shells with salt and invert the shells on paper towels to drain 15 minutes. Chill the shells, covered, 1 hour. Fill the shells with Smoked Salmon Spread (page 30), Cream Cheese and Bacon Filling (page 37), or Anchovy and Cream Cheese Filling (page 42), piping it through a pastry bag fitted with a decorative tip or using a ¼-teaspoon measuring spoon. Garnish the top of each stuffed tomato with a rinsed and drained caper or tiny piece of black olive and sprinkle lightly with minced fresh dill. Arrange the tomatoes on a platter. Cover them with a domed lid or inverted bowl and chill 1 hour. Garnish the platter with sprigs of watercress or Italian flat-leaf parsley and serve.

VARIATIONS:

Substitute Smoked Salmon and Avocado Dip (page 24) for the above fillings. Use the whole green peppercorns in that recipe to garnish the stuffed tomatoes.

Using a ¼-teaspoon measuring spoon or a small knife, fill the tomato shells with Guacamole (page 21) and garnish the tops with bacon slices, cooked crisp and crumbled into small bits.

Moisten the rim of each tomato shell with olive oil and dip it in finely minced parsley to make a green border. Fill the tomato shells with Hummus bi Tahini (page 19) and, if desired, garnish the center of each with a tiny dot of paprika. Alternatively, fill the shells with Serbian Herb Cheese Spread (page 28) or Herb Yogurt Cheese (page 57).

Fill the tomato shells with Cream Cheese and Mushroom Filling (page 37). Garnish the top of each with a tiny sprig of dill.

Fill the tomato shells with Seafood Salad Filling (page 40). Garnish the top of each with a tiny sprig of parsley.

Fill the tomato shells with Tabbouli (page 114).

Fill the tomato shells with Kibbeh (page 239) and garnish each with a tiny strip of green pepper or sprig of parsley.

Fill the tomato shells with Pesto Sauce (page 393). Or, halve the tomatoes and spoon a small amount of Pesto Sauce onto each tomato half.

LOMI LOMI CHERRY TOMATOES

In a bowl combine ¼ pound smoked salmon or lox, finely minced, 3 scallions, including 2 inches of the green tops, finely minced, and 1 small green pepper, seeded, deribbed, and finely minced. If desired, add a dash of Tabasco sauce and sprinkle with a little freshly squeezed and strained lime or lemon juice. Mix well. Using a ¼-teaspoon measuring spoon, fill the tomato shells with this mixture. If you like, mince the scooped-out tomato pulp and add it to the salmon mixture.

STUFFED ITALIAN PLUM TOMATOES

Once again, the more flavorful the tomatoes, the better the dish.

Prepare Caponata (page 138) with these changes: Sauté 2 medium garlic cloves, minced, along with the onion, omit the sugar, add ¾ teaspoon minced fresh thyme or ¼ teaspoon crushed dried thyme with the capers, and substitute black olives for the green olives.

Cut 1 pound Italian plum tomatoes in half lengthwise. Scoop out the seeds and let the tomatoes drain, inverted, on paper towels 15 minutes. Sprinkle the insides of the tomatoes with salt and freshly ground pepper to taste. Divide the eggplant mixture among the tomato shells, mounding it. Sprinkle the stuffed tomatoes with minced parsley and arrange them on a serving platter. Cover with a domed lid or inverted bowl and chill 1 hour before serving. Makes about 30.

SICILIAN BAKED STUFFED TOMATOES

This zestful antipasto *will satisfy body and soul.*

4 medium-sized firm, ripe tomatoes
 Salt
 Olive oil
1 small yellow onion, finely chopped
1 medium garlic clove, finely chopped
1 cup fresh soft breadcrumbs (made from French or Italian bread)
1 can (7 ounces) Italian tuna packed in olive oil, drained and broken into small pieces
4 anchovy fillets, drained and finely chopped
3 tablespoons finely chopped parsley, preferably Italian flat-leaf
1 tablespoon capers, rinsed, drained, and chopped
8 Mediterranean oil-cured black olives, finely chopped
1 tablespoon freshly grated imported Parmesan cheese
 Finely chopped parsley

Cut about ¼ inch off the top of each tomato. Using a teaspoon, scoop out the inside, leaving a ¼-inch-thick shell all around. Discard the seeds and reserve the pulp for another use. Sprinkle the cavities of the tomatoes with salt and let them drain, inverted, on paper towels.

Meanwhile, in a medium-sized, heavy skillet heat ¼ cup olive oil over moderate heat. Add the onion and garlic and sauté, stirring frequently, until the onion is soft but not browned. Add the breadcrumbs, tuna, and anchovy fillets and cook, stirring constantly, about 2 minutes. Remove the skillet from the heat and stir in the 3 tablespoons parsley, capers, and olives. Spoon the mixture into the tomatoes and sprinkle them evenly with the Parmesan cheese and a few drops of olive oil.

Brush a shallow baking dish just large enough to hold the stuffed tomatoes in one layer with olive oil. Arrange the tomatoes in the dish and bake them in a preheated 375°F oven about 25 minutes or until they are tender but still intact. Remove from the oven and cool. Carefully transfer the tomatoes to a serving platter. Sprinkle with a little parsley and serve at room temperature. Makes 4 servings.

ZUCCHINI SANDWICHES

Cut medium zucchini crosswise into ¼-inch-thick slices. Using a cookie cutter that is slightly smaller than the diameter of the slices, trim the zucchini into uniform circles, removing the peel. Spread half of the zucchini slices with any of the mixtures given below, using about 1 teaspoon for each slice and spreading it evenly to the edge of the slice. Top with the remaining zucchini slices to make cocktail-sized sandwiches. Brush the edges of each sandwich with Mayonnaise (page 387) and roll in finely chopped parsley. Arrange the sandwiches on a platter, cover, and chill 1 hour before serving.

Herb Butter (page 35)
Cheese Butter (page 36)
Anchovy and Cream Cheese Butter (page 36)
Shrimp Filling (page 40)
Anchovy and Cream Cheese Filling (page 42)
Prosciutto Filling (page 44)

ZUCCHINI IMAM BAYILDI

A top-drawer Middle Eastern appetizer for pedestrian pocketbooks, this is a less famous but equally delicious version of the renowned Eggplant Imam Bayildi (see Variation). The words imam bayildi (Turkish for "the priest fainted") refer to the origin of the latter dish. There are conflicting tales as to why the priest fainted on being served it. Some say that it was from sheer pleasure; in at least one account, however, he is said to have swooned from shock at learning how much olive oil his wife had used to make it. The recipe given here asks for an amount well short of the fainting point.

4 medium zucchini
1 bunch scallions, chopped
3 medium garlic cloves, finely chopped
½ cup finely chopped parsley
2 tablespoons finely chopped fresh mint leaves
2 tablespoons finely chopped fresh dill
  Salt to taste
1 large tomato, peeled, seeded, and chopped
⅓ cup olive oil
1½ tablespoons freshly squeezed and strained lemon juice
⅓ cup water
  Romaine or Boston lettuce leaves
1 lemon, cut into wedges

Slit the zucchini lengthwise on one side without quite cutting through, leaving 1 inch at each end uncut. Combine the scallions, garlic, parsley, mint, dill, and salt and mix well. Stuff the zucchini pockets with the mixture. Arrange the zucchini side by side, cut sides up, in a heavy saucepan or casserole. Spread any leftover stuffing mixture over the top. Add the tomato, olive oil, lemon juice, and water. Bring to a boil and cover. Reduce the heat to low and simmer 50 minutes or until tender, adding more water if necessary. Remove from the heat and let cool. Serve cold on the lettuce leaves, garnished with the lemon wedges. Makes 4 servings.

VARIATION:

EGGPLANT IMAM BAYILDI

Substitute 4 cylindrical eggplants (each 5 or 6 inches long) for the zucchini. Remove the stems and green tops from the eggplants. Peel each eggplant lengthwise in ½-inch strips, leaving ½-inch strips of skin in between to make a striped design. Sprinkle the eggplants generously with salt and let them drain in a colander 30 minutes. Rinse with cold water and pat dry with paper towels. Slit the eggplants in the same manner as the zucchini and proceed as directed.

HOT VEGETABLE APPETIZERS

ITALIAN STUFFED ARTICHOKE BOTTOMS

These will linger in your mind long after they are out of sight.

10 large artichokes
    Juice of 1 lemon, freshly squeezed and
      strained
 2 tablespoons butter
    Olive oil
¼ pound mushrooms, finely chopped
¼ cup finely chopped onion or shallots
 1 medium garlic clove, finely chopped
 2 tablespoons finely chopped parsley
 3 tablespoons finely chopped prosciutto
 6 tablespoons freshly grated imported
      Parmesan cheese
 1 cup fresh soft breadcrumbs (made from
      French or Italian bread)
    Salt and freshly ground pepper to taste
⅓ cup finely diced mozzarella cheese
   (optional)

Prepare and cook the artichokes as directed in the recipe for Stuffed Artichoke Salad (page 101). When cool enough to handle, pull off all the leaves and reserve them to be eaten at another time. Set the artichoke bottoms aside.

In a small, heavy skillet heat the butter and 1 tablespoon olive oil over medium-high heat. Add the mushrooms, onion or shallots, and garlic and sauté, stirring frequently, until lightly browned. Remove from the heat, add the parsley, prosciutto, 4 tablespoons of the Parmesan cheese, breadcrumbs, salt, and pepper and mix well. Taste and adjust the seasoning. Fill each artichoke bottom with a mound of the mixture, packing it firmly. Top the stuffed artichoke bottoms with the mozzarella, if used, and sprinkle evenly with the remaining 2 tablespoons Parmesan.

Pour a thin layer of olive oil into a shallow baking dish just large enough to hold the stuffed artichoke bottoms in one layer. Arrange the artichokes in the dish and bake in a preheated 375°F oven about 20 minutes or until the tops are lightly browned. Transfer to a heated platter and serve. Makes 10 servings.

VARIATION:

ITALIAN STUFFED MUSHROOMS

Substitute large mushroom caps, wiped with dampened paper towels, for the cooked artichoke bottoms. If desired, you may bake the stuffed mushrooms in tomato sauce as follows: Omit sprinkling them with the mozzarella and Parmesan cheese at the end. Instead of the olive oil, pour about 1 cup Tomato Sauce (page 398) into the baking dish, arrange the mushrooms over it, and spoon about ⅓ cup Tomato Sauce over the mushrooms. Bake as above and serve hot or at room temperature.

FRIED ARTICHOKE SLICES

Enthusiastic applause is certain to greet the appearance of these interestingly shaped, crunchy artichoke slices.

4 medium artichokes
1 egg
¼ cup water
½ teaspoon salt
¼ teaspoon freshly ground pepper
2 cups flavorless vegetable oil or olive oil, or 1 cup of each
1 cup breadcrumbs
Lemon wedges

Prepare each artichoke as follows: Peel the tough outer skin from the stem and trim the stem to 1 inch. Remove any coarse or discolored outer leaves and cut 1 inch off the top of the remaining leaves. Cut the artichoke in half lengthwise and remove the fuzzy choke and thorny pinkish leaves from the center. Holding each artichoke half firmly, carefully cut it lengthwise into ¼-inch-thick slices.

In a bowl beat the egg with the water, salt, and pepper until frothy. In a medium saucepan heat the oil to 375°F. Dip each artichoke slice in the egg mixture, then coat in the breadcrumbs. Fry the artichoke slices, a few at a time, in the hot oil, turning them once, about 1 minute or until they are golden brown and crisp. As each batch is done, transfer the slices with a wire skimmer or spoon to a baking sheet lined with paper towels and keep them warm in a preheated 200°F oven while you fry the remaining slices. Arrange the slices on a heated platter and garnish the platter with the lemon wedges. Serve at once. Makes about 24.

VARIATION:

4 cup breadcrumbs mixed with 3 tablespoons freshly grated imported Parmesan cheese and 1 tablespoon minced parsley for the plain breadcrumbs.

FALAFEL
Deep-Fried Fava Bean Balls

An Egyptian dish of ancient origin, falafel, or ta'amia, has long been popular throughout the Arab world. It consists of patties made from dried white fava beans (also known as broad beans), skillfully seasoned and deep-fried in oil. Falafel has also become a national snack in Israel, where chickpeas are substituted for the fava beans. The traditional way of serving it is in pita bread along with a vegetable salad or pickles and dressed with a sesame sauce (Taratoor bi Tahini, page 394) and, sometimes, a fiery red sauce. The following version makes a delightful cocktail hour treat.

1 pound dried white fava beans,
  preferably shelled (available at Middle
  Eastern groceries)
1 large red onion or 1 bunch scallions,
  very finely chopped (include 2 inches of
  the green tops of the scallions)
2 large garlic cloves, crushed
1 bunch parsley, finely chopped
1½ teaspoons cumin
1½ teaspoons coriander
  ½ teaspoon baking powder
  Salt and cayenne pepper to taste
  Flavorless vegetable oil for deep-frying
  Taratoor bi Tahini (page 394) (optional)

Soak the beans in cold water 24 hours. Drain and remove the skins if unshelled. Put the beans through the fine blade of a meat grinder. Add the onion or scallions, garlic, parsley, cumin, coriander, baking powder, salt, and cayenne pepper. Mix well and grind again. Pound the mixture to as smooth a paste as possible and let it rest, covered, 30 minutes. (Alternatively, finely grind the beans in a food processor fitted with the steel blade. Add the onion or scallions, garlic, parsley, cumin, coriander, baking powder, salt, and cayenne pepper and blend the mixture to as smooth a paste as possible. Transfer the mixture to a bowl and let it rest, covered, 30 minutes.) Form the paste into 1-inch balls. Arrange the balls on a plate and let them rest 15 minutes. Fry them in deep hot oil, a batch at a time, until richly browned, regulating the heat as necessary and being careful not to crowd the pan. Lift out the balls and with a slotted spoon transfer them to paper towels to drain.

Mound the *falafel* on a heated platter and set out a separate container of cocktail picks. Serve with the Taratoor bi Tahini, if desired, as an accompaniment to drinks. Makes 6 servings.

BABY EGGPLANTS WITH RATATOUILLE

Even a perennial favorite can use a new look now and then.

  4 baby eggplants (about ¼ pound each)
  Salt
  1 cup diced zucchini
  4 tablespoons olive oil
  1 cup finely sliced yellow onion
  *1 cup finely sliced green or red bell
    pepper, or ½ cup each*
*1½ cups peeled, seeded, and chopped
    tomatoes*
  2 teaspoons tomato paste
  2 medium garlic cloves, finely chopped
  *2 teaspoons finely chopped fresh basil, or
    ½ teaspoon crushed dried basil*
  *¾ teaspoon finely chopped fresh thyme,
    or ¼ teaspoon crushed dried thyme*
  ½ bay leaf
  Salt and freshly ground pepper to taste
  2 tablespoons finely chopped parsley
  Lettuce leaves

With a sharp knife, cut the eggplants in half lengthwise. Cut 3 or 4 gashes in the flesh of each eggplant half. Place the eggplants and zucchini on paper towels and sprinkle generously with salt. Let stand 30 minutes. Rinse and dry with fresh paper towels.

Arrange the eggplant halves, cut sides down, in a baking pan coated with 1 tablespoon of the olive oil. Brush the eggplant skins with 1 tablespoon of the remaining olive oil. Bake the eggplants in a preheated 400°F oven 10 to 15 minutes or until they are tender. Transfer the eggplants to a rack and let them cool. Scoop out the pulp with a spoon, leaving ¼-inch shells, being careful not to damage the shells. Chop the eggplant pulp coarsely and reserve the shells.

In a heavy enameled or stainless steel casserole heat the remaining 2 tablespoons oil over moderate heat. Add the onion and bell pepper and sauté, stirring frequently, until the onion is soft but not browned. Add the zucchini and eggplant pulp and cook, stirring, 3 minutes. Add the tomatoes, tomato paste, garlic, basil, thyme, bay leaf, salt, and pepper. Stir the mixture, cover, and cook over low heat 15 minutes. Uncover and cook the mixture over high heat, stirring, until almost all the liquid has evaporated. Remove and discard the bay leaf and stir in the parsley. Remove the *ratatouille* from the heat and divide it among the reserved eggplant shells, mounding it. Arrange the stuffed eggplant shells on a serving platter lined with the lettuce leaves. Serve warm or at room temperature. Makes 4 servings.

VARIATIONS:

During the last few minutes of cooking the *ratatouille,* stir in ½ cup diced prosciutto or drained flaked tuna (preferably imported tuna packed in olive oil) and ¼ cup sliced pitted Greek or Niçoise black olives.

Omit the lettuce leaves. Sprinkle the stuffed eggplant shells with freshly grated imported Parmesan cheese and dot them with unsalted butter. Arrange the eggplants in one layer in an oiled gratin dish and place them under a preheated broiler about 5 inches from the heat 3 minutes or until the tops are lightly browned. Serve hot.

EGGPLANT CANNELLONI

Sheer bliss for eggplant enthusiasts.

1¼ cups freshly grated mozzarella cheese
  ¾ cup (3 ounces) freshly grated imported
    Parmesan cheese
  ½ cup ricotta cheese
  3 ounces (about ¾ cup) prosciutto, finely
    chopped
  3 eggs
  1 to 2 tablespoons finely chopped parsley
    Salt and freshly ground pepper to taste
    All-purpose flour
  ½ teaspoon baking powder
  ⅛ teaspoon salt
  ½ cup milk
  1 tablespoon flavorless vegetable oil
  1 large eggplant (about 1½ pounds)
  6 tablespoons olive oil, more if needed
  1 cup Tomato Sauce (page 398)

In a medium bowl combine the mozzarella cheese, ½ cup of the Parmesan cheese, ricotta cheese, prosciutto, 2 of the eggs, parsley, salt, and pepper. Mix until well blended and smooth. Cover and chill.

In a small mixing bowl sift together ¼ cup flour, the baking powder, and the ⅛ teaspoon salt. Add the remaining egg, milk, and the 1 tablespoon vegetable oil and beat the batter until it is smooth. Pour the batter into a pie pan or other similar shallow pan and set aside.

Remove the stem and green top from the eggplant. Cut the eggplant lengthwise into 12 slices of equal thickness. In a large, heavy skillet heat 3 tablespoons of the olive oil over moderate heat. Dredge the eggplant slices lightly in flour and dip them into the batter, coating them evenly but thinly. Arrange several of the slices side by side in the skillet, being careful not to crowd the pan, and sauté until they are soft, turning to brown them lightly on both sides. Transfer to paper towels to drain. Repeat this procedure until all the eggplant slices are sautéed, adding more oil as necessary.

Divide the cheese mixture into 12 equal parts. Place each part across the center of an eggplant slice. Fold one of the narrow ends of each eggplant slice over the cheese filling and roll up like a jelly roll to close.

Arrange the filled eggplant slices, seam sides down, in a lightly oiled shallow baking-and-serving dish. Spoon the Tomato Sauce evenly over them. Bake, uncovered, in a preheated 375°F oven 15 to 20 minutes or until the cheese is melted and the eggplant slices are heated through. Sprinkle evenly with the remaining ¼ cup Parmesan cheese and serve hot. Makes 6 servings.

VARIATION:

Substitute a mixture of 4 tablespoons olive oil and 2 tablespoons butter for the olive oil, adding more olive oil and butter if necessary.

CHAMPIGNONS FARCIS AUX CRABES
Crab-Filled Mushrooms

These will elicit sighs of rapture from crab and mushroom devotees alike.

12 large mushrooms
 3 tablespoons butter
 1 tablespoon all-purpose flour
½ cup hot milk
   Salt and freshly ground pepper to taste
½ cup finely chopped shallots or scallions
   (include 2 inches of the green tops of
   the scallions)
 5 ounces crabmeat
 1 tablespoon Cognac
   Cayenne pepper to taste
 1 egg yolk
 3 tablespoons butter, melted
¼ cup freshly grated imported Parmesan
   cheese

Remove the stems from the mushrooms, chop them finely, and reserve. Wipe the mushroom caps with dampened paper towels and set aside.

In a small, heavy saucepan melt 1 tablespoon of the butter over moderate heat. Add the flour and cook 1 or 2 minutes without letting it brown, whisking constantly. Add the hot milk and cook, stirring, until the mixture comes to a boil and is thick and smooth. Add salt and pepper and remove from the heat.

In a medium saucepan melt the remaining 2 tablespoons butter over moderate heat. Add the shallots or scallions and reserved mushroom stems and sauté, stirring frequently, 4 to 5 minutes. Add the crabmeat, stir to blend, and add the Cognac. Add the white sauce, cayenne pepper, salt, and pepper and mix well. Stir in the egg yolk until well blended. Remove from the heat and set aside.

Arrange the mushroom caps, stem ends down, in a buttered baking dish just large enough to hold them in one layer. Brush them with 1½ tablespoons of the melted butter and bake in a preheated 400°F oven 10 minutes. Remove from the oven and let cool. Fill the cavities of the mushroom caps with the crabmeat mixture, mounding it. Arrange the stuffed mushrooms in the baking dish and sprinkle them with the Parmesan cheese and remaining 1½ tablespoons melted butter. Bake in a preheated 400°F oven 20 minutes. Serve hot. Makes 12.

CHINESE STUFFED MUSHROOMS

Appealing to both Eastern and Western palates.

20 dried Chinese mushrooms, 1 to 1½ inches in diameter
1 tablespoon imported soy sauce
1 tablespoon Chinese rice wine or pale dry Sherry
½ teaspoon sugar
Cornstarch
½ pound boneless pork shoulder, finely ground
4 peeled fresh water chestnuts or drained canned water chestnuts, finely chopped
1½ tablespoons finely chopped scallions, including 2 inches of the green tops
½ teaspoon grated peeled fresh ginger root
1 tablespoon peanut oil or flavorless vegetable oil
2 tablespoons bottled oyster sauce

In a bowl cover the mushrooms with hot water and let them soak 30 minutes. Drain, reserving ¼ cup of the mushroom water.

Remove and discard the mushroom stems. Pat the mushroom caps dry with paper towels and set aside.

In a bowl combine the soy sauce, wine, sugar, and 1 teaspoon cornstarch and stir until the cornstarch dissolves. Add the ground pork, water chestnuts, scallions, and ginger root and mix until the ingredients are thoroughly blended. Dust the stem sides of the mushrooms with cornstarch and fill them with the pork mixture, dividing it equally.

Place a large, heavy skillet over high heat for about 30 seconds. Pour in the oil, swirling it around in the skillet. Place the stuffed mushrooms side by side in one layer in the skillet. Reduce the heat to moderate and sauté the mushrooms 1 or 2 minutes until they are lightly browned. Add the reserved ¼ cup mushroom water to the skillet and bring to a boil. Cover the skillet, reduce the heat to low, and simmer very gently 15 minutes. Stir the oyster sauce into the pan liquid and baste each mushroom. Cover the skillet for a few seconds, then with a slotted spoon or spatula transfer the mushrooms to a heated platter. Serve hot. Makes 10 servings.

VARIATION:

Substitute large fresh mushroom caps for the dried mushrooms. Omit adding the mushroom water and oyster sauce to the skillet. Instead of braising the stuffed mushrooms, sauté them as follows: In a large, heavy skillet heat ½ cup peanut oil or flavorless vegetable oil over high heat. Lower the mushrooms, stuffed sides down, into the oil. Reduce the heat to moderate and sauté the mushrooms about 3 minutes on each side or until they are nicely browned and the filling is cooked. Drain the mushrooms on paper towels and serve.

SPANISH MUSHROOMS IN GARLIC SAUCE

½ pound mushrooms
3 tablespoons olive oil
2 medium garlic cloves, finely chopped
1½ tablespoons all-purpose flour
1 cup beef broth
½ dried hot red chili pepper, seeded and cut into 3 pieces
2 tablespoons finely chopped parsley
2 teaspoons freshly squeezed and strained lemon juice
Salt to taste

Trim off any tough ends of the mushroom stems. Wipe the mushrooms clean with dampened paper towels. If the mushrooms are large, halve or quarter them. Set aside.

In a medium-sized, heavy skillet or fire-proof casserole heat 2 tablespoons of the oil over medium-high heat. Add the garlic and sauté, stirring, until barely golden; do not let it brown. Immediately remove the pan from the heat and stir in the flour until smooth. Return to the heat and cook, stirring, 1 to 2 minutes. Gradually stir in the broth. Add the chili pepper, 1 tablespoon of the parsley, the lemon juice, and salt and cook, stirring, until the sauce is thick and smooth. Remove from the heat and set aside.

In a medium-sized, heavy skillet heat the remaining 1 tablespoon oil over high heat. Add the mushrooms and sauté, stirring frequently, until they are lightly browned. Add the mushrooms to the sauce and simmer 5 minutes. Taste and adjust the seasoning. Transfer to a heated serving bowl. Sprinkle with the remaining 1 tablespoon parsley and serve at once as a *tapa* (page 405). Makes 4 servings.

RUSSIAN MUSHROOMS IN SOUR CREAM

1½ pounds mushrooms
¼ cup butter
1 medium onion, finely chopped
Salt and freshly ground pepper to taste
2 cups sour cream, at room temperature
1 cup heavy cream, at room temperature
2 tablespoons dry Sherry
3 tablespoons finely chopped fresh dill

Trim off any tough ends of the mushroom stems. Wipe the mushrooms clean with dampened paper towels. If using button mushrooms, leave them whole. Quarter or slice larger mushrooms.

In a large, heavy skillet melt the butter over medium-high heat. Add the mushrooms and onion and sauté, stirring frequently, until the vegetables are lightly browned. Season with the salt and pepper. Add the sour cream and heavy cream, reduce the heat to low, and simmer very gently, stirring constantly, until heated through and smooth. Stir in the Sherry and sprinkle with 2 tablespoons of the dill. Taste and adjust the seasoning. Transfer to a heated serving dish, sprinkle with the remaining 1 tablespoon dill, and serve. Makes 6 servings.

BULGARIAN FRIED PEPPERS STUFFED WITH CHEESE

These provide a splendid starting point for a Balkan- or Middle Eastern-oriented meal.

12 medium-sized Italian finger-shaped
    frying peppers
¾ pound brindza cheese or feta cheese,
    crumbled
6 ounces pot cheese
4 eggs
    Freshly ground pepper to taste
2 tablespoons finely chopped parsley
    (optional)
½ cup all-purpose flour (approximately)
3 cups soft fresh breadcrumbs, made from
    homemade-type bread
    Flavorless vegetable oil for deep-frying

Arrange the peppers on the rack of a broiler pan and broil under a preheated broiler about 1 inch from the heat, turning them frequently until the skins are evenly blistered and charred. Remove the peppers from the oven and place them in a paper bag. Close the bag tightly and let the peppers steam until they are cool enough to handle. Peel and discard the charred skins. Cut out the stems and carefully scoop out the seeds, leaving the peppers intact.

Force the *brindza* or feta and the pot cheese through a food mill set over a bowl, or rub them through a medium-meshed sieve. Add 2 of the eggs and the ground pepper and beat vigorously with a wooden spoon until the mixture is well blended and smooth. Stir in the parsley, if used. Taste and adjust the seasoning. Using a pastry bag fitted with a small, plain tip, fill each roasted pepper with approximately 3 tablespoons of the cheese mixture. In a bowl lightly beat the remaining 2 eggs. Dredge each stuffed pepper in flour, gently shaking off any excess, dip into the beaten eggs, and roll on all sides in the breadcrumbs. Arrange the peppers side by side on a platter lined with waxed paper and refrigerate 30 minutes.

In a deep-fryer or large, heavy saucepan heat 3 inches oil to 375°F. Fry the stuffed peppers in the hot oil, 3 or 4 at a time, turning them about with a slotted spoon for 2 to 3 minutes or until they are golden brown. Transfer the peppers with the slotted spoon to paper towels to drain. Arrange them on a heated platter. Serve hot, either whole as a first course or cut crosswise into 3 or 4 slices as an accompaniment to drinks. Makes 12.

Note: Brindza, a soft white cheese similar to feta, is popular in central and eastern Europe. Also made in the United States, it is available in some specialty food shops.

CHEESE-CRUSTED POTATO SKINS WITH SALSA CRUDA

A relative rarity a decade or so ago, fried potato skins have become increasingly popular in recent years. Even those who ordinarily leave nutrition-packed baked potato skins on their plates are tempted by this Mexican-inspired appetizer.

    Salsa Cruda (page 399)
  5 large russet potatoes (about 3 pounds)
    Flavorless vegetable oil (for deep-frying),
    or ⅓ cup butter, melted (for oven frying)
    (approximately)
¾ cup (3 ounces) shredded sharp Cheddar
    cheese
¾ cup (3 ounces) shredded Monterey Jack
    cheese

Prepare the Salsa Cruda and set aside.

Scrub the potatoes and pierce each one with a fork. Bake them in a preheated 400°F oven about 1 hour or until tender. Remove the potatoes from the oven and let them stand until they are cool enough to handle.

Cut them lengthwise into quarters. With a spoon, carefully scoop the potato flesh from the skin, leaving a ⅛-inch-thick shell. (Save the flesh for another use.)

In a deep-fryer or deep, heavy skillet heat 2 inches oil to 400°F. Add the potato skins, about 5 at a time, and fry about 1 minute or until they are golden brown and crisp. As each batch is done, transfer the potato skins with a slotted spoon to paper towels to drain. Arrange the hot skins, cut sides up and side by side, in a single layer on a 12 by 15-inch baking sheet. (Alternatively, brush the potato skins inside and out with the melted butter. Arrange the skins, cut sides up and side by side, in a single layer on a 12 by 15-inch baking sheet. Bake in a preheated 500°F oven about 12 minutes or until they are lightly browned and crisp.)

Fill the potato skins with the cheeses, dividing equally. Broil under a preheated broiler about 4 inches from the heat 2 minutes or until the cheeses melt. Transfer to a heated platter and serve at once with the Salsa Cruda for dipping. Makes 4 to 6 servings.

AUSTRIAN CHEESE SOUFFLÉ IN TOMATOES

A glamorous offering that tastes as good as it looks.

> 4 large, firm tomatoes
> Salt and freshly ground pepper to taste
> 1½ tablespoons butter
> 2 tablespoons all-purpose flour
> ½ cup heavy cream or milk, heated
> 3 egg yolks
> Pinch freshly grated nutmeg
> ½ cup freshly grated imported Parmesan cheese, or ¼ cup each freshly grated Parmesan and Swiss cheese
> 2 teaspoons finely chopped parsley
> 1 teaspoon finely chopped chives
> 3 egg whites, stiffly beaten
> Freshly grated imported Parmesan cheese

Cut about ½ inch off the stem end of each tomato. Using a teaspoon, scoop out the insides, leaving a ¼-inch-thick shell all around. Discard the seeds and reserve the pulp for another use. Sprinkle the insides of the tomatoes with salt and pepper and let them drain, inverted, on paper towels.

In a medium-sized, heavy saucepan melt the butter over moderate heat. Add the flour and cook 1 or 2 minutes without letting it brown, whisking constantly. Add the cream or milk and cook, stirring, until the mixture comes to a boil and is thick and smooth. Remove from the heat and beat in the egg yolks, one at a time, incorporating each yolk completely before adding the next. Season with nutmeg, salt, and pepper, then stir in the ½ cup cheese, parsley, and chives. Fold in the egg whites.

Arrange the drained tomato shells in a buttered shallow baking dish just large enough to hold them comfortably. Fill the shells with the soufflé mixture, dividing equally. Sprinkle the tops with grated Parmesan cheese and place the tomatoes in a preheated 400°F oven. Immediately reduce the heat to 375°F and bake about 25 minutes or until the filling is golden brown. Serve at once. Makes 4 servings.

TAHU
Indonesian Fried Soybean Cubes

Tofu *lovers, take note.*

2 firm soybean cakes (dowfu or tofu*)*
2 tablespoons peanut oil or corn oil
   Sambal Kacang (page 395) and/or Colo
   Colo (page 399)

Pat the soybean cakes dry with a kitchen towel. Cut each cake into 9 cubes. In a wok or large, heavy skillet heat the oil over medium-high heat. Add the cubes and fry, turning them, until they are nicely browned on all sides. With a slotted spoon, transfer the cubes to paper towels to drain. Arrange the fried cubes on a platter and serve with the Sambal Kacang and/or Colo Colo for dipping. Makes 18.

RELISHES AND PICKLES

Throughout the world there has been an age-old tradition of preserving the summertime bounty of vegetables and fruits for the year ahead. Although "putting by" these zesty temptations is no longer a matter of necessity for most of us, in many homes it is still an annual ritual that generates a sense of achievement and satisfaction, both in the act itself and in its long-term benefits. Despite the abundance of commercial products available, homemade relishes and pickles are as a rule better-tasting and more economical.

Many of the piquant preparations that follow are not to be found in stores, so you can serve them proudly as unique specialties from your own kitchen. Offer them on a hors d'oeuvre tray or as part of an appetizer buffet and watch them quickly vanish.

PICKLED CUCUMBER

Popular throughout Scandinavia, this is a standard offering on the smörgåsbord.

    1 long, thin cucumber (known as
       European or English cucumber)
       Salt
    ⅓ cup white vinegar
    ⅓ cup water
    1 tablespoon sugar
    ¼ teaspoon freshly ground white pepper
    2 tablespoons finely chopped fresh dill

Slice the cucumber as thinly as possible. Arrange the slices in a thin layer in a shallow glass or china dish and sprinkle with 1 tablespoon salt. Place 2 or 3 china plates on top of the cucumber slices to press out excess water and bitterness and let them stand at room temperature several hours. Remove the plates and drain the cucumber slices thoroughly. Pat them dry with paper towels and arrange them in a clean shallow glass or china dish. In a small bowl beat together the vinegar, water, sugar, pepper, and salt to taste and pour over the cucumber slices. Sprinkle with the dill, cover, and chill 2 hours. Just before serving, drain off almost all of the liquid. Makes 4 to 6 servings.

VARIATIONS:

Substitute 2 medium-sized regular cucumbers for the European cucumber. Scrub the wax coating (if any) off the cucumbers and dry them. Or peel the cucumbers, if desired.

Instead of mixing the dill with the vinegar mixture, sprinkle the cucumber slices with minced fresh dill or parsley just before serving.

SPANISH MARINATED MUSHROOMS AND ONION

    ¾ pound medium mushrooms
    ¼ cup Sherry wine vinegar
    ¼ cup olive oil
    1 small garlic clove, finely chopped
    ¼ teaspoon crushed dried oregano
    ⅛ teaspoon crushed dried thyme
    ½ teaspoon salt
    1 small onion, thinly sliced
    1 tablespoon finely chopped parsley

Wipe the mushrooms clean with dampened paper towels, trim the stems, and set aside.

In a large enameled or stainless steel saucepan combine the vinegar, olive oil, garlic, oregano, thyme, and salt. Bring to a boil over moderate heat. Reduce the heat to low, cover, and simmer 5 minutes. Add the reserved mushrooms and onion and return to a boil. Remove from the heat and let stand, covered, 10 minutes. Uncover and allow to cool to room temperature. Transfer to a bowl, cover, and refrigerate several hours or up to 2 days, stirring occasionally.

With a slotted spoon, lift the mushrooms out of the marinade, draining them carefully, and arrange them on a platter or in a serving bowl. Sprinkle with the parsley and serve slightly chilled or at room temperature. Makes 6 servings.

RUSSIAN PICKLED MUSHROOMS

1 pound small mushrooms
⅔ cup wine vinegar
½ cup water
2 medium garlic cloves, crushed
2 whole cloves
5 whole peppercorns
½ bay leaf
1½ teaspoons salt
1 to 2 tablespoons olive oil or flavorless vegetable oil

Wipe the mushrooms clean with dampened paper towels, trim the stems, and set aside.

In a medium-sized enameled or stainless steel saucepan combine the vinegar, water, garlic, cloves, peppercorns, bay leaf, and salt. Add the reserved mushrooms, reduce the heat to low, and simmer, uncovered, 10 minutes, stirring the mushrooms from time to time. Remove from the heat and let the mushrooms cool in the liquid.

Spoon the mushrooms and the cooking liquid into a 1-quart jar. Slowly spoon the oil on top. Cover the jar tightly and refrigerate the mushrooms at least 6 days before using. Remove the garlic before serving. Serve the pickled mushrooms on a *zakuska* table or as an accompaniment to meat or fish. Makes 6 servings.

Note: One pound medium mushrooms, cleaned, stemmed, and halved, can be substituted for the small mushrooms.

JAPANESE MARINATED MUSHROOMS

A nice change on the relish tray.

36 small mushrooms
½ cup finely chopped onion
¼ cup white vinegar
3 tablespoons sake or dry Sherry
2 tablespoons imported soy sauce
2 tablespoons sugar
1 teaspoon salt

Wipe the mushrooms clean with dampened paper towels. Remove the stems and reserve them for another use. Place the mushroom caps in a bowl. Combine the remaining ingredients in a small saucepan. Stirring constantly, bring the mixture to a boil over high heat and pour over the mushrooms. Cover and let marinate in a cool place 24 hours, stirring occasionally. Drain the mushroom caps and arrange them on a platter or in a shallow serving bowl. Set out a separate small container of cocktail picks for spearing the mushrooms. Makes 36.

DANISH PICKLED BEETS

All of Scandinavia adores pickled beets, which form an indispensable component of any true smörgåsbord.

2 pounds small beets, scrubbed and
  trimmed
¾ cup cider vinegar or white wine vinegar
2 to 4 tablespoons sugar
¾ teaspoon salt
½ teaspoon mixed pickling spice

In a saucepan combine the beets with water to cover. Bring to a boil over high heat. Reduce the heat, cover, and simmer about 35 minutes or until the beets are tender. Drain the beets, reserving 1 cup of the cooking liquid. Peel off the skins and slice the beets. Place the sliced beets in a heatproof glass, enamel, or stainless steel bowl and set aside.

In a medium-sized enameled saucepan combine the reserved 1 cup cooking liquid and vinegar and bring to a boil. Add the sugar, salt, and mixed pickling spice and bring to a boil again, stirring constantly until the sugar and salt are dissolved. Pour the mixture over the beets, covering them completely. Allow to cool to room temperature, then cover the bowl with plastic wrap and chill at least 12 hours before serving. Makes 8 servings.

GIARDINIERA
Italian Pickled Vegetables

You can easily duplicate in your own kitchen the brightly colored mélange of pickled vegetables that is sold in Italian delicatessens, specialty food shops, and some supermarkets.

1 pound cauliflower, separated into florets (discard the leaves and center core)
½ pound pickling or small white boiling onions, peeled
1 bunch small carrots, peeled, cut in half lengthwise, and cut crosswise into 1½-inch-long pieces
½ small bunch celery, cut in half lengthwise and cut crosswise into 1½-inch-long pieces
1 green or red bell pepper, seeded, deribbed, and cut into 1-inch-wide strips
½ cup salt
2 quarts cold water
1 quart white wine vinegar
1¼ cups sugar
2 tablespoons mustard seed
1 tablespoon celery seed
1 small dried hot chili pepper

Combine the cauliflower, onions, carrots, celery, and green or red pepper in a large bowl. Dissolve the salt in the cold water and pour over the vegetables. Cover and refrigerate 12 to 18 hours. Drain, rinse in cold water, and drain again. Set aside.

In a large enameled or stainless steel saucepan combine the remaining ingredients. Bring to a boil, stirring until the sugar is dissolved, and boil 3 minutes. Add the vegetables and boil 10 minutes or until the vegetables are almost tender. Remove and discard the chili pepper. Using a slotted spoon, immediately pack the vegetables into 3 hot, sterilized pint jars (below). Run a spatula around the inside of each jar to release any air bubbles. Stir the boiling vinegar mixture to mix the seasonings, pour over the vegetables in the jars to within ½ inch of the rims, and seal. Store the *giardiniera* in a cool, dark, dry place 2 weeks before using. Refrigerate several hours to chill and crisp before serving. Keep refrigerated after opening. Makes 3 pints.

To sterilize jars: Wash Mason jars and their lids in hot, soapy water and rinse well in scalding water. Place the jars in a large kettle with a rack on the bottom. Cover them completely with hot (not boiling) water, bring to boil, and boil 20 minutes, then reduce the heat. Leave the jars in the hot water until ready to use, then remove them with tongs and drain. Do not boil the self-sealing lids; place them in a bowl, pour boiling water over them, and leave until ready to use. Wipe the jar rims with a clean, damp cloth. Fill and seal the jars while they are still hot so that they will not crack when the hot ingredients are poured into them. Allow the jars to cool thoroughly before storing.

ARMENIAN PICKLED VEGETABLES

Even the poorest home in the Middle Eastern countryside is sure to have a supply of pickles. During the summer, when vegetables are abundant, many families pack enormous amounts into large glass or earthenware jars to provide a sufficient quantity to last the coming year. These colorful taste-tempters are served as hors d'oeuvre or as an accompaniment to the main course, and a meal without at least one kind of pickle would be inconceivable.

1 small head cauliflower, separated into florets (discard the leaves and center core)

4 small carrots, quartered lengthwise and cut into 3- to 4-inch-thick pieces

¼ pound tender green beans, stemmed

2 green peppers, quartered, seeded, and deribbed

2 small beets, quartered

2 garlic cloves, peeled

4 sprigs fresh dill, or 2 sprigs each fresh basil, coriander, and tarragon

1 quart water

1 cup white wine vinegar

¼ cup salt (not iodized)

2 tablespoons mixed pickling spice (optional)

Pack the vegetables tightly into 2 sterilized quart jars (page 168), adding 1 garlic clove and 2 sprigs dill (or 1 sprig each basil, coriander, and tarragon) to each jar. In an enameled or stainless steel saucepan bring the remaining ingredients to a boil, stirring to dissolve the salt. Pour over the vegetables in the jars, covering them completely, and seal. Store in a cool, dark, dry place 3 to 4 weeks before using. Once opened, keep the jars in the refrigerator. Makes 2 quarts.

FRUITED TOMATO RELISH

A delightful sweet-and-sour relish for meat loaf and hamburgers (see Miniature Hamburgers, page 293).

8 medium-sized, ripe tomatoes, peeled, seeded, and diced
1 cup diced celery
2 medium onions, diced
1 medium-sized red bell pepper, seeded, deribbed, and diced
1 small green bell pepper, seeded, deribbed, and diced
2 small Bartlett pears, peeled, cored, and diced
2 medium peaches, peeled, pitted, and diced
1 small, tart apple, peeled, cored, and diced
1 cup cider vinegar
1 cup sugar
1 tablespoon mixed pickling spice, tied in a cheesecloth bag
1½ teaspoons, salt

Combine all the ingredients in a large enameled or stainless steel saucepan. Bring to a boil over moderate heat, stirring, until the sugar is dissolved. Reduce the heat to low and simmer the mixture, uncovered, stirring occasionally, about 1½ hours or until it is thick. Remove the spice bag and discard. Pack the relish into hot, sterilized jars (page 168) to within ¼ inch of the tops and seal. Makes about 4 pints.

FRUIT

A refreshingly delicious and utterly easy way to create premeal pleasure, especially in hot weather, is to serve fresh fruits as starters. Whether served singly, in combination, or in partnership with selected seafood, meats, or cheeses, they offer elegant and exceptional fare.

Perhaps the most popular of fruit appetizers are fruit cocktails made, preferably, with cut-up fresh fruits and berries. To make these appealing curtain raisers, mix tart fruits (natural appetite stimulators such as grapefruit, oranges, and pineapple), with blander fruits (such as apples, apricots, bananas, peaches, and pears). Present them in stemmed goblets, small bowls set in larger bowls of crushed ice, grapefruit or orange shells, or papaya halves. If you wish, spike them with wine or liqueur, garnish with fresh mint sprigs, or top with scoops of fruit ice or sherbet.

Your culinary repertoire can be notably enhanced by the inclusion of the following fruit appetizers, which will impart a measure of originality and a touch of the unexpected to your entertaining.

Additional recipes employing fruit can be found by consulting the Index.

PEARS WITH CHEESE

One of the simplest ways of producing an exquisite opener.

Spread cored, unpeeled thick slices of ripe Bartlett pear with any of the following mixtures and serve on a chilled platter.

Herb Cheese (page 51)
Gorgonzola Cheese and Prosciutto Spread (page 27)
Swedish Cheese Spread (page 28)
Prosciutto Filling (page 44)

PEARS WITH HAM AND CHEESE

Quick to make but long to stay in the memory.

For each serving, peel a small, ripe Bartlett pear without removing the stem. Place the pear, stem pointing upward, on a chilled appetizer plate and brush it lightly with fresh lemon juice to prevent it from darkening. Arrange alongside the pear 2 or 3 paper-thin slices of prosciutto, Smithfield ham, or Westphalian ham, rolled or rippled on the plate, and a few thin slices of Leyden, Edam, Taleggio, Emmenthal, or Gruyère cheese.

APPLES WITH ROQUEFORT

Spread cored, unpeeled red apple slices, each ¼ to ½ inch thick, with Roquefort Cheese Spread (page 27) and sprinkle with chopped toasted walnuts, if desired. Arrange on a chilled platter and serve.

PAPAYA WITH LIME

All that is needed is a little lime juice to bring papayas to their peak of perfection.

2 ripe papayas
½ cup freshly squeezed and strained lime juice

Halve the papayas lengthwise, remove the seeds, and peel. Cut crosswise into thick slices, then cut each slice in half and impale on a cocktail pick. Serve with a bowl of the lime juice for dipping. Makes 8 servings.

WEST AFRICAN FILLED PAPAYA HALVES

A particularly good starter if you're counting calories.

2 medium-sized ripe papayas
2 teaspoons freshly squeezed and strained lime juice
2 cups diced fresh fruit (pineapple, orange, banana, and sweet cherries)
4 lime wedges

Cut the papayas in half lengthwise and scoop out the seeds. Sprinkle each half with ½ teaspoon lime juice. In a bowl combine the diced fruit, then divide it among the papaya halves. Transfer each filled papaya half to an appetizer plate and serve with a wedge of lime. Makes 4 servings.

VARIATION:

Substitute lemon juice for the lime juice. Instead of filling the papaya halves with the above fruit, use a mixture of mandarin orange segments, halved pitted sweet cherries, and banana slices. Sprinkle with a little Grand Marnier and freshly squeezed and strained lemon juice. Garnish with chopped unsalted pistachio nuts and serve.

BRAZILIAN STUFFED PRUNES

In a bowl cover large dried prunes with Port, Sherry, or rum and let soak 2 hours. Drain and pat dry with paper towels, then carefully remove the pits. Using a pastry bag fitted with a small decorative tip, pipe Prosciutto Filling (page 44) or Cream Cheese and Bacon Filling (page 37) into the cavities of the prunes. Place each prune in a fancy little cup, arrange on a platter, and serve.

STUFFED GRAPES

These are real charmers.

Select ½ pound large seedless green grapes. With a small, sharp knife cut each grape ¾ of the way through from the stem end. Pat the grapes dry with paper towels. Using a pastry bag fitted with a small star tip, pipe Roquefort Cheese Spread (page 27, omitting the chives or scallion tops), Serbian Cheese Spread (page 28), or Yogurt Cheese (page 57) into the center of each grape, gently pressing the sides together. Line a serving platter with rinsed and dried fresh grape leaves or lemon leaves, if available. Arrange the stuffed grapes on the platter. Cover and chill 2 hours before serving. Makes about 40.

VARIATION:

The cheese mixture given for Stuffed Kumquats (following) also makes a delicious filling for the grapes.

STUFFED KUMQUATS

These exotic, eye-catching morsels can lend enchantment to any hors d'oeuvre table.

3 ounces cream cheese or Neufchâtel
    cheese, at room temperature
1 tablespoon dry Sherry
⅛ teaspoon salt or to taste
2 tablespoons finely chopped toasted
    blanched almonds, walnuts, or
    macadamia nuts
1 jar (1 pound 4 ounces) preserved whole
    kumquats
Parsley sprigs

In a small bowl beat the cream cheese or Neufchâtel cheese with the Sherry and salt until light and fluffy. Add the nuts and mix well.

Drain the kumquats. Using a sharp knife, cut them in half lengthwise and remove the seeds. Place about 1 teaspoon of the cheese mixture in each kumquat half, then sandwich the halves together. Cover and chill. Garnish with the parsley sprigs and serve. Makes about 25.

Note: About 25 fresh kumquats, cut in half and seeded, can be substituted for the preserved kumquats.

STUFFED DATES

Fill pitted dates with Prosciutto Filling (page 44), Cream Cheese and Bacon Filling (page 37), or a soft, creamy cheese such as Brie, Camembert, or *chèvre* (goat cheese). Arrange the stuffed dates on a baking sheet and bake them in a preheated 350°F oven about 5 minutes or just until the cheese is melted. Serve warm.

VARIATION:

Fill the dates with almond or hazelnut butter (available in specialty food shops) or peanut butter. Do not bake.

MEXICAN-STYLE CRANBERRY ICE

Inspired by the south-of-the-border fruit ices known as paletas, *this refreshing offering can begin, end, or come between the courses of a meal.*

> 1 pound (4 cups) cranberries, stemmed
>   and picked over
> 1½ cups water
> ⅔ cup sugar or to taste
> ½ teaspoon grated orange rind
> ½ cup freshly squeezed and strained
>   orange juice
> 1 tablespoon freshly squeezed and
>   strained lemon juice

In a large enameled or stainless steel saucepan combine the cranberries with the water. Cook, uncovered, over moderate heat until the skins pop, stirring frequently. With the back of a metal spoon, press the cranberries and liquid through a sieve set over a large bowl to remove the skins and seeds. Add the remaining ingredients to the cranberry pulp and stir until the sugar is dissolved. Pour the mixture into a 9-inch stainless steel baking pan. Cover with aluminum foil and freeze about 8 hours or until solid. Remove the ice from the freezer and let stand at room temperature until you can break it into small chunks. Process about one third of the ice at a time in a food processor until it turns into a smooth slush. Alternatively, place all the ice in a stainless steel bowl and smash it into very small pieces with a wooden spoon, then beat with an electric mixer until smooth. Cover with aluminum foil and freeze the ice until it is firm. Allow the ice to stand at room temperature 5 to 10 minutes to thaw slightly, then spoon it into stemmed goblets and serve. Makes about 3½ cups.

VARIATION:

MEXICAN-STYLE POMEGRANATE ICE

Remove the seeds from 8 to 10 large pomegranates (you will need 8 cups seeds) as follows: Peel and quarter the pomegranates. Break sections apart with your fingers and separate the seeds from the pulp. In the container of an electric blender or food processor whirl 2 cups seeds at a time until liquefied. Pour the pomegranate seeds and juice through a cheesecloth-lined wire strainer placed over a bowl and let drain. Reserve the juice (you will need 4 cups) and discard the seeds. To the pomegranate juice add ¾ cup sugar, 1½ teaspoons grated lemon rind, and 3½ tablespoons freshly

squeezed and strained lemon juice and stir until the sugar is dissolved. Pour the mixture into a 9-inch stainless steel baking pan and proceed as directed above. Makes about 5 cups.

SEAFOOD

Americans have not been great devotees of fish in the past. We seem always to have been fond of shellfish, however, especially shrimp, followed by crab and lobster, while oysters, clams, and scallops have their share of aficionados.

Part of the reason for our unfamiliarity with fish has doubtless been our limited understanding of how to prepare it. By being endlessly breaded and fried, or if not, almost certainly overcooked, its delicate flavor and texture have been abused or even utterly destroyed. Also, much of the population suffered from a decided lack of adventurousness when it came to food, hewing to the straight and narrow path of meat and potatoes. Besides, there were always all those annoying little bones!

Happily, several factors have contributed to an increase in our consumption of fish. One is definitely economic: although it is not cheap, fish is less expensive than many cuts of meat, and it contains little waste. Another is our growing awareness of the need for good nutrition, and here fish excels. It is low in fat and contains as much protein as meat, with only one half to two thirds the calories. A corollary to our concern for food value has been the increased emphasis on lighter, fresher foods and on preserving their natural tastes in cooking. Here again fish merits the spotlight. Easily prepared, it can be amply rewarding if treated with the gentle consideration it deserves.

The world of hors d'oeuvre encompasses a remarkable assortment of tempting appetizers using not only fresh but smoked and canned seafood. Among the most popular ready-to-eat items are smoked salmon and canned anchovies, sardines, herring, and smoked oysters. Perhaps the ultimate hors d'oeuvre of all is caviar—sturgeon roe—which is one of the most expensive foods on earth. Other, more reasonably priced fish roes—cod, lumpfish, whitefish, flying fish, and red-colored salmon—are also called caviar, although the term in its strict sense applies only to the eggs of the sturgeon.

For other recipes containing seafood please consult the Index.

A note on serving caviar: According to connoisseurs, fresh sturgeon caviar should be served from its own tin embedded in crushed ice and accompanied only with thin unbuttered white toast or thinly sliced unbuttered black bread (the caviar should be oily enough not to require any other fat). Lemon wedges may be grudgingly permitted. An ounce or two is considered sufficient for one person, but even this, due to sturgeon caviar's exorbitant cost, can deplete your finances if you plan to serve it to more than a few people. (Pasteurized sturgeon caviar, which is less expensive than fresh, still commands a princely sum.) The more moderately priced types of caviar, which are available fresh, frozen, and pasteurized, can be enjoyed with a greater variety of accompaniments, among them chopped hard-cooked eggs, chopped onions or chives, sour cream, and crackers.

Pasteurized caviar, which is what one finds on supermarket shelves, can be considerably improved by rinsing to reduce salt, dye content, and preservative taste. Place the caviar in a strainer with a mesh finer than the eggs and rinse gently under cool water about 2 minutes. Drain well, then cover and chill thoroughly until ready to serve. Stored airtight in the refrigerator, pasteurized caviar will keep up to five days.

COLD SEAFOOD APPETIZERS

MEXICAN SHRIMP COCKTAIL

Shrimp cocktail, a rather banal offering in many restaurants here in the United States, takes a bold and imaginative form in Mexico.

36 medium shrimp, cooked, shelled, and
   deveined
½ cup freshly squeezed and strained lime
   juice
2 medium tomatoes, peeled, seeded, and
   cut into small cubes
1 large, ripe avocado, peeled, pitted, and
   cubed
1 small mild white or red onion, finely
   chopped
1 or 2 serrano chilies or any fresh hot
   green chilies, seeded and finely
   chopped
2 pimentos, diced (optional)
12 small pitted green olives, halved
   (optional)
2 tablespoons finely chopped fresh
   coriander leaves or Italian flat-leaf
   parsley
3 tablespoons olive oil
   Salt and freshly ground pepper to taste

Combine all the ingredients in a large bowl and toss gently but thoroughly. Taste and adjust the seasoning. If made ahead, cover and chill up to 2 hours. Divide the shrimp mixture among 6 chilled cocktail glasses and serve cold. Makes 6 servings.

AVOCADOS STUFFED WITH SHRIMP SEVICHE

While the idea of "cooking" fish in citrus juice derives most probably from Polynesia, it has taken hold throughout Latin America, where it is known as *seviche*. This particular version of seviche hails from Acapulco.

Follow the recipe for Mexican Shrimp Cocktail (page 179) with these changes: Omit the avocado. Substitute 1 pound small raw shrimp, shelled and deveined, for the cooked shrimp. Combine them in a bowl with enough freshly squeezed lime juice to cover. Cover and refrigerate, stirring twice, about 4 hours or until the shrimp are opaque, then combine with the remaining ingredients. Cut 3 large, ripe avocados in half lengthwise. Remove the pits and discard. Place each avocado half on an individual serving plate lined with lettuce leaves. Drain the shrimp mixture. Fill the cavities of the avocado halves with the shrimp mixture, dividing it equally. Serve at once. Makes 6 servings.

VARIATION:

Substitute 1 pound scallops for the shrimp.

MARINATED BROILED SHRIMP PROVENÇAL

An excellent and uncomplicated example of Mediterranean cooking.

1½ pounds jumbo raw shrimp in their shells
½ cup olive oil
¼ cup breadcrumbs, toasted
¼ cup freshly grated imported Parmesan cheese
1 large garlic clove, crushed and finely chopped
2 tablespoons freshly squeezed and strained lemon juice
Salt and freshly ground pepper to taste
1 tablespoon finely chopped parsley

With a sharp knife, carefully split the shrimp lengthwise but leave unshelled. In a small bowl mix together ¼ cup of the olive oil, breadcrumbs, Parmesan cheese, and garlic and spread over the cut surfaces of the shrimp. Arrange the shrimp on the rack of a broiler pan and broil under a preheated broiler 3 to 4 inches from the heat about 4 minutes or until golden brown. Transfer the shrimp to a serving dish.

In a small bowl mix together the remaining ¼ cup olive oil, lemon juice, salt, and pepper and spoon over the shrimp. Cool to room temperature, then cover and refrigerate at least 2 hours or up to 24 hours. To serve, bring to room temperature and sprinkle with the parsley. Makes 4 servings.

AUSTRALIAN LOBSTER AND MELON COCKTAIL

An artful liaison in which subtle flavors and delicate textures mingle to felicitous effect.

1 medium-sized, ripe cantaloupe
1 pound cooked lobster meat, diced
1 cup South Seas Dressing (page 391) or Chutney Dressing (page 391)
Lettuce leaves
Lime wedges

Cut the cantaloupe in half. Scoop out and discard the seeds and fibers. With a melon-ball cutter, cut the cantaloupe flesh into balls and place them in a large mixing bowl. Add the lobster meat and dressing and toss gently but thoroughly. Taste and adjust the seasoning. Cover and chill 1 hour.

Line 6 individual glass bowls with the lettuce leaves and set them over ice. Divide the lobster and cantaloupe mixture among the bowls. Serve with the lime wedges. Makes 6 servings.

CRABMEAT AND CLAMS ON THE HALF SHELL

Two favorite hors d'oeuvre foods team up in this elegant appetizer.

12 medium-sized hard-shelled clams
½ cup dry white wine
 1 envelope unflavored gelatin
½ pound cooked crabmeat, flaked and
     picked over
 1 tablespoon freshly squeezed and
     strained lemon juice or to taste
     Salt, freshly ground pepper, and
     Tabasco sauce to taste
     Rock salt
     Red caviar
     Finely chopped parsley

Scrub the clams with a stiff brush or stainless steel scouring pad under cold running water, discarding any that have cracked shells or that are not shut tightly. In a large, heavy saucepan bring the wine to a boil over high heat. Add the clams, cover tightly, reduce the heat to moderate, and steam about 10 minutes or until the shells have opened. Discard any unopened clams. With tongs or a slotted spoon, remove the clams, shuck them, reserving the shells, and chop the meat. Strain enough of the clam broth to make 1 cup into a bowl through a fine sieve lined with a triple layer of dampened cheesecloth. Pour ¼ cup of the strained broth into a small saucepan, let it cool, then sprinkle the gelatin over it. Let stand 5 minutes to soften. Stir over low heat until the gelatin is dissolved, then stir in the remaining ¾ cup strained broth.

In a shallow bowl combine the chopped clams, crabmeat, the gelatin mixture, lemon juice, salt, pepper, and Tabasco sauce. Cover and chill the mixture about 30 minutes or until it is partially set, then mound it in the reserved clam shells. Arrange the filled shells on a layer of rock salt in a shallow serving dish. Cover and chill at least 2 hours or until the filling is set. Decorate each filled clam with ½ teaspoon red caviar and parsley. Makes about 24.

MUSSELS IN SHALLOT MAYONNAISE

In Europe the sweet, delicate flavor of the mussel is greatly savored. In America, however, this versatile mollusk is still relatively little known and remains unjustly neglected. Cleaning and preparation entail some time and effort, but mussel fanciers value the wait for the anticipatory pleasure it affords.

4 quarts mussels in their shells
1 cup dry white wine
   Bouquet Garni (page 197)
6 whole peppercorns
   Shallot Mayonnaise (page 388)

Scrub the mussels with a stiff brush or stainless steel scouring pad under cold running water. Scrape off the beards and rinse the mussels. Soak the mussels in cold water to cover for several hours to remove any sand. Lift the mussels out of the water into a sieve and rinse again under cold running water. Drain the mussels.

In a large, heavy saucepan or kettle combine the mussels, wine, Bouquet Garni, and peppercorns. Cover, bring to a boil, and cook over moderate heat about 10 minutes or until the mussels open. Discard any unopened mussels. With tongs or a slotted spoon, transfer the mussels to a platter and, when cool enough to handle, remove them from their shells. Spread the mussels on paper towels to drain and allow to cool to room temperature. In a bowl combine the mussels with enough Shallot Mayonnaise to bind them. Cover and chill before serving. Makes 6 servings.

Note: If desired, you can serve the mussels on the half shell, topping each one with a spoonful of the Shallot Mayonnaise.

VARIATIONS:

MUSSELS IN SAUCE VERTE

Substitute Sauce Verte (page 388) for the Shallot Mayonnaise.

MUSSELS IN CURRY MAYONNAISE

Substitute Curry Mayonnaise (page 388) for the Shallot Mayonnaise.

SPANISH MUSSELS IN ALMOND SAUCE

A devotee of mussels could live and die happily in Spain, where the virtues of this delectable shellfish have long been recognized. Prepared in the following manner, mussels please long-time aficionados and win new converts.

24 large mussels in their shells
24 almonds, blanched and toasted
1 slice white bread
½ cup olive oil
1 tablespoon wine vinegar
    Dash Tabasco sauce
    Salt and freshly ground pepper to taste

Clean, soak, rinse, and drain the mussels as directed in the recipe for Mussels in Shallot Mayonnaise (page 388).

Arrange the mussels in one layer in a baking pan. Place the pan in a preheated 450°F oven about 7 minutes or until the shells have opened. With tongs or a slotted spoon, transfer the mussels to a platter, discarding any unopened ones. Remove and discard the top shells and the black rims. Cover and chill the mussels.

Grind the almonds in an electric blender or in a food processor fitted with the steel blade. Add the remaining ingredients, cover, and blend the mixture until it is smooth. Spoon the almond sauce over the mussels. Cover and refrigerate at least 1 hour or until chilled before serving. Makes 4 servings.

VARIATIONS:

Instead of placing the mussels in the oven, you may combine them in a saucepan with ½ cup dry white wine or water and Bouquet Garni (page 197) and steam them as directed in the recipe for Mussels in Shallot Mayonnaise (page 388).

MUSSELS WITH SAUCE VINAIGRETTE

In a small bowl mix together Sauce Vinaigrette (page 387) or Lemon Vinaigrette (page 387) with 1 tablespoon each minced mild white or red onion, pimento, and parsley, and, if desired, 1 teaspoon capers, rinsed, drained, and minced. Substitute this sauce for the almond sauce.

MUSSELS WITH TOMATO SAUCE

Substitute Tomato Sauce (page 398) for the almond sauce. Serve hot or chilled. If serving hot, you would, of course, not chill the mussels at any point. After removing one shell from each bivalve, simply spoon the hot Tomato Sauce over the mussels and serve.

MIDIA DOLMA
Armenian Stuffed Mussels

If some cruel fate limited me to a single mussel appetizer, this would be my choice.

36 large mussels in their shells
½ cup olive oil
3 cups finely chopped onion
½ cup uncooked long-grain white rice, washed and drained
¼ cup dried currants
¼ cup pine nuts
½ teaspoon allspice
¼ teaspoon cinnamon
 Salt and freshly ground pepper to taste
2 cups water
1 tablespoon freshly squeezed and strained lemon juice
2 lemons, cut into wedges

Scrub the mussels with a stiff brush or stainless steel scouring pad under cold running water. Using a sharp knife, pry the shells open until loose but not separated. Remove the beards and any bits of black waste matter. Leaving the mussels in their shells, rinse carefully under cold running water to remove sand and clean the insides of the shells. Soak the mussels in cold water 1 hour.

Meanwhile, in a heavy skillet heat the oil over moderate heat. Add the onion and sauté until golden brown, stirring frequently. Remove from the heat and stir in the rice, currants, nuts, allspice, cinnamon, salt, and pepper. Mix well and set aside to cool.

Lift the mussels out of the water into a sieve and rinse again under cold running water. Drain well. Place 1 tablespoon of the rice mixture in each shell, then close it tightly by tying firmly with a piece of string.

Arrange the stuffed mussels side by side in layers in a heavy fireproof casserole. Pour in the water and lemon juice. Place an inverted plate over the top to keep the mussels from moving during cooking. Bring to a boil over moderate heat, then reduce the heat to low. Cover and simmer about 1 hour or until the rice stuffing is tender. Uncover and let the mussels cool to room temperature in the casserole. Using a slotted spoon, remove the mussels from the casserole, discarding the liquid in which they were cooked. Cut off the strings and arrange the mussels on a serving platter. Cover and chill. Serve cold, garnished with the lemon wedges. Makes 9 servings.

SCALLOPS IN SAUCE VERTE

½ cup dry white wine
½ medium onion, chopped
Bouquet Garni (page 197)
3 whole peppercorns
½ teaspoon salt
1 pound sea scallops
Lettuce leaves
Sauce Verte (page 388)
Finely chopped parsley

In a large saucepan combine the wine, onion, Bouquet Garni, peppercorns, and salt and bring to a simmer. Add the scallops and simmer, uncovered, about 5 minutes or until tender. Drain and cool. Arrange the scallops in a shallow bowl lined with the lettuce leaves. Cover with the Sauce Verte and sprinkle with the parsley. Cover and chill 2 hours before serving. Makes 6 servings.

VARIATIONS:

SCALLOPS IN HERB MAYONNAISE
Substitute Herb Mayonnaise (page 388), made with dill rather than tarragon, for the Sauce Verte and fresh dill for the parsley.

SCALLOPS IN CURRY MAYONNAISE
Substitute Curry Mayonnaise (page 388) for the Herb Mayonnaise.

SCALLOPS IN SAUCE VINAIGRETTE

Omit the lettuce and parsley. Substitute Garlic Vinaigrette (page 387) mixed with 1 tablespoon minced fresh dill for the Sauce Verte. Chill 4 hours, stirring occasionally. Drain the scallops and serve them with cocktail picks.

OYSTERS PLAKI

One of the most popular ways of serving oysters is on the half shell, with a squirt of fresh lemon juice and a few grindings of pepper. For something more unusual, however, try this Armenian recipe.

Plaki refers to an Armenian, Greek, and Turkish method of cooking vegetables or fish, usually with olive oil, tomatoes, parsley, and onion and/or garlic. The finished dish is served cold.

2 medium onions, cut in half lengthwise and thinly sliced
4 medium tomatoes, peeled, seeded, and chopped
⅓ cup water
⅓ cup finely chopped parsley
2 medium garlic cloves, finely chopped
2 tablespoons olive oil
1 tablespoon freshly squeezed and strained lemon juice
   Salt and freshly ground pepper to taste
12 large oysters, cleaned and shucked
1 lemon, quartered

Combine the onions, tomatoes, water, parsley, garlic, oil, lemon juice, salt, and pepper in a heavy saucepan. Bring to a boil and reduce the heat to low. Cover and simmer about 30 minutes or until the mixture is reduced to the consistency of a thick sauce. Scatter the oysters on top and continue to simmer about 10 minutes. Remove from the heat and cool. Serve slightly chilled, with the lemon wedges. Makes 4 servings.

VARIATION:

Substitute clams, mussels, or shrimp for the oysters.

SMOKED SALMON AND CRABMEAT ROLLS

Guests seem to delight in these.

> 2 ounces cream cheese, at room
>   temperature
> 2 tablespoons Mayonnaise (page 387)
> 1½ cups picked-over and flaked cooked
>   crabmeat
> 1 tablespoon finely chopped scallion,
>   including 2 inches of the green top
> 1 teaspoon finely chopped fresh dill
>   (optional)
> 1 teaspoon freshly squeezed and strained
>   lemon juice or to taste
>   Salt and freshly ground pepper to taste
> 1 teaspoon unflavored gelatin
> 1 tablesoon Cognac
> ½ pound thinly sliced smoked salmon

In a medium bowl beat together the cream cheese and Mayonnaise until light and fluffy. Add the crabmeat, scallion, dill (if used), lemon juice, salt, and pepper and blend well.

In a small, heatproof bowl sprinkle the gelatin over the Cognac and let stand 5 to 10 minutes to soften. Place the bowl in a small skillet containing 1 inch of simmering water and stir the mixture until the gelatin is dissolved, then stir it into the crabmeat mixture.

Spread the salmon slices with the crabmeat mixture. Beginning with a short end, roll up each slice tightly to form a cylinder. Arrange the rolls, seam sides down, on a platter. Cover with plastic wrap and chill at least 4 hours. To serve, using a sharp knife, cut the rolls crosswise into ¾-inch-thick slices and arrange them, cut sides up, on a chilled serving platter. Makes about 30.

SMOKED SALMON CORNETS

Expensive, and worth it.

Cut thin slices of smoked salmon into 1½-inch squares. Roll each square to form a cornet or cone and press the overlapping edges together, securing with a cocktail pick if necessary. Fill the cornets with caviar and sprinkle the edges of the salmon with minced parsley. Arrange the cornets attractively, spaced well apart, on a platter. Cover with plastic wrap and chill at least 1 hour. Just before serving, garnish the platter with sprigs of parsley or watercress.

VARIATIONS:

Omit the caviar and minced parsley. Fill the cornets with Smoked Salmon Spread (page 30) or Caviar and Cream Cheese Filling (page 42) piped through a pastry bag fitted with a fluted tip. Garnish the platter with sprigs of fresh dill, parsley, or watercress.

GRAVLAX
Swedish Dill-Cured Salmon

One of Scandinavia's most esteemed delicacies.

> 3 pounds center-cut fresh salmon, in one piece
> 1⅓ cups chopped fresh dill
> ¼ cup sugar
> ¼ cup coarse salt
> 2 tablespoons coarsely ground white pepper
> Mustard-Dill Sauce (page 390)

Have the fishmonger fillet the salmon, leaving the skin intact, so that you have 2 boneless matching sides. Rinse the fillets briefly under cold running water and pat dry with paper towels. Sprinkle ⅓ cup of the dill over the bottom of a flat-bottomed ceramic or glass dish just large enough to ac-commodate the salmon comfortably. Place 1 fillet, skin side down, over the dill. In a small bowl mix together the sugar, salt, and white pepper. Sprinkle half of this mixture evenly over the surface of the fillet and press the seasonings into the fillet. Sprinkle ½ cup of the remaining dill over the seasoning mixture and press it into the fillet. Sprinkle the remaining seasoning mixture over the flesh side of the second fillet, pressing it into the fillet. Carefully place this fillet, skin side up, over the fillet in the dish. Sprinkle the remaining ½ cup dill over the skin side of the top fillet. Cover the dish with plastic wrap. Place a small wooden plank or cutting board that fits inside the dish on top of the fish. Place a 3-pound weight on the plank or board. Chill the salmon 2 to 3 days, turning it every 12 hours.

Transfer the salmon fillets one at a time to a cutting board. Scrape off the seasonings and pat the fish dry with paper towels. With a long, sharp knife, cut the flesh diagonally across the grain into paper-thin slices, cutting it off the skin. Arrange the salmon slices on a platter and serve with the Mustard-Dill Sauce and thin slices of dark caraway rye bread. Makes 8 to 10 servings.

Note: If desired, you may garnish the platter with lemon slices, cherry tomatoes, and fresh dill sprigs.

HERRING PLATTER

Variations of this dish are encountered throughout Scandinavia as well as in Russia.

2 fillets of canned matjes *or pickled herring, drained*
2 hard-cooked eggs, finely chopped
1 small cucumber, peeled, seeded, and finely chopped, or ½ cup Pickled Cucumber (page 164)
½ cup finely chopped Danish Pickled Beets (page 166) or canned pickled beets
2 tablespoons finely chopped fresh dill
2 tablespoons finely chopped fresh chives
½ cup sour cream or Mayonnaise (page 387), or ¼ cup sour cream mixed with ¼ cup Mayonnaise

Arrange the herring fillets side by side on a chilled long platter. With a sharp knife, make diagonal cuts ½ inch apart through both fillets. Arrange the eggs, cucumber, and pickled beets in an attractive pattern around the herring. Sprinkle with the dill and chives and serve with the sour cream, Mayonnaise, or a combination of both. Makes 6 servings.

VARIATIONS:

Substitute slices or wedges of hard-cooked eggs for the finely chopped eggs. Or finely chop the whites and yolks separately and arrange alternate mounds of chopped egg white, egg yolk, cucumbers, beets, and minced parsley around the herring.

Other ingredients used to garnish the herring include thinly sliced rings of mild onion or scallion, green or black olives, capers, and salted or pickled mushrooms.

DANISH MARINATED HERRING IN SOUR CREAM SAUCE

In Scandinavia few other foods can rival herring in popularity.

3 salt herring fillets
 Milk

MARINADE FOR HERRING

½ cup dry white wine
2 medium onions, thinly sliced
3 tablespoons sugar
2 bay leaves
 Salt and freshly ground pepper to taste

SOUR CREAM SAUCE

1 cup sour cream
1 small mild red onion, thinly sliced
2 teaspoons finely chopped fresh dill

Rinse the herring fillets under cold running water and pat them dry with paper towels. Place the herring in a medium bowl and cover it with milk. Cover and refrigerate 24 hours, changing the milk from time to time. If the herring is very salty, soak it another 24 hours in fresh milk. Drain the herring well and pat dry with paper towels. Cut it crosswise into 1-inch pieces and pack tightly in an enamel, glass, or stainless steel bowl.

Combine all the ingredients for the marinade and pour the mixture over the herring. Cover and refrigerate overnight. Drain, reserving the marinade.

Combine all the ingredients for the Sour Cream Sauce, thinning with a little of the marinade, if you like. Pour over the herring. Cover and let marinate in the refrigerator 1 to 2 days before serving. Makes 6 servings.

RUSSIAN HERRING IN MUSTARD SAUCE

Russians are extraordinarily fond of herring, a love that can no doubt be traced to Scandinavian influence, for what was to become the Russian kingdom of Muscovy was founded by a Norseman named Rurik in the ninth century.

2 salt herring fillets, each weighing about
  ¼ pound
  Milk
5 tablespoons olive oil
2 tablespoons white wine vinegar
1½ tablespoons Dijon-style mustard
½ teaspoon sugar
¼ cup finely chopped scallions, including
  2 inches of the green tops
1 tablespoon finely chopped fresh dill
  Freshly ground pepper to taste
  Fresh dill sprigs

Rinse the herring fillets under cold running water and pat them dry with paper towels. Place the herring in a medium bowl and cover it with milk. Cover and refrigerate 24 hours, changing the milk from time to time. If the herring is very salty, soak it another 24 hours in fresh milk. Drain the herring well and pat dry with paper towels. Cut it crosswise into 1-inch pieces and place it in an enamel, glass, or stainless steel bowl.

In a small bowl combine the oil, vinegar, mustard, and sugar. Whisk the mixture until it is blended and pour over the herring. Sprinkle with the scallions, chopped dill, and pepper and toss. Cover and refrigerate 24 hours.

Transfer the herring and sauce to a serving dish and garnish with the dill sprigs. Makes 6 servings.

CAVIAR WITH CRÈME FRAÎCHE

A culinary marriage made in heaven.

1 jar (4 ounces) salmon caviar
1 cup Crème Fraîche (below)
2 scallions, including 2 inches of the green
   tops, finely chopped
   Thinly sliced black bread

Mound the caviar in the center of a serving platter and spoon the Crème Fraîche around the base of the mound. Sprinkle a narrow line of scallions around the caviar to form a border between it and the Crème Fraîche. Arrange the bread slices around the rim of the platter. Serve at once. Makes 8 servings.

CRÈME FRAÎCHE

1 cup heavy cream
1 teaspoon buttermilk, or 2 teaspoons sour
   cream

Combine the cream and buttermilk or sour cream in a jar. Cover the jar, shake the mixture, and let it stand at room temperature 24 hours or until thickened. Refrigerate in a tightly sealed jar. It will keep about 2 weeks. Makes about 1 cup.

ESCABECHE DE PESCADO

Marinated Sautéed Seafood with Orange and Green Pepper

A dish that is common to all Hispanic countries, where it exists in dozens of versions, escabeche *makes a splendid first course or buffet offering. This refreshingly original rendition is an inspired amalgam of sharp and fruity tastes and contrasting textures.*

1 pound red snapper fillets, cut into 4 by
    1½-inch pieces
½ pound bay scallops
9 tablespoons olive oil or flavorless
    vegetable oil
½ cup julienne-cut green pepper
2 tablespoons julienne-cut orange rind
2 tablespoons finely chopped scallions,
    including 2 inches of the green tops
¼ cup freshly squeezed and strained orange
    juice
1 tablespoon freshly squeezed and strained
    lime juice
1 tablespoon red wine vinegar
1 large garlic clove, finely chopped
1 teaspoon peeled and grated fresh ginger
    root
    Salt, freshly ground pepper, and Tabasco
    sauce to taste
1 navel orange, cut crosswise into ⅜-inch-
    thick slices
    Sauce Vinaigrette (page 387)
    Lettuce leaves
    Finely chopped parsley

Wash the red snapper fillets and scallops under cold running water. Drain and dry well with paper towels. In a heavy skillet heat 3 tablespoons of the oil over moderate heat. Add the snapper fillets and sauté, turning to brown lightly on both sides.

Transfer the fillets to a wide, shallow ceramic or glass dish.

Add 1 tablespoon of the remaining oil to the skillet and heat. Add the scallops and sauté 2 minutes, turning frequently. Transfer them to the dish.

Sprinkle the fish with the green pepper, orange rind, and the scallions. In a small ceramic or glass bowl mix together the remaining 5 tablespoons oil, orange juice, lime juice, vinegar, garlic, ginger root, salt, pepper, and Tabasco sauce. Pour the mixture over the fish, cover, and refrigerate at least 8 hours or overnight, basting from time to time.

Place the orange slices in a glass or china dish and spoon the Sauce Vinaigrette over them. Cover and refrigerate 1 hour. Serve the escabeche on individual plates lined with the lettuce leaves. Drain the orange slices and use them to garnish each serving along with the parsley. Makes 6 servings.

RUSSIAN FISH IN ASPIC

For an effective presentation use a fish-shaped mold for this.

5½ *cups water*
  2 *cups dry white wine*
  2 *medium carrots, peeled*
  1 *stalk celery with leaves, coarsely*
    chopped
  1 *medium onion, quartered*
  2 *sprigs parsley*
  6 *whole peppercorns*
  1 *tablespoon salt, more if needed*
  2 *cod or haddock steaks, cut about 1 inch*
    thick and weighing about 10 ounces
    each
  2 *envelopes unflavored gelatin*
  3 *egg whites, at room temperature*
  3 *egg shells, slightly crushed*
  2 *tablespoons freshly squeezed and*
    strained lemon juice, more if needed
  2 *tablespoons dry Sherry, more if needed*
  2 *small cucumbers*
    Lemon wedges
    Black olives
    Fresh dill or parsley sprigs

In a large enameled or stainless steel saucepan combine 5 cups of the water, the wine, carrots, celery, onion, the 2 sprigs parsley, peppercorns, and salt. Bring to a boil over high heat. Reduce the heat to low and simmer, partially covered, 1 hour. Strain the broth through a fine sieve set over a large bowl, pressing down on the vegetables with the back of a large spoon to extract all their juices before discarding them. You should have about 6 cups of liquid.

Pour 2 cups of the vegetable broth into an enameled or stainless steel saucepan. Reserve the remaining 4 cups. Bring the broth to a boil over high heat. Reduce the heat to low and add the fish steaks. Cover and poach 8 to 10 minutes or until the fish is tender. With a slotted spoon, carefully transfer the fish steaks to a platter. Strain the fish broth through a fine sieve lined with dampened cheesecloth and reserve. When the fish steaks are cool enough to handle, remove and discard the skin and bones, leaving the flesh in pieces as large as possible. Cover and refrigerate.

Pour the remaining ½ cup water into a small bowl and sprinkle the gelatin over it. Let stand 5 minutes to soften. In a medium saucepan combine the strained fish poaching liquid and the reserved 4 cups vegetable broth and reheat over low heat. Stir in the softened gelatin until it is completely dissolved. To clarify the broth, in a small bowl beat the egg whites until frothy. Whisk the beaten egg whites and crushed egg shells into the warm broth. Stir over moderate heat until the broth starts to boil up through the egg whites. Immediately remove from the heat and let the broth rest, undisturbed, 20 minutes. Line a fine sieve with a triple layer of dampened cheesecloth and set it over a deep bowl. Slowly pour the broth through the cheesecloth in batches, letting it drip slowly through the cloth without disturbing it. Discard the contents of the sieve. Stir the lemon juice and Sherry into the clarified broth. Taste and add more lemon juice, Sherry, and salt, if you like.

Pour a thin layer of the clarified broth into the bottom of a 6-cup loaf pan or mold. Chill about 20 minutes or until set. Meanwhile, score 1 of the cucumbers lengthwise with the tines of a fork, cut it crosswise into thin slices, and reserve. Peel the remaining cucumber and cut it crosswise into thin slices. Arrange the peeled cucumber slices, overlapping, in rows down the center of the set broth in the pan or mold. Spoon 3 or 4 tablespoons of the remaining broth over the cucumber slices. Chill about 20 minutes or until set. Arrange the pieces of cooked fish in the mold and carefully ladle the remaining broth into the mold. Cover and chill at least 3 hours or overnight.

Unmold the aspic as directed on page 29. Garnish it with the reserved cucumber slices, lemon wedges, and dill or parsley sprigs. Makes 6 servings as a first course, 10 to 12 as part of a *zakuska* table (page 413).

HOT SEAFOOD APPETIZERS

SHRIMP IN GARLIC SAUCE

Here is a simple but spirited Spanish appetizer or tapa (page 405) that is standard fare in many of the local taverns.

*¼ pound small shrimp, shelled and
  deveined
2 tablespoons olive oil
1 large garlic clove, halved
1 small piece hot chili pepper, or cayenne
  pepper to taste
Salt to taste
Lemon juice (optional)
Ali-Oli (page 389) (optional)
Finely chopped parsley (optional)*

Rinse the shrimp under cold running water and pat them thoroughly dry with paper towels.

In an individual earthenware casserole or flameproof dish heat the olive oil over moderate heat. Add the garlic, chili pepper or cayenne pepper, and shrimp and sauté, stirring, about 2 minutes or until the shrimp turn pink and are cooked through. Season with the salt and, if desired, squirt lightly with lemon juice, add a spoonful of Ali-Oli, and sprinkle with a little parsley. Serve sizzling hot directly from the casserole or dish. Makes 1 serving.

Note: To prepare more than 1 serving of this dish, use a wide, shallow casserole or skillet and multiply the recipe by the number of people to be served.

VARIATION:
   Substitute butter for the olive oil and add ½ bay leaf with the garlic.

SHRIMP IN GREEN SAUCE

This recipe also produces a delicious tapa.

1 pound large shrimp in their shells
1½ cups water
1 lemon slice
    Bouquet Garni (page 197)
4 whole peppercorns
    Salt to taste
    Freshly ground pepper to taste
    All-purpose flour
5 tablespoons olive oil
1 cup chopped parsley, preferably Italian
    flat-leaf
1 large garlic clove or to taste, chopped
¼ cup dry white wine
2 tablespoons finely chopped onion

Shell and devein the shrimp, leaving the tails attached; reserve shells. Rinse the shrimp under cold running water and pat them thoroughly dry with paper towels. Set aside.

In a small saucepan combine the shrimp shells, water, lemon slice, Bouquet Garni, peppercorns, and salt. Bring to a boil over high heat, reduce the heat, and simmer 15 minutes. Strain the broth into a bowl. Measure ¾ cup and reserve.

Sprinkle the shrimp with salt and pepper and coat with flour, shaking off the excess. In a large, heavy skillet heat 3 tablespoons of the oil over medium-high heat. Add the shrimp and sauté, stirring, about 2 minutes or until they begin to turn pink. With a slotted spoon, transfer the shrimp to a heated platter.

In the container of an electric blender combine the parsley, garlic, wine, reserved ¾ cup broth, and salt to taste. Cover and blend the mixture until it is smooth.

Add the remaining 2 tablespoons oil to the skillet and heat over moderate heat. Add the onion and sauté, stirring constantly, until soft but not browned. Stir in 1½ tablespoons flour and blend thoroughly. Gradually add the parsley mixture, stirring constantly, until thickened and smooth. Taste and adjust the seasoning. Return the shrimp to the skillet, turn them about with a spoon to coat them evenly with the sauce, and cook until just heated through. Transfer the shrimp and sauce to a heated serving dish and serve at once. Makes 4 servings.

BOUQUET GARNI

4 sprigs parsley
½ stalk celery with leaves
1 bay leaf
2 sprigs fresh thyme, or ¼ teaspoon dried thyme
1 sprig summer savory (optional)

If using fresh herbs, tie all the ingredients together with a string. If using dried herbs, tie them in a piece of cheesecloth.

GREEK SKEWERED SHRIMP

Light and enticing, this dish is simplicity itself and a perfect choice for a patio meal.

2 pounds medium shrimp, shelled and deveined
Lemon Vinaigrette (page 387)
½ cup (2 ounces) freshly grated imported Parmesan cheese

Rinse the shrimp under cold running water and pat them thoroughly dry with paper towels. Thread the shrimp on small bamboo skewers, leaving enough room at one end of each skewer to handle. Brush the shrimp liberally with the Lemon Vin-aigrette and dip in the cheese, coating well on all sides. Broil under a preheated broiler about 6 inches from the heat 2 to 3 minutes on each side, or until pink and cooked through. Serve hot. Makes about 10 servings.

HAWAIIAN SHRIMP KEBABS

If you wish, present these kebabs Honolulu style, arranged in advance on skewers so that guests can broil their own over a hibachi.

1 tablespoon cornstarch
1 cup pineapple juice
2 tablespoons honey
⅓ cup imported soy sauce
1 tablespoon white wine vinegar or cider vinegar
1 teaspoon peeled and grated ginger root
1 tablespoon toasted sesame seed (optional)
1 pound small shrimp, shelled and deveined

In a small enameled or stainless steel saucepan mix the cornstarch with a little of the pineapple juice, then combine with the remaining pineapple juice, honey, soy sauce, vinegar, ginger root, and sesame seed (if used). Cook over low heat, stirring constantly, until thickened.

Rinse the shrimp under cold running water and pat them thoroughly dry with paper towels. Thread the shrimp on small bamboo skewers, allowing 4 to 6 shrimp for each skewer, leaving enough room at one end to handle. Dip in the sauce and broil over charcoal or under a preheated broiler about 4 inches from the heat, turning frequently, about 5 minutes or until the shrimp are lightly browned on all sides. Serve at once. Makes 8 servings.

VARIATIONS:

You can marinate the shrimp in the sauce before broiling them: Cool the thickened sauce and combine it in a wide, shallow bowl with the shrimp. Turn the shrimp to coat thoroughly with the mixture. Cover and let marinate at room temperature 30 minutes to 1 hour, turning the shrimp twice. Remove the shrimp from the marinade, thread them on the skewers, and broil as directed.

HAWAIIAN SHRIMP AND VEGETABLE KEBABS

Use ½ pound shrimp. Arrange the shrimp on the skewers, alternating them with small pieces of green pepper and precooked tiny white onions, small mushroom caps, and cherry tomatoes. Dip in the sauce and broil as directed.

CHINESE SHRIMP BALLS

This is a close relative of the popular appetizer Chinese Shrimp Toast (page 285).

8 thin slices day-old firm, homemade-type white bread
1 egg white, lightly beaten
2 teaspoons pale dry Sherry
2 teaspoons cornstarch
½ teaspoon salt
½ teaspoon very finely chopped peeled ginger root
½ pound shrimp, shelled, deveined, and chopped to a fine paste
1 tablespoon very finely chopped fresh pork fat, bacon fat, or cooked Smithfield ham
¼ cup very finely chopped water chestnuts
1 scallion, including 2 inches of the green top, very finely chopped
4 cups peanut oil or corn oil Chinese Plum Sauce I (page 396), Chinese Plum Sauce II (page 397), or Roasted Szechuan Peppercorn-Salt (page 199)

Remove the crusts from the bread slices and cut the bread into ¼-inch cubes. Spread the cubes out in one layer on a baking sheet and let them dry in a cool, dry place for 2 hours, turning them from time to time. Transfer the bread cubes to a dish and set aside.

In a medium bowl beat the egg white until foamy. In a small bowl stir together the Sherry and cornstarch, then stir the mixture into the beaten egg white along with the salt and ginger. Add the shrimp, fat or ham, water chestnuts, and scallion and mix thoroughly until the ingredients form a paste. With oil-coated hands, form the shrimp mixture into walnut-sized balls and roll the balls in the bread cubes to cover them, pressing the bread slightly into the balls.

In a wok or deep-fryer heat the oil to 350°F. Add and fry the balls in 2 batches, turning them occasionally, 2 to 3 minutes or until golden brown. With a slotted spoon or skimmer, transfer the shrimp balls to paper towels to drain, then arrange them on a heated serving dish. Serve at once with the Plum Sauce or Peppercorn-Salt for dipping. Makes about 16.

ROASTED SZECHUAN PEPPERCORN-SALT

1 tablespoon whole Szechuan peppercorns (available in Oriental food markets)
⅓ cup salt

Combine the peppercorns and salt in a small, heavy skillet and cook over medium-low heat, stirring constantly, about 5 minutes or until the salt begins to brown and the peppercorns become fragrant. Be careful not to let the mixture burn. Remove from the heat and cool. Crush the mixture to a fine powder with a mortar and pestle, a kitchen mallet, or rolling pin. Store in an airtight jar. Makes about ⅓ cup.

DOMINICAN SHRIMP AND POTATO BALLS

A happy choice that won't last the happy hour.

2 medium baking potatoes, peeled and
    quartered
4 tablespoons butter, cut into ½-inch
    pieces
1 cup (4 ounces) freshly grated Muenster
    cheese
1 egg yolk
¼ cup finely chopped parsley
    Salt and freshly ground white pepper to
    taste
2 tablespoons butter
1 cup finely chopped onion
1 pound shrimp, shelled, deveined, and
    finely diced
½ cup all-purpose flour
1 egg, lightly beaten
1 cup soft fresh crumbs made from
    homemade-type white bread
    Flavorless vegetable oil for deep-frying
    Tomato Sauce (page 398)

Drop the potatoes into lightly salted boiling water to cover and cook briskly, uncovered, until they are tender. Drain the potatoes well, then mash them. Add the 4 tablespoons butter, the cheese, egg yolk, parsley, salt, and pepper and beat the mixture vigorously with a large wooden spoon until it is smooth. Taste and adjust the seasoning. Cover the bowl and set aside.

In a medium-sized, heavy skillet melt the 2 tablespoons butter over moderate heat. Add the onion and cook, stirring constantly, until soft but not browned. Add the shrimp and cook, stirring, 1 to 2 minutes or until they begin to turn pink; do not overcook. Remove from the heat, season with salt and pepper, and cool slightly. Form the potato mixture into 1-inch balls and stuff each with about 1 teaspoon of the shrimp mixture. Roll each stuffed ball lightly in flour, dip in beaten egg, then roll in breadcrumbs. Place the balls side by side on a tray or baking sheet lined with waxed paper and refrigerate them at least 30 minutes to set the coating.

In a deep-fryer heat 2 inches of oil to 375°F. Fry the balls, a batch at a time, in the hot oil, turning them frequently, 1 to 2 minutes or until they are golden brown on all sides. As each batch is done, transfer the balls with a slotted spoon to a baking sheet lined with paper towels and keep them warm in a preheated 200°F oven while you fry the remaining balls. Arrange the balls on a heated platter and serve at once with the Tomato Sauce for dipping. Provide cocktail picks for spearing the balls. Makes about 28.

CHANGURRO

Basque Crabmeat with Sherry and Brandy

Basque cuisine is considered by many to be the finest in Spain, and the height of the Basque culinary achievement is its seafood preparations. Here is a superlative example.

6 tablespoons butter
1 tablespoon olive oil
2 medium garlic cloves, cut in half
    lengthwise
1 medium onion, finely chopped
¾ cup finely chopped leeks (white parts
    only)
1 medium tomato, peeled, seeded, and
    coarsely chopped
3 tablespoons pale dry Sherry
3 tablespoons brandy
1 pound fresh crabmeat
3 tablespoons finely chopped parsley
½ teaspoon salt or to taste
¼ teaspoon freshly ground pepper
    Pinch cayenne pepper
1 cup fresh soft breadcrumbs (made from
    French or Italian bread)

In a large, heavy skillet heat 3 tablespoons of the butter and the oil over moderate heat. Add the garlic and sauté 1 to 2 minutes or until golden brown, stirring constantly, then remove and discard the garlic. Add the onion and leeks to the skillet and cook, stirring frequently, about 5 minutes or until they are soft but not browned. Stir in the tomato, Sherry, and brandy and bring to a boil over high heat. Cook, stirring, about 5 minutes or until most of the liquid in the skillet has evaporated and the mixture is thickened. Reduce the heat to low and stir in the crabmeat, 2 tablespoons of the parsley, salt, pepper, and cayenne pepper. Simmer, uncovered, 3 minutes. Taste and adjust the seasoning. Remove from the heat and set aside.

In a small skillet melt the remaining 3 tablespoons butter over moderate heat. Add the breadcrumbs and remaining 1 tablespoon parsley and cook, stirring, until all the butter has been absorbed and the crumbs have begun to separate and brown lightly. Remove from the heat and set aside.

Spoon the crabmeat mixture into 6 individual scallop shells or ramekins, dividing it equally. Sprinkle with the breadcrumb mixture and bake in a preheated 350°F oven about 15 minutes or until the crumbs are crisp and golden brown. Serve immediately. Makes 6 servings.

PORTUGUESE CLAMS WITH SAUSAGE AND HAM

Full of tantalizing aromas and lingering aftertastes, this immensely satisfying combination originates from the Portuguese province of Algarve, where fishing is a way of life.

  3 ounces *Portuguese* linguiça, *or substitute Spanish* chorizo *or any other garlic-seasoned smoked pork sausage*
16 *small hard-shelled clams*
¼ *cup olive oil*
  1 *medium onion, finely chopped*
  2 *medium garlic cloves, finely chopped*
½ *teaspoon paprika*
⅛ *teaspoon crushed dried hot red pepper or to taste*
    Freshly ground black pepper to taste
  1 *ounce* presunto *ham (Portuguese mountain-cured ham) or prosciutto, finely chopped*
⅓ *cup dry white wine*
  1 *medium tomato, peeled, seeded, and finely chopped*
  3 *tablespoons finely chopped parsley*
  1 *small bay leaf*
    Salt to taste

With a small, sharp knife remove the casing of the sausage. Crumble the meat and place it in a sieve. Lower the sieve into a saucepan of boiling water and boil rapidly 1 minute. Spread the sausage meat out on paper towels to drain.

Scrub the clams with a stiff brush or stainless steel scouring pad under cold running water, discarding any that have cracked shells or that are not shut tightly. Set aside.

In a large, heavy skillet heat the olive oil over moderate heat. Add the onion and sauté, stirring frequently, until soft but not browned. Add the garlic, paprika, red pepper, and black pepper and cook, stirring, about 1 minute. Add the sausage meat, ham, wine, tomato, parsley, and bay leaf and bring to a boil over high heat. Cook rapidly, stirring constantly, until most of the liquid in the skillet is evaporated and the mixture is thickened.

Arrange the clams, hinged sides down, over the meat and tomato mixture. Cover the skillet tightly and cook over moderate heat about 10 minutes or until the clams open. Taste and add salt if needed. With tongs or a slotted spoon, transfer the clams to heated individual casseroles or soup plates, discarding any unopened clams. Remove and discard the bay leaf and ladle the sauce over the clams. Serve at once. Makes 4 servings.

Note: Do not use Mexican *chorizos*, which are made with fresh pork. Also, avoid at all costs the so-called chorizos made with finely ground beef seasoned with chili powder, which are passed off as Mexican. No matter how vehemently salespeople insist that they are the real thing, do not give in!

SPANISH CLAMS A LA MARINERA

The Spanish have long harbored a special fondness for this dish, which is a familiar offering in many *tascas* (taverns). Although generally eaten as a *tapa* (page 405) in Spain, it makes an excellent first course, accompanied with a good dry white wine.

Follow the recipe for Portuguese Clams with Sausage and Ham (page 202) with these changes: Omit the sausage, paprika, hot red pepper, and ham and use 24 clams. If desired, reserve 1½ tablespoons of the parsley and sprinkle it over the clams just before serving. Serve with lemon wedges, if you like. Makes 4 servings.

ITALIAN STUFFED CLAMS

It must be against the law to be a bad cook in Italy.

12 large cherrystone clams
½ cup dry white wine
1¼ cups breadcrumbs
⅓ cup freshly grated imported Parmesan cheese
2 medium garlic cloves, crushed and finely chopped
2 tablespoons finely chopped fresh basil, or 2 teaspoons crushed dried basil
Salt and freshly ground pepper to taste
6 teaspoons olive oil
¾ cup Tomato Sauce (page 398)

Scrub the clams with a stiff brush or stainless steel scouring pad under cold running water, discarding any that have cracked shells or that are not shut tightly.

In a large, heavy skillet or saucepan combine the clams and wine. Cover tightly and cook over moderate heat about 10 minutes or just until the clams open and give up their juices. With tongs or a slotted spoon, transfer the clams to a platter, discarding any unopened ones. Strain the clam broth through a fine sieve lined with a triple layer of dampened cheesecloth into a bowl and set aside.

Break the clam shells apart, remove the clams from the shells, and reserve half the clam shells for stuffing. Chop the clams and place them in a mixing bowl. Add 1 cup of the breadcrumbs, the cheese, garlic, basil, salt, pepper, and enough of the clam broth to moisten. Toss lightly to mix. Stuff the clam shells with the clam mixture. Arrange the stuffed shells side by side in 1 layer in a shallow baking dish containing a little water. Sprinkle the tops evenly with the remaining ¼ cup breadcrumbs, then sprinkle each stuffed shell with ½ teaspoon olive oil and cover each with 1 tablespoon of the Tomato Sauce. Bake in a preheated 350°F oven about 20 minutes or until the clams are thoroughly heated and bubbling. Serve hot. Makes 4 servings.

SPANISH FRIED CLAMS

Scrub and steam small fresh clams as described in the recipe for Italian Stuffed Clams (page 203). When the shells have opened, remove the clams, roll in flour, dip in beaten egg, and deep-fry in hot olive oil. Serve hot on cocktail picks.

SPANISH FRIED MUSSELS

Follow the recipe for Spanish Fried Clams (above), substituting mussels for the clams. To clean mussels, see the recipe for Mussels in Shallot Mayonnaise (page 182).

GALICIAN SCALLOPS

This northern Spanish triumph is the sort of dish that remains in one's memory for a long time.

1 pound scallops
3 tablespoons olive oil
⅓ cup finely chopped onion
2 medium garlic cloves, finely chopped
2 tablespoons finely chopped parsley, preferably Italian flat-leaf
½ teaspoon crushed dried thyme
¼ teaspoon crushed dried hot red pepper or to taste
Salt and freshly ground black pepper to taste
2 cups sliced mushrooms
2 tablespoons Cognac
¾ cup dry white wine
½ cup Tomato Sauce (page 398)
Breadcrumbs
Butter

Rinse the scallops thoroughly under cold running water. Drain and pat dry with paper towels. Cut them in half lengthwise and set aside.

In a large, heavy skillet heat the oil over medium-high heat. Add the onion and garlic and sauté, stirring frequently, until soft but not browned. Add the scallops and sauté 2 minutes, stirring constantly. Sprinkle with the parsley, thyme, red pepper, salt, and black pepper. Add the mushrooms and cook, stirring, over moderate heat about 5 minutes.

In a small saucepan heat the Cognac briefly over medium-high heat. Pour into the skillet (making certain that it is not under an exhaust fan) and ignite, shaking the pan gently until the flame subsides. With a slotted spoon, transfer the scallops and mushrooms to a shallow baking dish. Add the wine and Tomato Sauce to the skillet and bring to a boil over medium-high heat. Reduce the heat to low and simmer 10 minutes. Spoon over the scallops and mushrooms. Sprinkle with breadcrumbs and dot with butter. Bake in a preheated 450°F oven about 10 minutes or until the tops are golden brown. Serve hot. Makes 4 servings.

SCALLOP, WATER CHESTNUT, AND BACON BROCHETTES

How to barbecue in style.

16 sea scallops
12 strips bacon, partially cooked and cut into pieces the same size as the scallops
16 small water chestnuts, cut in half lengthwise
½ recipe Teriyaki Sauce (page 399)

Rinse the scallops thoroughly under cold running water. Drain and pat dry with paper towels. Cut the scallops in half lengthwise. Alternate the bacon between the scallop halves and water chestnut slices on 32 bamboo skewers, each 5 to 6 inches long, leaving enough room at one end of each skewer to handle. Arrange the skewers side by side in one layer in a wide, shallow dish. Pour the Teriyaki Sauce over them, cover, and marinate 30 minutes at room temperature, turning the skewers several times.

Remove the skewers from the marinade and broil over charcoal or under a preheated broiler about 4 inches from the heat, turning frequently, 5 to 10 minutes or until the scallops are just cooked but not dry. Serve at once. Makes 8 servings.

VARIATIONS:

SCALLOP, PINEAPPLE, AND BACON BROCHETTES

Marinate rinsed, dried, and halved sea scallops in Teriyaki Sauce 30 minutes at room temperature. Thread the scallop halves on bamboo skewers, alternating them with pieces of bacon or Canadian bacon and cubes of fresh pineapple. Dip the skewers in the Teriyaki Sauce and broil as directed.

SCALLOP, GREEN PEPPER, TOMATO, AND BACON BROCHETTES

Marinate rinsed, dried, and halved sea scallops in Teriyaki Sauce 30 minutes at room temperature. Onto each bamboo skewer thread 1 tiny cherry tomato, 1 scallop half, 1 piece of bacon, 1 green pepper square, 1 more scallop half, and 1 more piece of bacon. Dip the skewers in the Teriyaki Sauce and broil as directed.

BAKED OYSTERS WITH PROSCIUTTO AND MUSHROOMS

I can imagine few tributes to the oyster as fine as this.

2 tablespoons butter
2½ ounces prosciutto, finely chopped
4 large mushrooms, finely chopped
2 shallots or scallions (include 2 inches of the green tops of the scallions), finely chopped
1 medium green or red bell pepper, seeded, deribbed, and diced
1 medium garlic clove, finely chopped
Finely chopped parsley, preferably Italian flat-leaf
¼ teaspoon crushed dried oregano
2 tablespoons dry white wine
Salt, freshly ground pepper, and cayenne pepper to taste
16 fresh oysters, thoroughly washed and scrubbed, shucked (reserve the liquor and shells)
Dash fresh lemon juice
Rock salt or well-washed pebbles
Mornay Sauce (page 397)
Freshly grated imported Parmesan cheese
Melted butter
Lemon wedges

In a medium-sized, heavy skillet melt the butter over medium-high heat. Add the proscuitto, mushrooms, shallots or scallions, bell pepper, garlic, 2 tablespoons parsley, oregano, wine, salt, pepper, and cayenne pepper. Sauté 2 minutes, stirring frequently. Remove from the heat, taste and adjust the seasoning, and set aside.

In a large saucepan combine the reserved oyster liquor, lemon juice, 3 quarts water, and salt to taste. Add the oysters and bring to a boil over high heat. Remove from the heat and allow the oysters to cool in the liquid.

Cover the bottom of a large, shallow baking pan with a bed of rock salt or pebbles. Clean and dry the reserved oyster shells. Fill each oyster shell with about 1 tablespoon of the prosciutto and mushroom mixture. Drain the oysters thoroughly. Place 1 oyster in each filled shell and cover with 1 tablespoon Mornay Sauce. Sprinkle with Parmesan cheese and drizzle with melted butter. Arrange the oysters side by side in one layer over the rock salt or pebbles. Broil under a preheated broiler about 4 inches from the heat until piping hot. Sprinkle with parsley and serve at once with the lemon wedges. Makes 16.

IKAN BAKR
Indonesian Barbecued Fish

1 pound fillet of tuna, swordfish, or similar firm-fleshed fish
¼ cup freshly squeezed and strained lemon juice
2 tablespoons Kecap Manis (page 400)
1 tablespoon peanut oil or corn oil
1 medium garlic clove, finely chopped
½ teaspoon sugar
½ teaspoon salt

Wash the fish under cold running water and dry thoroughly with paper towels. Cut the fish into 1-inch cubes.

Combine the remaining ingredients in a large bowl and stir until the sugar and salt are dissolved. Add the fish cubes, tossing them about to coat them well with the mixture. Cover and let marinate at room temperature 30 minutes, turning the cubes occasionally.

Broil the fish cubes over charcoal or under a preheated broiler approximately 3 inches from the heat, turning frequently, about 10 minutes or until lightly browned and firm. Arrange on a platter and serve warm or at room temperature. Makes about 16 cubes.

JANSSON'S FRESTELSE

Jansson's Temptation

A well-known Swedish specialty, often featured on the smörgåsbord.

    7 medium boiling potatoes, peeled and
       cut into strips 2 inches long and ¼ inch
       thick
  4½ tablespoons butter
    2 tablespoons flavorless vegetable oil
    3 to 4 medium-sized yellow onions, thinly
       sliced
   16 flat anchovy fillets, drained
       Freshly ground white pepper to taste
    2 tablespoons fine dry breadcrumbs
    1 cup heavy cream
    ½ cup milk

Place the potato strips in a large bowl of cold water to prevent them from darkening. In a large, heavy skillet heat 2 tablespoons of the butter and the oil over moderate heat. Add the onions and cook 10 minutes, stirring often, until they are soft but not browned.

Rub a 2-quart baking dish with ½ tablespoon of the remaining butter. Drain the potato strips and pat them dry with paper towels. Arrange alternate layers of potatoes, onions, and anchovies in the baking dish, beginning and ending with potatoes and seasoning each layer lightly with white pepper. Sprinkle the top layer of potatoes with the breadcrumbs and dot with the remaining 2 tablespoons butter, cut into ¼-inch bits.

Combine the cream and milk in a small saucepan. Heat the mixture over moderate heat until it barely simmers, then pour it carefully down the sides of the baking dish. Bake in a preheated 400°F oven about 45 minutes or until the potatoes are tender and almost all of the liquid is absorbed. Serve hot. Makes 6 servings.

RUSSIAN FISH CAKES

The mundane fish cake is here transformed into a delicacy redolent of dill and served with a lively mustard mayonnaise.

       Mustard Mayonnaise (page 388)
    7 tablespoons finely chopped fresh dill
    8 slices homemade-type white bread,
       trimmed of crusts
    1 cup milk
    2 pounds cod fillets, skinned and finely
       ground
    ⅓ cup finely grated onion
  1½ teaspoons salt or to taste
    ¼ teaspoon freshly ground white pepper
       All-purpose flour
    6 tablespoons Clarified Butter (page 288)
       or as needed

In a small serving bowl combine the Mustard Mayonnaise with 3 tablespoons of the dill. Cover and chill until ready to serve.

Soak the bread slices in the milk, squeeze out excess milk, and mash them in a large bowl. Add the cod, onion, the remaining 4 tablespoons dill, salt, and pepper and blend well. Form the mixture into flat round cakes 1½ to 2 inches in diameter. Dredge the cakes in flour, shaking off the excess.

In a large, heavy skillet melt 4 tablespoons of the Clarified Butter over high heat. Add the fish cakes, a batch at a time, reduce the heat to moderate, and sauté 1 to 2 minutes on each side or until golden brown, adding more butter as necessary. As the fish cakes are done, transfer them to a heated platter with a slotted spoon or spatula. Cover loosely with aluminum foil to keep them warm while you fry the remaining cakes. Serve hot, accompanied with the Mustard Mayonnaise and dill mixture. Makes about 24.

VARIATIONS:

Substitute Egg Sauce (page 390) for the Mustard Mayonnaise.

Substitute 4 tablespoons unsalted butter and 2 tablespoons flavorless vegetable oil for the Clarified Butter, adding more unsalted butter and oil if necessary.

CALAMARES A LA ROMANA
Fried Squid, Roman Style

Despite its name, this is a popular Spanish tapa (page 405).

1 pound fresh or frozen squid, cleaned, patted dry, and cut into thin rings
½ cup all-purpose flour or as needed
2 eggs
  Olive oil for deep-frying
  Salt
  Lemon wedges

Dredge the squid pieces in the flour, shaking off the excess. In a medium bowl lightly beat the eggs. Add the squid and mix to coat the pieces thoroughly.

In a deep-fryer or deep, heavy skillet heat about 2 inches oil to 375°F. Add the squid pieces, a few at a time, and fry, turning once, 2 to 3 minutes or until golden brown. As each batch is done, transfer the squid pieces with a wire skimmer or slotted spoon to a baking sheet lined with paper towels and keep warm in a preheated 200°F oven while you fry the remaining squid pieces. Sprinkle the fried squid lightly with salt and arrange them on a heated platter. Garnish with the lemon wedges and serve at once. Makes 8 servings.

FROGS' LEGS VALENCIANA

Effective propaganda for frogs' legs skeptics.

½ cup dry white wine
3 tablespoons freshly squeezed and
    strained lemon juice
1 tablespoon olive oil
1 medium garlic clove, crushed
1 tablespoon chopped parsley
½ teaspoon crushed dried thyme
    Salt to taste
4 whole peppercorns
1½ pounds medium frogs' legs (10 to 12
    pairs)
    Freshly ground pepper
    All-purpose flour
2 eggs, lightly beaten
    Fine breadcrumbs
    Olive oil or flavorless vegetable oil (or a
    combination of the two) for deep-frying

In a small bowl combine the wine, lemon juice, 1 tablespoon olive oil, garlic, parsley, thyme, salt, and peppercorns. Mix well. Arrange the frogs' legs in a shallow casserole just large enough to accommodate them in one layer. Pour the wine mixture over the legs. Cover and chill several hours.

Drain the frogs' legs thoroughly and pat them dry with paper towels. Season them on both sides with salt and pepper and dust with flour. Dip the legs in the beaten eggs, then in the breadcrumbs, coating evenly.

In a large, heavy skillet heat about ½ inch oil to 375°F. Add the frogs' legs to the skillet in batches and fry, turning them over until they are golden on both sides and cooked through. As each batch is done, transfer the legs with a slotted spoon to a baking sheet lined with paper towels and keep them warm in a preheated 200°F oven while you fry the remaining legs. Arrange the frogs' legs on a platter and serve at once. Makes 10 to 12 servings.

CHICKEN

Chicken must undoubtedly be one of the most cosmopolitan of birds, for there is no country worldwide where it does not occupy a prominent position in cookery. Highly adaptable, nutritious, and low in cost and calories, it forms the basis of many masterful creations in both classic and provincial cuisines. When planning a selection of appetizers one can choose from a wide range of fascinating international chicken preparations, as demonstrated by the recipes that follow.

For additional recipes featuring poultry please see the Index.

◇

COLD CHICKEN APPETIZERS

CIRCASSIAN CHICKEN

This famous dish enjoys popularity throughout the Middle East. It originally comes from Circassia, a region of the North Caucasus on the eastern coast of the Black Sea, whose inhabitants, especially the women, are noted for their striking beauty. Ground walnuts dominate the unusual sauce, which is used to dress the strips of chicken. Often served as a first course, it makes a fine buffet dish as well.

1 chicken (3 to 3½ pounds), cut into 6
  serving pieces
3 cups water
1 medium onion, cut into 8 wedges
1 stalk celery with leaves, coarsely
  chopped
1 carrot, scraped and coarsely chopped
3 sprigs parsley
½ bay leaf
4 whole peppercorns
  Salt
1½ cups shelled walnuts
⅓ cup finely chopped onion
3 slices firm white bread, torn into small
  pieces
  Paprika
  Freshly ground pepper to taste
1 tablespoon finely chopped parsley,
  preferably Italian flat-leaf (optional)

In a Dutch oven combine the chicken, water, onion wedges, celery, carrot, parsley sprigs, bay leaf, peppercorns, and 1 teaspoon salt. Bring to a boil over high heat. Reduce the heat to low, cover, and simmer about 45 minutes or until the chicken is just tender. Transfer the chicken to a plate and reserve. Strain the broth. In a large saucepan bring the strained broth to a boil over high heat. Boil rapidly, uncovered, until it is reduced to 1½ cups. Remove from the heat and cool slightly.

Combine the walnuts, chopped onion, bread, 1 teaspoon paprika, pepper, and the reduced broth in the container of an electric blender. Cover and blend until the mixture becomes a smooth purée. Taste and adjust the seasoning.

When the chicken is cool enough to handle, remove the skin and pull the meat away from the bones. Discard the skin and bones. Cut the meat into strips about ⅛ inch wide and 1½ inches long. Place the strips in a bowl, add half of the walnut sauce, and toss gently until the strips are well coated with the sauce. Mound the chicken on a platter, mask the top with the remaining walnut sauce, and sprinkle with paprika. Garnish with the finely chopped parsley, if desired. Serve at room temperature. Makes 6 servings as a first course, 12 as an hors d'oeuvre.

Note: A more traditional garnish for this dish is made from paprika and the oil of ground walnuts. To prepare, with a mortar and pestle pulverize ¼ cup shelled walnuts with ¾ teaspoon paprika. Place a small spoonful of the mixture at a time in a garlic press and squeeze the oil over the chicken.

CHICKEN AND HAM IN LETTUCE LEAVES

The following treatment turns modestly priced ingredients into an uncommonly engaging starter.

> Boston or Bibb lettuce leaves
> 2 slices white bread, trimmed of crusts
> 1 cup chicken broth
> 1½ pounds chicken breasts, skinned, boned, and ground
> 2 eggs
> 2 tablespoons finely chopped fresh dill
> 2 tablespoons heavy cream
> Salt and freshly ground pepper to taste
> 1 slice cooked ham, about ⅓ inch thick, cut into ⅓ by ⅓ by 2-inch strips
> All-purpose flour
> 2 tablespoons butter or as needed
> Fresh dill or watercress sprigs
> Herb Mayonnaise (page 388)

Wash the lettuce leaves under cold running water. Drain, dry with paper towels, and chill.

In a mixing bowl soak the bread in the broth, then pour off the broth and reserve. Shred the bread with a fork, add the chicken, eggs, dill, cream, salt, and pepper and mix well. Add just enough of the reserved broth to moisten the mixture, then cover and chill 2 hours to make it more manageable.

Shape the mixture into fingers about 3 inches long and 1½ inches in diameter. Form each finger around a stick of ham. Roll the fingers in flour, shaking off the excess. In a heavy skillet melt the butter over moderate heat. Add the fingers and sauté on all sides until they are lightly browned and crisp. Drain on paper towels and allow to cool to room temperature.

To eat, place a finger in the center of a lettuce leaf. Top with a sprig of dill or watercress and roll up. Dip into the Herb Mayonnaise. Makes 6 servings.

GERMAN CHICKEN, HAM, AND CHEESE ROULADES

A substantial and altogether winning appetizer.

    2 whole chicken breasts (about 1 pound
        each), skinned, boned, and halved
    4 thin slices Westphalian or Black Forest
        ham
    4 thin slices Gruyère or Emmenthaler
        cheese
    1 medium garlic clove, very finely chopped
    ¼ teaspoon crushed dried thyme,
        marjoram, or sage
        Freshly ground white pepper to taste
    ⅓ cup dry white wine
    ⅓ cup chicken broth
        Watercress or parsley sprigs

Place each chicken breast between sheets of plastic wrap and pound it lightly with the flat side of a cleaver or a wooden mallet until it is about ¼ inch thick. Trim the slices of ham and cheese so that they are the same size as the flattened pieces of chicken. Place a slice of ham on each piece of chicken and cover the ham with a slice of cheese. Season with the thyme, marjoram, or sage and white pepper. Roll up the pieces tightly and fasten with wooden picks, or tie securely with string.

Arrange the roulades in a greased baking dish just large enough to hold them comfortably in one layer and pour the wine and broth over them. Cover with aluminum foil. Bake in a preheated 350°F oven 35 to 40 minutes or until the chicken is tender. Transfer the roulades to a platter and cool to room temperature, then cover and chill. Remove the wooden picks or string. Slice the roulades crosswise into rounds and arrange on a chilled serving platter. Garnish with watercress or parsley sprigs and serve. Makes about 20.

VARIATION:

In a medium-sized, heavy skillet melt 2 tablespoons Clarified Butter (page 288), or heat a mixture of 1 tablespoon each butter and flavorless vegetable oil or olive oil over moderate heat. Add the roulades and sauté, turning to brown lightly on all sides. Add the wine and chicken broth and bring to a boil. Reduce the heat to low, cover, and simmer about 30 minutes or until the chicken is tender. Cool, chill, slice, and serve as directed above.

POLLO EN ESCABECHE
Dominican Pickled Chicken

2 pounds chicken breasts, skinned, boned, and cut into ¾-inch pieces
4 medium onions, thinly sliced
3 medium garlic cloves, finely chopped
1 bay leaf
1 teaspoon crushed dried oregano
  Salt, freshly ground pepper, and cayenne pepper to taste
¼ cup olive oil
2 tablespoons white wine vinegar

Dry the chicken pieces with paper towels. In a heavy casserole combine the chicken, onions, garlic, and bay leaf. Sprinkle with the oregano, salt, pepper, and cayenne pepper. Mix well. Pour the oil and vinegar evenly over the chicken and onion mixture. Cover and simmer gently about 35 minutes, stirring occasionally. If the onions are very watery, partially uncover the casserole for the last 10 minutes of cooking to reduce the sauce. Remove from the heat and cool to room temperature. Remove and discard the bay leaf. Transfer the chicken and onions to a serving dish, cover, and chill. Serve with romaine lettuce hearts and slices of tomato, avocado, pimento-stuffed olives, and radishes, or use as a filling for pita breads or *sope* shells (page 301). Makes 8 servings.

Hot Chicken Appetizers

CHICKEN, PEPPER, AND ONION KEBABS

These succulent kebabs are nothing short of first-rate.

¼ cup olive oil
2 tablespoons imported soy sauce
2 tablespoons honey
2 tablespoons brandy
3 medium garlic cloves, crushed and finely chopped
2 tablespoons finely chopped stemmed and seeded red chili pepper
2 whole chicken breasts (about 1 pound each), skinned, boned, and cut into ¾-inch cubes
1 green bell pepper, seeded, deribbed, and cut into ¾-inch squares
16 tiny white onions
¼ cup sesame seed, toasted (optional)*

In a medium glass or ceramic bowl combine the olive oil, soy sauce, honey, brandy, garlic, and chili pepper and mix well. Add the pieces of chicken and toss to coat thoroughly with the mixture. Cover and let marinate in the refrigerator several hours or overnight, turning the pieces occasionally.

Remove the pieces of chicken from the marinade and thread them on small bamboo skewers, alternating them with the green pepper squares and onions and leaving enough room at one end of each skewer to handle. Broil over charcoil or under a preheated broiler about 4 inches from the heat, turning and basting occasionally with the marinade, about 8 minutes or until the chicken is lightly browned. Arrange the skewered kebabs on a heated serving platter. Sprinkle with the toasted sesame seed, if desired, and serve at once. Makes 8 servings.

VARIATION:

CHICKEN, PEPPER, AND PINEAPPLE KEBABS

Substitute 16 cubes of fresh pineapple for the onions.

*To toast sesame seed: Spread the sesame seed in a shallow baking pan and bake in a preheated 350°F oven 10 to 15 minutes or until golden, stirring occasionally.

CARIBBEAN CHICKEN ROLLS

Sheer witchery—a real tropical stunner.

4 whole chicken breasts (about 1 pound
  each), skinned, boned, and halved
8 thin slices prosciutto
1 mango, peeled, flesh removed and cut
  into 8 strips, each about 1 inch wide
1 cup all-purpose flour
½ teaspoon salt
⅛ teaspoon freshly ground pepper
¼ teaspoon curry powder
  Pinch crushed dried thyme
2 cups grated fresh coconut
2 eggs, well beaten
  Flavorless vegetable oil for deep-frying
  Lime wedges
  Parsley sprigs

Place each chicken breast between sheets of plastic wrap and pound it lightly with the flat side of a cleaver or a wooden mallet until it is about ¼ inch thick. Put 1 slice of prosciutto on each slice of chicken, leaving a ½-inch border around the prosciutto; trim the prosciutto to fit if necessary. Place 1 mango strip over each slice of prosciutto. Trim the ends to within ½ inch of the ends of the chicken. Beginning from a long side, roll up the chicken, making certain that both the prosciutto and mango are securely enclosed inside the chicken, tucking in the ends of the chicken if necessary. Arrange the chicken rolls in one layer on a baking sheet and place them, uncovered, in the freezer 10 minutes to firm.

In a small bowl combine the flour, salt, pepper, curry powder, and thyme. Spread the mixture on a shallow plate. Spread the coconut on another shallow plate.

Remove the chicken rolls from the freezer. Roll each in the flour mixture and shake off the excess. Roll in the beaten eggs until thoroughly covered and let drain over a plate. Roll in the coconut, coating all sides evenly. Gently shake off the excess coconut. Arrange the chicken rolls on a plate, cover, and refrigerate about 30 minutes or until firm.

In a deep-fryer or deep, heavy skillet heat about 3 inches oil over medium-high heat to 375°F. Add 2 chicken rolls at a time to the pan and fry them in the hot oil, turning frequently, about 4 minutes or until lightly browned on all sides. With a slotted spoon, transfer the rolls to paper towels to drain.

Arrange the chicken rolls on a baking sheet and bake them in a preheated 350°F oven about 10 minutes or until the chicken is cooked through. To test for doneness, insert the tip of a small, sharp knife into the breast meat. There should be no trace of pink in the chicken.

Transfer the chicken rolls to a plate. With a sharp knife, cut each roll into 6 equal slices. Arrange the slices on a heated platter and garnish the platter with the lime wedges and parsley sprigs. Serve hot. Makes 48.

CANTONESE SESAME-NUT CHICKEN

1 egg white, lightly beaten
2 tablespoons medium dry Sherry
2 teaspoons imported soy sauce
2 tablespoons cornstarch
1 whole chicken breast (about 1 pound), skinned, boned, and cut into 1-inch pieces
¾ cup finely chopped blanched almonds or walnuts
¼ cup sesame seed
Peanut oil or corn oil for deep-frying
Salt or Roasted Szechuan Peppercorn-Salt (page 199)

In a bowl combine the egg white, Sherry, soy sauce, and 1 tablespoon of the cornstarch and mix until smooth. Add the chicken, tossing the pieces about to coat them well with the mixture. Cover and let marinate at room temperature 30 minutes, turning the pieces occasionally.

In a dish mix together the nuts, sesame seed, and remaining 1 tablespoon cornstarch. Coat the pieces of chicken with the nut mixture. In a wok or deep-fryer heat 2 to 3 inches oil to 350°F. Deep-fry the chicken pieces in batches, turning them occasionally with a slotted spoon, about 3 minutes or until they are golden brown. Transfer the chicken pieces to paper towels to drain and sprinkle lightly with salt or Roasted Szechuan Peppercorn-Salt. Arrange the chicken on a heated platter. Set out a small container of cocktail picks for spearing the chicken. Serve hot. Makes about 24.

CHINESE PAPER-WRAPPED CHICKEN AND HAM

Good things come in small packages.

2 tablespoons dry Sherry
2 tablespoons oyster sauce
1 tablespoon imported soy sauce
½ teaspoon imported sesame oil
1 small garlic clove, very finely chopped
½ teaspoon very finely chopped peeled fresh ginger root
¼ teaspoon sugar
Pinch freshly ground pepper
1 whole chicken breast (about 1 pound), skinned, boned, and halved
16 6-inch squares parchment paper (see Note on page 78)
16 very thin slices Smithfield or Black Forest ham, cut into 1½ by 3-inch rectangles
4 scallions, the green tops cut into 3-inch lengths, the white parts cut in half lengthwise
Flavorless vegetable oil
Parsley sprigs

In a small bowl combine the Sherry, oyster sauce, soy sauce, sesame oil, garlic, ginger root, sugar, and pepper. Set aside.

Holding your knife at a sharp angle, cut the chicken very thinly against the grain into 16 1½ by 3-inch rectangles. Add the chicken pieces to the sauce and let them marinate 30 minutes.

Place 1 square of parchment paper on your work surface, with a corner pointing toward you. Place 1 piece of marinated chicken horizontally in the center, cover it with 1 piece of ham, and top the ham with 2 or 3 pieces of scallion. Bring the bottom corner up over the filling. Fold the sides over and crease them. Lift up the portion nearest you (the bottom part enclosing the filling) and fold it over the sides, creasing it. Bring the top corner down and slide it all the way into the opening created by the previous folds, creasing thoroughly. Repeat this procedure with the remaining ingredients.

In a large, heavy skillet heat 2 to 3 inches oil to 370°F. Lower the packages, a few at a time, into the hot oil and fry about 2 minutes on each side. Drain on paper towels. Repeat with the remaining packages. Arrange the packages on a platter and garnish with the parsley sprigs. Serve them hot for guests to open at table. Makes 16.

APRICOT-GLAZED CHICKEN WINGS

Here chicken wings shake off their commonplace image.

12 chicken wings (about 2 pounds)
⅓ cup flavorless vegetable oil
2 tablespoons freshly squeezed and strained lemon juice
2 large garlic cloves, finely chopped
1 teaspoon crushed dried rosemary
1 teaspoon crushed dried thyme
1 small bay leaf, crumbled
1 teaspoon salt
Freshly ground pepper to taste
Apricot Glaze (below)
Scallion Brushes (Page 221)

Chop off the wing tips from the chicken wings and save for making soup stock. Cut each wing apart at the joint. In a medium glass or ceramic bowl combine the oil, lemon juice, garlic, rosemary, thyme, bay leaf, salt, and pepper. Add the chicken wings, tossing them about to coat them well with the mixture. Cover and let marinate at room temperature 1 hour or in the refrigerator several hours or overnight, turning the wings occasionally.

Drain the chicken wings and arrange them on a grill or on the rack of a broiler pan. Broil over charcoal or under a preheated broiler about 6 inches from the heat 5 minutes on each side. Baste the wings with the Apricot Glaze and continue to broil, turning and basting occasionally, about 8 minutes or until they are glazed and nicely browned. Arrange the wings on a heated serving platter, garnish with the Scallion Brushes, and serve at once. Makes 24.

APRICOT GLAZE

1 tablespoon butter
1 medium onion, finely chopped
2 tablespoons cider vinegar
1 cup apricot preserves
1 tablespoon imported soy sauce
2 teaspoons Dijon-style mustard
¼ teaspoon ginger
¼ teaspoon cloves
Salt and freshly ground pepper to taste

In a small enameled or stainless steel saucepan melt the butter over moderate heat. Add the onion and sauté, stirring frequently, until soft but not browned. Add the vinegar and cook, stirring, until the liquid in the pan is reduced to 1 tablespoon. Add the remaining ingredients and cook the mixture, stirring occasionally, about 8 minutes or until it is thickened. Purée the mixture through the coarse disk of a food mill into a bowl. Makes about 1 cup.

SCALLION BRUSHES

Trim off the roots and green tops of the scallions, leaving 3-inch lengths. Make 4 intersecting cuts 1 inch deep in both ends of the scallions and drop them into ice water. Refrigerate until the ends curl into brushlike fans. Drain well on paper towels before using.

CURRIED SESAME CHICKEN WINGS

The preparation of this appetizer is rather time-consuming, but the final outcome is well worth the effort.

12 chicken wings (about 2 pounds)
½ cup honey
¼ cup Dijon-style mustard
2 tablespoons butter, melted
1 teaspoon curry powder
1 teaspoon salt or to taste
¼ cup sesame seed, toasted (page 216)
   Coriander or parsley sprigs

Chop off the wing tips from the chicken wings and save for making soup stock. Cut each wing apart at the joint. For sections with 2 bones, remove the smaller bone by cutting it loose at both ends and pulling it out. Starting at one end of each piece (the narrow ends of the larger pieces), with a small knife scrape the meat down almost to the joint, then pull the meat inside out over the joint. Smooth the meat with your fingers.

In a small bowl combine the honey, mustard, melted butter, curry powder, and salt and stir until well blended. Reserve.

Arrange the chicken wings on a grill or on the rack of a broiler pan. Broil over charcoal or under a preheated broiler about 4 inches from the heat 5 minutes on each side. Baste the wings with the reserved sauce and continue to broil, turning and basting occasionally, about 10 minutes or until they are glazed and nicely browned.

Using the trimmed bones as handles, dip the wings in the toasted sesame seed and arrange them on a heated serving platter. Garnish with the coriander or parsley sprigs and serve. Makes 24.

SINGAPORE-STYLE CHICKEN SATAY

Sold by street vendors in Singapore, this exotic temptation can easily be duplicated at home.

¼ *cup imported soy sauce*
3 *tablespoons peanut oil or corn oil*
2 *medium garlic cloves, finely chopped*
2 *teaspoons curry powder*
2 *teaspoons sugar*
2 *whole chicken breasts (about 1 pound each), skinned, boned, and cut into ¾-inch cubes*
Singapore-Style Peanut Sauce (page 394)

In a medium bowl combine the soy sauce, peanut oil or corn oil, garlic, curry powder, and sugar and stir until the sugar is dissolved. Add the chicken, tossing the pieces about to coat them well with the mixture. Cover and let marinate in the refrigerator several hours or overnight, turning the pieces occasionally.

Thread the chicken pieces on small bamboo skewers, leaving enough room on one end of each skewer to handle. Broil over charcoal or under a preheated broiler about 2 inches from the heat, turning frequently, about 8 minutes or until the chicken is golden brown. Arrange the skewers on a heated serving platter. Serve at once with the Peanut Sauce. Makes 8 servings.

VARIATION:

SINGAPORE-STYLE BEEF OR LAMB SATAY

Substitute 1½ pounds boneless beef sirloin or leg of lamb, trimmed of excess fat and cut into ¾-inch cubes, for the chicken breasts.

YAKITORI

Japanese Broiled Chicken, Chicken Livers, and Scallions

A popular Japanese specialty that non-Japanese find delicious.

2 *whole chicken breasts (about 1 pound each), skinned, boned, and cut into 1-inch pieces*
8 *chicken livers, trimmed of fat and cut into 1-inch pieces*
8 *scallions, including 3 inches of the green tops, cut into 1- to 1½-inch lengths*
Teriyaki Sauce (page 399)
Kona sansho (Japanese pepper) (optional)

Thread the pieces of chicken, chicken livers, and scallions alternately on small bamboo skewers, leaving enough room at one end of each skewer to handle. Arrange the skewers side by side in a shallow dish large enough to hold them in one layer. Pour the Teriyaki Sauce over the skewered ingredients and let them marinate at room temperature 30 minutes, turning the skewers occasionally. Remove the skewers from the Teriyaki Sauce (reserve the sauce) and broil over hot coals in a hibachi or charcoal grill or under a preheated broiler about 3 inches from the heat, turning and basting occasionally with the reserved Teriyaki Sauce, 6 to 8 minutes or until the chicken is cooked but still juicy, not dry. Arrange the skewers on a heated serving platter and moisten each with a little of the Teriyaki Sauce. Sprinkle lightly with *kona sansho*, if desired, and serve. Makes 12 servings.

PARMESAN CHICKEN WINGS

There won't be any leftovers.

12 chicken wings (about 2 pounds)
½ cup unflavored yogurt
3 tablespoons freshly squeezed and strained lemon juice
1 tablespoon Dijon-style mustard
2 large garlic cloves, finely chopped
½ teaspoon crushed dried sage
½ teaspoon crushed dried oregano
Salt
Freshly ground pepper to taste
½ cup breadcrumbs
½ cup (2 ounces) freshly grated imported Parmesan cheese
Cayenne pepper to taste
Melted unsalted butter

Chop off the wing tips from the chicken wings and save for making stock. Cut each wing apart at the joint.

In a medium glass or ceramic bowl combine the yogurt, lemon juice, mustard, garlic, sage, oregano, 1 teaspoon salt, and pepper. Add the chicken wings, tossing them about to coat them well with the marinade. Cover and let marinate at room temperature 2 hours or in the refrigerator overnight, turning the wings occasionally.

In a shallow dish combine the bread-crumbs, Parmesan cheese, salt, pepper, and cayenne pepper. Drain the chicken wings and roll them in the crumb mixture, coating them thoroughly. Arrange the wings 1 inch apart in a well-buttered shallow baking pan and refrigerate 1 hour.

Dribble the wings with the butter, turning the pieces to coat completely, and bake them in a preheated 375°F oven 30 minutes or until they are golden brown. Transfer the chicken wings to a heated platter and serve. Makes 24.

VARIATION:

If desired, prepare the chicken wings as for Curried Sesame Chicken Wings (page 221).

SPANISH CHICKEN LIVERS IN SHERRY

Elegance at a bargain price.

12 chicken livers
 1 teaspoon salt or to taste
½ teaspoon paprika
   Freshly ground pepper to taste
   All-purpose flour
 2 tablespoons butter
¼ cup finely chopped onion
½ cup chicken broth
½ teaspoon Worcestershire sauce
 3 tablespoons dry Sherry
 1 tablespoon finely chopped parsley
   (optional)
   White toast slices

Clean the chicken livers, trimming off any fat and removing any dark or green spots. Dry them with paper towels and cut them in half. Season the chicken livers with salt, paprika, and pepper. Roll in flour, shaking off the excess. Set aside.

In a medium-sized, heavy skillet or flameproof casserole melt the butter over moderate heat. Add the onion and sauté, stirring frequently, until soft but not browned. Add the chicken livers and sauté, stirring, until they are lightly browned outside but still pink inside. Stir in 1 teaspoon flour until well mixed. Cook, stirring, 1 to 2 minutes. Gradually stir in the chicken broth, then add the Worcestershire sauce. Taste and adjust the seasoning. Stir in the Sherry and cook 1 to 2 minutes longer. Transfer to a heated serving dish and sprinkle with the parsley, if desired. Serve at once on toast as a *tapa* (page 405). Makes 4 servings.

RUSSIAN CHICKEN LIVERS IN SOUR CREAM

¾ *pound chicken livers*
  Salt and freshly ground pepper to taste
  All-purpose flour
3 *tablespoons butter*
1 *small onion, finely chopped*
¼ *pound mushrooms, sliced*
½ *cup sour cream*
1 *tablespoon finely chopped parsley*

Clean the chicken livers, trimming off any fat and removing any dark or green spots. Dry them with paper towels and cut them in half. Season the chicken livers with salt and pepper. Roll in flour, shaking off the excess. Set aside.

In a medium-sized, heavy skillet melt 1½ tablespoons of the butter over medium-high heat. Add the onion and mushrooms and sauté, stirring frequently, until lightly browned. Remove from the heat and set aside.

In a medium-sized, heavy skillet or flameproof casserole melt the remaining 1½ tablespoons butter over moderate heat. Add the chicken livers and sauté, stirring, until they are lightly browned outside but still pink inside. Reduce the heat to low and stir in 1 teaspoon flour until well blended. Season to taste with salt and pepper. Remove from the heat and let cool slightly, then gradually stir in the sour cream. Return to the heat and cook over low heat, stirring constantly, until the sauce thickens. Add the mushroom and onion mixture and cook gently, stirring, just until heated through. Taste and adjust the seasoning. Transfer to a heated serving dish or chafing dish and sprinkle with the parsley. Serve as part of a *zakuska* table (page 413). Makes 4 servings.

MEAT

The appreciation of good meat is universal, although one culture may extol the virtues of beef and another of lamb, while yet another sings the praises of pork. It is no wonder, then, that there exists a wealth of mouthwatering international meat appetizers to inspire the creative cook.

When considering meat hors d'oeuvre, one of the first things we are prone to think of is cold cuts. If you want to take advantage of the panorama of worthwhile offerings available, bypass the prepackaged items in your supermarket in favor of the abundant selection in ethnic delicatessens: Italian, German, French, Spanish, Scandinavian, Jewish, Polish, Middle Eastern, Latin American, and Oriental. The love of good sausage seems to be virtually worldwide, and many cultures have also perfected the art of curing hams. Delicatessen fare, served simply with some good breads, mustards, and pickles, makes robust and satisfying hors d'oeuvre and is a convenient choice for larger cocktail parties. Do not stop there, though, but explore the vast array *of other kinds of meat appetizers.*

You will discover that your options are not confined only to the cold variety. The choice of hot meat hors d'oeuvre extends far beyond cocktail-sized meatballs and frankfurters. For example, an exciting discovery can be the treasure trove of delights lovingly developed by generations of Eastern cooks, from the shores of the Levant through the steppes of central Asia and the Indian subcontinent to the Far East and South Pacific. Especially popular are miniature skewers of meat, vegetables, and fruit that are certain to tantalize and earn enthusiastic approval.

Besides the many recipes in this chapter, you will find other meat appetizers listed in the Index.

COLD MEAT APPETIZERS

CHARCUTERIE AND CHEESE PLATTER

Here's how to create a thoroughly gratifying appetizer with a minimum of effort.

Choose a selection of high-quality thinly sliced cold meats and cheeses from those suggested below. Arrange the slices on a large, flat serving platter. Garnish the platter with *cornichons* (French sour gherkins, available at specialty shops and some supermarkets), cherry tomatoes, and black and green olives. Serve with French bread, dark rye or pumpernickel bread, Dijon-style mustard, and a bowl of unsalted butter.

COLD MEATS	Bayonne ham
	Black Forest ham
	Westphalian ham
	Prosciutto
	Lyons sausage
	Hard cervelat
	Mortadella
	Soppressata

CHEESES   Italian Fontina
Provolone
Muenster
St. Paulin
Teleme
Emmenthal
Gruyère
Bucheron
Chabichou

CARPACCIO
Italian Raw Beef Slices

In contrast to Steak Tartare (page 238), which is a centuries-old classic, *carpaccio*—extremely thin slices of raw beef served with a mayonnaise sauce—is a classic born in this century. Said to have been created by Giuseppe Cipriani, founder of the famous Harry's Bar in Venice, for an ailing countess who was a favored customer, it was named after Vittorio Carpaccio, a celebrated fifteenth-century Venetian painter in whose works the color red figures prominently. Although most commonly found in restaurants, carpaccio can easily be prepared at home.

Freeze a ¾-pound raw fillet of beef, trimmed of all fat and membrane, in the freezing compartment of the refrigerator about 45 minutes or until it is firm. Remove the meat from the freezer and cut it into paper-thin slices. Divide the slices among individual serving plates, arranging them overlapping in a circle. Serve with Green Mayonnaise (page 388) or Mustard Mayonnaise (page 388). Makes 4 to 6 servings.

VARIATION:

MARINATED CARPACCIO

In a medium bowl combine ⅓ cup minced shallots, 1 tablespoon Dijon-style mustard, 1 tablespoon minced parsley, 1 tablespoon minced fresh basil or 1 teaspoon crushed dried basil, and 1 teaspoon each crushed dried rosemary and sage. Stir in ⅔ cup freshly squeezed and strained lemon juice or ⅓ cup each lemon juice and red wine vinegar. Add 1¼ cups olive oil in a slow, steady stream, whisking constantly. Season to taste with salt and freshly ground pepper. Layer the slices of beef in a shallow ceramic or glass dish, alternating with the sauce. Cover and let marinate in the refrigerator 6 hours or overnight. To serve, divide the beef slices among individual serving plates, arranging them in overlapping slices.

MATAMBRE
Argentine Stuffed Rolled Flank Steak

Matambre ("hunger killer") is a dish well known throughout Latin America, with Argentina claiming superiority in its preparation. It makes an excellent choice for a first course, buffet, or picnic.

4 pounds flank steak, trimmed
1 large onion, chopped
1 large garlic clove, crushed and finely chopped
3 tablespoons chopped parsley
1 bay leaf
¼ teaspoon crushed dried thyme
6 whole peppercorns
½ cup red wine vinegar
Freshly ground pepper to taste
1½ cups fresh soft breadcrumbs
3 to 4 tablespoons milk
1 bunch scallions, including 2 inches of the green tops, finely chopped
1 cup chopped cooked spinach
3 chorizo sausages (available at Hispanic markets and some specialty food shops) or Italian hot sausages, removed from the casings and crumbled

1 egg, beaten
Salt to taste
4 hard-cooked eggs, chopped
½ pound salt pork, cut into thin strips
Flavorless vegetable oil
2 cups beef broth

Pound the steak to a thin, square shape. In a shallow glass or earthenware dish large enough to hold the steak comfortably, combine the onion, garlic, 1 tablespoon of the parsley, bay leaf, thyme, peppercorns, and vinegar. Lay the steak in the marinade and turn it about until the meat is well coated. Cover and let the steak marinate at room temperature 4 to 5 hours, turning it over from time to time.

Remove the steak from the marinade, reserving the marinade. Lay the steak flat and sprinkle with the pepper. Soak the breadcrumbs in the milk. In a bowl combine the soaked breadcrumbs, scallions, spinach, sausages, remaining 2 tablespoons parsley, and beaten egg. Season with salt and pepper and mix well. Spread the mixture evenly over the meat to within 1 inch of the edge. Spread the chopped eggs on the mixture, pressing them lightly in place. Cover with the salt pork strips. Carefully roll up the steak like a jelly roll and tie it securely with kitchen string at about 1-inch intervals.

In a heavy casserole just large enough to hold the beef roll comfortably, heat a little oil over moderate heat. Add the beef roll and brown, turning until it is richly colored on all sides. Add the beef broth and reserved marinade. Cover and braise in a preheated 350°F oven about 3 hours or until tender, turning the meat occasionally and basting frequently. Allow to cool under a weight such as a heavy platter. Serve at room temperature in thin slices. Makes about 16 slices.

VITELLO TONNATO
Italian Cold Veal with Tuna Sauce

Esteemed in both Piedmont and Lombardy, this elegant specialty has earned an international reputation.

      1 leg of veal (about 4 pounds), boned and
         tied
 1½ cups dry white wine
      1 medium-sized yellow onion, quartered
      1 medium carrot, cut up
      1 stalk celery, cut up
      1 bay leaf
      6 sprigs parsley
      8 whole peppercorns
      1 can (3 ounces) Italian tuna packed in
         olive oil
         Olive oil
      3 to 5 flat anchovy fillets
      3 tablespoons freshly squeezed and
         strained lemon juice
      2 eggs
 3½ tablespoons capers, rinsed and drained
         Salt if needed
      2 tablespoons finely chopped parsley
         Lemon slices

Place the veal in a large, heavy saucepan or kettle. Add the wine, onion, carrot, celery, bay leaf, parsley, peppercorns, and just enough water to cover the meat. Bring to a boil, reduce the heat to low, cover, and simmer 1½ to 2 hours or until the veal is tender when pierced and a meat thermometer registers 170°F when inserted into the thickest part. Remove the pan from the heat and let the veal cool in the stock. Cover and chill.

Meanwhile, prepare the tuna sauce: Drain the oil from the tuna into a measuring cup and add enough additional olive oil to make 1 cup. In the container of an electric blender or a food processor combine the tuna, anchovy fillets, lemon juice, eggs, and 1½ tablespoons of the capers. Cover and blend until smooth. Gradually pour in the oil in a thin, steady stream until it is thoroughly blended. Taste and adjust the seasoning. Transfer the tuna sauce to a bowl, cover, and chill at least 3 hours.

When the meat is cold, lift it out of the stock and transfer it to a carving board. Strain the stock and refrigerate for another use. Trim the veal of any fat or gristle and cut the meat into thin, uniform slices. Spread a very thin layer of tuna sauce in the bottom of a large serving platter. Arrange the veal slices over the sauce so that they barely overlap and cover with the remaining sauce. Cover and refrigerate at least 24 hours. Shortly before serving, sprinkle with the parsley and garnish the platter with the lemon slices and remaining 2 tablespoons capers. Makes 16 servings.

VARIATIONS:

Substitute 1 frozen boneless turkey roast (about 4 pounds), thawed, for the veal.

Other possibilities for garnishing the platter include black olives (preferably Mediterranean olives), sliced or quartered hard-cooked eggs, dill gherkins, and radish roses.

JELLIED VEAL

Variations of this dish exist in Russia and Scandinavia.

> *2 pounds veal shoulder, cut into 2-inch*
> * pieces*
> *1 medium onion, quartered*
> *1 bay leaf*
> *5 whole peppercorns*
> *3 allspice berries*
> *2 cloves*
> *1½ teaspoons salt*
> *5¼ cups cold water*
> *1 tablespoon white vinegar*
> *2 egg whites, lightly beaten (if needed to*
> * clarify)*
> *1 envelope unflavored gelatin*
> *Bibb or Boston lettuce leaves (use the*
> * small, tender inner leaves of the Boston*
> * lettuce)*
> *Cucumber slices*
> *Lemon wedges*

In a large, heavy pot combine the veal, onion, bay leaf, peppercorns, allspice, cloves, salt, and 5 cups of cold water. Bring to a boil over moderate heat. Reduce the heat to low and simmer, partially covered, about 2 hours or until the veal is very tender, carefully skimming off any foam and scum that rise to the surface. With a slotted spatula, transfer the veal to a plate, and when it is cool enough to handle, remove the bones and gristle and discard. Cut the veal into ½-inch dice and set aside.

Strain the broth through a fine sieve set over a large bowl and let it rest about 10 minutes. With a large spoon, skim off and discard any fat from the surface. Strain the broth again through a sieve lined with a triple layer of dampened cheesecloth.

Pour the strained broth into a medium saucepan, add the vinegar, and bring to a boil. If the broth is cloudy, whip in the beaten egg whites and strain again. Sprinkle the gelatin over the remaining ¼ cup cold water and let stand about 5 minutes to soften, then stir the mixture into the hot broth until the gelatin is dissolved. Pour the broth into a rinsed and chilled 1½-quart loaf pan or mold and chill until syrupy. Stir in the diced veal, cover with aluminum foil, and chill at least 6 hours or until firm.

Unmold the jellied veal as directed on page 29. Garnish with the lettuce leaves, cucumber slices, and lemon wedges and serve. Makes 6 servings.

Note: Other garnishes for the jellied veal include hard-cooked egg slices, parsley sprigs, and carrot curls.

HAM AND CHEESE ROLLS

When it comes to hors d'oeuvre, ham's culinary versatility is little short of amazing.

Spread thin slices of Westphalian or Smithfield ham, each about 4 by 2 inches, with Roquefort Cheese Spread (page 27) or Herb Cheese (page 51). Beginning with a long side, roll up each slice firmly, jelly roll fashion. Wrap the rolls securely in aluminum foil and chill at least 3 hours. Shortly before serving, trim the ends, cut the rolls crosswise in half, and arrange them on a chilled serving platter.

VARIATIONS:

HAM AND PÂTÉ ROLLS

Substitute Chicken Liver Pâté (page 31, omitting the parsley sprigs) for the cheese filling. Dip the ends of each piece in finely chopped unsalted pistachio nuts, toasted blanched almonds, or parsley.

HAM AND MUSHROOM ROLLS

Substitute Cream Cheese and Mushroom Filling (page 37) for the cheese filling. Instead of cutting each roll in half, cut it into 4 equal pieces and spear each piece with a cocktail pick.

HAM CORNETS WITH ASPARAGUS

Roll thin slices of Westphalian or Smithfield ham, each about 3 by 3 inches, into cornet (cone) shapes. Secure the overlapping edges with cocktail picks, and, using a teaspoon, fill the centers with Curried Egg Filling (page 38). Place a bowl of Curry Mayonnaise (page 388) in the center of a large platter lined with lettuce leaves. Arrange the filled cornets along with chilled cooked asparagus spears in spokes around the mayonnaise. Garnish the platter with cherry tomatoes and large pitted black olives. Serve well chilled.

PROSCIUTTO WITH MELON

There is gastronomic beauty in the simplicity of this Italian classic.

1 large, ripe cantaloupe, honeydew, casaba, Persian, or Crenshaw melon, well chilled
12 thin slices prosciutto, loosely rolled
  Lemon wedges (optional)
  Freshly ground pepper (optional)

Cut the melon in half, remove the seeds and fibers, and cut each half into 6 wedges. With a sharp knife, cut the melon flesh away from the rind (discard the rind). Arrange the melon wedges around a large platter, alternating them with the slices of prosciutto. If desired, garnish the platter with the lemon wedges and grind a little pepper over the prosciutto, or set out a pepper mill nearby. Serve at once. Makes 12 servings.

PROSCIUTTO WITH FIGS

If you are fortunate enough to have access to fresh figs, savoring this great Italian favorite is an experience you will not want to miss.

12 ripe fresh green or purple figs, well chilled
*12 thin slices prosciutto, loosely rolled
Freshly ground pepper*

Trim off the very tip of the pointed end of each fig. Make shallow lengthwise cuts in the skin in 4 places as though you were going to cut the fig into quarters. Starting from the pointed end at what would be the top of a quarter and following the cuts carefully, peel back the skin in sections, leaving it attached at the base. Place the figs and prosciutto slices alternately around a large platter. Arrange the skin of each fig like the petals of a flower, with the fruit in the center. Grind a little pepper over the figs and prosciutto, or set out a pepper mill nearby. Serve at once. Makes 12 servings.

VARIATIONS:

If preferred, you can peel the figs completely and present them as above. Or cut each fig in half lengthwise and place a thin slice of prosciutto over each half.

HAM WITH PAPAYA

This and the following three recipes offer delectable alternatives to the traditional Italian combination of prosciutto with melon.

Cut a medium-sized, ripe, chilled papaya in half and remove the seeds. Peel the papaya and cut it into 2 by ½-inch pieces. Wrap a thin slice of prosciutto, Bayonne ham, or Westphalian ham around each piece of papaya and fasten with a cocktail pick, if necessary. Arrange the wrapped papaya pieces on a chilled platter and, if desired, grind a little pepper over them. Garnish the platter with wedges of lime and serve.

HAM WITH MANGO

With a stainless steel knife, peel 2 large mangoes and cut them lengthwise into ½-inch slices. Arrange the mango slices in the center of a serving platter and sprinkle them with freshly squeezed and strained lime juice. Arrange 8 very thin slices of prosciutto,

Bayonne ham, or Westphalian ham, folded loosely, around the mango slices and serve. Makes 4 servings as a first course.

VARIATION:

HAM AND MANGO TIDBITS

Cut the peeled mango flesh in ¾-inch cubes, wrap in thin strips of ham, and fasten with decorative picks. Serve as an accompaniment to cocktails.

HAM WITH PEARS

For each serving place 1 halved, cored, unpeeled, ripe Bartlett pear on a chilled appetizer plate and brush it lightly with freshly squeezed and strained lemon juice to prevent it from darkening. Arrange alongside the pear 2 or 3 paper-thin slices of prosciutto or Smithfield ham, rolled or folded accordion fashion. Grind a little pepper over all and serve.

VARIATION:

Substitute very thin slices of Genoa salami, rolled into cornet (cone) shapes, for the ham and omit the pepper. If preferred, cut the cored, unpeeled pear into lengthwise slices rather than in half.

HAM WITH DATES

Gently remove the pits from soft dried dates. Wrap a thin slice of prosciutto or Smithfield ham around each date and fasten with a cocktail pick. Arrange the rolls on a platter, grind a little pepper over them, and serve.

VARIATIONS:

Insert an apple slice (peeled or unpeeled) in each pitted date. Wrap the date with a strip of prosciutto. Or wrap each stuffed date with a slice of partially cooked bacon and bake in a preheated 400°F oven about 7 minutes or until the bacon is crisp and the dates are heated.

COLD MEAT AND MELON PLATTER

The time-honored Italian pairing of prosciutto with melon is beyond discussion, but here are a few other cold meats with which melon combines deliciously.

Cut a large, ripe, well-chilled cantaloupe, honeydew, casaba, Persian, or Crenshaw melon into thin wedges. Remove the seeds and fibers. With a sharp knife, cut the melon flesh away from the rind (discard the rind).

Arrange the melon wedges in the center of a large platter and sprinkle lightly with freshly squeezed and strained lemon or lime juice, if desired. Around the melon wedges arrange a selection of thinly sliced cold meats chosen from those suggested below, rolling some of the slices into cornet (cone) or cigarette shapes and folding some accordion fashion or into other decorative shapes. Garnish the platter with sprigs of watercress and serve at once with crusty French rolls and a bowl of unsalted butter.

COLD MEATS   Prosciutto
Bayonne ham
Westphalian ham
Smithfield ham
Cervelat
Genoa salami
Coppa
Mortadella
Smoked tongue
Bundnerfleisch
    (Swiss dried beef)

HAM AND FRUIT ON SKEWERS

Alternate bite-sized pieces of ham and fresh fruit such as pineapple, papaya, peaches, or green grapes on cocktail skewers. Arrange on a chilled platter and serve.

VARIATION:

Substitute homemade or best-quality pickled fruit such as pickled pineapple, peaches, cherries, grapes, or melon.

SALAMI CORNETS

Place 2 wire racks one on top of the other at right angles so that they form a grid. Cut finely grained large Italian salami into paper-thin slices. Cut each slice in half, twist it around your finger to form a cornet (cone), and brush the edges with beaten egg white. Press the edges firmly together to seal and place the cornet upright in a square of the grid. Using a pastry bag fitted with a fluted tip, pipe Herb Cheese (page 51) into the cornets. Refrigerate 1 hour. Arrange the filled cornets on a chilled platter and serve.

MORTADELLA PINWHEELS

Spread thin slices of mortadella with Herb Cheese (page 51). Roll up each slice firmly like a jelly roll. Wrap the rolls securely in aluminum foil and chill at least 3 hours. Shortly before serving, cut each roll crosswise into 4 equal pieces and spear each piece with a cocktail pick. Arrange the pinwheels on a chilled platter.

TONGUE WITH HORSERADISH SAUCE

A good buffet dish, variations of which turn up in Scandinavia as well as in Russia.

1 fresh beef tongue (2 to 3 pounds), trimmed of fat and gristle
1 medium onion, quartered
2 carrots, scraped and coarsely chopped
2 stalks celery with leaves, coarsely chopped
   Parsley sprigs
1 bay leaf
3 cloves, or 3 allspice berries
5 whole peppercorns
2 teaspoons salt
2 hard-cooked eggs, sliced
   Horseradish Sauce (page 389)

Scrub the tongue and rinse thoroughly under cold running water. Place it in a casserole just large enough to hold it and cover with cold water. Bring the water just to a simmer, skimming off the scum as it rises to the surface. When no more scum rises, add the onion, carrots, celery, 2 parsley sprigs, bay leaf, cloves or allspice, peppercorns, and salt. Simmer the tongue, partially covered, about 2 hours or until tender. Remove from the heat and let the tongue steep in its cooking liquid until it is cool enough to handle, then skin and cool to room temperature.

Slice the tongue thinly and arrange the slices in overlapping rows on a serving platter. Garnish with the egg slices and parsley sprigs and serve with the Horseradish Sauce. Makes 8 to 12 servings.

Note: Other garnishes for the tongue include lettuce leaves (use Bibb lettuce or the small, tender inner leaves of Boston lettuce), sliced fresh or pickled cucumber, sliced tomatoes, black olives, pickled small white onions, and pickled beets.

STEAK TARTARE

The preparation of this famous appetizer is not at all difficult, nor does it require the iron stomach of a Genghis Khan to be able to consume it happily. Although beef fillet or sirloin is often used, round steak is less expensive and possesses excellent flavor. Be sure to remove all fat and gristle; the meat must be absolutely lean. Also, use impeccably fresh meat and chop or grind it as close to serving time as possible.

1 pound top-quality beef fillet, sirloin, or round steak, trimmed of all fat and gristle and freshly chopped until fine-textured, or freshly ground twice
2 tablespoons finely grated mild onion
1 large garlic clove, crushed to a smooth purée
2 teaspoons Dijon-style mustard
2 teaspoons freshly squeezed and strained lemon juice
1 to 2 teaspoons Worcestershire sauce
½ cup finely chopped parsley
Salt, freshly ground pepper, and cayenne pepper to taste
Cherry tomatoes or lemon wedges
1 can (2 ounces) flat anchovy fillets, drained and chopped
½ cup capers, rinsed and drained
½ cup finely chopped shallots or mild white onion
½ cup finely chopped dill gherkins

In a medium mixing bowl combine the beef, grated onion, garlic, mustard, lemon juice, Worcestershire sauce, ¼ cup of the parsley, salt, pepper, and cayenne pepper. Mix until well blended. Taste and adjust the seasoning. Form the mixture into a mound and place it on a serving platter. Sprinkle it with the remaining ¼ cup parsley and garnish with the cherry tomatoes or lemon wedges. Surround the platter with small bowls filled with the remaining ingredients, to be added to each serving according to individual taste. Serve at once, accompanied with thin slices of pumpernickel or rye bread or buttered toast. Makes 6 servings.

VARIATION:

STEAK TARTARE BALLS

Omit the last 5 ingredients. Instead of forming the meat mixture into a mound, form it into small balls. Roll the balls in minced parsley or walnuts, or top each ball with a tiny cocktail onion or several capers. Arrange the balls on a platter and serve.

KOREAN STEAK TARTARE

An interesting switch from the standard steak tartare.

1 pound boneless beef sirloin or round
   steak, freshly ground twice or cut into
   matchstick strips
1½ tablespoons imported soy sauce
2 teaspoons sugar
¾ teaspoon imported sesame oil
1 teaspoon peanut oil or corn oil
1 tablespoon finely chopped scallions,
   including 2 inches of the green tops
1 very small garlic clove, crushed and
   finely chopped
1 teaspoon sesame seed, toasted (page
   216)
¼ teaspoon freshly ground pepper
   Salt to taste
   Narrow strips of pear

Place the meat in a large bowl. Combine all the remaining ingredients except the strips of pear in a small bowl and stir until well mixed, or put them in a jar, cover tightly, and shake vigorously. Pour over the meat and mix thoroughly. Taste and adjust the seasoning. Arrange on a platter and garnish with the strips of pear. Serve at once with thin slices of plain toast, rye or pumpernickel bread, or Melba toast. Makes 6 servings.

KIBBEH NAYYE
Raw Ground Lamb with Bulgur

Kibbeh is a mixture of bulgur and, usually, ground lamb. In its many forms it is a mainstay of life in Lebanon and Syria, eaten and enjoyed by everyone. Kibbeh Nayye is an estimable Arab version of steak tartare.

1 tablespoon olive oil or butter
¼ cup pine nuts
   Kibbeh (page 240)
   Paprika
1 lemon, cut into wedges

In a small, heavy skillet heat the oil or butter over moderate heat. Add the pine nuts, reduce the heat to low, and sauté, stirring, until lightly browned. Drain on paper towels.

Smooth the kibbeh onto a chilled flat serving platter and sprinkle lightly with paprika. Garnish with the sautéed pine nuts and lemon wedges and serve at once. Makes 4 servings.

VARIATIONS:

To the skillet in which you sautéed the pine nuts add 2 tablespoons olive oil or butter and heat over moderate heat. Add 2 medium onions, thinly sliced, and sauté, stirring frequently, until richly browned. Remove from the heat and combine with the sautéed pine nuts. Garnish the kibbeh with the mixture and lemon wedges and serve.

KIBBEH NAYYE BALLS

Instead of smoothing the kibbeh onto the platter, form it into 1-inch balls and top each ball with a sautéed pine nut. Arrange the balls on a platter lined with lettuce leaves. Sprinkle them lightly with olive oil and 2 minced scallions, including 2 inches of the green tops. Dust with the paprika, garnish with the lemon wedges, and serve with a bowl of chilled romaine lettuce hearts or Bibb lettuce leaves. To eat, place 1 or 2 kibbeh balls in the center of a lettuce leaf. Squeeze a little lemon juice over and eat out of hand.

KIBBEH

1 to 2 cups fine bulgur
½ pound very lean boneless leg of lamb, ground 3 times
1 small onion, grated
½ teaspoon cinnamon or allspice
Pinch freshly grated nutmeg
Salt, freshly ground pepper, and cayenne pepper to taste

Soak the bulgur in cold water to cover about 10 minutes. Drain and squeeze out as much moisture as possible with your hands. Combine the bulgur, lamb, onion, cinnamon or allspice, nutmeg, salt, pepper, and cayenne pepper in a mixing bowl. With hands moistened by occasionally dipping them into a bowl of lightly salted ice water, knead the mixture about 10 minutes or until it is well blended and smooth. Taste and adjust the seasoning.

GROUND MEAT AND EGG ROLLS

An Armenian version of a substantial appetizer that is enjoyed throughout the Middle East and Caucasus.

1 pound lean boneless beef or lamb,
   ground twice
1 medium onion, grated
1 medium garlic clove, crushed
3 tablespoons breadcrumbs
1 tablespoon chopped parsley
½ teaspoon curry powder (optional)
⅛ teaspoon cinnamon
⅛ teaspoon freshly grated nutmeg
   Salt and freshly ground pepper to taste
6 hard-cooked eggs, peeled
¼ cup tomato paste
¼ cup water
2 tablespoons melted butter
   Parsley sprigs

In a deep bowl combine the meat, onion, garlic, breadcrumbs, parsley, curry powder (if used), cinnamon, nutmeg, salt, and pepper and knead until thoroughly blended. Divide into 6 equal parts. Roll each egg in one part of the meat mixture to cover completely, making a round meatball. With hands moistened in water, smooth the surface of the balls and place side by side in a buttered shallow baking dish just large enough to hold them comfortably in one layer. Combine the tomato paste and water. Brush the rolls with the butter and spoon the tomato paste mixture over them. Bake in a preheated 450°F oven 15 minutes. Reduce the heat to 350°F and bake about 30 minutes longer or until browned, turning and basting with the pan juices from time to time. Remove from the oven and cool to room temperature, then cover and refrigerate until thoroughly chilled. Slice and arrange on a flat serving platter. Garnish with the parsley sprigs. Makes 6 servings.

CARNE FIAMBRE
Cold Beef, Ham, and Shrimp Sausage

A traditional buffet or picnic dish in the Dominican Republic, this makes a fine appetizer as well.

  1 pound lean ground beef, preferably ground round
  ¼ pound lean boneless ham, coarsely chopped
  ½ pound raw shrimp, shelled, deveined, and coarsely chopped
  1 medium onion, coarsely chopped
  2 medium garlic cloves, finely chopped
  1 fresh hot red or green pepper, seeded and finely chopped
  1 egg
  1¼ cups coarsely crumbled saltine crackers or as needed, crushed with a rolling pin
  2 teaspoons salt or to taste
  ¼ to ½ teaspoon freshly ground pepper
  ½ cup fresh green peas (about ½ pound before shelling), or ½ cup frozen green peas, thawed
  1 egg, well beaten
  1 large onion, thinly sliced
  1 bay leaf
    Pickled cucumbers
    Pimento-stuffed olives
    Sliced tomatoes
    Lettuce leaves

Put the beef, ham, shrimp, chopped onion, garlic, and hot pepper twice through the finest blade of a meat grinder. Or have your butcher grind the beef and ham together, then chop the shrimp, onion, garlic, and hot pepper as fine as possible yourself and combine them in a large bowl. Add the unbeaten egg, ¼ cup of the cracker crumbs, salt, and pepper and knead the mixture vigorously with a wooden spoon until it is smooth. The mixture should be firm enough to hold its shape; if necessary, beat in more cracker crumbs. Gently fold in the peas.

Spread the remaining 1 cup cracker crumbs on a piece of waxed paper and pour the beaten egg into a large, shallow baking dish. Form the meat mixture into a cylinder about 10 inches long and 3 inches in diameter and carefully roll the cylinder in the crumbs. When the meat is thickly coated on all sides, roll it in the beaten egg, then again in the crumbs.

Center the cylinder on a double thickness of cheesecloth about 20 inches long. Wrap the long sides of the cheesecloth over the meat, enclosing it completely and patting the cylinder into a smooth sausage shape. Twist the ends tightly and tie them securely with kitchen string.

In a heavy casserole large enough to accommodate the sausage comfortably, bring 3 quarts water to a boil over high heat. Add the sliced onion and bay leaf and carefully lower the sausage into the water. The water should cover the meat by 1 to 2 inches; if necessary, add more boiling water. Bring to a boil again, reduce the heat to low, cover, and simmer about 1 hour and 15 minutes or until the sausage is firm to the touch, adding more boiling water to keep the sausage covered throughout the cooking period.

Grasping the ends of the cheesecloth, lift the sausage out of the casserole and place it on a meat board. Allow it to cool to room temperature, then remove the sausage from the cheesecloth. To serve, cut the sausage crosswise into ⅓-inch-thick slices and arrange them on a platter. Accompany with the pickled cucumbers, pimento-stuffed olives, tomatoes, and lettuce leaves. Makes about 30 slices.

HOT MEAT APPETIZERS

HAWAIIAN BEEF, PINEAPPLE, AND MUSHROOM KEBABS

These kebabs are always winners at Island parties.

Marinate ¾-inch cubes of beef fillet or boneless top sirloin steak in Teriyaki Sauce (page 399) for 2 hours at room temperature. Remove the steak cubes from the marinade and thread them on small, wet bamboo skewers along with small chunks of fresh pineapple and small sautéed mushroom caps, starting and ending with the steak and leaving enough room at one end of each skewer to handle. Broil over charcoal or under a preheated broiler about 4 inches from the heat, turning frequently, about 4 minutes or until the meat is done to your taste. Arrange the skewered kebabs on a heated platter and serve at once.

VARIATION:

In a small saucepan combine the Teriyaki Sauce in which the steak was marinated with 2 teaspoons cornstarch dissolved in 2 tablespoons pineapple juice. Cook over low heat, stirring constantly, until the mixture is thickened. Serve as a dipping sauce for the kebabs.

PINCHOS MORUNOS
Moorish Brochettes

Middle Eastern influence is clearly discernible in this Spanish tapa.

2 tablespoons olive oil
2 tablespoons red wine vinegar or freshly squeezed and strained lemon juice
1 small garlic clove, finely chopped
1 small bay leaf, crumbled
½ teaspoon crushed dried thyme
½ teaspoon cumin
¼ teaspoon crushed red pepper or to taste Salt and freshly ground pepper to taste
1 pound boneless leg of lamb, trimmed of excess fat and cut into ¾-inch cubes

In a glass or ceramic bowl mix together the olive oil, vinegar or lemon juice, garlic, bay leaf, thyme, cumin, crushed red pepper, salt, and pepper. Add the lamb cubes and toss to coat them thoroughly with the mixture. Cover and refrigerate several hours, turning the meat from time to time.

Remove the lamb cubes from the marinade and thread them on small metal or wet bamboo skewers (about 5 inches long), leaving enough room at one end of each skewer to handle. Broil over charcoal (preferably) or under a preheated broiler about 4 inches from the heat, turning frequently, about 8 minutes or until the lamb is done to your taste. Arrange the brochettes on a heated platter and serve at once. Makes 4 servings.

VARIATIONS:
Omit the bay leaf, thyme, and cumin; instead use ¼ teaspoon each crushed dried oregano, basil, and rosemary. Thread the marinated lamb cubes on the skewers, alternating them with small squares of bacon, small mushroom caps, or bite-sized pieces of red bell pepper or onion.

Substitute 1 pound beef fillet or boneless top sirloin steak for the lamb.

Substitute 1 pound lean boneless pork loin for the lamb and use lemon juice rather than vinegar.

CARNITAS

Mexican Pork Cubes

An unpretentious appetizer that shows off an economical cut of meat to good advantage.

Cut 1 pound boneless pork shoulder, trimmed, into 1-inch cubes. Mix 1 medium garlic clove, puréed, with ¾ teaspoon salt and freshly ground pepper to taste. Rub the pork cubes thoroughly with the mixture and let them stand at room temperature 1 hour. Spread the pork cubes on a rimmed baking sheet. Bake in a preheated 350°F oven about 1 hour or until they are nicely browned and crisp, stirring occasionally and draining off the fat as it accumulates. Drain the pork cubes briefly on paper towels. Transfer them to a heated serving platter and serve hot with cocktail picks, accompanied with a bowl of Guacamole (page 21) or Salsa Cruda (page 399) for dipping. Makes about 20.

CHINESE BARBECUED PORK, CHICKEN LIVER, AND SCALLION ROLLS

A lively preparation that provides a most agreeable contrast of flavors and textures.

12 chicken livers
*½ cup hoisin sauce ***
*¼ cup canned plum sauce ***
¼ cup imported soy sauce
¼ cup Chinese rice wine or dry Sherry
3 tablespoons sugar
2 large garlic cloves, crushed
1 teaspoon imported sesame oil
1 pound boneless pork loin, trimmed of excess fat and cut into 24 thin slices
24 scallion pieces, each 1 inch long

*Available at Oriental groceries and some supermarkets.

Clean the chicken livers, trimming off any fat and removing any dark or green spots. Dry them with paper towels and cut them in half.

In a medium saucepan combine the chicken livers with boiling water to cover and let stand 1 minute. Drain the livers and set aside.

In a medium bowl combine the hoisin sauce, plum sauce, soy sauce, rice wine or Sherry, sugar, garlic, and sesame oil and stir until the ingredients are well blended. Transfer half the mixture to another medium bowl. Add the pork slices to one of the bowls and the reserved chicken livers to the other, turning them to coat them well with the mixture. Let marinate at room temperature 20 to 30 minutes.

Drain the pork and the livers, reserving the marinade. Wrap 1 chicken liver half and 1 scallion piece in a slice of pork and fasten the pork with a wooden pick. Repeat this procedure with the remaining chicken liver halves, scallions, and pork slices. Arrange the pork, chicken liver, and scallion rolls on a lightly oiled rimmed baking sheet and brush them with the reserved marinade. Broil under a preheated broiler about 5 inches from the heat, basting twice with the marinade, about 5 minutes on each side or until cooked through and richly browned. Arrange the rolls on a heated platter and serve at once. Makes 24.

CHINESE ROAST PORK

This perennial favorite tastes best when barbecued over charcoal, although it is also quite good when prepared in an oven. A fixture on Chinese restaurant menus, it is not difficult to make at home.

2 pounds boneless pork loin or butt, trimmed of excess fat and cut into strips about 6 inches long, 2 inches wide, and 1 inch thick
3 tablespoons imported soy sauce
1 tablespoon dry Sherry
2 tablespoons freshly squeezed and strained orange juice or unsweetened pineapple juice
2 tablespoons bean paste (also known as bean sauce, yellow bean sauce, or brown bean sauce)*
2 tablespoons ketchup
1 tablespoon sugar
1 tablespoon honey
2 large garlic cloves, coarsely chopped
½ teaspoon five-spice powder*

*Available at Oriental groceries and some supermarkets.

Lay the pork strips flat in a large, shallow dish. In a small bowl combine the remaining ingredients and stir until well blended. Pour the mixture over the pork strips, coating them thoroughly on all sides. Cover and let marinate 2 to 3 hours at room temperature or 5 to 6 hours in the refrigerator, turning the strips occasionally.

Remove all but the uppermost rack from your oven. Fill a large, shallow roasting pan with 1 to 2 inches of water and place it on the floor of the oven to catch the drippings of the pork strips as they roast and to prevent the oven from smoking. Preheat the oven to 350°F.

Insert a meat hook, curtain hook, or other S-shaped hook fashioned from heavy-duty wire into one end of each pork strip. Hang the strips, spaced far enough apart so that they do not touch each other, from the top rack of the oven over the water-filled pan. (Remember that the rack is hot, so be careful when you hang the pork strips on it.) Roast the strips 1 hour. Raise the oven heat to 425°F and roast about 10 minutes longer or until the pork strips are richly browned.

Remove the pork from the oven, take out the hooks, and cut the strips crosswise into thin slices. Arrange the slices in overlapping layers on a platter and serve hot, at room temperature, or cold. Makes about 30 slices.

CHINESE BARBECUED SPARERIBS

For this dish buy lean ribs in whole racks from a butcher rather than packaged ones, which are cracked and folded over and contain too much fat and gristle.

2 racks spareribs, uncut, each about 2 pounds
½ cup imported soy sauce
½ cup hoisin sauce *
2 teaspoons bean paste (also known as bean sauce, yellow bean sauce, or brown bean sauce) *
2 tablespoons dry Sherry
1 tablespoon freshly squeezed and strained orange juice or unsweetened pineapple juice
1 teaspoon sugar
1 teaspoon honey
1 tablespoon ketchup
3 large garlic cloves, coarsely chopped Chinese Plum Sauce I or II (page 396 or 397)
Chinese mustard

*Available at Oriental groceries and some supermarkets.

Trim off any excess fat and gristle from the spareribs. Remove the overlapping piece of meat on the bony side, if any, and reserve it for making stock.

Place the spareribs in a long, shallow dish large enough to hold them comfortably. In a small bowl combine the soy sauce, hoisin sauce, bean paste, Sherry, orange or pineapple juice, sugar, honey, ketchup, and garlic and stir until the ingredients are well blended. Brush the spareribs with the mixture, coating them evenly on both sides. Cover and let the ribs marinate 2 to 3 hours at room temperature or 4 to 5 hours in the refrigerator, turning and basting them occasionally.

Remove all but the uppermost rack from your oven. Fill a large, shallow roasting pan with 1 inch of water and place it on the floor of the oven to catch the drippings of the spareribs as they roast and to prevent the oven from smoking. Preheat the oven to 375°F.

Using meat hooks, curtain hooks, or other S-shaped hooks fashioned from heavy-duty wire, insert 4 hooks across the width of each rack of spareribs at regular intervals through the thick side. Hang the two racks, spaced far enough apart so that they do not touch each other, from the top rack of the oven over the water-filled pan. (Remember that the oven rack is hot, so be careful when you hang the spareribs on it.) Roast the spareribs 45 minutes. Raise the oven heat to 425°F and roast about 15 minutes longer or until the spareribs are crisp and richly browned.

Separate each rack into individual ribs. Arrange the ribs on a platter and serve with the plum sauce and Chinese mustard. Makes 8 servings.

Note: If the ribs are large, transfer them to a chopping board and, with a cleaver, chop each in half crosswise before serving.

VARIATIONS:

Instead of roasting the ribs in a 425°F oven the last 15 minutes, transfer them to the broiler and broil about 5 inches from the heat 6 to 7 minutes on the meat side and about 5 minutes on the bony side. Or, for a very special flavor, broil the ribs over charcoal, turning often, until they are crisp and browned.

SPARERIBS SOUTH PACIFIC

Experiencing these richly glazed and succulently moist spareribs is a sensation not to be missed.

2 pounds pork back ribs
4 quarts water
3 medium onions, quartered
4 medium garlic cloves, halved
2 tablespoons salt
¾ cup fresh pineapple chunks, puréed
¾ cup sugar
¾ cup cider vinegar
⅓ cup imported soy sauce
2 medium garlic cloves, finely chopped
1 tablespoon finely grated orange rind
2 tablespoons freshly squeezed and
    strained orange juice
¾ teaspoon dry mustard
¾ teaspoon peeled and finely grated fresh
    ginger root
¼ cup amber or dark rum
1 unpeeled orange, thinly sliced
    Parsley sprigs

Have your butcher slit each rack of ribs lengthwise so that the rib bones are 2 to 2½ inches long. Remove the overlapping piece of meat on the bony side, if any, and reserve it for making stock.

In a large, heavy saucepan combine the water, onions, halved garlic cloves, and salt. Bring to a boil, add the ribs, and simmer, uncovered, 25 minutes.

Meanwhile, in a small, heavy saucepan combine the pineapple, sugar, vinegar, soy sauce, finely chopped garlic, orange rind, orange juice, mustard, and ginger root and simmer 5 minutes, stirring to dissolve the sugar. Stir in the rum and simmer 2 minutes longer.

Drain the ribs well and transfer them to a heatproof shallow dish just large enough to hold them comfortably. Immediately pour the pineapple mixture over them, coating them evenly on all sides. Cover and refrigerate several hours or overnight, turning and basting the ribs from time to time.

Shortly before serving, arrange the ribs, still coated with the pineapple mixture, curved sides down on a rimmed baking sheet lined with aluminum foil. Bake in a preheated 400°F oven 25 minutes. Turn the ribs over, brush with the remaining glaze, and bake about 10 minutes or until richly browned. Separate the ribs and arrange them on a heated platter. Garnish with the orange slices and parsley sprigs and serve at once. Makes 8 servings.

RUMAKI

Bacon-Wrapped Chicken Livers and Water Chestnuts

Polynesian in origin, rumaki *has become cosmopolitan.*

    6 chicken livers
        Teriyaki Sauce (page 399)
    12 slices lean bacon, cut in half crosswise
    12 water chestnuts, cut in half
        Chinese Plum Sauce I or II (page 396 or
        397) (optional)

Clean the chicken livers, trimming off any fat and removing any dark or green spots. Dry them with paper towels and cut into quarters.

In a glass or ceramic bowl marinate the chicken livers in the Teriyaki Sauce 1 hour. Drain well. Wrap a half slice of bacon around each quartered chicken liver and water chestnut half and fasten with a wooden pick.

Arrange the *rumaki* on a rack in a shallow baking pan. Bake in a preheated 425°F oven about 10 minutes, turning once, or broil under a preheated broiler about 4 inches from the heat, turning frequently, about 4 minutes or until the bacon is crisp and golden. Drain on paper towels and replace the wooden picks with cocktail picks. Arrange the rumaki on a heated platter and serve hot with the plum sauce for dipping, if desired. Makes 24.

VARIATIONS:

BACON-WRAPPED SHRIMP

Substitute 24 medium shrimp, shelled and deveined, for the chicken livers. Omit the water chestnuts and plum sauce.

BACON-WRAPPED LOBSTER

Substitute the meat from 2 boiled lobster tails, cut into 24 cubes, for the chicken livers and, if desired, 24 chunks of fresh pineapple for the water chestnuts. Omit the plum sauce.

BACON-WRAPPED SCALLOPS

Substitute 24 small scallops or 12 large scallops, halved, for the chicken livers. Omit the Teriyaki Sauce, water chestnuts, and plum sauce.

BACON-WRAPPED OYSTERS

For the chicken livers substitute 24 freshly shucked oysters that have been marinated for 1 hour in fresh lemon juice seasoned with a dash of Tabasco sauce. Omit the Teriyaki Sauce, water chestnuts, and plum sauce.

BACON-WRAPPED KUMQUATS

Fill the cavities of 24 well-drained preserved kumquats with coarsely chopped peanuts. Substitute these for the chicken livers. Omit the Teriyaki Sauce, water chestnuts, and plum sauce.

BACON-WRAPPED STUFFED PRUNES

For the chicken livers substitute 24 pitted dried prunes that have been soaked in Port at least 2 hours and stuffed with toasted blanched almonds. Omit the Teriyaki Sauce, water chestnuts, and plum sauce.

BACON-WRAPPED FIGS

Substitute 24 fresh figs for the chicken livers. Omit the Teriyaki Sauce, water chestnuts, and plum sauce.

HONOLULU HAM AND PAPAYA KEBABS

½ pound lean cooked ham, cut into ¾-inch cubes
1 large, ripe papaya, peeled, seeded, and cut into ¾-inch cubes
3 tablespoons butter, melted
2 tablespoons freshly squeezed and strained lemon or lime juice
2 teaspoons sugar
½ teaspoon cinnamon
Pinch ginger

Thread the ham cubes on small, wet bamboo skewers, alternating them with the papaya cubes and leaving enough room at one end of each skewer to handle. Combine the remaining ingredients in a small bowl. Dip the skewers in the seasoned butter and broil, preferably over charcoal, 3 to 4 inches from the heat, turning and basting occasionally with the butter, about 6 minutes or until the ham and papaya are glazed and lightly browned. Arrange the skewers on a heated platter and serve hot. Makes 8 servings.

VIETNAMESE PORK PATTIES IN LETTUCE LEAVES

This Southeast Asian creation is sure to find many fans in the Western Hemisphere.

> *1 pound lean boneless pork, ground twice*
> *8 water chestnuts, finely chopped*
> *1 large garlic clove, crushed and finely chopped*
> *1 scallion, including 2 inches of the green top, finely chopped*
> *1 tablespoon imported soy sauce*
> *2 teaspoons flavorless vegetable oil*
> *1½ teaspoons freshly squeezed and strained lemon juice*
> *½ teaspoon peeled and finely grated fresh ginger root*
> *¼ teaspoon Chinese hot chili oil* *
> *¼ teaspoon sugar*
> *⅛ teaspoon salt*
> *24 Bibb lettuce leaves*
> *½ cup chopped fresh scallions, including 2 inches of the green tops*
> *½ cup chopped fresh coriander leaves*
> *½ cup chopped fresh mint leaves*
> *Dipping Sauce*

In a large bowl combine the pork, water chestnuts, garlic, scallion, soy sauce, vegetable oil, lemon juice, ginger root, hot chili oil, sugar, and salt. Mix thoroughly. Form the mixture into 24 sausage-shaped patties, each about 2 inches long and ¾ inch thick. Thread the patties on wet bamboo skewers, leaving a few inches bare at each end. Broil over charcoal or under a preheated broiler about 3 inches from the heat, turning frequently, 10 to 12 minutes or until the meat is crisped, browned, and cooked through.

Invite each guest to sprinkle a lettuce leaf with some of the scallions, coriander leaves, and mint leaves. Slide each pork patty off the skewer onto a lettuce leaf. To eat, wrap the leaf around the patty and dip into the sauce. Makes 8 servings.

DIPPING SAUCE

> *½ cup imported soy sauce*
> *¼ cup freshly squeezed and strained lemon juice*
> *3 tablespoons water*
> *2 medium garlic cloves, finely chopped*
> *2 teaspoons sugar*
> *1 teaspoon oyster sauce* *
> *1 teaspoon peeled and finely chopped fresh ginger root*
> *⅛ teaspoon cayenne pepper or to taste*

*Available at Oriental groceries and some supermarkets.

Combine all the ingredients in a small saucepan and bring to a boil over moderate heat, stirring constantly to dissolve the sugar. Reduce the heat to low and simmer 5 minutes. Remove from the heat and let cool. Divide among 8 small bowls.

PAKISTANI MEATBALLS

Richly flavored and exceptionally good.

1 pound lean boneless lamb or beef, ground twice
3 slices firm white bread, trimmed of crusts, soaked in water, squeezed dry, and crumbled
1 small onion, finely chopped
1 egg, lightly beaten
2 tablespoons milk
1 teaspoon peeled and grated fresh ginger root
½ teaspoon cumin
⅛ teaspoon cardamom
⅛ teaspoon cinnamon
    Pinch cloves
    Salt and cayenne pepper to taste
    Mint or Coriander Leaf Chutney with Yogurt (page 392)

In a medium bowl combine all the ingredients except the chutney. Knead until the mixture is well blended and smooth. Taste and adjust the seasoning. Cover and refrigerate at least 1 hour.

With hands moistened in water, shape the meat mixture into 1-inch balls. Thread the balls on long metal or wet bamboo skewers, leaving a few inches bare at each end. Broil over charcoal or under a preheated broiler about 4 inches from the heat, turning frequently, about 10 minutes or until the meat is done to your taste. Using a fork, push the meatballs off the skewers and arrange them on a heated platter. Serve at once with the chutney. Provide a small container of cocktail picks for spearing the meatballs. Makes about 30.

HAWAIIAN MEATBALL AND PINEAPPLE KEBABS

1 tablespoon imported soy sauce
1 teaspoon dry Sherry
½ teaspoon peeled and finely grated fresh ginger root
½ teaspoon sugar
1 small garlic clove, crushed and finely chopped
1 scallion, including 2 inches of the green top, very finely chopped
¾ pound lean ground beef
24 small chunks fresh pineapple (approximately)
Chinese Plum Sauce I or II (page 396 or 397)

In a medium bowl combine the soy sauce, Sherry, ginger root, sugar, garlic, and scallion and stir until the sugar is dissolved. Add the beef and knead until the mixture is well blended and smooth. Form the mixture into tiny balls. Thread the meatballs alternately with the pineapple cubes on small, wet bamboo skewers, starting and ending with a meatball and leaving enough room at one end of each skewer to handle. Broil over charcoal or under a preheated broiler about 4 inches from the heat, turning frequently, about 7 minutes or until the meat is done to your taste. Arrange the kebabs on a heated platter and serve at once with the plum sauce for dipping. Makes 6 servings.

KEFTEDAKIA
Greek Meatballs

Even a Stoic would be tempted.

2 slices firm white bread, trimmed of crusts and torn into small pieces
¼ cup dry red wine
1 pound lean ground beef
1 medium onion, finely grated
1 large garlic clove, crushed and finely chopped
2 tablespoons finely chopped parsley
1 tablespoon finely chopped fresh mint leaves
½ teaspoon cinnamon or allspice
Salt and freshly ground pepper to taste
½ cup all-purpose flour (approximately)
3 tablespoons olive oil, more if needed

Soak the bread in the wine about 5 minutes. In a large bowl combine the soaked bread and wine, ground beef, onion, garlic, parsley, mint, cinnamon or allspice, salt, and pepper. Knead until the mixture is well blended and smooth. Taste and adjust the seasoning. Cover and refrigerate at least 1 hour.

With hands moistened in water, shape the mixture into 1-inch balls. Roll the balls lightly in the flour.

In a large, heavy skillet heat the olive oil over moderate heat. Add the meatballs in batches and sauté them, turning frequently, about 10 minutes or until they are evenly browned on all sides, adding more oil to the skillet if necessary. As each batch is cooked, transfer the meatballs with a slotted spoon to a casserole or baking dish lined with paper towels and keep warm in a preheated 200°F oven while you cook the remaining meatballs. Arrange the meatballs on a heated platter. Serve hot with a small container of cocktail picks nearby for spearing the meatballs. Makes about 30.

VARIATIONS:

Instead of soaking the bread in wine, soak it in ¼ cup *ouzo* or other anise-flavored liqueur, then squeeze the bread dry (discard the ouzo) and combine with the other ingredients in the bowl, substituting ½ to 1 teaspoon crushed dried oregano for the cinnamon or allspice.

If desired, rather than grating the onion, mince it and sauté in 2 tablespoons olive oil over moderate heat, stirring often, until soft but not browned, then add to the bowl.

The *keftedakia* may be served with Herb Garlic Yogurt Sauce (page 392), using mint, or Skordalia (page 393).

POLPETTE
Italian Meatballs

An enduring favorite.

*2 slices French or Italian bread, trimmed
    of crusts and torn into small pieces*
½ cup milk
1 pound lean boneless beef, ground twice
*¼ pound sweet Italian sausage, casing
    removed*
1 egg, lightly beaten
*⅓ cup freshly grated imported Parmesan or
    Romano cheese*
*2 tablespoons finely chopped parsley,
    preferably Italian flat-leaf parsley*
2 large garlic cloves, very finely chopped
1 teaspoon finely grated lemon rind
¼ teaspoon allspice
*1 teaspoon salt or to taste
    Freshly ground pepper to taste*
*3 tablespoons olive oil or flavorless
    vegetable oil, more if needed
    Tomato Sauce (page 398)*

Soak the bread in the milk about 5 minutes, then squeeze it dry and discard the milk. In a large bowl combine the soaked bread, ground beef, sausage, egg, grated cheese, parsley, garlic, lemon rind, allspice, salt, and pepper. Knead until the mixture is well blended and smooth. With hands moistened in water, shape the mixture into 1-inch balls. Arrange the meatballs in one layer on a tray or baking sheet, cover them with plastic wrap, and chill at least 1 hour.

In a large, heavy skillet heat the oil over moderate heat. Add the meatballs in batches and sauté, turning frequently, about 10 minutes or until they are evenly browned on all sides, adding more oil to the skillet if necessary. As each batch is cooked, transfer the meatballs with a slotted spoon to a casserole or baking dish lined with paper towels and keep warm in a preheated 200°F oven while you cook the remaining meatballs. Serve the meatballs in a chafing dish with the Tomato Sauce. Provide a small container of cocktail picks for spearing the meatballs. Makes about 36.

VARIATION:

Substitute ¾ pound lean beef and ½ pound veal, both ground twice, for the beef and sausage and ½ teaspoon each crushed dried basil and oregano and ¼ teaspoon freshly grated nutmeg for the lemon rind and allspice.

CATALONIAN MEATBALLS

These hauntingly aromatic and marvelously savory meatballs are certain to bring forth shouts of ¡olé! from your guests.

2 slices firm white bread, trimmed of
  crusts and torn into small pieces
½ cup milk
1½ pounds lean boneless beef, ground
  twice, or 1 pound lean boneless beef
  and ½ pound lean boneless pork,
  ground twice
1 egg, lightly beaten
1 medium onion, finely grated
2 large garlic cloves, crushed and finely
  chopped
4 tablespoons finely chopped parsley
½ teaspoon crushed dried thyme
1 teaspoon cumin
⅛ teaspoon hot Spanish paprika
  Salt and freshly ground pepper to taste

¾ cup all-purpose flour (approximately)
  Olive oil
2 large onions, thinly sliced
1 green bell pepper, seeded, deribbed,
  and thinly sliced
1 red bell pepper, seeded, deribbed, and
  thinly sliced
¼ teaspoon crushed dried hot red pepper
  or to taste
4 large, ripe tomatoes, peeled, seeded,
  and finely chopped
1 tablespoon tomato paste
1 bay leaf
4 pimento-stuffed olives, sliced

Soak the bread in the milk about 5 minutes, then squeeze it dry and discard the milk. In a large bowl combine the soaked bread, meat, egg, grated onion, garlic, 2 tablespoons of the parsley, thyme, cumin, paprika, salt, and pepper. Knead until the mixture is well blended and smooth. With hands moistened in water, shape the mixture into 1-inch balls. Roll the balls lightly in the flour.

In a large, flameproof casserole or deep, heavy skillet heat 3 tablespoons olive oil over moderate heat. Add the meatballs in batches and sauté, turning frequently, about 10 minutes or until they are well-browned on all sides, adding more oil to the pan if necessary. As each batch is cooked, transfer the meatballs with a slotted spoon to a dish and set aside while you cook the remaining meatballs.

When all the meatballs are cooked, pour off all but 2 tablespoons of the fat from the pan. (If the oil has burned, discard it completely and add 2 additional tablespoons oil to the pan and heat.) Add the sliced onions and sauté over moderate heat, stirring frequently, until they are golden brown. Add the bell peppers and crushed red pepper and cook about 3 minutes, scraping the bottom of the skillet with a wooden spoon. Add the tomatoes, tomato paste, bay leaf, salt, and pepper and bring to a boil. Reduce the heat to low and return the meatballs to the pan. Cover the pan and transfer it to a preheated 350°F oven. Braise the meatballs about 40 minutes, basting them occasionally with the pan juices. Transfer the meatballs and sauce to a chafing dish. Sprinkle with the remaining 2 tablespoons parsley and the olives and serve with a small container of cocktail picks nearby for spearing the meatballs. Makes about 45.

LATIN AMERICAN MEATBALLS

Meatballs, known as albóndigas, *are very popular throughout Latin America, where they vary from country to country. This version is the one that tastes most like home to a Venezuelan.*

  1 pound lean boneless beef, ground twice
  ¼ pound boiled ham, ground twice
  1 medium onion, finely chopped
  ½ cup fresh breadcrumbs
  2 eggs, lightly beaten
    Salt and freshly ground pepper to taste
  3 tablespoons flavorless vegetable oil, more
    if needed
  1 onion, coarsely chopped
  4 medium-sized, ripe tomatoes, peeled,
    seeded, and coarsely chopped
  1 tablespoon chopped parsley
  1 cup dry white wine

In a bowl combine the beef, ham, finely chopped onion, breadcrumbs, eggs, salt, and pepper. Mix thoroughly and shape into ¾-inch balls.

In a large, heavy skillet heat the oil over moderate heat. Add the meatballs in batches and sauté, turning frequently, about 8 minutes or until they are evenly browned on all sides, adding more oil if necessary. As each batch is browned, transfer the meatballs with a slotted spoon to a flameproof casserole or saucepan.

In a blender or food processor combine the coarsely chopped onion, tomatoes, parsley, wine, salt, and pepper. Blend until the mixture is smooth. Pour over the meatballs, cover, and simmer over low heat about 20 minutes or until the meatballs are cooked. Serve the meatballs and sauce in a chafing dish, or drain the meatballs well and arrange them on a heated platter (reserve the sauce for another use). Provide a small container of cocktail picks for spearing the meatballs. Makes about 36.

VARIATION:

Stuff the meatballs with small pimento-stuffed olives as follows: Shape a little of the meat mixture around each stuffed olive, rolling between your palms to make a smooth ball about 1 inch in diameter. Cook and serve as directed above.

KÖTTBULLAR
Swedish Meatballs

A dish for which Sweden is justly renowned.

½ cup fresh breadcrumbs (made from rye,
    pumpernickel, or firm white bread,
    trimmed of crusts)
2 tablespoons milk
5 tablespoons butter, more if needed
½ cup finely chopped onion
1 large garlic clove, finely chopped
    (optional)
¾ pound boneless beef, ground twice
¼ pound boneless veal, ground twice
¼ pound lean boneless pork, ground twice
1 egg, lightly beaten
¼ teaspoon freshly grated nutmeg
¼ teaspoon allspice
4 tablespoons finely chopped fresh dill
    Salt and freshly ground pepper to taste
2 tablespoons flavorless vegetable oil, more
    if needed
2 tablespoons all-purpose flour
1 cup beef broth
¾ cup heavy cream

Soak the breadcrumbs in the milk about 5 minutes. Meanwhile, in a small, heavy skillet melt 1 tablespoon of the butter over moderate heat. Add the onion and garlic, if used, and sauté, stirring frequently, until the onion is soft but not browned. In a large bowl combine the beef, veal, pork, sautéed onion and garlic, soaked breadcrumbs, egg, nutmeg, allspice, 1 tablespoon of the dill, salt, and pepper. Knead until the mixture is well blended and smooth. With hands moistened in water, shape the mixture into 1-inch balls. Arrange the meatballs in one layer on a tray or baking sheet. Cover them with plastic wrap and chill at least 1 hour.

In a large, heavy skillet heat 2 tablespoons of the remaining butter and the oil over moderate heat. Add the meatballs in batches and sauté, turning frequently, until they are evenly browned on all sides. Reduce the heat to low and continue to cook the meatballs, uncovered, turning them often and adding more butter and oil to the skillet as needed, about 8 minutes or until they are fully cooked. The meatballs are done if they show no trace of pink inside when one is broken open with a knife. As each batch is cooked, transfer the meatballs with a slotted spoon to a dish and set aside while you cook the remaining meatballs.

In another large, heavy skillet or a flameproof casserole melt the last 2 tablespoons butter over moderate heat. Add the flour and cook about 1 minute without letting it brown, whisking constantly. Gradually add the beef broth and cook the mixture, stirring, until it comes to a boil, thickens, and is smooth. Reduce the heat to low and stir in the heavy cream, 2 tablespoons of the remaining dill, salt, and pepper. Simmer, stirring, 2 to 3 minutes. Add the meatballs to the pan and simmer, partially covered, 5 to 10 minutes. Transfer the meatballs and sauce to a chafing dish and sprinkle with the remaining 1 tablespoon dill. Serve with a small container of cocktail picks nearby for spearing the meatballs. Makes about 36.

VARIATION:

To serve the meatballs as part of a *smörgåsbord*, make them without the sauce. Use 3 tablespoons butter (more if needed) and 1 tablespoon dill and omit the flour, beef broth, and heavy cream. Form the meat mixture into ¾-inch balls, sauté them as directed above, and serve on a heated platter with the cocktail picks nearby. Makes about 48.

MEATBALLS STROGANOV

1 pound lean boneless beef, ground twice
½ cup breadcrumbs
¼ cup milk
1 egg
1 garlic clove, crushed and finely chopped
  Salt and freshly ground pepper to taste
2 tablespoons butter, more if needed
1 tablespoon flavorless vegetable oil, more
  if needed
  Stroganov Sauce (page 261)

In a large bowl combine the beef, breadcrumbs, milk, egg, garlic, salt, and pepper. Knead until the mixture is well blended and smooth. Taste and adjust the seasoning. With hands moistened in water, form the mixture into 1-inch balls.

In a large, heavy skillet heat the butter and oil over moderate heat. Add the meatballs in batches and sauté, turning frequently, about 10 minutes or until they are evenly browned on all sides, adding more butter and oil to the skillet if necessary. Reduce the heat to low, cover, and continue to cook the meatballs about 6 minutes. As each batch is cooked, transfer the meatballs with a slotted spoon to a casserole or baking dish lined with paper towels and keep warm in a preheated 200°F oven while you cook the remaining meatballs. Serve the meatballs in a chafing dish with the Stroganov Sauce. Provide a small container of cocktail picks for spearing the meatballs. Makes about 30.

STROGANOV SAUCE

2 tablespoons butter
1 small onion, finely chopped
2 tablespoons all-purpose flour
1 cup beef broth
2 tablespoons finely chopped fresh dill
  Salt and freshly ground pepper to taste
½ cup sour cream, at room temperature

In a small, heavy saucepan melt the butter over moderate heat. Add the onion and sauté, stirring frequently, until soft but not browned. Add the flour and cook about 1 minute without letting it brown, whisking constantly. Gradually add the beef broth and cook the mixture, stirring constantly, until it comes to a boil, thickens, and is smooth. Stir in the dill and season with salt and pepper. Remove from the heat and stir in the sour cream. Taste and adjust the seasoning.

CHINESE MEATBALLS AND KUMQUATS IN SWEET AND SOUR SAUCE

One of the most unusual variations on the meatball theme you will find.

1 pound lean boneless pork, ground twice
1 tablespoon finely chopped scallion
  (white part only)
1 tablespoon imported soy sauce
2 teaspoons dry Sherry
2 teaspoons imported sesame oil
½ teaspoon sugar
¾ teaspoon salt
⅛ teaspoon freshly ground pepper
1 egg, lightly beaten
1 tablespoon cornstarch
1 tablespoon all-purpose flour
3 cups plus 1½ tablespoons peanut oil or
  flavorless vegetable oil
1 medium-sized green pepper, seeded,
  deribbed, and cut into ¾-inch squares
16 preserved kumquats, halved
  Sweet and Sour Sauce (page 262)
1 teaspoon cornstarch dissolved in 2
  teaspoons water

In a large bowl combine the pork, scallion, soy sauce, Sherry, sesame oil, sugar, ½ teaspoon of the salt, and pepper. Knead until the mixture is well blended and smooth. Add the egg and mix well. Sprinkle with the cornstarch and flour and blend thoroughly. With hands moistened in water, shape the mixture into 1-inch balls.

Heat a wok or large deep-fat fryer over high heat until hot. Add 3 cups of the oil and heat to 375°F. Add the meatballs in batches and deep-fry, turning frequently, 1 to 2 minutes. Reduce the heat to moderate and continue to fry the meatballs, turning often until they are evenly browned on all sides. As each batch is cooked, transfer the meatballs with a slotted spoon to a casserole or baking dish lined with paper towels and keep warm in a preheated 200°F oven while you cook the remaining meatballs.

Pour off the oil remaining in the wok, or heat a large, heavy skillet over high heat until hot. Add the remaining 1½ tablespoons oil to the wok or skillet and heat 15 seconds. Add the green pepper squares and sprinkle with the remaining ¼ teaspoon salt. Cook about 2 minutes or until the pepper squares are slightly softened, stirring constantly and reducing the heat to moderate after the initial few seconds. Add the kumquats and turn them about in the hot pan several times. Add the Sweet and Sour Sauce and cook, stirring, until it is hot. Give the cornstarch mixture a quick stir to recombine it and add to the pan. Cook, stirring constantly, until the sauce begins to thicken. Add the meatballs, raise the heat, and cook, stirring quickly, until the sauce glazes the contents of the pan smoothly. Transfer to a chafing dish and serve with a small container of cocktail picks nearby. Makes about 8 servings.

VARIATION:

Substitute 1 cup fresh pineapple chunks for the kumquats.

SWEET AND SOUR SAUCE

¼ cup distilled white vinegar
3 tablespoons imported soy sauce
2 tablespoons dry Sherry
3 tablespoons ketchup
5 tablespoons sugar
½ teaspoon salt
2 tablespoons peanut oil or flavorless vegetable oil
1 large garlic clove, lightly crushed
1 tablespoon cornstarch dissolved in 3 tablespoons water
1 tablespoon imported sesame oil
½ cup water

In a small bowl combine the vinegar, soy sauce, Sherry, ketchup, sugar, and salt and stir the mixture until the sugar is dissolved. Reserve.

Heat a large, heavy skillet over high heat until hot. Reduce the heat to moderate. Add the peanut oil or flavorless vegetable oil and swirl it about in the skillet. Add the garlic and turn it a few times in the oil. Gradually add the reserved vinegar mixture, stirring, until it comes to a boil. Reduce the heat to low. Working quickly, stir the sesame oil thoroughly into the cornstarch mixture and add the mixture to the skillet. Cook, stirring, until the sauce begins to thicken. Add the water, a little at a time, and cook, stirring, until the sauce is smooth and bubbly. Remove and discard the garlic.

KIBBEH, GREEN PEPPER, AND TOMATO KEBABS

Those who are find of bulgur will welcome this and the following appetizer. For a cold *kibbeh* appetizer, please see page 240.

Prepare Kibbeh (page 240), adding 1 medium garlic clove, puréed, with the onion and substituting ¼ teaspoon cumin or to taste for the cinnamon or allspice and nutmeg. Shape the mixture into ¾-inch balls and thread them on small, wet bamboo skewers along with tiny cherry tomatoes and bite-sized squares of green pepper, beginning and ending with kibbeh balls and leaving enough room at one end of each skewer to handle. Brush the kebabs with olive oil or melted butter and broil over charcoal or under a preheated broiler about 4 inches from the heat, turning frequently, about 6 minutes or until the kibbeh balls are evenly browned and crisp on all sides. Arrange the kebabs on a heated platter and serve at once. Makes 8 to 12 servings.

FRIED STUFFED KIBBEH

One cannot recommend this particular kibbeh too highly.

¾ cup olive oil
2 tablespoons pine nuts
1 small onion, finely chopped
¼ pound lean boneless leg or shoulder or lamb, ground
⅛ teaspoon cinnamon or allspice
Salt and freshly ground pepper to taste
Kibbeh (page 240)

To make the stuffing, in a small, heavy skillet heat 2 tablespoons of the oil over moderate heat. Add the pine nuts and sauté, stirring, until golden brown. With a slotted spoon transfer the nuts to a plate and set aside. Add the onion to the oil remaining in the skillet and sauté, stirring frequently, until soft but not browned. Add the lamb and, breaking it up with a fork, cook until lightly browned. Drain off any excess fat from the skillet. Stir in the reserved pine nuts, cinnamon or allspice, salt, and pepper and mix well. Taste and adjust the seasoning, remove from the heat, and set aside.

With hands moistened in cold water, shape the *kibbeh* mixture into 1-inch balls and stuff each as follows: Hold a ball in the palm of your left hand. Place your right thumb in the center and press to make an opening. Continue pressing gently but firmly with your thumb all around the inside wall while rotating the ball in the palm of your left hand until it is hollowed out. Gently press a small spoonful of the stuffing into the opening. With moistened hands, re-shape the kibbeh around the stuffing to enclose it securely and form the ball into an oval shape.

In a large, heavy skillet heat the remaining oil over moderate heat. Add the stuffed kibbeh in batches and fry, turning frequently, until they are richly browned and crisp on all sides. As each batch is cooked, transfer the kibbeh with a slotted spoon to a baking dish lined with paper towels and keep warm in a preheated 200°F oven while you cook the remaining kibbeh. Arrange the kibbeh on a heated platter and serve. Makes about 30.

Note: The fried stuffed kibbeh are also good served at room temperature.

SPANISH CHORIZO SAUSAGE IN RED WINE

1 pound Spanish chorizo sausage (available in Hispanic markets and some specialty food shops), cut into ¼-inch-thick slices
¼ cup dry red wine
2 tablespoons chopped parsley
2 medium garlic cloves, finely chopped
   French bread cubes

Arrange the sausage slices in one layer in an attractive shallow baking dish. Pour in the wine and sprinkle with the parsley and garlic. Bake, uncovered, in a preheated 450°F oven 10 minutes. Serve hot directly from the dish, accompanied with the bread cubes for soaking up the sauce. Makes 4 servings.

RUSSIAN KIDNEYS IN MADEIRA

This and the following recipe should help to convert those who faint at the mere mention of kidneys.

  *2 pounds young veal or lamb kidneys,
    trimmed of fat
    All-purpose flour
  3 tablespoons unsalted butter
  3 slices bacon, cut into 1-inch pieces
  ½ cup finely chopped yellow onion
  ½ cup dry Madeira
  ½ cup heavy cream
    Salt and freshly ground pepper to taste
  2 tablespoons finely chopped parsley*

Rinse the kidneys and pat them dry with paper towels. Cut them crosswise into thin slices. Dredge the slices lightly in flour, shaking off the excess.

In a large enameled skillet melt the butter over moderate heat. Add the kidneys and sauté, stirring frequently, about 5 minutes or until they are evenly browned on both sides but still pink inside. Transfer the kidneys and their pan drippings to a heated platter and set aside.

Wipe the skillet dry with paper towels. Add the bacon to the skillet and sauté over moderate heat about 5 minutes or until the edges start to brown. Add the onion and reduce the heat to low. Sauté the onion in the rendered bacon fat, stirring frequently, about 5 minutes or until it is golden. Add the Madeira and heat, scraping up any browned bits that cling to the bottom and sides of the skillet. Simmer, uncovered, about 5 minutes or until the liquid in the pan is reduced by half. Stir in the heavy cream and simmer, stirring constantly, about 2 minutes or until the sauce is heated through.

Return the kidneys and the juices left on the platter to the skillet and stir to coat them thoroughly with the sauce. Cook briefly over moderate heat just until heated through. Season with the salt and pepper. Transfer to a chafing dish or a heated serving dish and sprinkle with the parsley. Serve as a first course or on a *zakuska* table (page 413). Makes 6 to 8 servings.

SPANISH KIDNEYS IN SHERRY

6 tablespoons olive oil
1 medium onion, finely chopped
2 medium garlic cloves, finely chopped
1 small bay leaf
2 tablespoons all-purpose flour
½ cup beef or chicken broth
2 tablespoons finely chopped parsley
2 pounds veal kidneys, split lengthwise in
    half, trimmed of all fat, and cut into 1-
    inch cubes
    Salt and freshly ground pepper to taste
½ cup dry Sherry

In a medium-sized, heavy skillet heat 4 tablespoons of the olive oil over moderate heat. Add the onion, garlic, and bay leaf and sauté, stirring frequently, until the onion is soft but not browned. Add the flour and mix well. Pour in the broth and cook, stirring constantly, until the mixture comes to a boil and is thick and smooth. Stir in the parsley, reduce the heat to low, and simmer 2 to 3 minutes. Remove from the heat and reserve.

In a large enameled skillet heat the remaining 2 tablespoons oil over moderate heat. Season the kidneys with salt and pepper and cook them in the oil, stirring frequently, 4 to 5 minutes or until they are evenly browned on both sides but still pink inside. Transfer the kidneys to a heated plate and pour the Sherry into the skillet. Bring to a boil over high heat, scraping up any brown particles clinging to the bottom and sides of the skillet. Return the kidneys to the skillet, stir in the reserved onion sauce, and bring to a boil. Reduce the heat to low and simmer 1 to 2 minutes. Taste and adjust the seasoning. Transfer to a heated serving dish and serve at once as a *tapa* (page 405). Makes 6 to 8 servings.

FORSHMAK

Baked Herring, Meat, and Potato Appetizer

A familiar specialty on the zakuska *table (page 413).*

  2 salt herring fillets (about ¼ pound each)
    Milk
  2 large, firm boiling potatoes (about 1
    pound), peeled
  2 tablespoons unsalted butter
  ½ cup finely chopped onion
  3 eggs, separated, at room temperature
  2 cups finely diced cooked ham, veal, or
    beef roast
  1 cup sour cream
  ¼ cup finely chopped fresh dill
    Freshly ground pepper to taste
    Tomato Sauce (page 398) (optional)

Rinse the herring fillets under cold running water and pat them dry with paper towels. Place the fillets in a medium bowl and add enough milk to cover them. Cover and refrigerate 24 hours, changing the milk from time to time. If the herring is very salty, soak it another 24 hours in fresh milk. Drain the herring well and pat dry with paper towels. Chop finely and set aside.

In a medium-sized, heavy saucepan combine the potatoes with salted water to cover. Bring to a boil over high heat. Reduce the heat to moderate, cover, and cook about 25 minutes or until the potatoes are tender. Drain the potatoes and place them in a shallow bowl. Mash them with a fork or potato masher to a medium-coarse consistency and set aside.

In a small, heavy skillet melt the butter over moderate heat. Add the onion and sauté, stirring frequently, until golden. In a large bowl beat the egg yolks lightly. Add the chopped herring, mashed potatoes, sautéed onion, diced cooked meat, sour cream, dill, and pepper and mix well. In a medium bowl beat the egg whites until they are stiff but not dry. Fold gently but thoroughly into the herring mixture. Turn the mixture into a buttered shallow 1½-quart baking dish. Bake, uncovered, in a preheated 400°F oven about 30 minutes or until the top is golden brown. Serve hot or at room temperature as part of a *zakuska* table (page 413), accompanied with the Tomato Sauce, if desired. Makes 8 servings.

CANAPÉS AND SANDWICHES

A tempting assortment of artistically assembled canapés and cocktail sandwiches can provide ideal fare for parties and receptions.

A canapé (literally, a "couch" or "sofa" in French) is a bite-sized, open-faced sandwich, the base of which serves as a platform for other ingredients that make up the topping and garnish. Although most commonly bread, the base can also be a thin pastry, crisp bland cracker, or even a vegetable or fruit.

The bread used for canapés must be a sturdy, close-grained sandwich loaf that is firm enough to be sliced thin. If freshly baked, allow it to stand unwrapped at room temperature for 24 hours to stale a bit and become even firmer. Although white bread is most versatile, it can be replaced by firm loaves of whole wheat, rye, or pumpernickel. The bread can be plain, freshly toasted, slowly dried (Melba toast), or fried golden brown in butter. Other breads that can lend interesting flavor and texture to canapés include tiny French rolls, thin French bread known as "flutes," pita bread, lavash (*Armenian cracker bread*), *Scandinavian crispbread, and miniature bagels. Instructions for using these breads will be found in individual recipes in this chapter.*

Canapé shapes range from simple squares, circles, or triangles to fanciful forms made with canapé or small cookie cutters. The size of a canapé is generally 1½ to 2 inches in diameter, if a circle, or the equivalent in other shapes, although it can be smaller or larger. To mass-produce bread-based canapés quickly and efficiently, cut a whole loaf of bread into thin lengthwise slices, then spread the slices and cut them into desired shapes. For a recipe using this technique, please see Shrimp Canapés I (page 272).

Plain or toasted bread canapé bases are usually coated with butter to help insulate them against sogginess and to provide an adhesive surface to which toppings can be anchored. Use the best quality, freshest butter available. Cream it and spread it evenly all the way to the edges of each bread base. Flavored butters (pages 34-37) are sometimes substituted for regular butter, contributing their own distinctive tastes.

Toppings and garnishes lend irresistible appeal to canapés. Toppings cover a wide spectrum encompassing seafood,

poultry, meat, eggs, cheese, vegetables, and fruit and consist of two types: a soft topping or coating that spreads easily without being runny, such as flavored butters, cheese spreads, meat or fish pastes, finely-textured egg, seafood, or meat salads, Steak Tartare (page 238) or Kibbeh Nayye (page 239), and caviar; and a firm topping, such as slices or strips of meat, fish, cheese, vegetables, or fruit.

When preparing untoasted bread-based canapés, the topping must be applied as soon as the loaf is sliced in order to prevent the bread from drying out. When the topping or garnish consists of flavored butter, the canapé should be chilled briefly to allow the butter to harden.

Canapés call for garnishes; garnishes, happily, call for imagination rather than prolonged toil in the kitchen. They contribute eye-catching flashes of color and interesting texture while imparting a contrasting nuance of flavor. Garnishes can range from a simple addition of fresh herbs, capers, olives, pimentos, radishes, or pickles to truffles and elegant swirls of flavored butters or mayonnaise. Using a set of truffle cutters, you can fashion tiny tulips, rosettes, hearts, stars, or other whimsical shapes from some of these. A pastry bag with assorted tips through which various creamy mixtures are piped can also give a professional look to canapés.

It is best not to prepare any bread-based canapés in advance but to assemble them at the last possible moment. Canapés made with untoasted bread can, however, be prepared up to two hours ahead and stored in the refrigerator under a domed cover.

The closed sandwich has long been an American culinary institution. It is therefore not surprising that a miniature, more tailored version, the cocktail sandwich, has become a standard offering on the appetizer tray. Closely related to the English tea sandwich, it is distinguished by a refined simplicity. The bread used should be firm-textured and very thinly sliced, with crusts removed, and the sandwiches cut into classic shapes: squares, triangles, fingers, diamonds, or rounds. Their exact size will depend on their shape; for example, 2 slices of bread with a filling will yield 4 cocktail sandwiches when cut into squares, triangles, or fingers. Most canapé spreads can be used for cocktail sandwiches.

Among the most intriguing-looking party sandwiches are those consisting of several layers of bread joined together with spreads that harden when chilled. Ribbon and checkerboard sandwiches (page 276) are two examples of this genre.

For best results have bread sliced by machine at a bakery. Alternatively, use a very sharp knife to cut bread at home. Bread will cut more easily if it has been chilled. Chilling is particularly recommended when preparing rolled sandwiches, for which very thinly sliced, freshly baked bread must be used. Other types of sandwiches are easier to make if the bread is a day old.

If party sandwiches are prepared several hours in advance, cover them with a dampened tea towel or plastic wrap and refrigerate until serving time. When storing, it is advisable not to mix different kinds but to wrap each kind separately to prevent the mingling of odors.

COLD CANAPÉS AND SANDWICHES

TOMATO CANAPÉS WITH GUACAMOLE AND BACON

Spread thin slices of toasted sourdough or French rolls with butter. Cover each with a thin slice of firm, ripe tomato cut to size. Top with a spoonful of Guacamole (page 20). Sprinkle with chopped crisp-cooked bacon.

VARIATIONS:

Substitute Shellfish and Avocado Filling (page 41) for the Guacamole. Omit the bacon.

Substitute Curried Crabmeat Filling (page 39) or Crabmeat and Avocado Filling (page 40) for the Guacamole. Omit the bacon, if desired.

Substitute Shrimp Filling (page 40) for the Guacamole. Omit the bacon.

Substitute Pesto Sauce (page 393) or Pesto Mayonnaise (page 388) for the Guacamole. Omit the bacon.

AVOCADO-CAVIAR CUPS

These will impart a festive note to the canapé tray.

Trim the crusts from thinly sliced white bread. Flatten each slice with a rolling pin and cut it into 4 equal squares. Brush 1¾-inch muffin cups with melted butter. Carefully press each bread square into a muffin cup. Bake in a preheated 400°F oven about 8 minutes or until lightly toasted. Transfer the toast cups to a wire rack to cool. Prepare Avocado Dip as directed in the recipe for Avocado Dip with Caviar (page 22). Fill the toast cups with the dip. Garnish each cup with ½ teaspoon of the red or black caviar.

YUGOSLAV STUFFED CUCUMBER CANAPÉS

Peel cucumbers with a fluted vegetable knife and cut them into ¾-inch-thick slices. Remove some of the seeds from the center of each slice to make tiny cups. Using a pastry bag fitted with a small fluted tip, pipe Serbian Cheese Spread (page 28) into the cucumber cups. Place the cups on dark rye or pumpernickel rounds. Garnish with finely chopped chives or paprika.

SHRIMP CANAPÉS I

Making canapés in quantity usually requires time and patience. For a quicker and easier method, try this and Smoked Salmon and Black Olive Canapés (page 273).

On a cutting board remove the crust from one of the long sides of 1 loaf unsliced white or whole wheat bread, using a serrated bread knife to cut straight down with a sawing motion. Cut the loaf lengthwise into ¼-inch-thick slices. Trim the remaining crusts. Spread each slice with Parsley and Cream Cheese Butter (page 35). Arrange 1 pound cooked, shelled, and deveined small shrimp over the buttered bread in diagonal rows. Border the bread slices with Anchovy and Cream Cheese Butter (page 36) piped through a pastry bag fitted with a star tip. Chill the slices 30 minutes. To serve, cut diagonally across each bread slice between the rows of shrimp, then cut each slice in half. Makes about 84.

SHRIMP CANAPÉS II

Prepare Shrimp Paste (page 29). Have ready 12 small shrimp, cooked, shelled, deveined, and halved lengthwise. Put half a shrimp in each of 24 well-buttered 1¼-inch miniature muffin cups. Divide the Shrimp Paste among the cups, filling each cup ¾ full. Smooth the tops, cover the cups, and chill at least 4 hours. Using a 1½-inch round fluted cutter, cut out 24 rounds from toasted white bread slices. Run the tip of a sharp knife around the edge of each cup to loosen the contents. Invert the cups onto the toast rounds. Transfer the canapés to a serving platter. Makes 24.

VARIATION:
Substitute Curried Crabmeat Filling (page 39) or Shrimp Filling (page 40) for the Shrimp Paste.

OYSTER CANAPÉS

Spread small rounds of white bread with Mustard Butter (page 35). Top each round with a chilled raw oyster dipped in Mayonnaise (page 387). Garnish with sieved hard-cooked egg yolk mixed with finely chopped chives.

FRENCH OYSTER CANAPÉS

Spread small squares of white bread with butter. Center on each a small oyster that has been poached in dry white wine about 3 minutes and thoroughly drained. Border each square with a ribbon of caviar and garnish with Mustard Mayonnaise (page 388) piped through a pastry bag fitted with a small fancy tip.

SMOKED SALMON AND AVOCADO CANAPÉS

Spread small rounds of white toast with butter. Spread half of each round with Smoked Salmon Spread (page 30) and the remaining half with mashed avocado mixed with a little fresh lemon juice. Mark the division with a strip of pimento.

SWEDISH SMOKED SALMON AND ASPARAGUS CANAPÉS

Spread small rectangles of white bread with butter. Cover with thin slices of smoked salmon. Top with cooked white asparagus tips and garnish with dill sprigs.

ANCHOVY AND PIMENTO CANAPÉS

Spread small squares of white toast with Anchovy Butter (page 36). Cover with alternating strips of anchovy fillets and pimento. Garnish with slices of green olives.

SMOKED SALMON AND BLACK OLIVE CANAPÉS

1 round loaf unsliced rye or sourdough bread
Anchovy and Cream Cheese Butter (page 36)
½ pound smoked salmon
24 pitted black olives, sliced
12 sprigs parsley

Remove the top and bottom crusts from the bread. Cut the loaf lengthwise into 3 thick slices and trim away the crusty edges. Spread each slice with Anchovy and Cream Cheese Butter.

Cut the salmon into 36 strips, each approximately ¼ inch wide. Roll each strip into a coil and reserve 12 of the coils. Arrange the remaining 24 coils around the edges of the bread slices, allowing 8 coils per slice. Place 3 olive slices in the shape of a pyramid between each coil. Cluster 4 of the reserved salmon coils and 4 parsley sprigs in the center of each bread slice. Decorate each slice with a border of the Anchovy and Cream Cheese Butter piped through a pastry bag fitted with a small fancy tip.

To serve, cut a circle about 1½ to 2 inches from the outside edge of each bread slice. Cut this outside rim into 16 equal pieces. Cut the center of each bread slice into 4 wedges. Makes 60.

CAVIAR CANAPÉS

Spread small rounds of white toast or unsweetened brioche with whipped cream cheese. Cover with caviar. Garnish with sieved hard-cooked egg and finely chopped chives.

DANISH CAVIAR CANAPÉS

Spread thin slices of white bread with butter and cut into heart shapes. Cover with red caviar. Garnish with leek or scallion rings.

FRENCH SMOKED EEL CANAPÉS

Spread small rounds of white bread with Mustard Butter (page 35). Top with thin round slices of smoked eel (available in specialty shops). Surround the eel with a border of sieved hard-cooked egg yolk and surround the egg yolk with a border of finely chopped chives.

CHICKEN LIVER BAGELETTES

Split and toast frozen Lender's Bagelettes, thawed. Spread with Chicken Liver Pâté (page 31), omitting the parsley sprigs. Top each with a small ring of red onion and sprinkle with finely chopped hard-cooked egg or crumbled crisp-cooked bacon.

KOREAN STEAK TARTARE CANAPÉS

Spread small rectangles of white or rye toast with Korean Steak Tartare (page 239). Garnish with narrow strips of pear.

FRENCH ASPIC CANAPÉS

Few canapés can rival these for sheer elegance.

Spread thin slices of white bread, cut the length of the loaf, with butter. Spread a very thin layer of Dijon-style mustard over the butter. Cover the bread with very thin slices of cold cooked ham, tongue, turkey breast, liver pâté, or smoked salmon. Brush the surfaces with a thin coating of cold but still liquid Quick Aspic (below) and chill about 10 minutes or until the aspic is set. Cut each slice of bread into rounds, squares, triangles, ovals, or crescents. Garnish each canapé with small cutouts of chilled truffle slices and hard-cooked egg white cut in flower shapes. Brush each canapé with aspic and chill the canapés again until the aspic is set. Brush each canapé a third time with aspic and, while the aspic is still liquid, decorate the edges of the canapés with a thin border of creamed butter piped through a pastry bag fitted with a small fancy tip.

QUICK ASPIC

2 cups cold, fat-free flavorful stock (fish, chicken, or beef, depending on the substance to be glazed)
1 egg white, lightly beaten
1 egg shell, slightly crushed
1 envelope unflavored gelatin
¼ cup dry Sherry, Sercial Madeira, or dry white wine

Pour the stock into a 1-quart saucepan. Stir the beaten egg white into the stock. Add the egg shell. Heat slowly to boiling about 15 minutes, stirring several times during the first few minutes. When the stock boils, remove it from the heat and let stand, undisturbed, 15 minutes. Strain the stock through a colander or sieve lined with several layers of dampened cheesecloth. Allow it to stand 15 minutes. In a small bowl sprinkle the gelatin over the Sherry, Madeira, or white wine. Let stand 5 minutes to soften. Add the gelatin mixture to the stock and stir over low heat until the gelatin is dissolved. Let stand at room temperature until ready to use. If the mixture jells before it is used, it may be reheated over low heat. Makes about 2 cups.

RIBBON SANDWICHES

With a sharp knife, trim the crust from a chilled unsliced rectangular loaf of firm, fine-textured light or dark bread. Cut the loaf lengthwise into ¼-inch-thick slices. To make each 4-layer ribbon loaf, use 4 slice of bread. Spread each slice with butter; butter both sides of the 2 slices that will be used in the center of the loaf. Spread 3 of the slices evenly with a cold creamy filling (chapter 4). Stack them on top of each other and cover with the remaining slice of bread, buttered side down. Press the layers together gently but firmly to make a compact loaf. Stack the remaining bread slice in the same manner. Wrap the stacks in a dampened tea towel or plastic wrap and chill at least 2 hours. To serve, cut the loaf crosswise into ½-inch-thick slices, then cut each slice in half either diagonally, to make triangles, or crosswise, to make rectangles.

Note: Alternate slices of light and dark bread can be used in the same sandwich, as can fillings that contrast both in flavor and color.

TRI-COLOR CHECKERBOARD SANDWICHES

With a sharp knife, trim the crusts from 2 chilled unsliced rectangular loaves of firm, fine-textured bread, one white, the other dark. Cut the loaves lengthwise into ½-inch-thick slices. Beginning with a slice of white bread, butter and stack the slices, using Herb Butter (page 35). Alternate the bread colors, ending on top with an unbuttered slice of dark bread. Press gently but firmly to make a compact loaf. Wrap in a dampened tea towel or plastic wrap and chill at least 1 hour to firm the butter.

Remove the loaf from the refrigerator and unwrap. Cut the loaf crosswise at ½-inch intervals to form ribboned slices. Spread a ribboned slice evenly with a thick layer of Herb Butter. Top with a second slice, turned around so that the dark strips rest directly over the white strips. Spread it evenly with a thick layer of the butter. Layer and butter the remaining ribboned slices in the same manner, leaving the top slice unbuttered. Press the loaf gently but firmly. Wrap and chill at least 2 hours. To serve, cut the loaf crosswise into ½-inch-thick slices, then cut each slice diagonally in half to make triangles.

Note: Other colored spreads, such as Avocado Butter (page 35), Parsley and Cream Cheese Butter (page 35), or a whipped cream cheese mixture colored with herbs can be substituted for the Herb Butter.

FINNISH SANDWICH LOAF

Present this beautifully decorated party loaf whole on a buffet, or slice it and serve as an appetizer.

  *1 large rectangular loaf rye or firm, fine-
    textured whole wheat bread (about 2
    pounds), chilled
    Butter, at room temperature
  ½ recipe Ham Filling (page 44)
  ½ recipe Egg Filling (page 38)
  ½ recipe Smoked Salmon Spread (page 30)
    Roquefort Cheese Frosting (page 278)
    Rolled thin slices of lean cooked ham
    Cooked shrimp
    Thin slices of long, thin cucumber
    (known as European or English
    cucumber)
    Cherry tomatoes
    Parsley or watercress sprigs*

With a sharp knife, trim the crust from the bread. Cut the loaf lengthwise into 4 equally thick slices.

To assemble the loaf, butter the bottom slice of bread, then spread it evenly with the Ham Filling. Cover with the second slice of bread, butter it, and spread evenly with the Egg Filling. Cover with the third slice of bread, butter it, and spread evenly with the Smoked Salmon Spread. Cover with the fourth slice of bread. Press the layers gently but firmly to make a compact loaf. Wrap the loaf in a dampened tea towel or plastic wrap and chill several hours or overnight. Unwrap the loaf and place it on a rectangular serving platter. Frost the top and sides with the Roquefort Cheese Frosting. Garnish the top of the loaf and the platter with the ham rolls, shrimp, cucumber slices, cherry tomatoes, and parsley or watercress sprigs. Chill the loaf thoroughly.

To serve, cut crosswise into ½- to ¾-inch-thick slices. These sandwiches are eaten with a fork. Makes 12 to 16 servings.

ROQUEFORT CHEESE FROSTING

3 ounces Roquefort cheese, crumbled
¼ cup butter, at room temperature
3 tablespoons sour cream
3 tablespoons Mayonnaise (page 387)
1 tablespoon finely chopped chives
1 tablespoon finely chopped parsley
1 tablespoon finely chopped fresh dill
Few drops Tabasco sauce (optional)

Combine all the ingredients in a bowl and beat until the mixture is well blended and smooth. Cover and chill.

JOURBROT
Austrian Sandwich Loaf

This luxurious offering is well worth the time and patience it demands.

12 slices firm, fine-textured white bread, each 7 inches long, 3 inches wide, and ½ inch thick
Butter, at room temperature
Chicken Liver Pâté (page 31), omitting the parsley sprigs
2 truffles, diced (optional)
4 hard-cooked eggs, sieved
¼ cup Mayonnaise (page 387)
2 tablespoons very finely chopped mild white onion
2 tablespoons finely chopped chives
Salt and freshly ground pepper to taste
1½ pounds cream cheese, at room temperature
2 tablespoons sour cream
6 ounces caviar
2 ounces anchovy paste
1 cup toasted blanched almonds, chopped
12 rolled anchovy fillets
Unpeeled chopped radishes
Parsley sprigs

With a sharp knife, trim the crusts from the bread slices. Place 3 of the slices end to end on a long board or tray. Butter them and spread evenly with a ½-inch-thick layer of the Chicken Liver Pâté, which has been mixed with the truffles, if used. Cover with 3 additional slices of bread end to end, butter them, and chill.

In a small bowl cream ¼ cup butter. Add the eggs, Mayonnaise, onion, chives, salt, and pepper and blend well. Taste and adjust the seasoning. Spread the second layer of bread with this mixture. Cover with 3 more slices of bread, butter them, and chill again.

In a medium bowl beat ½ pound of the cream cheese with the sour cream until light and fluffy. Fold in the caviar until thoroughly mixed. Spread the third bread layer with this mixture. Cover with the remaining 3 slices of bread and chill.

Whip the remaining 1 pound cream cheese with the anchovy paste. Spread the loaf thickly with some of this anchovy cream and press the chopped almonds on the 4 sides. Decorate the top of the loaf with rosettes of the remaining anchovy cream, piped through a pastry bag fitted with a fancy tip, and the anchovy fillets. Sprinkle with the radishes. Garnish the board or tray with the parsley sprigs. Chill the *jourbrot* thoroughly.

To serve, cut crosswise into ⅜-inch-thick slices. These sandwiches are eaten with a fork. Makes about 60 slices.

PINWHEEL SANDWICHES

With a sharp knife, trim the crust from a chilled unsliced rectangular loaf of firm, fine-textured white or whole wheat bread. Spread one long side of the loaf with butter and cut off a very thin slice. Spread the slice with filling.* Beginning at the narrow end, roll up the bread tightly like a jelly roll. Following this same procedure, prepare as many rolls as needed. Wrap the rolls in a dampened tea towel or plastic wrap and chill at least 2 hours. Close to serving time, cut the rolls crosswise into ⅓-inch-thick slices.

*You can use such fillings as Herb Butter (page 35), Parsley and Cream Cheese Butter (page 35), a mixture of mashed soft Camembert cheese and minced radishes, or minced watercress mixed with salt and fresh lemon juice to taste and blended with just enough Mayonnaise to bind.

STUFFED PINWHEEL SANDWICHES

Follow the recipe for Pinwheel Sandwiches (above), spreading the slices of bread with butter and filling.* Arrange a row of pimento-stuffed olives or a strip of dill gherkin along one narrow end of each bread slice before rolling it up. When the sandwiches are cut, each will have a slice of olive or gherkin in the center of the pinwheel.

*You can use any cold creamy filling (chapter 4) that is compatible with pimento-stuffed olives and dill gherkins.

MOSAIC SANDWICHES

With a canapé or small cookie cutter, cut diamond shapes out of thin slices of light and dark bread trimmed of crusts. Spread half of the light and half of the dark diamonds with butter and a cold creamy filling (chapter 4). Using a tiny diamond cutter, cut holes in the center of each of the remaining bread diamonds. Place these diamonds on top of the whole diamonds. The fillings will show through.

Note: Other shapes, such as circles, triangles, or squares, or any combination of these, can be used.

VARIATION:
You can use matching cut-out pieces of bread to cover the fillings that show through the center openings of the sandwiches. Insert light cut-outs into dark centers and dark cut-outs into light centers.

SEAFOOD SALAD SANDWICHES

Lightly butter thin slices of white or whole wheat bread. Spread half of the slices with Seafood Salad Filling (page 40). Cover with the remaining bread slices, buttered sides down. Gently press each sandwich, trim the crusts, and cut into 4 squares or triangles. Cover the sandwiches with a dampened tea towel or plastic wrap and chill at least 1 hour.

VARIATION:
Use slices of whole wheat bread for the bottoms of the sandwiches and white bread for the tops, or vice versa.

CHICKEN AND ALMOND SANDWICHES

Butter 1½-inch rounds of white bread, challah, or brioche. Spread half of the rounds with Curried Chicken Filling (page 43). Cover with the remaining bread rounds, buttered sides down. Brush the edge of each sandwich with Mayonnaise (page 387) and roll it in finely chopped toasted blanched almonds.

HAM AND WATERCRESS SANDWICHES

Spread very thin slices of pumpernickel bread with Herb Mayonnaise (page 388). Cover half of the slices with very thin slices of Westphalian or Smithfield ham or prosciutto. Top with a layer of watercress leaves, and top the watercress with the remaining bread slices, mayonnaise sides down. Gently press each sandwich, trim the crusts, and cut into 4 squares or triangles, or lengthwise into thirds. Cover the sandwiches with a dampened tea towel or plastic wrap and chill at least 1 hour.

SAVORY CORNUCOPIAS

Trim the crusts from a chilled loaf of thinly sliced white or whole wheat bread. Cut each slice into 2½-inch squares. Lightly butter both sides of the squares and fold them into cornucopias, securing the overlapping opposite corners with food picks. Arrange the horns on an ungreased baking sheet and bake in a preheated 350°F oven about 10 minutes or until lightly toasted. Remove from the oven and cool. Remove the food picks. Fill the cornucopias with any cold creamy filling (chapter 4) piped through a pastry bag fitted with a fluted tip.

BRIOCHE BASKET WITH COCKTAIL SANDWICHES

An enchanting cocktail hour treat, worth every minute of the time it takes to prepare.

> *Pâte à Brioche (below)*
> *1 egg yolk*
> *1 tablespoon milk*
> *Butter, at room temperature*
> *Chicken Liver Pâté (page 31), omitting the parsley sprigs*
> *Curried Chicken and Almond Filling (page 43)*
> *Parsley sprigs*

Prepare the Pâté à Brioche. On a lightly floured board form three fourths of the dough into a smooth ball and place it in a buttered 2-quart brioche pan. With your fingers, make a cone-shaped indentation in the center of the ball about 2½ inches in diameter at the top and about 2 inches deep. Shape the remaining dough into a teardrop and insert it, pointed end down, into the indentation in the ball. Cover the dough with a kitchen towel and let it rise in a warm place free from drafts until it reaches the top of the pan.

Beat the egg yolk with the milk. With a soft brush, paint the brioche with the mixture. Bake in a preheated 350°F oven about 45 minutes or until a rich golden brown. (If after 20 minutes the top of the brioche appears to be browning too rapidly, cover it very loosely with aluminum foil.) Remove the brioche from the oven and let stand 10 minutes. Turn it out onto a wire rack and let stand 24 hours.

With a sharp pointed knife, cut off enough of the top of the brioche to leave a flat surface. Reserve the top. Hollow out the brioche: Carefully cut around the sides to within about 1 inch of the bottom, leaving a border 1 inch thick. Slice the cut-out in half, loosen the halves carefully, and remove them. Remove the crust from the reserved top. To make the cocktail sandwiches, cut the scooped-out halves and top of the brioche into thin slices, then cut the slices into small triangles. Butter the triangles. Spread one fourth of the triangles with the Chicken Liver Pâté and one fourth with the Curried Chicken and Almond Filling. Top them with the remaining triangles, buttered sides down. Fill the brioche basket with the sandwiches and place the basket on a serving platter. Garnish with the parsley sprigs. Makes about 16 cocktail sandwiches.

VARIATIONS:

Substitute very thin slices of smoked salmon, prosciutto, Italian salami, or smoked tongue for the above fillings.

A commercially made brioche can be substituted for the homemade brioche.

PÂTE À BRIOCHE
(BRIOCHE DOUGH)

¼ cup warm water (110°F)
1 package active dry yeast
½ teaspoon plus 2 tablespoons sugar
4 cups sifted all-purpose flour
4 eggs
½ cup butter, at room temperature, cut into pieces
1½ teaspoons salt
½ cup lukewarm milk (95°F)

Pour the warm water into a small bowl. Sprinkle it with the yeast and ½ teaspoon sugar. Let the mixture stand about 5 minutes, then stir to dissolve the yeast.

Place 3 cups of the flour in a large bowl. Make a well in the center and add the eggs, butter, remaining 2 tablespoons sugar, and salt. Combine the dissolved yeast with the lukewarm milk and add it to the bowl. Mix the ingredients together until they form a soft dough.

Transfer the dough onto a lightly floured board and knead in the remaining 1 cup flour, a little at a time. Continue to knead the dough about 10 minutes or until it is smooth and elastic and no longer sticks to the board. Place the dough in a lightly greased bowl and turn over to grease the top. Cover loosely with a kitchen towel and let the dough rise in a warm place free from drafts 1½ to 2 hours or until doubled in bulk.

Punch down the dough, transfer it to a lightly floured board, and knead briefly to release air.

OPERA CLUB SANDWICHES

It is anyone's guess as to why these Scandinavian sandwiches are so named.

Assemble each sandwich as follows: Spread a slice of party rye bread with whipped cream cheese. Cover with a layer of red or black caviar. Spread a second slice of bread on both sides with whipped cream cheese with chives. Place it over the layer of caviar and sprinkle it with salt and freshly ground pepper to taste. Cover the bread with slices of smoked salmon or smoked sturgeon cut to size and top with paper-thin slices of cucumber sprinkled with finely chopped fresh dill. Spread a third slice of bread with Mayonnaise (page 387) and place it, mayonnaise side down, over the cucumber slices. Secure the sandwich with food picks at all 4 corners, then halve or quarter diagonally. Impale pitted black olives or cocktail onions on the food picks and serve.

STUFFED ROLLS

Trim the ends from long, narrow loaves of French bread or narrow rectangular hard French rolls and carefully scoop out the soft insides, leaving a shell about ¼ inch thick (reserve the soft bread for other uses). Stuff the shells with any cold thick savory filling (chapter 4), pressing firmly to prevent air pockets. Wrap each stuffed roll with aluminum foil and chill several hours. To serve, cut the chilled rolls crosswise into ⅜- to ½-inch-thick slices. Arrange the slices on a chilled platter and garnish the platter with radish roses, olives, and gherkins or pickled sweet cherry peppers.

Note: You can use 4 by 1¾-inch brown-and-serve rolls for this recipe. Bake the rolls following the package directions, cool them, and proceed as instructed above.

STEAK TARTARE LOAF

Trim the crust from a very narrow loaf of French bread. Working from each end in turn, carefully scoop out the soft insides, leaving a shell about ¼ inch thick (reserve the soft bread for other uses). With a narrow spatula, coat the cavity with butter. Chill the loaf about 20 minutes or until the butter firms. Pack the hollowed loaf with the meat mixture used in the recipe for Steak Tartare (page 238), pressing it firmly to prevent air pockets. Wrap the stuffed loaf in aluminum foil and chill several hours. To serve, cut the chilled loaf crosswise into ½-inch-thick slices. Arrange the slices on a chilled platter. Top each slice with a dollop of sour cream and garnish with 1 teaspoon of black caviar. Serve at once.

Note: The very thin loaves of French bread known as *flutes* are ideal for this recipe, but if they are unavailable you may substitute long, narrow French rolls.

HOT CANAPÉS AND SANDWICHES

MUSHROOM CANAPÉS

If you're partial to mushrooms, don't overlook these outstanding canapés.

2 tablespoons olive oil
2 tablespoons finely chopped shallots or white parts of scallions
1 pound mushrooms, finely chopped
3 tablespoons Madeira
⅓ cup heavy cream
2 ounces cream cheese, cut into small pieces
1 egg yolk, at room temperature
2 tablespoons finely chopped prosciutto
1 tablespoon freshly squeezed and strained lemon juice
¾ teaspoon finely chopped fresh thyme, or ¼ teaspoon crushed dried thyme
⅛ teaspoon freshly grated nutmeg
Salt and freshly ground pepper to taste
24 thin slices white bread
¼ cup freshly grated imported Parmesan cheese

In a large, heavy skillet heat the oil over moderate heat. Add the shallots or scallions and sauté until soft but not browned, stirring frequently. Add the mushrooms and sauté, stirring, until lightly browned. Add the Madeira and cook, stirring often, until it evaporates. Add the cream and cook until it is absorbed. Add the cream cheese and stir until it is melted. Stir in the egg yolk, prosciutto, lemon juice, thyme, nutmeg, salt, and pepper. Remove from the heat, taste and adjust the seasoning, and set aside.

Trim the crusts from the bread slices. Using a 1½-inch fluted round cutter, cut 2 circles from each slice. Arrange the circles on a baking sheet. Cover them with the mushroom mixture, allowing equal portions for each circle. Sprinkle evenly with the grated cheese, dividing it equally among the canapés. Bake in a preheated 400°F oven about 10 minutes or until lightly browned. Serve at once. Makes 48.

ROQUEFORT CANAPÉS

Arrange small rounds of pumpernickel or French bread on an ungreased baking sheet. Toast them under a preheated broiler about 4 inches from the heat until they are golden brown on one side. Spread the untoasted sides with Roquefort Cheese and Walnut Spread (page 27). Broil, watching closely, until the tops are bubbling and lightly browned. Serve at once.

CHINESE SHRIMP TOAST

Long a favorite on Chinese restaurant menus, this can easily be made at home. Use bread that is firm-textured and at least a day old; otherwise it will become greasy from absorbing too much oil. For another form of this appetizer, see Chinese Shrimp Balls (page 198).

8 thin slices slightly stale firm-textured white bread
1 egg white, lightly beaten
2 teaspoons pale dry Sherry
2 teaspoons cornstarch
½ teaspoon salt
½ teaspoon very finely chopped peeled ginger root
½ pound shrimp, shelled, deveined, and chopped to a fine paste
1 tablespoon very finely chopped fresh pork fat, bacon fat, or cooked Smithfield ham
¼ cup very finely chopped water chestnuts
1 scallion, including 2 inches of the green top, very finely chopped
2 teaspoons sesame seed
4 cups peanut oil or corn oil

Trim the crusts from the bread slices. Cut each slice into 4 squares or triangles. Arrange them side by side on a tray or baking sheet and set aside.

In a medium bowl beat the egg white until foamy. In a small bowl stir together the Sherry and cornstarch, then stir the mixture into the beaten egg white along with the salt and ginger. Add the shrimp, fat or ham, water chestnuts, and scallion and mix thoroughly until the ingredients form a paste. Spread about ½ tablespoon of the shrimp mixture evenly and firmly over each bread square or triangle. Sprinkle the sesame seed evenly over the tops and press it down lightly with the blade of a wide knife.

In a wok or deep-fryer heat the oil to 375°F. Fry the squares or triangles in batches, shrimp sides down, about 2 minutes. Turn over and fry about 1 minute or until the bread is golden brown and crisp. Drain on paper towels. Keep warm in a 200°F oven until all are fried. Serve at once. Makes 32.

BRANDIED LOBSTER CANAPÉS

Trim the ends from a rectangular French roll (sweet or sourdough) and cut the roll into ½-inch-thick slices. Arrange the slices on an ungreased baking sheet and toast under a preheated broiler about 4 inches from the heat until they are lightly browned on one side. Spread the untoasted sides of the slices with butter and spoon about 1 tablespoon Brandied Lobster Filling (page 287) over each. Sprinkle the slices evenly with shredded Gruyère cheese. Place the slices under the preheated broiler until the cheese is melted and lightly browned.

BRANDIED LOBSTER FILLING

  2 tablespoons butter
  3 tablespoons all-purpose flour
1½ cups hot milk
1½ tablespoons tomato paste
  ¼ cup brandy
  ¼ cup finely chopped parsley
  1 teaspoon finely chopped fresh tarragon,
    or ⅛ teaspoon crushed dried tarragon
    Pinch freshly grated nutmeg
    Salt and freshly ground pepper to taste
  ½ pound diced cooked lobster meat

In a medium-sized, heavy saucepan melt the butter over low heat. Add the flour and cook 1 to 2 minutes, whisking constantly. Add the hot milk and cook, stirring, 1 minute or until the mixture comes to a boil and is thick and smooth. Remove from the heat, add the tomato paste, and mix thoroughly. Stir in the brandy, parsley, tarragon, nutmeg, salt, and pepper. Add the lobster meat, return the pan to the heat, and simmer gently a few minutes, stirring occasionally. Taste and adjust the seasoning. Makes about 2 cups.

SNAIL CROUSTADES

With snails it's usually either love or hate. If love, this appetizer is for you. If hate, chances are that not even this recipe will change your mind.

  1 loaf (1 pound) day-old unsliced firm,
    fine-textured white bread
    Clarified Butter (page 288), melted
 24 canned snails (escargots), rinsed, patted
    dry, and chopped
  ½ cup dry white wine
  ½ cup chicken broth
  ¼ cup finely chopped shallots
1½ teaspoons finely chopped fresh thyme,
    or ½ teaspoon crushed dried thyme
  1 bay leaf
  ¾ cup heavy cream
  2 medium garlic cloves, finely chopped
  2 tablespoons butter
    Finely chopped parsley
    Salt and freshly ground pepper to taste

Trim the crust from the bread, then cut the loaf crosswise into 1½-inch-thick slices. Cut the slices into 1½-inch cubes. Spread the cubes in one layer on a tray or baking sheet. Set aside 2 hours in a cool, dry place, turning them from time to time.

Carefully hollow out each cube with a small knife, leaving a shell ¼ inch thick.

Cut off the sharp edges of the corners, if desired. Brush all the surfaces except the undersides with the Clarified Butter and arrange the croustades on an ungreased baking sheet. Bake them in a preheated 325°F oven about 20 minutes or until they are golden.

In a medium-sized enameled or stainless steel saucepan combine the snails, wine, chicken broth, shallots, thyme, and bay leaf. Cook, uncovered, over high heat until the liquid in the pan is reduced to about 3 tablespoons. Add the heavy cream and garlic and cook, uncovered, over high heat until the liquid in the pan is reduced to about ⅓ cup. Stir in the butter, 2 tablespoons finely chopped parsley, salt, and pepper. Remove and discard the bay leaf. Taste and adjust the seasoning.

Divide the mixture among the croustades. Heat the filled croustades on the baking sheet in a preheated 325°F oven about 10 minutes or until they are heated through. Transfer them to a serving platter and sprinkle with finely chopped parsley. Serve at once. Makes about 16.

VARIATION:

Substitute ¾ teaspoon minced fresh tarragon or ¼ teaspoon crushed dried tarragon for the bay leaf and omit the garlic. Add 1½ tablespoons Pernod with the butter and parsley.

CLARIFIED BUTTER

In a heavy saucepan melt 1 pound butter over low heat, taking care not to allow it to burn. Skim off the foam with a spoon as it rises to the top. Remove from the heat and set aside about 3 minutes, then slowly and carefully pour the clear liquid into a container, discarding the creamy residue at the bottom of the pan. Cover and refrigerate. Makes about ¾ pound.

CROSTINI ALLA TOSCANA

Tuscan Chicken Liver Toast

Always a hit both in and out of Italy.

Butter
1 small onion, finely chopped
1 small garlic clove, finely chopped
   (optional)
8 chicken livers, cleaned and dried with
   paper towels
1 sprig sage
   Salt and freshly ground pepper to taste
2 rectangular hard French rolls
   Finely chopped parsley (optional)

In a small, heavy skillet melt ¼ cup butter over moderate heat. Add the onion and garlic, if used, and sauté until soft but not browned, stirring frequently. Add the chicken livers, sage, salt, and pepper and cook until the livers are firm but still pink inside.

Discard the sage and transfer the livers to a small bowl. Mash them to a paste with a fork. Add the onion and pan juices and mix well. Taste and adjust the seasoning.

Trim the ends from the rolls and cut the rolls into ¼-inch-thick slices. Arrange the slices on an ungreased baking sheet and toast in a preheated broiler about 4 inches from the heat until they are golden brown on one side. Spread the untoasted sides with butter and the liver paste and bake in a preheated 400°F oven about 8 minutes or until heated. Serve warm, sprinkled with parsley, if desired. Makes about 24.

VARIATIONS:

A pinch of crushed dried sage or marjoram may be substituted for the fresh sage.

A few drops of freshly squeezed lemon juice and 1½ tablespoons freshly grated imported Parmesan cheese may be added to the liver paste along with the cooked onion.

ITALIAN-STYLE SPINACH TOAST

Here is a recipe to entice those who are skeptical about spinach.

1 pound fresh spinach
½ cup water
½ pound mushrooms
¼ cup butter
⅔ cup finely diced prosciutto
   Salt and freshly ground pepper to taste
¼ cup Clarified Butter (page 288)
6 slices white bread, crusts removed
⅔ cup freshly grated imported Parmesan
   cheese

Wash the spinach thoroughly under cold running water, discarding the stems and bruised leaves. Drain. Coarsely chop the spinach and combine it with the water in a large saucepan. Bring to a boil over high heat. Reduce the heat to low, cover, and simmer 5 minutes or until the spinach is wilted. Transfer to a colander and allow the spinach to drain and cool. Set aside.

Finely slice the mushroom caps, reserving the stems for another use. In a large, heavy skillet melt the butter over high heat. Add the mushrooms and sauté, stirring frequently, until they are lightly browned. Add the spinach, reduce the heat to moderate, and cook, stirring, about 3 minutes or until all the moisture has evaporated. Stir in the prosciutto, cover, and cook about 3 minutes or until the prosciutto is heated through. Season with the salt and pepper. Remove from the heat and set aside.

In a large, heavy skillet melt the Clarified Butter over moderate heat. Add the bread slices and sauté, turning them to brown lightly on both sides. Arrange the bread slices on a baking sheet. Cover them with the spinach mixture, allowing equal portions for each slice. Sprinkle the slices evenly with the grated cheese. Place the baking sheet under a preheated broiler about 4 inches from the heat, watching closely, until the cheese is lightly browned. Serve at once. Makes 6.

MOZZARELLA IN CARROZZA

Italian Fried Cheese Sandwiches

The cheese used for this robust sandwich should be made of whole milk for smoother melting and richer flavor. Purchase it from a store where it is sold in bulk and where you are sure it will be fresh.

12 slices firm-textured white bread
6 slices (¼ inch thick) whole milk
  mozzarella cheese
2 eggs
1 teaspoon water
  Pinch salt
  Fine crumbs made from day-old white
  bread
  Olive oil
8 to 10 oil-packed flat anchovy fillets,
  drained and finely chopped
1 medium garlic clove, finely chopped
1 tablespoon freshly squeezed and
  strained lemon juice

Using biscuit cutters, shape the bread and cheese into circles, making the cheese rounds about ½ inch smaller in diameter than the bread rounds. Place the mozzarella rounds between the bread rounds to make 6 sandwiches.

In a shallow dish beat together the eggs, water, and salt. Dip each sandwich into the beaten egg mixture, turning until both sides of the bread and all the edges are evenly moistened. Roll the edges of the sandwich in the breadcrumbs until they are completely covered with the crumbs. Place the sandwiches on a platter and set aside.

In a large, heavy skillet heat 1 inch olive oil until hot but not smoking. Fry the sandwiches in the hot oil about 1 minute on each side or until they are golden brown. With tongs or 2 spatulas, remove them to paper towels to drain. Transfer the sandwiches to heated individual serving dishes.

In a small bowl combine the anchovies, garlic, and lemon juice. In a small saucepan heat ¼ cup olive oil over moderate heat. Add the anchovy mixture and stir about ½ minute. Remove from the heat and spoon a little of the sauce over each sandwich. Serve at once. Makes 6.

VARIATIONS:

The bread and cheese can be cut into triangles or rectangles instead of circles, if desired.

Other firm cheeses, such as Italian Fontina, Monterey Jack, Emmenthaler, Edam, Gouda, Cheddar, Muenster, or provolone, can be substituted for the mozzarella.

PEAR AND CHEESE SANDWICHES

Use a baguette or other long, slender loaf of French bread for this inviting first course.

3 large, ripe pears
  Juice of 1 lemon, freshly squeezed and strained
1 small mild red onion, thinly sliced (optional)
1 baguette, about 18 inches long
  Parsley-Cheese Filling (page 38)
2 cups (½ pound) freshly shredded imported Parmesan cheese
1 teaspoon freshly ground pepper or to taste

Peel and core each pear and cut it into 12 to 16 slices. Brush the slices with the lemon juice to prevent darkening and set aside. If using the onion, separate it into rings. Reserve 30 of the largest rings (save the remaining onion for another use).

Cut the *baguette* in half lengthwise. Place the baguette halves, cut sides up, on a rimless baking sheet and broil them 6 inches from the heat about 6 minutes or until golden. If the halves sag in the center, turn them over and broil, crusts side up, about 3 minutes or until they straighten out.

Remove the baguette halves from the oven. Cover them with equal portions of Parsley-Cheese Filling and top with the reserved onion rings. Drain the pear slices and arrange them diagonally across each baguette half. Sprinkle evenly with the Parmesan cheese, then the pepper.

Return the baguette halves to the baking sheet and broil 8 inches from the heat about 4 minutes or until the cheese begins to melt. Cut each half into 5 pieces and serve at once on heated individual plates. Makes 10 servings.

ITALIAN CLAMS ON TOAST

36 medium cherrystone clams
2 tablespoons olive oil
2 tablespoons butter
1 medium-sized green or red bell pepper, seeded, deribbed, and very thinly sliced
   Pinch all-purpose flour
2 medium garlic cloves, crushed and finely chopped
2 tablespoons finely chopped parsley
¼ teaspoon crushed dried oregano
⅛ teaspoon crushed dried basil
   Pinch crushed red pepper or to taste
   Salt and freshly ground pepper to taste
1 medium tomato, peeled, seeded, and chopped
6 slices Italian or French bread, each about ½ inch thick

Open the clams, reserving the juice, and coarsely chop the meat.

In a small, heavy skillet heat the oil and butter over moderate heat. Add the pepper slices and sauté 5 minutes, stirring frequently. Add the chopped clams and cook, stirring, about 3 minutes. Add the flour, garlic, parsley, oregano, basil, crushed red pepper, salt, and pepper. Stir in the tomato and the reserved clam juice. Bring to a boil, reduce the heat, and simmer, uncovered, about 10 minutes, stirring occasionally. Taste and adjust the seasoning.

Toast the bread slices and arrange them on a heated serving platter. Spoon the clam mixture over the toasted slices, dividing it equally. Serve at once. Makes 6.

MINIATURE BISCUITS WITH HAM

Prepare Miniature Baking Powder Biscuits (below). Carefully split the biscuits while still warm. Spread them with butter and, if desired, Dijon-style mustard. Sandwich them with very thin slices of Smithfield or Westphalian ham or prosciutto cut to size. Serve warm.

MINIATURE BAKING POWDER BISCUITS

    2 cups sifted all-purpose flour
    3 teaspoons double-acting baking powder
    ¾ teaspoon salt
    ⅓ cup shortening
    ⅔ cup milk (approximately)

Sift together the flour, baking powder, and salt into a large bowl. Cut in the shortening with a pastry blender or 2 knives, working quickly until the mixture resembles very coarse cornmeal. While stirring lightly with a fork, add enough milk to achieve a dough that is just moist enough to leave the sides of the bowl and form a mound. Turn onto a lightly floured board and knead lightly about 30 seconds. Roll out the dough ¼ to ⅜ inch thick. Using a floured 1½-inch biscuit cutter, cut the dough into rounds, being careful not to twist the cutter. Place the rounds 1 inch apart on an ungreased baking sheet and bake in a preheated 450°F oven about 10 minutes or until golden. Makes 24 to 30.

MINIATURE HAMBURGERS

In this diminutive incarnation even the lowly hamburger can be a charming addition to an hors d'oeuvre table.

Season 1 pound lean beef round steak, ground twice, with salt and freshly ground pepper to taste. Form it into about 20 tiny hamburger patties, each 2 inches in diameter. Broil the patties in a preheated broiler about 4 inches from the heat a few minutes on each side until done to your taste. Alternatively, roll the patties lightly in flour and sauté them in 1 tablespoon each butter and corn oil or olive oil.

Prepare Miniature Hamburger Buns (below) and split them horizontally. Place a hamburger patty on the bottom half of each bun and top with a small spoonful of Fruited Tomato Relish (page 170). Cover with the top half of the bun. Serve the miniature hamburgers immediately. Makes about 20.

VARIATION:

Thin slices of Italian plum tomato and mild red or white onion may be substituted for the Fruited Tomato Relish. Top each hamburger with a slice of onion and a slice of tomato.

MINIATURE HAMBURGER BUNS

1 cup warm water (110°F)
1 package active dry yeast
1 tablespoon sugar
1½ teaspoons salt
1½ tablespoons melted butter or flavorless vegetable oil
2⅔ cups unsifted all-purpose flour plus 1 teaspoon for glaze
¼ cup cold water

Pour the warm water into a medium mixing bowl and sprinkle with the yeast. Let the mixture stand 5 minutes, then stir in the sugar, salt, and melted butter or oil. Add 2 cups of the flour, a cup at a time, beating thoroughly with a large spoon or an electric mixer at medium speed until well blended and smooth. Gradually add the remaining ⅔ cup flour, mixing it in with a spoon or an electric mixer.

Turn out the dough onto a lightly floured board and knead thoroughly, sprinkling occasionally with just enough flour to keep it from sticking. When it is smooth and elastic, form it into a ball and place in a lightly greased bowl. Turn the dough over to grease the top. Cover loosely with a kitchen towel and let rise in a warm place free from drafts about 1 hour or until doubled in size.

Punch down the dough and divide it into 20 equal pieces. Form each piece into a smooth ball and place about 2 inches apart on greased and floured baking sheets. Cover lightly with kitchen towels and let rest 30 minutes at room temperature, then flatten each ball to a circle about 2 inches in diameter. Cover and let rise in a warm place 45 to 55 minutes, or until doubled in size.

Meanwhile, in a small saucepan blend the remaining 1 teaspoon flour with the cold water until smooth. Bring to a boil over moderate heat, stirring constantly, until the mixture thickens. Remove the flour glaze from the heat, cover, and set aside.

Bake the buns in a preheated 425°F oven about 15 minutes or until golden brown. Remove from the oven and immediately brush the tops and sides of the buns lightly with the flour glaze. Serve warm, or let cool on wire racks. Makes 20.

VARIATION:

MINIATURE SAUSAGE BUNS

Instead of shaping the pieces of dough into balls, form them into sausage-shaped logs, smoothing the ends.

TINY MEATBALLS IN MINIATURE BUNS OR BISCUITS

Carefully split Miniature Hamburger Buns (page 294) or Miniature Baking Powder Biscuits (page 293). Fill with Köttbullar (page 259) or other cocktail-sized meatballs (chapter 14). Serve at once.

PORTUGUESE LINGUIÇA ROLLS

Everything a sausage lover could ask for.

> 1 pound Portuguese linguiça *sausages (or substitute Spanish* chorizo *or any other garlic-seasoned smoked pork sausages), cut into cubes*
> 1 medium onion, finely chopped
> Olive oil
> 12 small French rolls, or 20 Miniature Sausage Buns (above)

In a large, heavy skillet sauté the *linguiça* and onion in a little olive oil, stirring frequently, until nicely browned. Drain off any excess fat. Split the rolls or buns without cutting all the way through, leaving one edge as a hinge. Carefully open the rolls or buns. Pull out some of the soft insides and reserve for another use. Divide the linguiça mixture among the rolls or buns and serve. Makes 12 or 20.

FILLED COCKTAIL POPOVERS

Enough of a novelty to be a treat.

>   1 large egg
>   ½ cup unsifted all-purpose flour
>   ½ cup milk
>   ¼ teaspoon salt
>   1½ teaspoons corn oil, or 1½ teaspoons
>   butter, melted and cooled
>   Melted butter for brushing tiny tart
>   pans
>   Any of the hot cream fillings on pages
>   45–48

Combine the egg, flour, milk, salt, and corn oil or butter in the container of an electric blender and blend until smooth. (Or combine the ingredients in a mixing bowl and beat with an electric mixer until smooth.) Generously brush 16 tiny tart pans, each 1¾ inches wide and 1 inch deep, with the melted butter. Half fill the buttered pans with the batter, dividing equally. Set the half-filled tart pans on a baking sheet and bake in a preheated 400°F oven (without peeking!) about 20 minutes or until richly browned and puffed. Remove the popovers from the pans and cool them on a wire rack a few minutes.

Slit each popover on the side and stuff with one of the fillings. Arrange the filled popovers on a baking sheet and reheat in a preheated 400°F oven about 5 minutes. Serve at once. Makes 16.

VARIATION:

Instead of a hot cream filling, substitute Seafood Salad Filling (page 40), Shellfish and Avocado Filling (page 41), Clam and Cream Cheese Filling (page 41), or Spinach, Mushroom, and Ham Filling (page 44). Cool the popovers, slit and stuff them, and serve.

TORTILLA AND PITA APPETIZERS

Both Mexico and the Middle East have sent many culinary pleasures our way, not the least of which are their time-honored breads, tortillas, and pita. Revered in their native lands, where they are as much the staff of life today as they were thousands of years ago, these classic breads have been enthusiastically adopted by millions of Americans.

Tortillas and pita can be featured in a host of hearty and spirited appetizers that are ideal for casual entertaining. The following selection of recipes offers interesting innovations along with a few traditional favorites.

$\diamond$

HOMEMADE TORTILLA CHIPS

12 corn tortillas
   Flavorless vegetable oil for deep-frying
   Salt to taste

Arrange the tortillas in a stack and cut into 8 equal wedges. In a deep-fryer or large, heavy saucepan or skillet heat 2 inches oil to 375°F. Add the tortilla wedges, a stack at a time, stirring to separate. Fry, turning them with a slotted spoon until they are crisp. Transfer them to paper towels to drain. Sprinkle with the salt and serve warm or at room temperature. Makes 96 chips.

VARIATION:

Instead of frying the tortillas, you can toast them. Spread the tortilla wedges in single layers on large baking sheets and sprinkle them with salt. Bake in a preheated 400°F oven 10 minutes. Remove from the oven, turn each wedge over, and bake about 3 minutes longer.

CHORIZO-CHEESE TORTILLA WEDGES

2 Mexican or Spanish chorizo sausages
   (available at Hispanic markets and some
   specialty food shops)
6 flour tortillas (about 7 inches in diameter)
2 cups (½ pound) shredded sharp Cheddar
   cheese

Remove the casings from the sausages and crumble the meat into a small, heavy skillet. Cook over moderate heat, stirring, until lightly browned. Drain and keep warm. Arrange the tortillas on ungreased baking sheets and sprinkle them evenly with the cheese to within about ½ inch of the edges. Top with the cooked *chorizo* meat, dividing equally. Bake in a preheated 425°F oven about 8 minutes or until the edges are crisp and lightly browned. With kitchen shears, cut each tortilla into 8 wedges and serve hot. Makes 48.

MIDDLE EASTERN-STYLE TORTILLA PIZZA WEDGES

A fruitful alliance between Mexico and the Arab world.

1 pound lean ground lamb
4 scallions, finely chopped (include 2
    inches of the green tops)
1 medium tomato, peeled, seeded, and
    finely chopped
3 tablespoons pine nuts (optional)
2 medium garlic cloves, crushed and finely
    chopped
½ teaspoon cumin
½ teaspoon allspice
    Salt and freshly ground pepper to taste
8 flour tortillas (each about 7 inches in
    diameter)
1 cup (¼ pound) grated Monterey Jack
    cheese

Combine the lamb, scallions, tomato, pine nuts (if used), garlic, cumin, allspice, salt, and pepper in a bowl and mix well.

Arrange the tortillas on lightly greased baking sheets. Top with the meat mixture, dividing equally and spreading it evenly to the edges. Sprinkle evenly with the cheese. Bake in a preheated 425°F oven about 15 minutes or until the meat is browned and the edges are crisp. With kitchen shears, cut each tortilla into 8 wedges and serve hot. Makes 64.

SPICY TORTILLA TORTES

This particular appetizer should more than satisfy a stubborn craving for tortillas.

10 flour tortillas (about 8 inches in
    diameter)
 4 cups (1 pound) shredded sharp Cheddar
    cheese
 1 can (7 ounces) peeled and diced green
    chilies, drained
⅔ cup thinly sliced scallions (include 2
    inches of the green tops)
½ cup pimento-stuffed olives, sliced
    Mexican seasoning
 1 tablespoon butter, melted

Place 1 tortilla on a lightly greased, rimmed baking pan. Sprinkle evenly with about 1 cup of the cheese, then sprinkle the cheese with about 1 tablespoon each of the chilies, scallions, and olives. Lightly dust with the Mexican seasoning. Cover with a tortilla and continue layering until you have used 4 tortillas. Top the stack with 1 more tortilla and brush it with some of the melted butter. Build another torte with the remaining 5 tortillas and fillings. Bake in a pre-heated 400°F oven about 30 minutes or until lightly browned. Cut into wedges and serve at once. Makes 8 servings.

MINIATURE PICADILLO TOSTADAS

These make a winning hors d'oeuvre as well as provide a reason to have another margarita.

1 can (5½ ounces) round flat tortilla chips
  (about 2½ inches in diameter)
  Picadillo (below)
2 cups (½ pound) grated Monterey Jack or
  Cheddar cheese
½ cup sour cream or unflavored yogurt
1 avocado, peeled and cut into slices about
  1 inch long
2 medium tomatoes, diced

Arrange the tortilla chips on an ungreased baking sheet. Spoon about 1 tablespoon Picadillo on each chip. Sprinkle the cheese evenly over the chips. Place the baking sheet under a preheated broiler about 4 inches from the heat, watching closely, until the cheese is melted and lightly browned. Top each chip with a spoonful of sour cream or yogurt and garnish with a slice of avocado and several pieces of tomato. Serve at once. Makes about 50.

PICADILLO

2 tablespoons corn oil or flavorless
  vegetable oil
1 medium onion, chopped
½ cup chopped green pepper
2 large garlic cloves, finely chopped
1 pound lean ground beef
2 medium tomatoes, peeled, seeded, and
  finely chopped
⅔ cup chopped pimento-stuffed olives
⅓ cup seedless raisins
2 tablespoons brown sugar
1½ tablespoons white wine vinegar
¼ teaspoon cinnamon
⅛ teaspoon cloves
  Salt and freshly ground pepper to taste

In a heavy skillet heat the oil over moderate heat. Add the onion and sauté until soft but not browned, stirring frequently. Add the green pepper and garlic and cook, stirring, about 3 minutes. Add the ground beef and cook, stirring and breaking it up with a fork, until browned and crumbly. Add the tomatoes, olives, raisins, brown sugar, vinegar, cinnamon, cloves, salt, and pepper and cook, stirring, about 8 minutes or until most of the liquid has evaporated but the mixture is still moist. Remove from the heat. Taste and adjust the seasoning. Keep warm.

SOPES

Sopes *are an unusual south-of-the-border appetizer that combine, on a small tortilla-like shell, several popular Mexican foods: refried beans, cheese, a tomato-meat sauce, and guacamole or shredded lettuce. They are a sure bet to delight tortilla aficionados.*

SOPE SHELLS

2 cups masa harina *(corn tortilla flour)*
½ teaspoon salt
½ teaspoon chili powder
2 tablespoons flavorless vegetable oil
1 cup plus 2 tablespoons water
   Flavorless vegetable oil for frying the shells

FILLING

Frijoles Refritos *(page 303)*
Freshly grated imported Parmesan cheese
Tomato-Chorizo Sauce *(page 302)*
Guacamole *(page 20)*
Radish slices

To make the *sope* shells, in a mixing bowl combine the *masa harina*, salt, and chili powder. Add the 2 tablespoons oil and the water and mix with a spoon until a stiff dough is formed. Divide the dough into 1½-inch pieces and shape each piece into a flat circle about 3 inches in diameter. Cook the circles in a lightly greased, heavy skillet set over moderate heat about 2 minutes on each side or until they are no longer doughy. Remove from the skillet, and when cool enough to handle pinch up the edges of each partially-cooked circle to form a narrow rim. When all the shells are made, cook them on the flat side, several at a time, in ⅛ inch oil over high heat, about 2 minutes or until golden brown on the bottom. Drain on paper towels.

Spread about 2 tablespoons of the beans on each sope shell and sprinkle with 1 teaspoon cheese. Spoon 1 tablespoon Tomato-Chorizo Sauce over the cheese and top with 1 tablespoon Guacamole. Garnish with the radish slices and serve. Makes about 16.

VARIATION:

For cocktail-sized sopes, make them half the size as above, using half as much filling for each. Makes about 32.

TOMATO-CHORIZO SAUCE

1 tablespoon butter
1 small onion, finely chopped
1 large tomato, peeled, seeded, and finely
    chopped
⅛ teaspoon crushed dried oregano
    Salt to taste
3 Mexican or Spanish chorizo sausages
    (available at Hispanic markets and some
    specialty food shops)

In a small, heavy saucepan melt the butter over moderate heat. Add the onion and sauté, stirring frequently, until soft but not browned. Add the tomato, oregano, and salt and cook gently about 8 minutes, stirring occasionally. Meanwhile, remove the casings from the sausages and crumble the meat into a small, heavy skillet. Fry slowly, stirring, until the fat renders out, then brown slightly over low heat. Drain the sausages and add them to the saucepan. Cook gently about 5 minutes, stirring occasionally, until the mixture is thickened.

VARIATION:

Substitute ¾ cup diced cooked pork, chicken, shrimp, or crabmeat for the browned *chorizos*.

FIESTA NACHOS

Nachos, a favorite appetizer both in Mexico and our Southwest, can range from a simple assembly of cheese melted onto crisp-fried tortillas and enlivened with green chilies to the more elaborate but still easily prepared version below.

1 pound lean ground beef, or ½ pound
    each lean ground beef and chorizo
    sausage, casing removed
1 large yellow onion, finely chopped
    Salt and Tabasco sauce to taste
    Frijoles Refritos (page 303)
1 can (4 ounces) peeled green chilies,
    seeded and chopped
3 cups (12 ounces) shredded Monterey
    Jack or mild Cheddar cheese, or 1½ cups
    (6 ounces) of each
¾ cup prepared green or red taco sauce
¼ cup finely chopped scallions, including 2
    inches of the green tops
1 cup pitted black olives
    Guacamole (page 20)
1 cup sour cream or unflavored yogurt
1 mild red pickled cherry pepper
    Fresh coriander or parsley sprigs
    Tortilla chips

In a heavy skillet crumble the ground beef and sausage, if used. Add the onion and cook over medium-high heat, stirring constantly until the meat is browned. Spoon off and discard excess fat. Season with the salt and Tabasco sauce. Set aside.

Spread the Frijoles Refritos in a large, shallow oval or rectangular ovenproof serving dish or platter (about 10 by 15 inches). Spread the meat mixture over the beans and sprinkle with the chilies. Top evenly with the cheese, then drizzle with the taco sauce. Bake in a preheated 400°F oven about 25 minutes or until thoroughly heated through.

Remove from the oven and quickly decorate with the scallions and olives. Mound the Guacamole in the center and top with the sour cream or yogurt. Place the cherry pepper in the center of the sour cream or yogurt and garnish with the coriander or parsley sprigs. Still working quickly, surround the bean mixture with the tortilla chips, tucking them just around the edges to create a petaled flower effect. Serve immediately. To eat, scoop up the bean mixture with the tortilla chips. If possible, keep the platter hot on an electric warming tray while serving. Makes 10 servings.

FRIJOLES REFRITOS
Refried Beans

2 tablespoons flavorless vegetable oil
1 tablespoon butter
1 small yellow onion, finely chopped
1 medium garlic clove, finely chopped (optional)
2 cups cooked pinto or kidney beans
½ cup cooking liquid from the beans or as needed
Salt to taste

In a large, heavy skillet heat the oil and butter over moderate heat. Add the onion and garlic, if used, and sauté until golden brown, stirring frequently. Add the beans, ½ cup of the bean liquid, and the salt. Cook, stirring and mashing the beans with a wooden spoon or a fork until the mixture is thickened, adding more liquid, a little at a time, if it seems too dry.

DOMINICAN PICKLED CHICKEN IN PITA

An inspired coupling of Caribbean and Middle Eastern tastes.

1½ cups shredded romaine lettuce
2 small tomatoes, seeded and diced
1 large avocado, peeled and diced
½ cup pimento-stuffed olives, sliced
6 radishes, trimmed and thinly sliced
8 small pita breads, each about 4 inches in diameter, halved crosswise and heated
Pollo en Escabeche (page 215)

Fill small dishes with the shredded lettuce, tomatoes, avocado, olives, and radishes. Present the pita bread in a basket. Invite guests to fill each pita half with chicken and condiments as desired. Makes 16 sandwiches.

VARIATION:

DOMINICAN PICKLED CHICKEN IN SOPE SHELLS

Prepare *Sope* Shells (page 301). Fill each shell with a portion of the chicken. Top the chicken with some of the lettuce, and top the lettuce with some of the tomatoes, avocado, olives, and radishes. Serve at once.

TINY MEATBALLS IN PITA

Here is a welcome departure from the usual presentation of cocktail meatballs.

Fill small pita breads (about 4 inches in diameter), halved crosswise and lightly toasted, with Keftedakia (page 254), Polpette (page 255), or Catalonian Meatballs (page 256). Serve at once.

SHRIMP PIZZA WEDGES

Several years ago I was delighted to discover that pita bread can be used to make a quick and luscious version of pizza.

2 tablespoons olive oil
1 medium garlic clove, finely chopped
2 medium-sized, ripe tomatoes, peeled, seeded, and finely chopped
1 tablespoon fresh basil leaves, finely chopped, or 1 teaspoon crushed dried basil
   Salt and freshly ground pepper to taste
2 pita breads, each about 6 inches in diameter, split to make 4 circles
½ pound shrimp, cooked, shelled, and deveined
½ pound mozzarella cheese, thinly sliced
½ cup freshly grated imported Parmesan cheese or to taste

In a large, heavy skillet heat the oil over moderate heat. Add the garlic and sauté until soft but not browned. Add the tomatoes and cook, uncovered, about 15 minutes or until the mixture is thickened, stirring frequently. Sprinkle with the basil and season with the salt and pepper. Remove from the heat.

Arrange the pita circles, rough sides up and slightly apart, on a large, ungreased jelly roll pan. Spread them with the tomato sauce, top with the shrimp, and cover with the cheese slices, dividing equally. Sprinkle evenly with the grated cheese. Bake in a preheated 450°F oven about 12 minutes or until the cheese is melted and lightly browned. Cut each circle into 8 wedges and serve. Makes 32.

VARIATION:

Substitute 3 small pita breads, each about 4 inches in diameter, for the regular-sized pita breads. Cut each circle into 6 wedges. Makes 36.

MEXICAN-STYLE BEEF PIZZA WEDGES

Another successful collaboration between our neighbor to the south and the Middle East.

1 pound lean beef round steak, ground
¼ pound mushrooms, thinly sliced
1 medium garlic clove, finely chopped
4 canned peeled green chilies, finely chopped
½ teaspoon salt or to taste
3 pita breads, each about 6 inches in diameter, split to make 6 circles
Olive oil
1 medium onion, chopped
1 small green pepper, seeded, deribbed, and chopped
1 small can (2¼ ounces) sliced black olives, drained
½ cup (2 ounces) shredded Monterey Jack cheese
½ cup (2 ounces) freshly grated imported Parmesan cheese
1 medium-sized, ripe avocado
1 cup sour cream or unflavored yogurt

In a heavy skillet cook the beef over moderate heat, stirring and breaking it up with a fork until browned and crumbly. Drain off any excess fat. Add the mushrooms, garlic, chilies, and salt and cook 3 minutes, stirring constantly. Remove from the heat.

Arrange the pita circles, rough sides up and slightly apart, on 2 large, ungreased jelly roll pans. Brush each circle lightly with olive oil. Spread the meat mixture over the circles, then scatter the onion and green pepper over the meat mixture, dividing equally. Distribute the olive slices over the tops and cover with a layer of the shredded cheese. Sprinkle with the grated cheese. Bake in a preheated 450°F oven about 12 minutes or until the cheese is melted.

Peel the avocado and cut into very thin slices. Arrange over the tops of the pizzas. Garnish with the sour cream or yogurt. Cut each circle into 8 wedges and serve. Makes 48.

PEPPERONI AND GREEN PEPPER PIZZA WEDGES

½ recipe Tomato Sauce (page 398)
2 tablespoons olive oil
1 medium-sized green pepper, seeded, deribbed, and cut into strips
½ pound pepperoni (Italian dried sausage), thinly sliced
2 pita breads, each about 6 inches in diameter, split to make 4 circles
6 ounces mozzarella cheese, thinly sliced

Prepare the Tomato Sauce.

In a small, heavy skillet heat the oil over moderate heat. Add the green pepper and sauté about 3 minutes or until lightly browned, stirring frequently. Remove from the skillet and drain. Add the *pepperoni* to the skillet and sauté slightly until browned. Remove from the skillet and drain.

Place the pita circles, rough sides up and slightly apart, on a large, ungreased jelly roll pan. Spread them with the tomato sauce, then the pepperoni slices, green pepper strips, and cheese slices, dividing equally. Bake in a preheated 450°F oven about 10 minutes or until the cheese is melted and lightly browned. Cut each circle into 8 wedges and serve. Makes 32.

VARIATION:

Substitute 3 small pita breads, each about 4 inches in diameter, for the regular-sized pita breads. Cut each circle into 6 wedges. Makes 36.

MUSHROOM AND BACON QUICHE

This is my simplified version of quiche, which substitutes pita bread for the traditional pastry.

Pita-Lined Pie Plate (page 308)
1 tablespoon butter
½ cup sliced mushrooms
3 scallions, thinly sliced (include 2 inches of the green tops)
1 small garlic clove, finely chopped
4 strips bacon, cooked crisp and crumbled
¾ cup (3 ounces) shredded Gruyère or Swiss cheese
2 eggs
½ cup half-and-half
1 teaspoon Dijon-style mustard
¼ teaspoon salt or to taste

Prepare the pita-lined pie plate and set aside. In a small, heavy skillet melt the butter over moderate heat. Add the mushrooms, scallions, and garlic and sauté until lightly browned, stirring frequently. Remove from the heat and spoon the mixture evenly over the pita circle. Distribute the bacon over the mushroom mixture. Sprinkle the cheese over the bacon.

In a mixing bowl beat the eggs just until foamy, then beat in the half-and-half, mustard, and salt until well blended. Pour over the mushroom, bacon, and cheese mixture. Bake, uncovered, in a preheated 375°F oven about 30 minutes or until the quiche is puffed and lightly browned and a knife inserted in the center comes out clean. Remove from the oven and let stand 10 minutes at room temperature before serving. Makes 4 servings.

VARIATION:

Substitute ½ cup diced cooked ham or prosciutto for the bacon.

PITA-LINED PIE PLATE

1 pita bread, 6 inches or more in diameter

With a sharp knife, carefully slit the pita all the way around to make two circles. Place one circle, smooth side down, in an ungreased 8-inch glass pie plate, trimming the edges as necessary to fit the bottom (reserve the second circle for another use).

PANCAKES

Almost every country has its own version of the pancake. French crêpes, Hungarian palacsinta, Russian blini, Jewish blintzes, Scandinavian plättar, and even our own unpretentious flapjacks are just some of the examples of this universally beloved category of food, whose origins can be traced as far back as the days of ancient Egypt.

The most renowned of all pancakes are crêpes, which, for all their elegance and delicacy, are simple to prepare, remarkably sturdy, and highly versatile, accommodating a seemingly infinite variety of fillings, sauces, and seasonings. Although crêpes turn up most frequently as entrées and desserts, they can perform equally well as appetizers. Regular-sized crêpes make a sophisticated sit-down first course. Baked in miniature rounds, they provide charming and innovative hors d'oeuvre to serve with cocktails. They can also be utilized in other, more unusual ways when assembling appetizers, such as tartlike containers for quiche-type fillings, as wrappings for

Chinese egg rolls, and, crisped in the oven, as bases for dips and spreads.

The multi-talented palacsinta are to the Hungarians what crêpes, their close relatives, are to the French. There seem to be nearly as many renditions of this pancake in Hungary as there are cooks. Palacsinta can come to the table in soups, as entrées, and as desserts as well as hors d'oeuvre.

Blini, small, delicate yeast pancakes usually made with buckwheat, have sustained Russian peasants and princes for at least a thousand years. Most often served as an appetizer, they are prodigiously consumed with the combination of passion and reverence that Russians manifest toward the foods they hold most dear.

Not only blini but all of the pancakes in this chapter should meet with enthusiastic approval. They comprise a round-the-world sampler that begs to be tried.

MINIATURE CRÊPES

These can easily be made in a heavy, cast-iron Swedish pancake pan. Available in the housewares sections of department stores or in specialty kitchenware shops, the pan can be used to cook seven 3-inch crêpes simultaneously. Wrapped around savory fillings, the diminutive rounds make innovative party appetizers.

½ cup sifted all-purpose flour
1 egg
⅓ cup milk
⅓ cup water
¼ teaspoon salt
1 tablespoon butter, melted
2 tablespoons butter (approximately), melted, for brushing the pancake pan

Put the flour, egg, milk, water, salt, and 1 tablespoon melted butter in the container of an electric blender. Cover and blend at high speed 1 minute. Scrape down the sides of the container with a rubber spatula and blend again about 30 seconds or until smooth. (Or in a mixing bowl, blend the egg and flour with an electric beater or wooden spoon, then beat in the milk, water, melted butter, and salt.) Cover and refrigerate the batter 2 hours.

Heat a Swedish pancake pan over moderate heat, testing it with drops of cold water. When they splutter and evaporate instantly, the pan is ready. Brush each indentation lightly with melted butter. Stir the crêpe batter with a wire whisk or spoon. Remove the pan from the heat and, using a measuring tablespoon, dip up about 2 teaspoons of the batter and pour into each indentation. Quickly tilt the pan in all directions to allow the batter to cover the indentations completely and evenly. The batter will adhere to the pan and begin to firm up almost immediately. Return the pan to the heat and cook the crêpes 30 to 60 seconds or until the undersides are nicely browned. Turn them over with a narrow spatula, using your fingers to help, and cook about 30 seconds or until very lightly browned on the other sides. (You will note that the sides cooked first are more attractive than the second sides, which are speckled with brown spots and which are meant to remain unexposed.) Remove the crêpes from the pan and stack them on a plate. Repeat with the remaining batter, brushing the indentations lightly with butter each time if it seems necessary and stacking the crêpes as they are cooked. Makes about 35.

Note: If you do not own a Swedish pancake pan, you can use a 10-inch heavy skillet. Heat the skillet over moderate heat until drops of water flicked onto the surface evaporate at once. Brush it lightly with melted butter. Remove the skillet from the heat and, using a measuring tablespoon, dip up about 2 teaspoons of the batter and slowly pour it into the hot skillet, spreading it into a 3-inch circle (you can cook about 4 miniature crêpes at a time). Return the pan to the heat and cook the crêpes as directed above.

The crêpes can be made ahead and refrigerated or frozen. Stack them between layers of waxed paper, wrap securely in aluminum foil, and refrigerate up to several days or freeze as long as 3 months. If frozen, thaw overnight in the refrigerator or a few hours at room temperature. To prevent tearing the crêpes, be certain that they are completely thawed before using them. If your recipe does not call for heating filled crêpes in the oven, warm the refrigerated or thawed crêpes, still in their foil wrapping, in a preheated 300°F oven until heated through before filling and serving.

VARIATIONS:

MINIATURE HERB CRÊPES I

Stir 2 teaspoons each finely chopped fresh chives and parsley into the crêpe batter until well blended.

MINIATURE HERB CRÊPES II

Stir 1 teaspoon each finely chopped fresh dill, chives, and parsley into the crêpe batter until well blended.

MINIATURE SPINACH CRÊPES

Stir ¼ pound fresh spinach, cooked, squeezed dry, and finely minced or puréed, and ⅛ teaspoon freshly grated nutmeg into the crêpe batter until well blended.

MINIATURE COPENHAGEN-STYLE CRÊPES

Prepare Miniature Herb Crêpes II (pages 310–11) and Smoked Salmon Spread (page 30), using ¼ pound smoked salmon and substituting 2 tablespoons sour cream for the lemon juice. Place about 1½ teaspoons of the salmon mixture horizontally along the center of the speckled side of each crêpe and roll the crêpe into a cylinder. Arrange the filled crêpes on a platter. Dribble with melted butter and serve at once. Makes about 35.

VARIATIONS:

Substitute 1 cup Caviar and Cream Cheese Filling (page 42) or Anchovy and Cream Cheese Filling (page 36) for the Smoked Salmon Spread.

MINIATURE ITALIAN-STYLE CRÊPES

Prepare Miniature Crêpes (pages 310–11) and Gorgonzola Cheese and Prosciutto Spread (page 27) or Prosciutto Filling (page 44). Place about 1½ teaspoons of either mixture horizontally along the center of the speckled side of each crêpe and roll the crêpe into a cylinder. Arrange the filled crêpes on a platter and serve. Makes about 35.

MINIATURE VIENNESE-STYLE CRÊPES

Prepare Miniature Crêpes (pages 310–11) and 1 cup Spinach, Mushroom, and Ham Filling (page 44). Place about 1½ teaspoons of the filling horizontally along the center of the speckled side of each crêpe and roll the crêpe into a cylinder. Arrange the filled crêpes on a platter and serve. Makes about 35.

MINIATURE MEXICAN-STYLE CRÊPES

Prepare Miniature Herb Crêpes I (pages 310–11) and Shrimp and Avocado Filling (page 39). Place about 1½ teaspoons of the filling horizontally along the center of the speckled side of each crêpe and roll the crêpe into a cylinder.

Arrange the filled crêpes on a platter. Combine 2 tablespoons butter, melted, 1 tiny garlic clove, crushed to a smooth purée, dash freshly squeezed lemon juice, and salt and freshly ground pepper to taste. Dribble the warm butter sauce over the crêpes. If desired, garnish the platter with avocado slices and a few whole shelled and deveined cooked shrimp. Serve at once. Makes about 35.

MINIATURE SWISS-STYLE CRÊPES I

Prepare Miniature Herb Crêpes I (pages 310–11) and Cream Cheese and Mushroom Filling (page 37), adding 2 tablespoons freshly grated imported Parmesan cheese. Place about 1½ teaspoons of the filling in the center of the speckled side of each crêpe. Fold two opposite sides of the crêpe over the filling, then roll up to enclose the filling completely. Secure with a wooden pick.

Arrange the filled crêpes, seam sides down and slightly apart, on a buttered ovenproof platter. Brush the tops of the crêpes with melted butter. Bake, uncovered, in a preheated 350°F oven 10 to 15 minutes or until heated through. Serve at once. Makes about 35.

MINIATURE SWISS-STYLE CRÊPES II

Prepare Miniature Spinach Crêpes (page 312) and 1 cup Chicken Liver and Mushroom Filling (page 43). Fill, bake, and serve the crêpes as directed in the recipe for Miniature Swiss-Style Crêpes I (above). Makes about 35.

MINIATURE CRÊPES WITH CREAM FILLING

Prepare Miniature Herb Crêpes I (pages 310–11) and 1 cup of any of the hot cream fillings on page 363. Fill, bake, and serve the crêpes as directed in the recipe for Miniature Swiss-Style Crêpes I (above). Makes about 35.

VARIATIONS:

Substitute Miniature Spinach Crêpes (page 212) for the Miniature Herb Crêpes I and use 1 cup Cream Filling with Ham and Cheese (page 45), Cream Filling with Shellfish (page 46), or Cream Filling with Chicken Livers and Mushrooms (page 45).

RAKOTT SONKÁSPALACSINTA
Hungarian Layered Ham Pancakes

Prepare Crêpes (below) and 2 recipes Ham Filling (page 44). Place 1 crêpe, speckled side down, in a lightly buttered shallow ovenproof dish and spread with a thin layer of the Ham Filling. Cover with another crêpe and continue to stack the filling and crêpes, ending with a crêpe. Dot the top with about 1 tablespoon butter and bake in a preheated 375°F oven about 20 minutes or until heated through. With a large spatula, transfer the stacked crêpes to a heated serving platter. Garnish with sour cream and a dusting of paprika. Cut into wedges and serve at once. Makes 8 servings.

VARIATION:

Substitute Miniature Crêpes (page 310) for the Crêpes. Arrange them in stacks of 4 on a lightly buttered shallow baking pan, spreading a thin layer of the Ham Filling between each. Dot the tops with butter and bake about 10 minutes. With a small spatula, transfer the stacked crêpes to heated individual plates, allowing 1 stack for each guest. Garnish as above and serve at once.

CRÊPES

2 cups sifted all-purpose flour
4 eggs
1 cup milk
1 cup water
½ teaspoon salt
¼ cup butter, melted
2 tablespoons butter (approximately), melted, for brushing the crêpe pan

Put the flour, eggs, milk, water, salt, and ¼ cup butter in the container of an electric blender. Cover and blend at high speed 1 minute. Scrape down the sides of the container with a rubber spatula and blend again about 15 seconds or until smooth. (Or in a mixing bowl, blend the eggs and flour with an electric beater or wooden spoon, then beat in the milk, water, salt, and melted butter.) Cover and refrigerate the batter 2 hours.

Heat a 6- to 7-inch crêpe pan or heavy skillet over high heat, testing it with drops of cold water. When it splutters and evaporates instantly, the pan is ready. Brush the pan lightly with melted butter. Reduce the heat to moderate. Stir the crêpe batter with a wire whisk or spoon. Remove the pan from the heat and, using a small ladle, immediately pour about 2 tablespoons of the batter into the pan (just enough to coat the bottom of the pan thinly). Tilt the pan quickly in all directions to allow the batter to cover the bottom completely. The batter will adhere to the pan and begin to firm up almost instantly. At once pour off any excess batter back into the bowl and note the correct amount for the next crêpe. The cooked crêpes should be no more than 1/16 inch thick. If the batter seems too heavy (that is, if it spreads too slowly in the pan), thin it by stirring in a little more milk or water. Place the pan over moderate heat and cook about 1 minute or until the underside of the crêpe is nicely browned. If any holes appear in the crêpe, spoon on a little batter just to cover. Turn it over with a narrow spatula, using your fingers to help, and cook 30 to 60 seconds, or until very lightly browned on the other side. (You will note that the side cooked first is more attractive than the second side, which is a spotty brown and which is meant to remain unexposed.) Slide the crêpe onto a plate. Repeat with the remaining batter, greasing the pan lightly each time if it seems necessary and stacking the crêpes as they are cooked. Makes about 24.

HAM AND PÂTÉ CRÊPES WITH CHEESE SAUCE

A continental triumph your guests will rave about.

12 crêpes (page 314)
12 thin slices ham (Bayonne, prosciutto, Westphalian, or Smithfield)
    Chicken Liver Pâté (page 31), omitting the parsley sprigs
1 cup (1/4 pound) finely grated Gruyère cheese
1 cup heavy cream, lightly whipped
    Salt, freshly ground white pepper, and cayenne pepper to taste

Place 1 crêpe, speckled side up, on your work surface. Arrange 1 slice of ham on the crêpe and spread it with a thin layer of Chicken Liver Pâté. Fold in the sides of the crêpe and roll it up. Repeat this procedure with the remaining crêpes, ham slices, and pâté. Arrange the crêpes, seam sides down, in a buttered flameproof dish and cover with aluminum foil. Heat the crêpes in a preheated 350°F oven 15 minutes. Fold the grated cheese into the whipped cream. Season with the salt, white pepper, and cayenne pepper. Remove the aluminum foil and nap the crêpes with the cheese sauce. Place them under the broiler 4 to 6 inches from the heat until the sauce is golden and bubbly. Serve at once. Makes 12.

ITALIAN-STYLE SPINACH-CHEESE CRÊPES

This recipe combines a classic filling for manicotti with the convenience of crêpes.

1 tablespoon flavorless vegetable oil
1 large onion, finely chopped
1 medium garlic clove, finely chopped
1½ pounds fresh spinach, cooked,
    squeezed dry, and chopped
2 cups (1 pound) ricotta cheese
½ cup (2 ounces) freshly grated imported
    Parmesan cheese
2½ cups (10 ounces) shredded Italian
    Fontina, Gruyère, or Monterey Jack
    cheese (approximately)
3 eggs
1 teaspoon freshly squeezed and strained
    lemon juice
½ teaspoon freshly grated nutmeg
    Salt and freshly ground pepper to taste
16 crêpes (page 310)

In a heavy skillet heat the oil over moderate heat. Add the onion and garlic and sauté until soft, stirring frequently. Transfer the contents of the skillet to a mixing bowl. Add the spinach, ricotta, Parmesan, 1½ cups of the shredded cheese, eggs, lemon juice, nutmeg, salt, and pepper and mix well.

Divide the filling among the crêpes, spooning it down the center of each. Roll up tightly to enclose the filling. Arrange the filled crêpes in one layer in a shallow casserole or in individual ramekins. Cover with aluminum foil and bake in a preheated 375°F oven about 20 minutes or until heated through. Remove the foil and sprinkle with the remaining 1 cup shredded cheese, using 1 tablespoon for each crêpe. Bake about 5 minutes or until the cheese melts. Serve at once. Makes 8 servings.

CRÊPE QUICHES WITH BACON

Quiche is given a new look here with the substitution of crêpes for the standard pastry crust.

18 crêpes (page 310), each 5 inches in
    diameter
8 ounces cream cheese, cut into small
    chunks, at room temperature
½ cup heavy cream
1 egg
1 egg yolk
¼ cup (1 ounce) grated sharp Cheddar
    cheese or Gruyère cheese
2 tablespoons finely chopped chives
6 slices bacon, cooked crisp and finely
    crumbled
    Salt and freshly ground pepper to taste

Prepare the crêpes in a 5-inch heavy skillet, using about 1½ tablespoons batter for each crêpe. Place the cream cheese in a large mixing bowl. Gradually beat in the cream, then the whole egg and egg yolk until the mixture is well blended and smooth. Add the grated Cheddar or Gruyère cheese, chives, bacon, salt, and pepper and mix well.

Lightly grease 18 muffin cups (each 2½ inches in diameter). Lay 1 crêpe over the top of a muffin cup. Place a large spoonful of the cheese mixture in the center and push down gently with the back of a spoon. Repeat this procedure with the remaining crêpes and cheese mixture. Bake in a pre-heated 375°F oven about 30 minutes or until the centers are just firm. Cool the quiches in the cups on a rack 5 to 10 minutes. Run a narrow spatula down around the sides to loosen, then remove the quiches from the cups and serve. Makes 18.

VARIATIONS:

CRÊPE QUICHES WITH HAM
Substitute ¼ pound cooked ham, finely diced, for the bacon.

CRÊPE QUICHES WITH SHELLFISH
Substitute ¾ cup finely diced cooked lobster meat or picked over and flaked cooked crabmeat for the bacon.

BLINI
Buckwheat Pancakes

The toppings given here are among the most traditional for these beloved Russian pancakes. Some others often used are sardines, smoked whitefish, fresh or marinated mushrooms, chopped or thinly sliced hard-cooked eggs, and dill. Vodka is the usual accompaniment, although Russians have undoubtedly also consumed countless bottles of Champagne in the line of duty. Be sure to eat blini while they are still hot since they toughen as they cool.

½ cup warm water (110°F)
1½ packages active dry yeast
2 cups all-purpose flour, sifted
½ cup buckwheat flour, sifted
2 cups warm milk (110°F)
3 egg yolks, lightly beaten
1 teaspoon sugar
½ teaspoon salt
3 tablespoons butter, melted and cooled
2 cups sour cream
3 egg whites
Clarified Butter (page 288), melted
1 pound red or black caviar, or 1 pound thinly sliced smoked salmon, sturgeon, or herring fillets
Thinly sliced scallions, including 2 inches of the green tops (optional)

Pour the water into a small bowl and sprinkle it with the yeast. Let the mixture stand 2 to 3 minutes, then stir to dissolve the yeast. Set in a warm place free from drafts about 5 minutes or until the mixture almost doubles in volume.

In a large mixing bowl combine the all-purpose flour and ¼ cup of the buckwheat flour. Make a well in the center and pour in 1 cup of the warm milk and the yeast mixture. With a large wooden spoon, gradually stir the flour into the liquid ingredients, then beat until the mixture is well blended and smooth. Cover loosely with a kitchen towel and let rise in a warm place free from drafts about 3 hours or until doubled in size.

Stir the batter well and beat in the remaining ¼ cup buckwheat flour. Cover and let rise in a warm place free from drafts 2 hours. Stir the batter again and gradually beat in the remaining 1 cup warm milk, egg yolks, sugar, salt, 3 tablespoons melted and cooled butter, and 3 tablespoons of the sour cream.

In a medium mixing bowl beat the egg whites until they form stiff peaks. Fold them gently but thoroughly into the batter. Cover and let rise in a warm place free from drafts 30 minutes.

Heat a griddle or large, heavy skillet over moderate heat. Brush it lightly with Clarified Butter. Drop the batter by tablespoonfuls onto the pan without crowding. Cook the blini until they are golden brown on the bottoms. Turn and brown the other sides. Transfer the blini to an ovenproof dish and keep them warm in a preheated 200°F oven while you cook the remaining pancakes in the same manner, buttering the pan as necessary.

Serve the blini hot, stacked in two piles with the edges slightly overlapping and loosely covered with a napkin. Accompany with melted Clarified Butter, the remaining sour cream, caviar or smoked fish, and, if desired, the scallions. To eat, spread each pancake with Clarified Butter, top with a mound of caviar or a slice of smoked fish and a spoonful of sour cream and, if you like, garnish with a few slices of scallion. Makes about 42.

FILLED MANDARIN PANCAKES

A sure conversation maker, this recipe utilizes the same thin pancakes that are called for in the celebrated Chinese classic Peking duck.

> *Mandarin Pancakes (below), prepared in advance and reheated*
> *Pork Filling (page 321)*
> *Chicken Filling (page 322)*
> *Egg and Shrimp Filling (page 322)*
> *2 bunches scallions, including 2 inches of the green tops, cut into thin slivers about 2½ inches long*
> *2 heads Boston lettuce (use only the inner leaves), or 1 bunch fresh coriander or watercress*
> *Chinese Plum Sauce I (page 396), Chinese Plum Sauce II (page 397), or canned hoisin sauce (available in Oriental food markets)*
> *Chinese hot mustard*

Place the heated pancakes, the three fillings, scallions, lettuce leaves or coriander or watercress, plum or hoisin sauce, and mustard on the table.

Assemble each pork pancake as follows: Lay a pancake flat on a plate. Spread it with a little of the plum or hoisin sauce. Place a few strips of the pork along the middle of the pancake and top with a few scallion slivers. Add some lettuce, coriander, or watercress. Fold the lower end of the pancake over the filling, then bring both sides over to enclose. Roll up the pancake cigarette fashion. Pick up with your fingers to eat.

Make chicken pancakes in the same manner as pork pancakes, substituting Chicken Filling for the pork. Omit the scallion slivers.

Make egg and shrimp pancakes in the same manner as pork pancakes, substituting Egg and Shrimp Filling for the pork and mustard for the plum or hoisin sauce. Makes 4 to 6 servings.

MANDARIN PANCAKES

> *2 cups sifted all-purpose flour*
> *¾ cup boiling water*
> *1 to 2 tablespoons imported sesame oil*

Sift the flour into a mixing bowl and make a well in the center. Pour the boiling water into the well. Using a wooden spoon, gradually mix together the water and flour until a soft dough is formed. Transfer the dough to a lightly floured surface and knead about 10 minutes, or until smooth and elastic. Cover with a damp kitchen towel and let rest 15 minutes. On a lightly floured board roll out the dough into a circle about ¼ inch thick. With a 2½-inch cookie cutter cut the dough into circles. Knead scraps together, roll out again, and cut more circles. Brush half of the circles lightly with the sesame oil. Top them, sandwich fashion, with the remaining unoiled circles. With a rolling pin flatten each pair into a 6-inch circle, rotating the sandwich as needed in a clockwise direction as you roll so that the circle keeps its shape. Turn it once to roll both sides. Take care not to allow creases to form in the pancakes as you roll. Cover the pancakes with a dry towel.

Heat an ungreased 8-inch skillet over medium-high heat. Cook the pancakes, one at a time, in the skillet, turning them over as they puff up and little bubbles appear on the surface. Cook them on the other side in the same manner. Do not allow the pancakes to brown; although a few light brown spots will do no harm, they become dry and brittle if overcooked. As each pancake is done, gently separate the halves while still warm. Stack and keep covered while you make the remaining pancakes. Serve the pancakes at once, or wrap them in aluminum foil and refrigerate up to 2 days.

To reheat the pancakes for serving, either remove them from the foil and steam them in a steamer for 10 minutes or warm them, still wrapped in foil, in a preheated 350°F oven about 10 minutes. Serve in a napkin-lined basket to keep warm. Makes 24.

PORK FILLING

1 pound pork tenderloin
1 small onion, finely chopped
1 medium garlic clove, finely chopped
⅓ cup imported soy sauce
2 tablespoons dry Sherry
4 slices fresh ginger root

Place the pork in a bowl. Combine the remaining ingredients and pour the mixture over the pork. Cover and refrigerate at least 4 hours or overnight. Remove the meat from the marinade and roast, uncovered, in a preheated 375°F oven, basting occasionally with the marinade, about 40 minutes or until a meat thermometer in the center registers 175°F. Cool, then cut into thin strips and arrange on a serving platter.

CHICKEN FILLING

1½ pounds chicken breasts, skinned,
   boned, and cut into 1½-inch pieces
1 bunch leeks, or 2 bunches scallions
   (include 2 inches of the green tops of
   the scallions)
2 tablespoons dry Sherry
1 tablespoon imported soy sauce
1 teaspoon cornstarch
½ teaspoon sugar
1 tablespoon peanut oil or flavorless
   vegetable oil

Dry the chicken pieces with paper towels and set aside. Wash the leeks or scallions well. Trim away the tough green portions of the leeks. Cut into 2-inch lengths, then cut into ¼-inch-thick strips. Reserve. In a small pitcher or bowl combine the Sherry, soy sauce, cornstarch, and sugar and mix well.

In a wok or heavy skillet heat the oil over medium-high heat. Add the chicken, then the leeks or scallions and cook, stirring, about 4 minutes or until the chicken is just tender. Stir the Sherry mixture to blend together and add to the pan. Cook, stirring, about 1 minute. Transfer to a heated serving bowl.

EGG AND SHRIMP FILLING

8 eggs
⅓ cup milk
¾ teaspoon salt
½ teaspoon peeled and grated fresh ginger
   root
1 tablespoon peanut oil or flavorless
   vegetable oil
6 ounces cooked and shelled tiny shrimp
½ cup fresh peas or ½ cup frozen peas,
   thawed

In a mixing bowl combine the eggs, milk, salt, and ginger root and beat with a fork until well blended. In a wok or heavy skillet heat the oil over medium-high heat. Add the egg mixture and cook, stirring, until partially set. Add the shrimp and peas and cook about 1 minute, or until the eggs are softly scrambled. Transfer to a heated serving dish.

FRITTERS AND CROQUETTES

For all their tempting appearance, fritters and croquettes often turn out to consist of simple components, or they can be the exalted reincarnations of yesterday's leftovers. Fritters, puffed crisp composites of batter and ingredients that are fried in deep fat, can make delectable choices for any course of a meal, from appetizer to dessert. Served warm and small enough to be eaten in one bite from a food pick, they are certain to lend a festive note to an hors d'oeuvre tray. Croquettes are a combination of minced or puréed savory foods bound with butter, cream, egg yolks, or a thick sauce, shaped, coated with egg and breadcrumbs, and then deep-fried. While eminently suitable as entrées, they too can function beautifully as winning hors d'oeuvre.

Familiarizing yourself with the preparation of fritters and croquettes can greatly enrich your repertoire with inexpensive but imaginative and flavorful treats.

FRITTO MISTO

*In Italy, where frying is an art, fritto misto
(mixed fry) is encountered most everywhere
in great variety, many areas having their
own special versions. The ingredients can
be few or many in number, even to the
point of forming an entire meal, and can
consist of vegetables, seafood, meat,
cheese, or a combination. First they are
sliced thinly or divided into bite-sized
pieces, then coated with a light batter and
fried crisp and golden in oil, after which
they are thoroughly drained and served at
once while still hot, an exercise in
forbearance for the cook, who must fry so
that guests can immediately and
enthusiastically fall to.*

BATTER

  1 cup sifted all-purpose flour
  ¾ cup lukewarm water
  2 tablespoons olive oil
  ½ teaspoon salt
  2 egg whites

  2 pounds assorted vegetables and seafood,
      prepared as directed below
      All-purpose flour for dredging
      Flavorless vegetable oil for deep-frying
      Salt for sprinkling on the fritto misto
      Lemon wedges
      Large parsley sprigs

In a large mixing bowl stir together the
flour, water, olive oil, and salt until they
have combined to make a batter the consistency of heavy cream; do not beat or over-
stir. Let the batter stand at room temperature about 2 hours. (The egg whites will
be beaten and added to the batter just before it is used.)

Dry the pieces of vegetables and seafood
thoroughly with paper towels. Lightly
dredge them in flour, shaking off the excess.

Beat the egg whites until stiff, then fold
them gently into the batter.

In a deep-fryer or deep, heavy skillet heat
about 3 inches oil to 375°F. Dip the pieces
of vegetables and seafood, several at a time,
into the batter, then fry them in the hot oil,
turning them until they are golden brown on
all sides. As each batch is done, transfer the
deep-fried pieces of vegetables and seafood
with a wire skimmer or slotted spoon to a
baking sheet lined with paper towels and
keep them warm in a preheated 250°F oven
while you fry the remaining pieces.

Sprinkle the fritters lightly with salt and
arrange them on a heated platter. Garnish
the platter with the lemon wedges and either fresh parsley sprigs or parsley sprigs
that have been rinsed, thoroughly dried (but

not coated with batter), and briefly fried in the hot oil. Serve at once. Makes 8 to 12 servings.

VEGETABLES AND SEAFOOD FOR FRITTO MISTO

SMALL EGGPLANTS: Remove stem and green top but do not peel. Cut in half lengthwise, then cut crosswise into ¼- to ½-inch-thick slices. Sprinkle the slices generously with salt and let them drain in a colander at least 30 minutes. Squeeze gently but firmly to remove as much of their moisture as possible.

ZUCCHINI: Cut crosswise into ¼- to ½-inch-thick slices. Salt and drain as directed for eggplant slices (above).

SCALLIONS: Trim and leave whole (include 1 inch of the green tops), or cut into 2- to 3-inch lengths.

SMALL ONIONS: Cut into ¼-inch rings.

CAULIFLOWER: Break into small florets.

GREEN PEPPERS: Remove the seeds and ribs and cut into ¼- to ½-inch-thick strips or rings.

TENDER YOUNG GREEN BEANS: Trim and leave whole.

TOMATOES: Use only the firmest ripe tomatoes. Do not peel. Cut into ½-inch-thick slices and discard the seeds.

SHRIMP: Shell and devein, leaving the tails attached. Butterfly the shrimp by cutting them three-quarters of the way through along their inner curves and carefully spreading them open. Flatten them slightly with the side of a knife.

CRABMEAT: Choose large pieces of lump crabmeat.

LOBSTER OR ROCK LOBSTER TAIL: Cut the meat into ½-inch-thick pieces.

OYSTERS: Leave whole.

SCALLOPS: Leave small scallops whole, but cut large ones in half crosswise.

SMELTS OR OTHER TINY FISH: Clean and remove the heads.

TEMPURA

This Japanese favorite, which has achieved international fame, is actually European in origin, the deep-frying of batter-coated vegetables and seafood having been introduced into Japan by the Portuguese late in the sixteenth century.

TEMPURA SAUCE

  1 cup water
  2 tablespoons dried bonito flakes (available
    in Oriental markets)
  ⅓ cup Japanese soy sauce
  ⅓ cup mirin (syrupy rice wine, available in
    Oriental markets and some
    supermarkets)*

  1 pound assorted vegetables, prepared as
    directed below
  1 pound assorted fish and shellfish,
    prepared as direct below

TEMPURA BATTER

  2 eggs
  2 cups cold water
  2½ cups sifted all-purpose flour

  4 cups flavorless vegetable oil, or 3 cups
    flavorless vegetable oil and 1 cup
    imported sesame oil
  Freshly grated daikon (Japanese white
    radish)
  Freshly grated peeled ginger root

*One-third cup *sake* or dry Sherry, sweetened with 1 teaspoon sugar, may be substituted for the *mirin*.

Prepare the Tempura Sauce: In a small saucepan bring the water to a boil. Add the bonito flakes and cook rapidly, uncovered, 3 minutes. Strain. This stock is known as *dashi*. Combine the *dashi* with the soy sauce and *mirin*. Pour the sauce into individual small bowls.

Dry the pieces of vegetables and seafood with paper towels.

Prepare the Tempura Batter: In a large mixing bowl beat the eggs with the water. Gradually add the flour, stirring lightly. Do not overmix; the batter should be lumpy and some flour should remain floating on the surface.

In a wok or deep-fryer heat the oil to 360°F. For best results fry mild-flavored vegetables and seafood and then proceed to the stronger flavors. Dip the pieces of vegetables and seafood, several at a time, into the batter, then gently drop them into the hot oil. Fry, turning them until they are light gold on all sides. As each batch is done, transfer the *tempura* with a wire skimmer or slotted spoon to a baking sheet lined with paper towels and keep them warm in a preheated 250°F oven while you fry the remaining pieces.

Serve the tempura hot. Offer each person an assortment of vegetables and seafood with a bowl of the Tempura Sauce for dipping. The grated *daikon* and ginger root should be served on separate dishes, to be added to the sauce as desired. Makes 8 to 12 servings.

VEGETABLES AND SEAFOOD FOR TEMPURA

SMALL EGGPLANTS: Remove stem and green top; peel. Cut in half lengthwise, then cut crosswise into ¼-inch-thick slices.

SCALLIONS: Trim and cut into 2- to 3-inch lengths, including 1 inch of the green tops.

GREEN PEPPERS: Remove the seeds and ribs and cut into thin strips or rings.

TENDER YOUNG GREEN BEANS: Trim and leave whole.

MUSHROOM CAPS: Leave whole.

SLENDER SWEET POTATOES: Peel and cut crosswise into ⅛-inch-thick slices.

CARROTS: Peel and cut into approximately 1½-inch lengths, each about ⅛ inch thick.

ASPARAGUS TIPS: Leave whole or cut in half crosswise.

SNOW PEAS: Snap off the tips and remove the strings. Leave whole.

SHRIMP: Shell and devein, leaving the tails attached. Butterfly the shrimp by cutting them three-quarters of the way through along their inner curves and carefully spreading them open. Flatten them slightly with the side of a knife.

LOBSTER: Remove the meat and cut it into ½-inch-thick pieces.

SCALLOPS: Leave small scallops whole, but cut large ones in half crosswise.

CLAMS: Shell and leave whole unless they are very large, in which case cut them in half.

OYSTERS: Shell and leave whole unless they are very large, in which case cut them in half.

FISH FILLETS: Use white-meat fish such as flounder, sole, whiting, or bass and cut into 1½-inch pieces.

SMELTS: Leave whole.

PAKORAS
Indian Vegetable Fritters

Pakoras *might be considered India's counterpart to Japan's tempura. They are generally served with tea, but there is no law that says they cannot be offered with drinks.*

BATTER

  1 cup chickpea flour (available at Hispanic
    and Oriental markets)
¼ teaspoon baking soda
½ teaspoon salt
¼ teaspoon turmeric
¼ teaspoon cumin
⅛ teaspoon cayenne pepper
⅛ teaspoon freshly ground black pepper
⅔ cup cold water (approximately)
  1 pound assorted vegetables, prepared as
    directed below
    Flavorless vegetable oil for deep-frying
    Salt and freshly ground pepper for
    sprinkling on the pakoras
    Mint or Coriander Leaf Chutney with
    Yogurt (page 392)

Prepare the batter: Sift the chickpea flour, baking soda, salt, turmeric, cumin, cayenne pepper, and black pepper into a medium mixing bowl. Gradually add enough water to make a thick batter, stirring until well blended and smooth.

Use any or all of the vegetables. Dry the vegetable pieces thoroughly with paper towels.

In a wok or deep-fryer heat 2 to 3 inches oil to 360°F. Dip the vegetable pieces, several at a time, into the batter, then gently drop them into the hot oil. Fry, turning them until they have turned a golden brown on all sides. As each batch is cooked, transfer the *pakoras* with a wire skimmer or slotted spoon to a baking sheet lined with paper towels and keep them warm in a preheated 250°F oven while you fry the remaining pieces.

Sprinkle the pakoras lightly with salt and pepper and arrange them on a heated platter. Serve hot, accompanied with a bowl of the chutney for dipping. Makes 8 to 12 servings.

VARIATION:

Finely chop the vegetables and stir them into the batter. For each pakora, scoop up a spoonful of the vegetable and chickpea flour batter and, with a second spoon, scrape the batter into the hot oil. Deep-fry the pakoras in batches as directed above.

VEGETABLES FOR PAKORAS

MEDIUM POTATOES: Peel and cut crosswise into 1/16- to 1/8-inch-thick slices.

CAULIFLOWER: Break into small florets.

GREEN PEPPERS: Remove the seeds and ribs and cut into thin strips or rings.

SMALL ITALIAN FINGER PEPPERS: Remove the seeds and ribs and cut in half lengthwise.

MEDIUM ONIONS: Peel and cut crosswise into 1/16- to 1/8-inch-thick rings.

ASPARAGUS TIPS: Leave whole or cut in half crosswise.

SMALL EGGPLANTS: Remove stem and green top but do not peel. Cut in half lengthwise, then cut crosswise into 1/4- to 1/2-inch-thick slices. Sprinkle the slices generously with salt and let them drain in a colander at least 30 minutes. Squeeze gently but firmly to remove as much of their moisture as possible.

ZUCCHINI: Cut crosswise into 1/4- to 1/2-inch-thick slices. Salt and drain the slices as directed for eggplant slices (above).

OKRA: Trim stem ends and use whole.

CHEESE BEIGNETS WITH APPLE SAUCE

3 medium-sized, tart apples (such as Granny Smiths), peeled, cored, and cut into eighths
1 tablespoon dry Sherry
12 crêpes (page 310)
3/4 cup Roquefort Cheese Spread (page 27) or Gorgonzola Cheese and Prosciutto Spread (page 27)

BATTER

1 cup all-purpose flour
2 tablespoons cornstarch
1 teaspoon double-acting baking powder
1/2 teaspoon salt
2 eggs
1 egg yolk
1/2 cup water
2 teaspoons flavorless vegetable oil

Flavorless vegetable oil for deep-frying
Parsley sprigs

Combine the apples and Sherry in a medium-heavy saucepan. Cover and cook over low heat, stirring occasionally, about 10 minutes or until the apple wedges are soft but still intact. With a wooden spoon, chop and mash the apples into a chunky sauce.

Transfer to a serving bowl, cover, and refrigerate until chilled.

Form each beignet as follows: Lay 1 crêpe, speckled side up, on your work surface. Place 1 tablespoon of the cheese mixture in the center of the crêpe. Fold the sides of the crêpe envelope fashion to enclose the filling securely, making a square packet. Arrange the crêpe packets, folded sides down, in one layer on a tray or flat platter. Cover and refrigerate at least 2 hours or overnight.

Prepare the batter: Sift the flour, cornstarch, baking powder, and salt into a medium bowl. In a small bowl whisk the eggs, egg yolk, water, and the 2 teaspoons oil until blended. Gradually stir the egg mixture into the flour mixture just until smooth; do not overmix.

In a deep-fryer or deep, heavy saucepan heat 4 inches oil to 375°F. Dip 3 or 4 crêpe packets, one at a time, into the batter. Turn the packets with 2 forks to coat them well, but do not allow them to soak. Fry the packets in the hot oil, turning occasionally, about 4 minutes or until they are puffed and lightly browned. Transfer the packets with a wire skimmer or slotted spoon to a baking sheet lined with paper towels and keep them warm in a preheated 200°F oven while you fry the remaining packets. Arrange the beignets on a heated platter and garnish the platter with the parsley sprigs. Serve at once with the chilled apple sauce. Makes 12.

STUFFED MUSHROOM FRITTERS

Ultimate bliss for mushroom lovers.

 2 tablespoons butter
¼ cup finely chopped shallots
½ pound lean boneless beef, ground twice
⅔ cup fresh breadcrumbs
½ cup heavy cream
 1 egg, lightly beaten
 2 tablespoons finely chopped fresh chives
¼ teaspoon crushed dried tarragon
   Salt and freshly ground pepper to taste
36 large mushrooms
   Flavorless vegetable oil for deep-frying
   Fritter Batter (page 331)
   Salt to taste
   Shallot Mayonnaise (page 388), omitting the capers (optional)

In a small, heavy skillet melt the butter over moderate heat. Add the shallots and sauté, stirring frequently, until soft but not browned. Transfer the shallots to a medium bowl. Add the ground beef, breadcrumbs, cream, egg, chives, tarragon, salt, and pepper and mix well.

Remove the stems from the mushrooms and reserve them for another use. Wipe the mushroom caps with dampened paper towels. Stuff each cap with about 1 rounded tablespoon of the meat mixture, smoothing the top.

In a deep-fryer heat 2 inches oil to 375°F. Dip the stuffed mushrooms, 6 at a time, into the Fritter Batter and fry them in the hot oil, turning, 3 to 4 minutes or until they are lightly browned all over. As each batch is done, transfer the mushrooms with a wire skimmer or slotted spoon to a baking sheet lined with paper towels. Sprinkle them with salt and keep them warm in a preheated 300°F oven with the door ajar while you fry the remaining stuffed mushrooms. Transfer the mushrooms to a heated platter and serve at once with the Shallot Mayonnaise, if desired. Makes 36.

FRITTER BATTER

1 cup all-purpose flour
¼ teaspoon salt
2 tablespoons butter, melted and cooled, or 2 tablespoons flavorless vegetable or olive oil
2 egg yolks
1 cup flat beer, milk, or water
2 egg whites

Sift the flour and salt into a medium bowl. Make a well in the center and pour in the melted and cooled butter or oil, egg yolks, and beer, milk, or water. Whisk the ingredients together, then gradually blend into the flour. Continue to whisk the batter until it is smooth, but do not overwork the mixture. Cover the bowl and let the batter rest at room temperature 1 to 2 hours. Just before using the batter, beat the egg whites until they begin to form stiff peaks, then gently fold them into the batter.

PARMESAN ZUCCHINI FRITTERS

2 cups sifted all-purpose flour
3 teaspoons double-acting baking powder
Salt and freshly ground pepper to taste
½ cup freshly grated imported Parmesan cheese
½ cup finely chopped parsley
1¼ cups milk
2 eggs, lightly beaten
1 large garlic clove, crushed and finely chopped
1 pound small zucchini
Flavorless vegetable oil for deep-frying

Sift the flour, baking powder, salt, and pepper into a medium bowl. Stir in the Parmesan cheese and parsley. Make a well in the center and pour in the milk, beaten eggs, and garlic. Whisk the center ingredients together, then gradually blend them into the flour. Continue to whisk the batter until it is smooth, but do not overwork the mixture. Set aside.

Cut the zucchini in half crosswise, then slice lengthwise into strips about ¼ inch thick. Dry the strips thoroughly with paper towels.

In a deep-fryer heat 2 inches oil to 375°F. Dip the zucchini strips, a few at a time, into the batter and fry them in the hot oil, turning them until they are golden brown on both sides. As each batch is done, transfer the fritters with a wire skimmer or slotted spoon to a baking sheet lined with paper towels and keep them warm in a preheated 200°F oven while you fry the remaining fritters. Arrange the fritters on a heated platter and serve at once. Makes about 32.

COCONUT SHRIMP WITH CURRY SAUCE

This Polynesian hors d'oeuvre will bring forth exclamations of delight at both Oriental and Occidental gatherings.

2 pound large uncooked shrimp in their shells
⅓ cup freshly squeezed and strained lemon juice
2 teaspoons curry powder
¼ teaspoon ginger
1 teaspoon salt or to taste
2 cups sifted all-purpose flour
2 teaspoons double-acting baking powder
1 cup milk
¼ cup cornstarch
2 cups shredded fresh coconut
Flavorless vegetable oil for deep-frying
Curry Sauce (page 398)

Shell and devein the shrimp, leaving the tails attached to serve as handles for dipping. Rinse the shrimp under cold running water and pat them thoroughly dry with paper towels. In a large bowl mix together the lemon juice, curry powder, ginger, and salt. Add the shrimp and turn them to coat thoroughly with the mixture. Cover and let marinate at room temperature about 2 hours, turning the shrimp about in the marinade twice. Drain the shrimp, reserving the marinade, and pat them dry with paper towels.

In a medium bowl mix together the flour, baking powder, and milk until smooth. Stir the reserved marinade into the batter. Dredge the shrimp with the cornstarch, dip in the batter, and roll in the coconut.

In a wok or deep-fryer heat 2 inches oil to 375°F. Fry the shrimp, a batch at a time, in the hot oil, turning them until they are golden brown all over. As each batch is done, transfer the shrimp with a wire skimmer or slotted spoon to a baking sheet lined with paper towels and keep them warm in a preheated 200°F oven while you fry the remaining shrimp. Transfer the shrimp to a heated platter and serve at once with a bowl of the Curry Sauce for dipping. Makes about 30.

STUFFED LOBSTER FRITTERS

½ cup finely chopped Smithfield ham or prosciutto
2 tablespoons finely chopped shallots or scallions (include 2 inches of the green tops of the scallions)
1 tablespoon finely chopped parsley
1 egg, lightly beaten
Salt and freshly ground pepper to taste
½ cup dry breadcrumbs, or as needed
4 lobster tails (½ pound each), boiled and chilled
⅓ cup freshly squeezed and strained lemon juice
Flavorless vegetable oil for deep-frying
Fritter Batter (page 331)

In a bowl combine the ham, shallots or scallions, parsley, egg, salt, and pepper. Add enough breadcrumbs to bind the mixture. Cover and chill.

Remove the meat from the lobster tails, discarding the shells. Cut the meat crosswise into 1-inch pieces. In a bowl combine the pieces of lobster meat with the lemon juice. Cover and let marinate 30 minutes at room temperature, turning them once.

Make a slit halfway down the center of each piece of lobster. Place 1 rounded teaspoon of the ham mixture in each slit and press the opening together.

In a deep-fryer heat 2 inches oil to 375°F. Dip the stuffed lobster pieces, a batch at a time, in the Fritter Batter and fry them in the hot oil, turning them until they are golden on all sides. As each batch is done, transfer the lobster fritters with a wire skimmer or slotted spoon to a baking sheet lined with paper towels and keep them warm in a preheated 200°F oven while you fry the remaining stuffed lobster pieces. Arrange the pieces on a heated platter and serve at once. Makes about 24.

CRAB FRITTERS

½ recipe Pâte à Chou (page 361), using only 2 tablespoons butter and adding 6 drops Tabasco sauce along with the butter
6 ounces (about 1 cup) cooked crabmeat, picked over and flaked
1 tablespoon finely chopped fresh chives
Flavorless vegetable oil for deep-frying
Guacamole (page 21)

While the Pâte à Chou is still warm, stir in the crabmeat and chives until blended. Cool about 15 minutes.

In a deep-fryer heat 2 inches oil to 370°F. Carefully drop rounded teaspoonfuls of the crabmeat mixture into the hot oil without crowding the pan. Fry the fritters about 3 minutes, turning them until they are golden all over. As each batch is done, transfer the fritters with a wire skimmer or slotted spoon to a baking sheet lined with paper towels and keep them warm in a preheated 200°F oven while you fry the remaining fritters. Arrange the fritters on a heated platter and serve at once with the Guacamole for dipping. Provide cocktail picks for spearing the fritters. Makes about 36.

INDONESIAN FISH FRITTERS

3 eggs
2 scallions, finely chopped, including 2
  inches of the green tops
1 teaspoon salt
1½ teaspoons coriander
½ teaspoon cumin
1 tablespoon cornstarch
½ cup grated fresh coconut
2 teaspoons freshly squeezed and strained
  lemon juice
1 pound sole or flounder fillets, ground
  into a paste
  Flavorless vegetable oil

In a large bowl beat the eggs. Add the scallions, salt, coriander, cumin, cornstarch, coconut, lemon juice, and fish and blend well.

In a large, heavy skillet heat 1 inch oil to 360°F. Carefully drop rounded teaspoonfuls of the fish mixture into the hot oil without crowding the pan. Fry the fritters, turning them until they are golden brown all over. As each batch is done, transfer the fritters with a wire skimmer or slotted spoon to a baking sheet lined with paper towels and keep them warm in a preheated 200°F oven while you fry the remaining fritters. Arrange the fritters on a heated platter and serve at once. Makes about 60.

SPANISH COD AND POTATO FRITTERS

If you love the flavor of salt cod, you will find these fritters a great treat.

½ pound salt cod
1 pound boiling potatoes
2 medium garlic cloves, finely chopped
1 tablespoon finely chopped parsley
  Salt and freshly ground pepper to taste
2 egg yolks
  Olive oil or flavorless vegetable oil

Place the cod in a glass, enameled, or stainless steel bowl, cover it with cold water, and soak 24 hours, changing the water occasionally. Drain the cod, rinse under cold running water, and combine it in a saucepan with the unpeeled potatoes. Add enough water to cover and bring to a boil over medium-high heat. Reduce the heat to low, cover, and simmer about 30 minutes or until the potatoes are tender. Drain thoroughly. Peel the potatoes and force them through a sieve into a medium bowl. Shred the cod, discarding any remaining skin and bones, and add to the potatoes along with the garlic, parsley, salt, and pepper. Mix well. Stir in the egg yolks and blend thoroughly.

In a large, heavy skillet heat 1 inch oil to 375°F. Carefully drop rounded teaspoonfuls of the cod and potato mixture into the hot oil without crowding the pan. Fry the fritters, turning them until they are golden brown all over. As each batch is done, transfer the fritters with a wire skimmer or slotted spoon to a baking sheet lined with paper towels and keep them warm in a preheated 200°F oven while you fry the remaining fritters. Arrange the fritters on a heated platter and serve at once. Provide cocktail picks for spearing the fritters. Makes about 40.

CHINESE STUFFED CHICKEN WINGS

All it takes is a bit of imagination to turn a humble cut of chicken into a delicacy.

    12 large chicken wings
     2 tablespoons imported soy sauce
     1 teaspoon sugar
     1 whole Chinese star anise

BATTER

    2 tablespoons cornstarch
    1 tablespoon all-purpose flour
    ¼ teaspoon salt
    1 egg, well beaten
    1 tablespoon water

    6 scallion pieces, each about 2¾ inches
       long (use the white parts of large
       scallions)
    12 strips Smithfield ham, each 2¾ inches
       long and ¼ inch thick
       Flavorless vegetable oil for deep-frying

For this recipe you will need only the middle section of each chicken wing, the part with two bones. To prepare, chop off the wing tips from the chicken wings. Cut each wing apart at the joint. Reserve the larger section and the wing tips for another use.

In a saucepan just large enough to accommodate the middle sections of the wings combine the soy sauce and sugar and stir to dissolve the sugar. Add the chicken wing sections and star anise and pour over boiling water to cover. Bring the mixture to a boil over high heat. Cover and simmer 10 minutes over moderate heat, turning the wing sections occasionally. Remove from the heat and allow the wing sections to steep in the liquid until they are cool enough to handle.

Meanwhile, prepare the batter. In a small bowl combine the cornstarch, flour, and salt, then stir in the beaten egg until the mixture is smooth. Stir in the water until well blended. Cover the bowl and set aside.

Drain the chicken wing sections and pat them dry with paper towels. Bone each wing section as follows: Make a lengthwise slit along the underside. Lift and twist out the two bones, being careful not to tear the skin on the other side. Cut each scallion piece in half lengthwise. Stuff each wing section with half a scallion and 1 strip of ham.

In a wok or deep-fryer heat 2 inches oil to 375°F. Dip the stuffed chicken wings, a few at a time, into the batter and fry them in the hot oil, turning, about 3 minutes or until they are golden brown on all sides. As each batch is done, transfer the wings with a wire skimmer or slotted spoon to a baking sheet lined with paper towels and keep them warm in a preheated 200°F oven while you fry the remaining wings. Cut each wing into 2 pieces and arrange the pieces on a heated platter. Serve at once with cocktail picks. Makes 24.

HAM FRITTERS

1 tablespoon olive oil
¼ cup finely chopped onion
⅓ cup finely chopped Westphalian or Smithfield ham
½ recipe Pâte à Chou (page 361), using only 2 tablespoons butter
Flavorless vegetable oil for deep-frying

In a small, heavy skillet heat the olive oil over moderate heat. Add the onion and sauté, stirring frequently, until it just begins to turn golden. Add the sautéed onion and ham to the Pâte à Chou and blend well.

In a deep-fryer heat 2 inches oil to 375°F. Carefully drop rounded teaspoonfuls of the batter into the hot oil without crowding the pan. Fry the fritters, turning them until they are golden brown on all sides. As each batch is done, transfer the fritters with a wire skimmer or slotted spoon to a baking sheet lined with paper towels and keep them warm in a preheated 200°F oven while you fry the remaining fritters. Arrange the fritters on a heated platter and serve at once. Provide cocktail picks for spearing the fritters. Makes about 30.

VARIATION:

HAM AND CHEESE FRITTERS

Omit the olive oil and onion. Substitute ¼ cup each finely chopped prosciutto and freshly grated imported Parmesan or Gruyère cheese for the ham.

MUSHROOM AND CHEESE CROQUETTES

Cream Filling with Mushrooms and Cheese (page 46)
Melted butter
2 eggs
1 tablespoon *flavorless vegetable oil*
Pinch each salt and freshly ground pepper
10 *tablespoons all-purpose flour*
3 *cups loosely packed stale white breadcrumbs*
Flavorless vegetable oil for deep-frying

Spread the filling into a buttered shallow dish to form a smooth layer 1 inch thick. Coat the surface very lightly with melted butter. Cover and refrigerate until firm.

In a shallow bowl beat the eggs with the 1 tablespoon oil and salt and pepper until well blended. Cut the chilled cream filling into 1-inch cubes. Roll each cube, one at a time, in the flour, shaking off the excess. Dip it in the egg mixture, let it drain briefly, then roll in the breadcrumbs. With the flat side of a knife, pat the crumbs into place to help them adhere. When all the cubes are done, roll each one again in the egg mixture and once more in the breadcrumbs. Let the croquettes stand, uncovered, on a platter about 1 hour to dry and firm the coating.

In a deep-fryer heat 2 inches oil to 385°F. Fry the croquettes, several at a time, in the hot oil, turning them until they are nicely browned on all sides. As each batch is done, transfer the croquettes with a slotted spoon to a baking sheet lined with paper towels and keep them warm in a preheated 200°F oven while you fry the remaining croquettes. Arrange the croquettes on a heated platter and serve at once. Makes about 30.

SHELLFISH CROQUETTES

Follow the recipe for Mushroom and Cheese Croquettes (page 338), substituting Cream Filling with Shellfish (page 46) for the Cream Filling with Mushrooms and Cheese. Makes about 30.

HAM AND CHEESE CROQUETTES

Follow the recipe for Mushroom and Cheese Croquettes (page 338), substituting Cream Filling with Ham and Cheese (page 45) for the Cream Filling with Mushrooms and Cheese. Makes about 30.

TOKYO-STYLE CRAB CROQUETTES

Although the ingredients in this and the following recipe are not particularly suggestive of Japanese cuisine, various kinds of freshly fried croquettes happen to be popular fare in Tokyo.

2 medium-sized, thick-skinned potatoes (about ¾ pound)
1 tablespoon butter
¼ cup finely chopped onion
½ cup finely chopped mushrooms
2 tablespoons brandy
2 eggs, lightly beaten
½ teaspoon salt
⅛ teaspoon freshly ground pepper
½ pound (about 1½ cups) cooked crabmeat, picked over and flaked
⅓ cup all-purpose flour (approximately)
1 egg, beaten with 2 tablespoons water
1½ cups coarse dry breadcrumbs*
Flavorless vegetable oil for deep-frying
Prepared mustard
Imported soy sauce or chili sauce

Peel the potatoes and cook them in lightly salted boiling water until tender. Drain the potatoes well, mash them, and set aside.

In a large, heavy skillet melt the butter over moderate heat. Add the onion and

---

*To prepare the coarse dry breadcrumbs, trim the crusts from 8 slices firm white bread. Cube the bread slices, then whirl, about 1 cup at a time, in an electric blender or food processor, turning the machine on and off just until coarse crumbs are formed. Spread the breadcrumbs in a shallow, rimmed baking pan. Bake them in a preheated 325°F oven, stirring frequently, 15 to 20 minutes or until they are thoroughly dry but not brown. Remove from the oven and allow to cool to room temperature.

mushrooms and sauté, stirring frequently, until the juices have evaporated. Add the brandy (making certain that the skillet is not under an exhaust fan), ignite, and stir until the flames die.

Remove the skillet from the heat and add the potatoes, 2 eggs, salt, and pepper. Mix well. Stir in the crabmeat. Spread the mixture in a buttered 8-inch-square pan. Cover and chill.

Cut the crab mixture into 32 equal pieces. Roll each piece in flour, shaking off the excess, gently form it into a cylinder or ball, and place it on a platter or tray. Dip one croquette at a time into the egg and water mixture, let it drain briefly, and then roll in the breadcrumbs. Pat the crumbs into place with the flat side of a knife to help them adhere. Return the croquette to the platter or tray.

In a deep-fryer heat 2 inches oil to 375°F. Fry the croquettes, several at a time, in the hot oil, turning them until they are nicely browned on all sides. As each batch is done, transfer the croquettes with a slotted spoon to a baking sheet lined with paper towels and keep them warm in a preheated 200°F oven while you fry the remaining croquettes. Arrange the croquettes on a heated platter and serve at once with the mustard and soy sauce or chili sauce. Makes 32.

TOKYO-STYLE CHICKEN CROQUETTES

2 medium-sized, thick-skinned potatoes (about ¾ pound)
1 whole chicken breast (about 1¼ pounds)
1 tablespoon butter
1 small onion, finely chopped
½ cup finely chopped mushrooms
½ teaspoon crushed dried thyme
½ teaspoon salt
¼ teaspoon freshly ground pepper
1 egg, lightly beaten
⅓ cup all-purpose flour (approximately)
1 egg, beaten with 2 tablespoons water
1½ cups coarse dry breadcrumbs (page 339)
    Flavorless vegetable oil for deep-frying
    Prepared mustard
    Imported soy sauce or chili sauce

Peel the potatoes and cook them in lightly salted boiling water until tender. Drain the potatoes well, mash them, and set aside.

In a saucepan combine the chicken with 1 cup water. Cover and simmer about 30 minutes or until the chicken is tender. Allow it to cool, then remove the skin and bones and finely chop the meat.

In a large, heavy skillet melt the butter over moderate heat. Add the onion and mushrooms and sauté, stirring frequently, until the juices have evaporated. Add the chicken and cook, stirring, until it is heated through. Remove the skillet from the heat and add the potatoes, thyme, salt, pepper, and the 1 egg. Mix well. Spread the mixture in a buttered 8-inch-square pan. Cover and chill.

Shape, fry, and serve the croquettes as directed in the recipe for Tokyo-Style Crab Croquettes (page 339). Makes 32.

SAVORY PASTRIES, PASTA, AND RICE

Over the centuries savory pastries have taken many forms, both rustic and refined, in almost every corner of the globe. A goodly number seem to be related, bridging the cuisines of various nations. One example of such a kinship is illustrated by the similarities that exist between Middle Eastern sanbusak, *Indian* samosas, *Russian* pirozhki, *and Latin American* empanadas.

Savory pastries come in a profusion of shapes and sizes and rank among the most elegant and intriguing of appetizers. They are certain to be greeted with equal enthusiasm at both family meals and company gatherings. While they may require a little effort and practice to produce, the end result should inspire you to try your hand at them often.

In addition to the many recipes for savory pastries outlined in this chapter, you will find a few featuring pasta that function as admirable meal-openers when served in small portions. Also included are recipes for two exotic rice preparations, one an unusual Bedouin *creation and the other a Japanese spe-cialty,* sushi, *that has gained much favor here in recent years.*

CHEESE PASTRIES

⅔ cup butter, at room temperature
1⅓ cups (5 to 6 ounces) grated sharp
　　Cheddar cheese
⅓ cup freshly grated imported Parmesan
　　cheese
2 cups all-purpose flour
1 teaspoon salt
1 teaspoon sweet Hungarian paprika
½ teaspoon baking powder
⅓ cup heavy cream, chilled
　　(approximately)
1 egg yolk, lightly beaten with 2
　　teaspoons water
　　Sesame seed
　　Poppy seed
　　Caraway seed
　　Sliced blanched almonds

In a large mixing bowl blend the butter with the cheeses. Into another mixing bowl sift together the flour, salt, paprika, and baking powder. Add the flour mixture to the butter mixture alternately with the heavy cream, blending until a soft dough is formed. Shape the dough into a ball, wrap it in waxed paper, and chill 1 hour.

Roll out the dough on a lightly floured surface to ⅛-inch thickness. With cookie cutters, cut it into diamonds, squares, crescents, and rounds, each about 1½ inches across. As you cut the shapes, arrange them slightly apart on lightly buttered baking sheets and brush them with the egg yolk and water mixture. Sprinkle the diamonds with the sesame seed, the squares with the poppy seed, the crescents with the caraway seed, and the rounds with the almonds. Bake the pastries in a preheated 375°F oven about 12 minutes or until golden and puffed. Serve warm. Makes about 72.

VARIATIONS:

If desired, cut the dough into only one shape and sprinkle it with any one of the seeds or with the nuts given above.

CHEESE STARS

Omit the sesame seed, poppy seed, caraway seed, and almonds. Substitute grated Gruyère cheese for the Cheddar and ⅛ teaspoon cayenne pepper or to taste for the paprika. Instead of cutting the dough into the above shapes, cut it into star shapes with a 1½-inch star cutter. Sprinkle the center of each star with finely chopped salted pistachio nuts.

OLIVE-FILLED CHEESE BALLS

Each of these diminutive pastries conceals a piquant surprise within and provides a charming cocktail hour treat.

3 tablespoons butter, at room temperature
¾ teaspoon dry mustard
¼ teaspoon paprika, or pinch cayenne pepper
¼ teaspoon salt
1 cup (4 ounces) grated sharp Cheddar cheese
½ cup unsifted all-purpose flour (approximately)
16 jumbo pimento-stuffed green olives (approximately), drained and dried with a paper towel

In a mixing bowl cream the butter. Add the mustard, paprika or cayenne pepper, and salt and mix well. Beat in the cheese until thoroughly blended, then stir in the flour until a smooth dough is formed. Wrap about 1 teaspoon of dough around each olive, covering it completely and rolling it between your palms to make a smooth ball. Arrange the balls 1 inch apart on an ungreased baking sheet and chill, loosely covered, at least 1 hour. Bake in a preheated 400°F oven about 15 minutes or until golden brown. Remove from the oven and allow the olives to cool a few minutes before serving. Makes about 16.

VARIATION:

Substitute ¼ teaspoon crushed dried oregano for the paprika or cayenne pepper and, if desired, pitted black olives for the pimento-stuffed green olives.

NÜRNBERG FILLED CHEESE ROUNDS

¾ cup plus 2 tablespoons unsalted butter, at room temperature
1½ cups (6 ounces) finely grated Emmenthal or Gruyère cheese
1¾ cups all-purpose flour
1 large egg yolk, lightly beaten
1½ teaspoons sweet Hungarian paprika
1 teaspoon salt
⅛ teaspoon cayenne pepper
1 egg yolk, lightly beaten with 2 teaspoons water
Coarse salt
Caraway seed
Roquefort Cheese Spread (page 27)

In a large mixing bowl blend together the butter and Emmenthal or Gruyère cheese. Add the flour, egg yolk, paprika, salt, and cayenne pepper and stir the dough until it is smooth. Cover and chill 1 hour or until it is firm enough to handle. Shape the dough into a 6-inch square on a sheet of waxed paper and chill, wrapped in waxed paper, 1 hour.

Roll out the dough to ¼-inch thickness between 2 sheets of waxed paper. Remove the top sheet, and with a 1¼-inch fluted cutter cut the dough into rounds. As you cut the rounds, arrange them ½ inch apart on baking sheets lined with parchment paper. If necessary, place the dough in the freezing compartment of your refrigerator about 10 minutes to keep it firm. Gather the scraps, roll them out, and continue to make rounds as directed until all the dough is used. Brush half the rounds with the egg yolk and water mixture and sprinkle them liberally with the coarse salt and caraway seed. Bake the rounds in a preheated 375°F oven about 12 minutes or until golden and slightly puffed. Using a spatula, transfer the rounds to wire racks and allow to cool.

Spread the flat side of a plain round evenly with some of the Roquefort Cheese Spread and top it with a glazed round, flat side down, sandwich fashion. Repeat this procedure with the remaining rounds and cheese spread. Arrange the rounds on a serving board or platter and serve at once. Makes about 70.

VARIATION:

Substitute Ham Filling (page 44) for the Roquefort Cheese Spread.

FILLED CORNETS

These whimsical pastries with eye and taste appeal will make a cocktail party hum with conversation.

> 2⅔ cups all-purpose flour
> ½ teaspoon sugar
> ¼ teaspoon salt
> 1 cup plus 2 tablespoons butter, chilled and cut into small pieces
> 1 tablespoon lard, cut into small pieces
> 9 tablespoons ice water (approximately)
> Cream Filling with Goat Cheese (page 346)
> 3 tablespoons freshly grated imported Parmesan cheese

Sift together the flour, sugar, and salt into a mixing bowl. Cut in the butter and lard with a pastry blender or 2 knives, working quickly, until the mixture resembles fine crumbs. Sprinkle with half of the water and, with a fork, blend it into the flour and butter mixture. Sprinkle with just enough of the remaining water to allow you to form the ingredients into a ball with your hands. To ensure an even blending of fat and flour, transfer the dough to a lightly floured surface and, using the heel of your hand, smear it out in straight lines. Form the dough again into a ball, wrap it in waxed paper, and refrigerate at least 1 hour.

Meanwhile, prepare the filling and set aside. Liberally grease a baking sheet and cornet molds. Divide the dough into 2 equal parts and refrigerate 1 part. Roll out the other piece of dough on a lightly floured surface into an 8 by 18-inch rectangle. Trim the edges with a fluted pastry wheel or a sharp knife. Cut the pastry into 18 8-inch strips, each about ¾ to 1 inch wide. Wrap each strip around a cornet mold in an overlapping design resembling a small horn. Moisten the end of the strip with a drop of water and press to seal. Arrange the cornets, tips pointing up or sealed sides down, on the baking sheet. Repeat this procedure with the remaining piece of dough. Chill the cornets, loosely covered, at least 30 minutes.

Bake the cornets in a preheated 425°F oven 15 minutes. Reduce the heat to 350°F and bake about 10 minutes longer or until the cornets are lightly browned. Transfer the cornets, still wrapped around their molds, to wire racks and allow to cool 15 minutes. Carefully slip the molds out of the pastry and return the cornets to the wire racks. Let cool to room temperature.

With a spoon or pastry bag fitted with a ½-inch plain tip, fill the cornets with the Cream Filling with Goat Cheese. Return the cornets to a greased baking sheet and sprinkle the openings with the Parmesan cheese. Bake in a preheated 425°F oven 6 to 8 minutes or until the pastries are heated through. Serve at once. Makes 18.

CREAM FILLING WITH GOAT CHEESE

  5 tablespoons butter
  5 tablespoons all-purpose flour
1½ cups milk, heated
  ¾ cup heavy cream, heated
  3 eggs, lightly beaten
  6 ounces chèvre (French goat cheese), crumbled
  ½ teaspoon freshly grated nutmeg
  1 teaspoon salt or to taste
  ¼ teaspoon freshly ground pepper

In a heavy saucepan melt the butter over low heat. Add the flour and cook 2 to 3 minutes without letting it brown, whisking constantly. Add the milk and cream and cook, stirring, until the mixture comes to a boil. Simmer gently 15 minutes. Slowly stir the sauce into the beaten eggs. Return the mixture to the saucepan and, stirring constantly, bring to a boil over medium-high heat. Stir in the cheese, nutmeg, salt, and pepper.

Taste and adjust the seasoning. Cover the sauce with aluminum foil if not using it immediately.

TIROPETES

Greek Phyllo Pastry Triangles

The memory of these ethereal, crisp golden pastries will linger on as a near-Proustian experience.

> 12 sheets phyllo pastry, each 12 by 16 inches
> ¾ cup butter, melted
> Cheese Filling (below), or Spinach and Cheese Filling (page 348)

Cut the phyllo sheets into 4 strips, each 16 by 3 inches. Cover the cut phyllo sheets with a barely dampened kitchen towel to prevent drying. Brush 2 strips with melted butter and carefully lay one over the other, buttered sides up. Place about 2 teaspoons filling on a bottom corner and fold over to form a triangle. Continue folding in triangles the length of the strip. Secure the seam by brushing with melted butter. Place seam side down on a lightly buttered baking sheet. Repeat this procedure with the remaining phyllo strips and filling. Brush the tops of the triangles with melted butter.

Bake in a preheated 350°F oven about 15 to 20 minutes or until golden brown. Serve hot. Makes 24.

VARIATION:

For smaller-sized triangles, cut the phyllo into 6 strips, each 16 by 2 inches, and use 1½ teaspoons filling for each triangle. Makes 36.

CHEESE FILLING

> 1 egg
> ½ cup small-curd cottage cheese, drained, or ¼ pound Muenster cheese, grated
> 2 ounces feta cheese, finely crumbled or grated
> 1 tablespoon finely chopped parsley (optional)
> Salt to taste

In a mixing bowl beat the egg lightly with a fork. Add the cheeses and beat vigorously with a spoon until the mixture is well blended and smooth. Stir in the parsley, if used. Taste and add salt, if needed. Cover and refrigerate. Makes about 1 cup.

VARIATIONS:

Use 3 ounces each feta cheese and cottage or Muenster cheese instead of the above amounts. Fresh dill, mint, or chives to taste can be substituted for the parsley.

SPINACH AND CHEESE FILLING

3 tablespoons olive oil or butter
½ cup finely chopped onion
2 tablespoons finely chopped scallions,
   including 2 inches of the green tops
1 pound fresh spinach, washed, thoroughly
   drained, and finely chopped
2 tablespoons finely chopped fresh dill
2 tablespoons finely chopped parsley
¼ teaspoon salt
   Freshly ground pepper to taste
¼ pound feta cheese, finely crumbled or
   grated
2 eggs, lightly beaten

In a heavy skillet heat the oil or butter over moderate heat. Add the onion and scallions and sauté, stirring frequently, until soft but not browned. Stir in the spinach. Cover and cook gently a few minutes, stirring occasionally. Add the dill, parsley, salt, and pepper and cook, uncovered, stirring almost constantly until the spinach is tender and most of the liquid in the skillet has evaporated. Transfer the contents of the skillet to a mixing bowl and cool to room temperature. Add the cheese and gradually beat in the eggs. Taste and adjust the seasoning.

VARIATION:

Substitute 2 ounces each feta cheese and small-curd cottage cheese, drained, for the feta.

MEAT PASTRIES

Here is an appetizer that will quickly vanish amid a chorus of bravos.

Quick Puff Pastry (page 349)
3 tablespoons unsalted butter
¼ cup finely chopped shallots
1 medium garlic clove, finely chopped
1 pound ground veal
½ pound lean ground pork
⅓ cup dry breadcrumbs
⅓ cup heavy cream
¼ cup Cognac
¼ cup chopped unsalted pistachio nuts
¼ cup finely chopped parsley
2 tablespoons green peppercorns, rinsed
   and finely chopped
½ teaspoon crushed dried thyme
   Pinch freshly grated nutmeg
1 teaspoon salt
1 egg, lightly beaten with 2 teaspoons
   water

Prepare the Quick Puff Pastry.

In a large, heavy skillet melt the butter over moderate heat. Add the shallots and garlic and sauté, stirring frequently, until soft but not browned. Add the veal and pork and, breaking them up with a fork, cook until browned and crumbly. Transfer the contents of the skillet to a medium bowl and let stand at room temperature about 10 minutes. Add the breadcrumbs, cream, Cognac, pistachio nuts, parsley, green peppercorns, thyme, nutmeg, and salt and mix well. Taste and adjust the seasoning. Cover and refrigerate about 3 hours or until chilled. Knead the mixture with your hands until the meat is finely crumbled. Form it into 60 logs, each 2 inches by ½ inch. Arrange the logs on a baking sheet and chill about 30 minutes or until firm.

Cut the puff pastry rectangle crosswise in half. Wrap one half in plastic wrap and refrigerate. Roll out the second half on a lightly floured surface into a 13½ by 11¼-inch rectangle. Using a ruler, mark the pastry into 30 2¼-inch squares. Cut the squares. Place 1 meat log in the center of each square. Moisten the lower edge of each square with cold water. Enclose the meat log in the pastry, sealing the seam securely with your fingertips. Place on an ungreased baking sheet. Repeat this procedure with the remaining pastry and meat logs. Chill the pastries 15 minutes.

Brush the tops of the pastries with the egg and water mixture. With the tip of a small knife, make 3 diagonal cuts in the top of each pastry. Bake in a preheated 425°F oven 15 minutes. Lower the oven temperature to 375°F and bake 10 to 15 minutes longer, or until the pastries are golden. Serve hot. Makes 60.

QUICK PUFF PASTRY

4 cups sifted all-purpose flour
1¾ cups unsalted butter, chilled and cut
  into small pieces
2 teaspoons salt
1 cup plus 2 tablespoons ice water

Place the flour in a large bowl. With a pastry blender or 2 knives, cut the butter into the flour, working quickly, until the butter is in coarse pieces about the size of peas. Dissolve the salt in the ice water. Gradually stir into the flour mixture with a fork just until the mixture begins to hold together. Form the dough into a ball.

On a lightly floured surface pat the dough into an 8 by 6-inch rectangle. Wrap in plastic wrap and chill 45 minutes. On a lightly floured surface roll out the dough lengthwise into a 14 by 6-inch rectangle. Fold the top third of the dough over the center third, then fold the bottom third over the top third. Chill 15 minutes. Give the pastry a one-quarter turn so that an open side of the dough faces you. Repeat the process of rolling, folding, chilling, and turning the dough 3 more times. Cover and refrigerate the pastry dough until ready to use.

EMPANADILLAS
Spanish Meat Turnovers

Empanadas, pastries with fillings of seafood, meat, vegetables, or a combination of these, enjoy immense popularity throughout Spain. In miniature they are known as *empanadillas* and make ideal buffet and cocktail fare as well as admirable *tapas* (page 405).

Prepare 2 recipes Short Crust Pastry (page 364), sifting 1 teaspoon baking powder with the flour and salt and substituting 6 tablespoons each butter and lard for the butter. Prepare Meat Filling (below). On a lightly floured surface roll out the pastry ⅛ to ¹⁄₁₆ inch thick. With a 3-inch cookie cutter cut out circles. Place 1 rounded teaspoon of the Meat Filling in the center of one half of each circle. Moisten the edges of the circle with a finger dipped in cold water. Fold over the other half to make a half-moon shape and press the edges with a fork to seal.

In a deep-fryer or large, heavy saucepan heat 2 to 3 inches of flavorless vegetable oil to about 370°F. Add the turnovers in batches and deep-fry, turning them frequently with a slotted spoon, 3 to 4 minutes or until golden brown. Drain on paper towels. Alternatively, arrange the turnovers slightly apart on an ungreased baking sheet. Brush the tops with 1 egg yolk, lightly beaten with 1 teaspoon water, and prick with the tines of a fork. Bake in a preheated 400°F oven about 20 minutes or until golden brown. Serve hot. Makes about 30.

VARIATION:

SPANISH CHORIZO TURNOVERS
In a food processor fitted with the steel blade or in an electric blender finely chop ½ pound *chorizo* (garlic sausage, available in Hispanic markets and some specialty food shops). Transfer to a bowl and beat in 1 egg. Substitute this mixture for the Meat Filling.

MEAT FILLING

1 tablespoon olive oil
1 medium onion, finely chopped
1 medium garlic clove, finely chopped
2 ounces chorizo (see Variation, page 350)
    or other garlic-seasoned smoked pork
    sausage, chopped
1 pound ground veal
¼ cup dry white wine
3 tablespoons tomato paste
1 pimento, finely diced
1 tablespoon finely chopped green Spanish
    olives
1 tablespoon finely chopped parsley
    Salt and freshly ground pepper to taste

In a large, heavy skillet heat the oil over moderate heat. Add the onion and garlic and sauté, stirring frequently, until the onion is soft but not browned. Add the *chorizo* and cook, stirring often, about 5 minutes. Add the veal and, breaking it up with a fork, cook until browned and crumbly. Stir in the remaining ingredients. Reduce the heat to low and simmer, stirring occasionally, until the liquid in the skillet has evaporated and the meat is tender. Taste and adjust the seasoning. Remove from the heat and allow to cool.

EMPANADAS
Argentine Turnovers

Empanadas have found a warm welcome in Latin America, where they exist in numerous variations, having become as much a part of the food scene as sandwiches in North America. This unusual rendition, which combines meat and fruit to very happy effect, should win you many compliments.

Prepare 2 recipes Short Crust Pastry (page 364), sifting 1 teaspoon baking powder with the flour and salt and substituting 6 tablespoons each butter and lard for the butter. Prepare the filling (page 352). On a lightly floured surface roll out the pastry to about ⅛-inch thickness and with a 5-inch round cutter cut out circles. Place about 1 tablespoon filling in the center of one half of each circle. Moisten the edges of the circle with a finger dipped in cold water. Fold over the other half to make a half-moon shape and pinch the edges together to seal. Curve the turnover slightly to form a crescent shape. Brush the tops of the turnovers with 1 egg lightly beaten with ½ teaspoon water and prick with the tines of a fork. Arrange the turnovers slightly apart on an ungreased baking sheet. Bake in a preheated 375°F oven about 30 minutes or until golden brown. Serve hot. Makes about 10.

FILLING

1 tablespoon butter
1 small onion, finely chopped
½ medium-sized green pepper, seeded, deribbed, and finely chopped
½ pound lean ground beef
1 small tomato, peeled, seeded, and finely chopped
½ large pear, peeled, cored, and finely chopped
1 large peach, peeled, pitted, and finely chopped
2 tablespoons dry white wine
2 teaspoons finely chopped chives (optional)
Salt and freshly ground pepper to taste

In a medium-sized, heavy skillet melt the butter over moderate heat. Add the onion and green pepper and sauté until soft but not browned, stirring frequently. Add the beef and, breaking it up with a fork, cook until browned and crumbly. Stir in the remaining ingredients. Reduce the heat to low and simmer, stirring occasionally, until the liquid in the skillet has evaporated and the meat is tender. Taste and adjust the seasoning. Remove from the heat and allow to cool.

EMPANADITAS
Latin American Cocktail Turnovers

When made cocktail size, Latin American empanadas become empanaditas. These turnovers can be made either with pie pastry and (usually) deep-fried or with puff pastry and baked. For the latter version frozen patty shells can be successfully used, as illustrated in this recipe.

Mushroom and Cheese Filling (page 353)
1 package frozen patty shells (6 patty shells), thawed

Prepare the filling and set aside. Slightly overlap the patty shells on a lightly floured surface, then roll them out to ⅛- to ¹⁄₁₆-inch thickness. With a 3-inch cookie cutter cut out circles. Place about 1½ teaspoons filling in the center of one half of each circle. Moisten the edges of the circle with a finger dipped in cold water. Fold over the other half to make a half-moon shape and press the edges together to seal. Repeat this procedure with the pastry scraps.

Arrange the empanaditas slightly apart on an ungreased baking sheet. Prick the tops with the tines of a fork and bake in a preheated 400°F oven about 20 minutes or until golden. Serve at once. Makes about 24.

MUSHROOM AND CHEESE FILLING

2 tablespoons butter
1 small onion, finely sliced
6 ounces mushrooms, chopped
¼ cup chopped black olives
½ teaspoon paprika
  Salt and cayenne pepper to taste
1½ cups (6 ounces) grated Monterey Jack
  or Cheddar cheese

In a heavy skillet melt the butter over moderate heat. Add the onions and mushrooms and cook, stirring frequently, until the vegetables are golden brown and the liquid in the skillet has evaporated. Stir in the olives, paprika, salt, and cayenne pepper. Remove from the heat and allow to cool. Stir in the cheese. Taste and adjust the seasoning.

PASTELILLOS
Puerto Rican Meat Pies

At any party these will disappear rapidly along with the planter's punch.

3 tablespoons corn oil or flavorless
  vegetable oil
½ pound lean ground pork
2 ounces smoked ham, ground or finely
  chopped
½ cup finely chopped onion
1 large garlic clove, finely chopped
2 tablespoons finely chopped parsley
¼ teaspoon crushed dried oregano
½ teaspoon salt or to taste
¼ teaspoon freshly ground pepper
1 teaspoon white wine vinegar
½ cup water
1½ tablespoons tomato paste
2 tablespoons seedless raisins, chopped
1 teaspoon capers, drained
6 black olives, finely chopped
1 hard-cooked egg, finely chopped
¼ teaspoon crushed red pepper flakes
2 recipes Short Crust Pastry (page 364)
  Flavorless vegetable oil for deep-frying

In a heavy skillet heat the oil over moderate heat. Add the pork, ham, onion, garlic, parsley, oregano, salt, pepper, and vinegar and cook, stirring, until the pork is no longer pink. Stir in the water and tomato paste. Cover and cook 30 minutes. Stir in the raisins and capers and cook 5 minutes. Remove from the heat and transfer the contents of the skillet to a large mixing bowl. Add the olives, egg, and crushed red pepper flakes and toss the ingredients until thoroughly combined. Taste and adjust the seasoning and allow to cool.

On a lightly floured surface roll out the pastry to 1/16-inch thickness. Cut it into circles with a 2½-inch cookie cutter. Place about 1 teaspoon of the meat mixture in the center of one half of each circle. Moisten the edges of the circle with a finger dipped in cold water. Fold over the other half to make a half-moon shape and press the edges together to seal.

In a deep-fryer or large, heavy saucepan heat 2 to 3 inches oil to 375°F. Add the *pastelillos* in batches and deep-fry, turning them with a slotted spoon, about 3 minutes or until they are golden brown. Drain on paper towels and serve hot. Makes about 50.

SANBUSAK
Middle Eastern Turnovers

A dearly loved Middle Eastern pastry whose roots stretch deep into the past.

PASTRY

> ½ cup flavorless vegetable oil
> ½ cup butter
> ½ cup warm water
> 1 teaspoon salt
> 3½ cups all-purpose flour, sifted
>   (approximately)
>   Meat Filling (page 355) or Cheese
>   Filling (page 355)
> 1 egg, lightly beaten
>   Sesame seed (optional)

Prepare the pastry: Combine the oil and butter in a small heatproof bowl and heat over boiling water until the butter is melted. Stir in the warm water and salt and pour into a large mixing bowl. Gradually add the flour, stirring with your hand, until the mixture holds together and forms a soft ball (you may need to add a little more flour).

On a lightly floured surface roll out the dough 1/8 to 1/16 inch thick. With a 3-inch cookie cutter cut out circles. Place 1 rounded teaspoon filling in the center of one half of each circle. Moisten the edges of the circle with a finger dipped in cold water. Fold over the other half to make a half-moon shape and pinch the edges together to seal. Brush the surface with the beaten egg and sprinkle lightly with the sesame seed, if desired.

Arrange the pastries slightly apart on an ungreased baking sheet. Bake in a preheated 375°F oven about 30 minutes or until golden. Serve straight from the oven. Makes about 30.

VARIATION:

Omit brushing the pastries with the beaten egg and sprinkling them with the sesame seed. Instead of baking the pastries, fry them slowly in Clarified Butter (page 288) until golden on both sides and cooked through, or deep-fry in hot flavorless vegetable oil.

MEAT FILLING

2½ tablespoons flavorless vegetable oil
⅓ cup pine nuts
1 large onion, finely chopped
1 pound lean ground lamb or beef
1 large tomato, peeled, seeded, and chopped
2 tablespoons finely chopped parsley
½ teaspoon allspice or cinnamon
Salt and freshly ground pepper to taste

In a large, heavy skillet heat the oil over moderate heat. Add the pine nuts and sauté just until golden, stirring constantly. With a slotted spoon, remove the pine nuts and reserve. Add the onion to the oil remaining in the skillet and sauté until soft and a pale golden color, stirring frequently. Add the meat and, breaking it up with a fork, cook until browned and crumbly. Add the tomato, parsley, allspice or cinnamon, salt, and pepper and cook, stirring occasionally, until the liquid in the skillet has evaporated and the meat is tender. Stir in the reserved sautéed pine nuts. Taste and adjust the seasoning. Remove from the heat and allow to cool.

CHEESE FILLING

1 pound cheese, freshly grated *
2 eggs, lightly beaten
Freshly ground white pepper

In a bowl mix the cheese with the beaten eggs and season to taste with the pepper.

*Use Greek Halumi, Gruyère, Cheddar, Edam, Gouda, or a mixture of any of these with a little imported Parmesan.

PIROZHKI
Russian Turnovers

Mountains of these wonderful little pastries are a familiar sight on the zakuska table (page 413).

SOUR CREAM PASTRY

1¾ cups sifted all-purpose flour
½ teaspoon baking powder
½ teaspoon salt
½ cup unsalted butter, chilled and cut
　　into small pieces
½ cup sour cream
1 egg, beaten

MEAT FILLING

1 tablespoon butter
1 medium onion, finely chopped
½ pound lean ground beef
1 hard-cooked egg, finely chopped
1 tablespoon finely chopped fresh dill
　　Salt and freshly ground pepper to taste

1 egg, lightly beaten with 1 teaspoon water

Prepare the pastry: Sift together the flour, baking powder, and salt into a mixing bowl. With a pastry blender or 2 knives, cut in the butter, working quickly, until the mixture resembles coarse crumbs. In a small bowl mix the sour cream with the egg. Stir into the flour and butter mixture until well blended. Knead the dough on a lightly floured surface 1 minute. Form the dough into a ball, wrap in plastic wrap, and refrigerate 1 hour or overnight.

Prepare the filling: In a medium-sized, heavy skillet melt the butter over moderate heat. Add the onion and sauté until soft but not browned, stirring frequently. Add the meat and, breaking it up with a fork, cook until browned and crumbly. Remove from the heat. Add the egg, dill, salt, and pepper and mix well. Taste and adjust the seasoning.

On a lightly floured surface roll out the pastry to ⅛-inch thickness. With a 3-inch cookie cutter cut out circles. Place 1 rounded teaspoon filling in the center of one half of each circle. Brush the edges of the dough with some of the egg and water mixture. Fold over the other half to make a half-moon shape and press the edges together to seal.

Arrange the *pirozhki*, slightly apart, on a greased and floured baking sheet. Brush them with the egg and water mixture and prick the top of each pastry once with a wooden pick. Bake in a preheated 400°F oven 15 to 20 minutes or until golden brown. Serve hot. Makes about 40.

VARIATION:

Substitute Crème Fraîche (page 191) for the sour cream.

SAMOSAS

Indian Meat Pastries

A popular snack in India, these spicy, meat-filled pastries make delicious appetizers.

YOGURT PASTRY

2 cups all-purpose flour, sifted
1 teaspoon salt
¼ cup butter, melted
⅓ cup unflavored yogurt (approximately)

FILLING

1 tablespoon butter or flavorless vegetable oil
1 medium onion, finely chopped
1 large garlic clove, finely chopped
1 teaspoon peeled and grated fresh ginger root (optional)
½ pound lean ground lamb or beef
1 small tomato, peeled, seeded, and finely chopped
2 teaspoons imported Madras curry powder or to taste
¾ teaspoon salt or to taste
⅛ teaspoon cayenne pepper or to taste
2 tablespoons finely chopped parsley, coriander, or mint
Flavorless vegetable oil for deep-frying
Mint or Coriander Leaf Chutney with Yogurt (page 392)

Prepare the pastry: Sift together the flour and salt into a bowl. Stir in the melted butter and enough yogurt to make a dough. Knead gently until smooth. Cover and set aside 30 minutes.

Meanwhile, prepare the filling: In a heavy skillet heat the butter or oil over moderate heat. Add the onion, garlic, and ginger root (if used) and sauté 5 minutes, stirring frequently. Add the meat and, breaking it up with a fork, sauté until browned. Add the tomato, curry powder, salt, and cayenne pepper. Cook about 10 minutes, stirring occasionally. Mix in the parsley, coriander, or mint and remove from the heat. Drain off excess fat and liquid. Taste and adjust the seasoning and allow to cool.

On a lightly floured surface roll out the dough ⅛ to ⅟₁₆ inch thick. With a 4-inch cookie cutter cut out circles. Cut each circle in half. Moisten the edges of each semicircle with a finger dipped in cold water. Fold each semicircle in half and press the straight edges together to form a cone. Fill the cone with 1 rounded teaspoon of the filling and press the curving top edges of the cone together to seal it.

In a deep-fryer or large, heavy saucepan heat 2 to 3 inches oil to 375°F. Add the *samosas* in batches and deep-fry, turning them with a slotted spoon, 2 to 3 minutes or until they are golden brown. Drain on paper towels. Serve hot, accompanied with a bowl of the chutney for dipping. Makes about 60.

CHICKEN LIVER PASTRIES

½ recipe Cream Cheese Pastry (page 359)
  Chicken Liver Filling (page 359)
1 egg white, lightly beaten
1 egg, lightly beaten with 1 tablespoon water

Remove the Cream Cheese Pastry from the refrigerator and let stand at room temperature 10 minutes before rolling. Divide the pastry into two equal parts. Work with one part at a time, refrigerating the second until you are ready to use it. On a lightly floured surface roll out each part into a rectangle about 10 by 4 inches and about ⅛ inch thick. Spoon ½ cup of the Chicken Liver Filling down the center of each rectangle, smoothing it into a cylinder shape with a spatula. Fold one long side of the pastry up over the filling and press slightly. Brush the other side with some of the egg white and draw it up to overlap the first. Press lightly to seal in the filling. Brush the insides of the open ends of the rolls with egg white. Pinch them together to seal. Arrange the rolls, seam sides down, on a baking sheet. Chill, loosely covered, 1 hour.

Cut the rolls diagonally into 1-inch-thick slices and arrange them slightly apart on the baking sheet. Brush the tops with the egg and water mixture. Bake in a preheated 325°F oven 25 to 30 minutes or until golden brown. Makes about 20.

CREAM CHEESE PASTRY

¼ pound cream cheese, at room temperature
½ cup butter, at room temperature
1 cup sifted all-purpose flour (approximately)
¼ teaspoon salt

Combine the cream cheese and butter in a bowl until thoroughly blended and smooth. Gradually add the flour and salt, blending with a spatula, fork, or your fingertips until the ingredients form a smooth dough. Wrap the dough in waxed paper and refrigerate several hours or overnight.

CHICKEN LIVER FILLING

¼ cup butter
1 medium onion, finely chopped
1 medium garlic clove, finely chopped
½ pound chicken livers
1 hard-cooked egg
2 tablespoons finely chopped parsley
1 tablespoon Cognac
Salt and freshly ground pepper to taste

In a medium-sized, heavy skillet melt the butter over moderate heat. Add the onion and garlic and sauté, stirring frequently, until soft but not browned. Raise the heat, add the chicken livers, and cook briskly, turning to brown on all sides. Transfer the livers to a chopping board and chop them with the egg until very fine. Stir in the parsley and Cognac. Season with the salt and pepper. Allow to cool before using.

SAUCISSON EN BRIOCHE

Sausage in Pastry

A bit of a production, but a rewarding one.

SAUSAGE

1¼ pounds pork shoulder, coarsely ground
¼ pound pork fat, coarsely ground
½ cup Cognac, apple brandy, or bourbon
2 medium garlic cloves, finely chopped
1 tablespoon finely chopped fresh rosemary
1½ teaspoons crushed dried thyme
1½ teaspoons salt
1½ teaspoons freshly ground pepper

BRIOCHE DOUGH

¼ cup warm water (110°F)
¾ package active dry yeast
 2 teaspoons sugar
½ cup butter, melted
¾ teaspoon salt
 2 cups all-purpose flour, more if needed
 2 eggs

 1 egg yolk, beaten with 1½ tablespoons
   heavy cream
  Dijon-style mustard
  Cornichons (French sour gherkins)

Prepare the sausage: In a large bowl combine the pork, pork fat, Cognac, apple brandy, or bourbon, garlic, rosemary, thyme, salt, and pepper. In a small skillet sauté a spoonful of the mixture until cooked through, taste it, and adjust the seasoning of the remaining meat mixture if needed.

Form the mixture into a sausage-shaped roll about 7 inches long and 2 inches in diameter. Wrap the sausage in a double thickness of cheesecloth. Twist the ends of the cheesecloth tightly and tie them with string. Poach the sausage in a pot of boiling salted water just to cover 40 minutes or to an internal temperature of 170°F. Remove the sausage from the pot and refrigerate, still in the cheesecloth, overnight.

Prepare the brioche dough: Pour the warm water into a small bowl and sprinkle it with the yeast and sugar. Let the mixture stand about 10 minutes or until foamy. In a large mixing bowl blend the melted butter with the salt. Add the flour, eggs, and yeast mixture and beat by hand until well blended and smooth, adding more flour if necessary. Place the dough in a buttered bowl and turn over to grease the top. Cover loosely with a kitchen towel and let rise in a warm place free from drafts about 1½ hours, or until doubled in bulk.

Remove the cheesecloth from the sausage. Punch down the dough and roll it out on a lightly floured surface to ⅓-inch thickness. Place the sausage in the center of the dough and wrap neatly, turning in the ends and then bringing the sides together to overlap. Place seam side down on a buttered baking sheet. Brush with the egg yolk and cream mixture. Bake in a preheated 375°F oven about 35 minutes or until golden brown. Allow to cool slightly. Cut into slices about ¾ inch thick and serve with the mustard and *cornichons*. Makes about 10 servings.

VARIATION:

Substitute a 1-pound garlic-flavored sausage (such as Italian *coteghino* or French *saucisson à l'ail)* for the sausage mixture.

COCKTAIL PUFFS

These elegant little appetizers seem far more complicated to prepare than they actually are. The shells, made with pâte à chou (cream puff pastry), can be filled with a wide assortment of savory mixtures. Several suggestions are given on the following pages.

Pâte à Chou (below)
1 egg, lightly beaten with ½ teaspoon water

With a pastry bag or spoon, form mounds of *pâte à chou* 1 inch in diameter and spaced 2 inches apart on lightly buttered baking sheets. Lightly brush the tops of the puffs with the egg and water mixture, being careful not to let it run down the puffs and onto the baking sheets, as this will prevent the puffs from rising. Bake the puffs in a pre-heated 425°F oven about 20 minutes or until golden brown and crisp. Remove them from the oven and pierce each puff with a small knife to let out steam. Return the puffs to the hot, turned-off oven for about 10 minutes or until the interiors of the puffs are dry. Transfer them to a wire rack to cool. Use the puffs in any of the ways described below. Makes about 48.

PÂTE À CHOU (CREAM PUFF PASTRY)

1 cup water
½ cup butter, cut into pieces
¼ teaspoon salt
1 cup sifted all-purpose flour
4 eggs

In a heavy saucepan bring the water, butter, and salt to a rolling boil over high heat. When the butter has melted, add the flour all at once. Remove from the heat and beat with a wooden spoon until the mixture is well blended, clings together, and comes away from the sides of the pan. Beat in the eggs, one at a time, beating well after each addition, until the paste is smooth and shiny. Allow the paste to rest 15 minutes before shaping and baking.

Note: Any leftover *pâte à chou* can be refrigerated or frozen. Before using, bring to room temperature, then beat over hot water until the paste is just lukewarm. Be careful not to overheat; otherwise the mixture will not puff properly.

SWEDISH CHEESE PUFFS

Cut off the top of each puff and reserve. Spoon or pipe Swedish Cheese Spread (page 28) into the puffs and sprinkle with finely chopped salted pistachio nuts. Replace the tops of the puffs, slanting them to the side. If desired, serve on a large platter lined with watercress.

CREAM CHEESE AND MUSHROOM PUFFS

Split each puff horizontally and fill one half with Cream Cheese and Mushroom Filling (page 37). Cover with the other half.

SHELLFISH AND AVOCADO PUFFS

Cut off and discard the top of each puff to make an opening. Fill the puffs with Shellfish and Avocado Filling (page 41), mounding it. Sprinkle the puffs with finely chopped parsley.

WHIPPED CREAM CHEESE AND CAVIAR PUFFS

Cut off and discard the top of each puff to make an opening. Fill the puffs with whipped cream cheese seasoned with a little grated onion and top them with chilled black caviar. If desired, garnish each filled puff with a tiny strip of lemon rind.

HAM PUFFS

Slit each puff on the side and fill with Ham Filling or Prosciutto Filling (page 44) piped through a pastry bag fitted with a ¼-inch tip.

CHICKEN LIVER AND MUSHROOM PUFFS

Slit each puff on the side and fill with Chicken Liver and Mushroom Filling (page 43) piped through a pastry bag fitted with a ¼-inch tip.

VARIATION:

Substitute Chicken Liver Pâté (page 31, omitting the parsley sprigs) for the Chicken Liver and Mushroom Filling.

HOT COCKTAIL PUFFS

Cut off the top of each puff and reserve. Spoon any of the hot cream fillings (pages 45-48) into the puffs and replace the tops. Arrange the filled puffs on a baking sheet and bake in a preheated 425°F oven 2 to 3 minutes or until heated. Serve at once.

COCKTAIL CHEESE PUFFS

Prepare Pâte à Chou (page 361), adding ⅛ teaspoon freshly ground pepper and a pinch of freshly grated nutmeg along with the salt. After beating in the eggs, beat in ⅔ cup Gruyère and ⅓ cup imported Parmesan cheese, both freshly grated. Form the puffs as in the recipe for Cocktail Puffs (page 361). After brushing the puffs with the egg and water mixture, sprinkle each one with a little grated Parmesan. Serve hot or cold. Makes about 48.

VARIATIONS:

OLIVE-STUFFED COCKTAIL CHEESE PUFFS

Allow the puffs to cool. Slit the side of each puff and insert 1 small pimento-stuffed olive.

HERB COCKTAIL CHEESE PUFFS

Substitute Cheddar cheese for the Gruyère cheese, if you wish. Add 1 teaspoon dry mustard, 1 teaspoon crushed dried basil, oregano, or thyme, ⅛ teaspoon cayenne pepper, and, if desired, 2 tablespoons caraway or poppy seed along with the cheeses.

TARTLETS WITH HOT FILLINGS

Tartlets, hot or cold, make particularly noteworthy hors d'oeuvre.

Short Crust Pastry (page 364)
Any of the hot cream fillings on pages 45-48
Freshly grated imported Parmesan cheese
Melted butter

Roll out the pastry on a lightly floured board to ⅛-inch thickness. Have ready about 18 tartlet tins, 2 to 2½ inches across the top and about ¾ inch deep. With a cookie cutter cut out circles from the pastry, each ¾ inch larger than the tins. Fit the circles into the tins and press the pastry gently against the bottoms and sides. Trim the excess pastry from the edges. Prick the bottoms and sides of the pastry shells at ¼-inch intervals with a fork to prevent the pastry from blistering during baking. Chill 30 minutes.

Line the chilled pastry shells with buttered aluminum foil. Fill them with raw rice or dried beans and bake in a preheated 400°F oven 7 minutes. Remove from the oven and remove the foil and rice or beans. Prick the bottoms and sides of the shells again with a fork. Return them to the oven and bake about 3 minutes or until they just begin to color. Carefully remove the shells from the tins and cool on wire racks.

Fill the partially baked pastry shells with the filling of your choice. Sprinkle the tops with the cheese and top each with a drop of melted butter. Arrange the tartlets on a baking sheet and bake in a preheated 450°F oven about 5 minutes or until the filling is lightly browned on top. Arrange on a platter and serve at once. Makes about 18.

SHORT CRUST PASTRY

> 1 cup sifted all-purpose flour
> ¼ teaspoon salt
> ½ cup unsalted butter, chilled and cut into
>   small pieces
> 3 tablespoons ice water (approximately)

Sift the flour and salt into a mixing bowl. Cut in the butter with a pastry blender or 2 knives, working quickly until the mixture resembles fine crumbs. Add half of the water and, working quickly, blend it into the flour and butter mixture with a fork. Add just enough of the remaining water for you to be able to shape the dough into a firm ball with your hands. Wrap the dough in waxed paper or plastic wrap and chill 2 hours.

Note: When baking small tart shells blind (empty), you can substitute 1 beaten egg for ¼ cup of the butter. This makes a firmer pastry that is less likely to shrink.

TARTLETS WITH COLD FILLINGS

Prepare pastry shells as directed in the recipe for Tartlets with Hot Fillings (page 363), but after you have removed the foil and rice or beans and pricked the shells again, return them to the oven and bake about 8 minutes or until the shells are lightly browned. Carefully remove the fully baked shells from their tins and cool on wire racks. Fill the cooled shells with any of the following fillings. Arrange on a platter and serve. Makes about 18.

COLD FILLINGS FOR TARTLETS

Roquefort Cheese Spread (page 27)

Gorgonzola Cheese and Prosciutto Spread (page 27)

Swedish Cheese Spread (page 28)

Cream Cheese and Mushroom Filling (page 37)

Caviar and Cream Cheese Filling (page 42)

Chicken Liver and Mushroom Filling (page 43)

Ham Filling (page 44)

Spinach, Mushroom, and Ham Filling (page 44)

TARTALETAS DE ENSALADILLA
Spanish Tuna and Vegetable Tartlets

1 can (7 ounces) white tuna in oil, drained and flaked

2 tablespoons finely chopped parsley

2 teaspoons grated white mild onion

1 teaspoon capers, rinsed, drained, and finely chopped

1 teaspoon wine vinegar

2 medium-sized red potatoes, cooked, peeled, and finely diced

¼ cup cooked peas

¼ cup finely diced cooked carrots

1 hard-cooked egg, finely chopped

⅔ cup Mayonnaise (page 387), or as needed
   About 50 fully baked and cooled tartlet shells (page 363)

1 pimento, cut into small strips

In a large bowl combine the tuna, parsley, onion, capers, and vinegar and mix well. Add the potatoes, peas, carrots, egg, and Mayonnaise and toss gently but thoroughly. Taste and adjust the seasoning. Divide the mixture among the tartlet shells. Garnish with the pimento strips, arrange on a platter, and serve. Makes about 50.

VARIATIONS:

Substitute fully baked and cooled barquette shells (page 366) for the tartlet shells.

SHELLFISH AND VEGETABLE TARTLETS

Substitute 1 cup finely diced cooked, shelled, and deveined shrimp, crabmeat, or lobster meat for the tuna.

HAM AND VEGETABLE TARTLETS

Substitute 1 cup finely diced *serrano* ham or prosciutto for the tuna.

ANCHOVY AND EGG TARTLETS

Instead of the tun and vegetable mixture use this one: In a bowl combine 4 cans (2 ounces each) anchovy fillets, drained and finely chopped, 8 hard-cooked eggs, sieved, ½ cup Mayonnaise (page 387), and ½ cup finely chopped chives. Blend thoroughly. Taste and adjust the seasoning. Makes enough filling for about 48 tartlets.

BARQUETTES

Barquettes *are open tarts shaped like small boats, hence their name. You can find individual barquette tins, either plain or fluted, in lengths from 1½ to 5¾ inches in the housewares sections of department stores or in specialty kitchenware shops.*

Short Crust Pastry (page 364)

On a lightly floured board roll out the pastry to ⅛-inch thickness. Cut out ovals to fit 1½-inch-long barquette tins. (To make a pattern, invert a tin on paper and trace the outline, then add ¼ inch extra all around.) Fit the pastry ovals into the tins. Prick the bottoms and sides of the pastry shells at ¼-inch intervals with a fork to prevent the pastry from blistering during baking. Chill 30 minutes.

Line the chilled pastry shells with buttered aluminum foil. Fill them with raw rice or dried beans and bake in a preheated 400°F oven 7 minutes. Remove from the oven and remove the foil and rice or beans. Prick the bottoms and sides of the shells again with a fork.

To make barquettes with hot fillings, return the shells to the oven and bake about 3 minutes or until they just begin to color. Carefully remove the shells from the tins and cool on wire racks. Fill and bake the barquettes as directed in the recipe for Tartlets with Hot Fillings (page 363), using any of the fillings given in that recipe. Arrange on a platter and serve.

To make barquettes with cold fillings, return the shells to the oven and bake about 8 minutes or until the shells are lightly browned. Carefully remove the fully baked shells from the tins and cool on wire racks. Fill the cooled shells with any of the fillings suggested in the recipe for Tartlets with Cold Fillings (page 364). Arrange on a platter and serve. Makes about 24.

BARQUETAS DE CAVIAR

Brazilian Caviar Barquettes

With these little boats you'll be sure to make a splash the next time you entertain.

Prepare fully baked and cooled *barquette* shells as directed in the recipe for Barquettes (page 366). Fill the shells with red or black caviar. Top each barquette with a dab of sour cream and garnish with finely chopped chives. Arrange the barquettes on a platter and serve at once. Makes about 24.

VARIATION:

BRAZILIAN SEAFOOD BARQUETTES

Substitute Seafood Salad Filling (page 40) or Crabmeat and Avocado Filling (page 40) for the caviar. Garnish each barquette with a small pitted black olive. Omit the sour cream and chives.

MINIATURE CRAB QUICHES

These tiny filled pastry cups make winsome hors d'oeuvre that are easy to handle as finger food. The flaky pastry shells can be baked in advance. Just before serving, fill and bake as directed.

Short Crust Pastry (page 364)
3 ounces (1 cup) cooked crabmeat, picked over to remove any pieces of shell and flaked
½ cup (2 ounces) grated Swiss cheese
2 small eggs
½ cup half-and-half
Pinch freshly grated nutmeg
Salt and freshly ground pepper to taste

On a lightly floured surface roll out the pastry to ⅛-inch thickness. With a 3-inch cookie cutter cut out circles. Carefully fit the circles into small tart pans or muffin cups that measure about 1½ inches across the bottoms. Prick the circles at intervals with a fork to prevent the pastry from blistering during baking. Chill 30 minutes. Bake the pastry shells in a preheated 400°F oven about 8 minutes or until the pastry has barely started to color.

Remove the pastry shells from the oven and allow to cool. Divide the crabmeat and cheese among them. In a mixing bowl beat the eggs, then beat in the half-and-half, nutmeg, salt, and pepper until well blended. Spoon a small quantity of the egg mixture into each pastry shell, filling it nearly to the top. Bake the filled shells in a preheated 400°F oven about 15 minutes or until the filling is puffed, lightly browned, and firm. Remove from the oven and let cool 5 minutes. Carefully remove the quiches from the pans and place them on wire racks to cool a few minutes more. Serve warm or cold. Makes about 18.

Note: For a quiche made with pita bread see page 307.

VARIATIONS:

MINIATURE HAM QUICHES
Substitute 3 ounces (½ cup) finely chopped cooked ham for the crabmeat.

MINIATURE BACON QUICHES
Substitute 3 strips bacon, cooked crisp and crumbled, for the crabmeat.

SAVORY CHEESECAKE

An interesting choice for a buffet or first course. Although not sweet, it is quite rich, so serve small portions.

Whole Wheat Pastry (page 369)
1 pound Camembert or blue cheese, at room temperature
8 ounces cream cheese, at room temperature
3 eggs
Toasted sliced almonds, walnut halves, or pecan halves

Prepare the Whole Wheat Pastry.

If using Camembert cheese, leave on the rind. Cut the cheeses into 1-inch chunks. In a large bowl beat the eggs with an electric mixer until well blended. Add the chunks of cheese, a few at a time, beating until thoroughly blended and smooth. Spoon the mixture into the pastry-lined pan. Bake in a preheated 350°F oven 25 to 30 minutes or until the center of the cheesecake is almost firm. Transfer the cheesecake to a wire rack and allow to cool to room temperature.

The cheesecake can be served at once or, if made ahead, covered and chilled, then returned to room temperature before serving. To serve, remove the sides of the pan. Garnish the top of the cheesecake with the toasted nuts. Cut the cheesecake into thin wedges. Makes 12 to 16 servings.

VARIATIONS:

Substitute plain soft white *chèvre* (French goat cheese), trimmed of any hard rind, for the Camembert or blue cheese and thinly sliced radishes or small watercress sprigs for the nuts.

Substitute feta cheese for the Camembert or blue cheese and whole black Greek olives for the nuts.

WHOLE WHEAT PASTRY

1 cup whole wheat flour
6 tablespoons butter, chilled and cut into
  small pieces
1 egg

Place the flour in a mixing bowl. Cut in the butter with a pastry blender, 2 knives, or your fingers, working quickly, until the mixture resembles coarse cornmeal. With a fork, stir in the egg until blended. Form the dough into a ball. Press the dough evenly over the bottom and about 1¾ inches up the sides of a 9-inch round cheesecake pan or a round cake pan with a removable bottom. Bake in a preheated 350°F oven about 20 minutes or until golden brown.

COCKTAIL PIZZA SQUARES

This and the following recipe should leave pizza fans wreathed in smiles.

¾ cup plus 2 tablespoons warm water
  (110°F)
1 package active dry yeast
1½ tablespoons corn oil
¾ teaspoon salt
2⅔ cups unsifted all-purpose flour
2 pounds ripe tomatoes, peeled, seeded,
  and chopped
¼ pound Italian sausage
2 tablespoons olive oil
1 teaspoon crushed dried oregano
1 teaspoon crushed dried basil
  Freshly ground pepper to taste
1 pound mozzarella cheese, sliced
2 cans (2 ounces each) flat anchovy fillets
  packed in oil, drained

Pour the warm water into a large mixing bowl and sprinkle it with the yeast. Let the mixture stand 2 or 3 minutes, then stir to dissolve the yeast. Add the corn oil, ¼ teaspoon of the salt, and the flour and mix until the ingredients are well blended and form a soft dough. Transfer the dough onto a lightly floured surface and knead thoroughly, sprinkling occasionally with just enough flour to keep it from sticking. When it is smooth and elastic, form it into a ball and place it in a lightly greased bowl. Turn the dough over to grease the top. Cover loosely with a kitchen towel and let rise in a warm place free from drafts about 1½ hours or until doubled in size.

Meanwhile, combine the tomatoes and remaining ½ teaspoon salt in a heavy saucepan. Cover and simmer about 10 minutes or until very soft. Remove from the heat and set aside. In a heavy skillet cook the sausage in a little water 5 minutes. Drain and continue to cook, turning to brown lightly on all sides. Transfer to a plate and cool. Slice the sausage and set aside.

Grease a 15 by 10 by 1-inch jelly roll pan. Punch down the dough, transfer it to a lightly floured surface, and form it into a ball. Roll the dough into a long strip about the size of the pan. Place the dough in the pan, pressing and stretching it with your fingers until it touches the sides of the pan all around. Spread the tomatoes over the dough and sprinkle evenly with the olive oil, oregano, basil, and pepper. Lay the cheese slices over the tomatoes. Arrange the sausage slices over one-third of the cheese. Arrange the anchovies over another third, leaving the remaining third with cheese only. Bake the pizza in a preheated 500°F oven 15 to 20 minutes or until lightly browned. Cut into squares and serve. Makes about 36.

VARIATIONS:

Other toppings, such as cooked artichoke hearts, thin slices of prosciutto, Italian salami, pepperoni, or any good cured sausage, and slices of mushrooms or green pepper brushed with olive oil, can be used.

One loaf (1 pound) frozen bread dough can be substituted for the homemade dough. Thaw as directed on the package.

Substitute Tomato Sauce (page 398) for the cooked tomatoes.

PESTO PIZZA

A delectable departure from the usual tomato-flavored pizza.

    1 package active dry yeast
    2 teaspoons sugar
 2⅔ cups warm water (110°F)
    ⅓ cup olive oil
    1 tablespoon salt
 5½ cups all-purpose flour (approximately)
    Cornmeal
    1 egg, lightly beaten with 1 tablespoon
    water
    Pesto Sauce (page 393)

In a large bowl dissolve the yeast and sugar in ⅔ cup of the warm water. Let the mixture stand about 10 minutes or until foamy. Stir in the remaining 2 cups warm water, olive oil, and salt. Mix in 5 cups of the flour, 1 cup at a time, beating thoroughly with a wooden spoon after each addition, until the dough comes away from the sides of the bowl. Sprinkle your work surface with the remaining ½ cup flour. Transfer the dough onto the surface and knead thoroughly, sprinkling occasionally with just enough flour to keep it from sticking. When it is smooth and elastic in texture, form it into a ball and place it in a lightly greased bowl. Turn the dough over to grease the top. Cover loosely with a kitchen towel and let rise in a warm place free from drafts about 1½ hours or until doubled in size.

Grease two 14-inch pizza pans or heavy-bottomed baking sheets. Sprinkle with cornmeal and set aside. Punch down the dough and transfer it to a lightly floured surface. Knead briefly and form into a ball. Return to the bowl, cover with the towel, and let stand in a warm place free from drafts about 1½ hours or until it is again doubled in size.

Punch down the dough and transfer it to a lightly floured surface. Divide it into 2 equal parts. Roll or pat each part into a 14-inch circle. Transfer to the prepared pans. Pinch up the edges of the dough to form shallow rims. Brush twice with the egg and water mixture. Spread the Pesto Sauce evenly over the crusts, dividing equally. Let stand in a warm place free from drafts about 30 minutes. Bake the pizzas in a preheated 400°F oven 25 to 30 minutes or until the crusts are lightly browned. Remove from the oven and let stand 5 minutes at room temperature. Cut into wedges and serve. Makes 2 14-inch pizzas.

VARIATION:

Arrange the slices of Italian Fontina, Bel Paese, or mozzarella cheese over the Pesto Sauce before baking.

PISSALADIÈRE NIÇOISE

Niçoise Onion Tart with Anchovies and Black Olives

Pissaladière is to Provence what pizza is to Italy. In Nice it is made either like pizza (on a flat round of dough) or in a pastry shell. This recipe is an example of the latter type.

2 recipes Short Crust Pastry (page 364)
6 tablespoons olive oil
2 pounds onions, thinly sliced (about 6 cups)
4 large tomatoes, peeled, seeded, and coarsely chopped
2 large garlic cloves, finely chopped
1 teaspoon crushed dried thyme
1 teaspoon crushed dried rosemary
1 bay leaf
Salt and freshly ground pepper to taste
3 tablespoons stale breadcrumbs
¼ cup freshly grated imported Parmesan cheese
2 cans (1 ounce each) flat anchovy fillets, drained
Pitted black olives (preferably Mediterranean)

On a lightly floured surface roll out the pastry into an 18 by 13-inch rectangle. Fit the pastry into a 15 by 10 by 1-inch jelly roll pan and crimp the edges decoratively. Prick the bottom of the shell with a fork and chill the shell.

In a large, heavy skillet heat 4 table-spoons of the oil over moderate heat. Add the onions, reduce the heat to low, and cover the skillet with a buttered round of waxed paper and the lid. Cook the onions, stirring occasionally, about 30 minutes. Add the tomatoes, garlic, thyme, rosemary, bay leaf, salt, and pepper. Cover and cook over low heat 10 minutes. Uncover and cook over medium-high heat, stirring, about 10 minutes longer or until most of the liquid has evaporated. Remove from the heat and allow to cool.

Sprinkle the breadcrumbs over the bottom of the pastry shell. Spread the onion mixture evenly over the breadcrumbs, then sprinkle the Parmesan cheese evenly over the onion mixture. Arrange the anchovy fillets in a lattice pattern over the top and place an olive in the center of each square formed by the anchovies. Sprinkle the pissaladière with the remaining 2 table-spoons oil. Bake in a preheated 425°F oven about 35 minutes or until the crust is golden brown. Cut into squares and serve. Makes about 15 servings.

LUMPIA

Philippine Deep-Fried Pork, Shrimp, and Vegetable Rolls

Authentically, lumpia *wrappers—available in Philippine food markets—are used for this appetizer, but the more easily obtainable won ton wrappers make a very acceptable substitute.*

>   *Lumpia Filling (below)*
>   *Dipping Sauce (page 374)*
> *1 pound (about 90) ready-made won ton wrappers (available at Oriental groceries and some supermarkets), thawed if frozen*
>   *Flavorless vegetable oil*

Prepare the Lumpia Filling and Dipping Sauce as directed. Drain the juices from the filling, reserving ¼ cup. Stir ¼ cup of the Dipping Sauce into the filling.

Cover the won ton wrappers with a barely dampened kitchen towel to keep them from drying.

To assemble the *lumpia*, place about 1 teaspoon filling near the lower corner of a won ton wrapper. Fold the corner over the filling to cover it, then tuck in the sides and roll up. Repeat this procedure with the remaining wrappers and filling. Place the lumpia ½ inch apart on baking sheets or trays and cover them with a dry kitchen towel.

In a large, heavy skillet or deep-fryer heat ¼ inch oil to 375°F over moderate heat. Add the lumpia, seam sides down, in batches and fry, turning frequently, 1 to 2 minutes or until golden brown and crisp. With a slotted spoon, transfer the lumpia as they brown to a baking sheet lined with paper towels and keep them warm in a 250°F oven until all are fried.

Stir the reserved ¼ cup juices from the filling into the Dipping Sauce and reheat to boiling over high heat. Serve hot with the warm lumpia. Makes about 90.

LUMPIA FILLING

>   *¾ pound lean ground pork*
>   *1 medium onion, finely chopped*
>   *3 medium garlic cloves, finely chopped*
>   *6 ounces shelled and deveined raw shrimp, chopped*
>   *2 tablespoons finely chopped cooked ham*
>   *½ cup coarsely chopped bean sprouts*
>   *¼ cup finely chopped water chestnuts*
> *1½ tablespoons imported soy sauce*

Crumble the pork into a large, heavy skillet. Add the onion and garlic and sauté the mixture over moderate heat, stirring constantly, until the pork is browned and finely crumbled and the onion is soft. Add the shrimp and ham and cook, stirring, 2 minutes. Add the bean sprouts and water chestnuts and cook, stirring, 2 minutes. Stir in the soy sauce and remove from the heat.

DIPPING SAUCE

¼ cup firmly packed brown sugar
2 tablespoons cornstarch
½ cup cold water
½ cup freshly squeezed and strained
    orange juice or pineapple juice
3½ tablespoons white wine vinegar
3½ tablespoons imported soy sauce
1 tablespoon flavorless vegetable oil
2 medium garlic cloves, finely chopped

In a small bowl mix together the brown sugar and cornstarch. Stir in the water, orange or pineapple juice, vinegar, and soy sauce until well blended.

In a small saucepan heat the oil over moderate heat. Add the garlic and sauté, stirring constantly, until golden. Add the cornstarch mixture and cook, stirring, until the sauce boils and thickens.

DIM SUM

A specialty of southeastern China (particularly Canton), *dim sum* encompass a variety of dishes including steamed, baked, and fried filled packets made with many kinds of doughs and containing skillfully seasoned mixtures of meat, seafood, vegetable, sweet paste, or preserves. In the Cantonese dialect dim sum broadly means "touch the heart," indicating that they are meant to be enjoyed as light snacks whenever the heart desires. In old China these delicacies were savored in teahouses along with black or green tea; today there are also many restaurants outside of China that specialize in serving them. Even though dim sum are considered snacks or light meals in Chinese cuisine, they make outstanding appetizers and brunch dishes for Western entertaining.

EGG ROLLS

Egg rolls can often be crude and greasy affairs in many so-called Chinese restaurants in America, but when properly prepared they are delicate and delightful.

Shrimp and Pork Filling (page 376), or Chicken and Vegetable Filling (page 376)

16 ready-made Cantonese egg roll wrappers (available at Oriental groceries and many supermarkets), thawed if frozen

1 egg, lightly beaten

4 cups peanut oil or flavorless vegetable oil for deep-frying

Chinese Plum Sauce I or II (page 396 or 397)

Chinese mustard

Prepare the filling of your choice.

Cover the egg roll wrappers with a barely dampened kitchen towel to keep them from drying. Assemble each egg roll as follows: Lay an egg roll wrapper on a flat surface with a corner pointing toward you. Place about ¼ cup filling on it, about 2½ inches above the lower corner. Form it with your fingers into a compact cylinder about 4 inches long and 1 inch in diameter, the length lying horizontal to you. Roll the lower flap tightly over the filling and tuck the point under it. Roll over once to enclose the filling. Bring each of the two side flaps, one at a time, securely across the enclosed filling, making certain that there are no unnecessary wrinkles. Press the points down firmly (the wrapper will now look like an open envelope). Brush the remaining exposed area of dough with some of the beaten egg, then roll up the wrapper firmly into a tight, neat package. Place the egg rolls, seam sides down and ½ inch apart, on a tray or baking sheet and cover with a dry kitchen towel.

In a wok or deep-fryer heat the oil to 375°F. Add the egg rolls, 4 at a time, and deep-fry, turning frequently, 3 to 4 minutes or until golden brown and crisp. As they brown, transfer them with a slotted spoon to a baking sheet lined with paper towels and keep them warm in a 250°F oven until all are fried. With a heavy, sharp knife cut each egg roll diagonally into 3 sections. Serve at once, accompanied with the Plum Sauce and Chinese mustard. Makes 16 egg rolls (48 pieces).

VARIATION:

SPRING ROLLS

Substitute 16 ready-made Shanghai spring roll wrappers (available at Oriental food markets) for the egg roll wrappers. Serve the rolls as soon as they are fried; keeping them warm in the oven will toughen them and dry them out.

SHRIMP AND PORK FILLING

3 tablespoons peanut oil or flavorless
    vegetable oil
½ pound lean ground pork
1 tablespoon Chinese rice wine or dry
    Sherry
1 tablespoon imported soy sauce
½ teaspoon sugar
½ pound shrimp, shelled, deveined, and
    finely diced
3 medium mushrooms, thinly sliced
2 cups finely chopped celery
½ pound fresh bean sprouts, washed,
    drained, and dried with paper towels
2 teaspoons salt
1 tablespoon cornstarch dissolved in 2
    tablespoons cold water

Heat a wok or large, heavy skillet over high heat 30 seconds. Add 1 tablespoon of the oil, swirl it about in the pan, and heat 30 seconds. Reduce the heat to moderate. Add the pork and sauté, stirring constantly, 2 minutes or until it changes color. Add the rice wine or Sherry, soy sauce, sugar, shrimp, and mushrooms and sauté, stirring continuously, 1 minute or until the shrimp turn pink. Transfer the contents of the pan to a bowl and set aside.

Add the remaining 2 tablespoons oil to the pan, swirl it about, and heat 30 seconds over high heat. Reduce the heat to moder-ate. Add the celery and sauté, stirring constantly, 5 minutes. Add the bean sprouts and salt and mix well. Return the pork and shrimp mixture to the pan and stir until the ingredients are thoroughly combined. Cook, stirring constantly, until the liquid begins to boil. Spoon off and discard any liquid remaining in the pan in excess of 2 or 3 tablespoons. Stir the cornstarch and water mixture to recombine it and add it to the pan. Cook, stirring constantly, until the cooking liquids have thickened. Transfer the contents of the pan to a bowl and allow to cool to room temperature.

CHICKEN AND VEGETABLE FILLING

6 dried Chinese black mushrooms
3 tablespoons peanut oil or flavorless
    vegetable oil
1½ cups thinly shredded chicken meat
⅓ cup thinly shredded bamboo shoots
4 scallions, finely chopped, including 2
    inches of the green tops
1 cup fresh bean sprouts, washed,
    drained, and dried with paper towels
2 teaspoons imported soy sauce
½ teaspoon sugar
1½ teaspoons salt
2½ teaspoons cornstarch

In a small bowl soak the mushrooms in hot water to cover about 15 minutes, or until they are soft. Drain the mushrooms, remove and discard the stems, and shred the caps. Reserve.

Heat a wok or large, heavy skillet over high heat 30 seconds. Add the oil, swirl it about in the pan, and heat 30 seconds. Reduce the heat to medium-high. Add the chicken, bamboo shoots, and scallions and sauté, stirring constantly, 1 minute. Add the reserved mushrooms and bean sprouts and sauté, stirring, 1 minute. Add the soy sauce, sugar, salt, and cornstarch and cook, stirring, 1 minute. Transfer the contents of the pan to a colander and allow to drain. Let cool to room temperature.

PORK, SHRIMP, AND MUSHROOM TURNOVERS

4 dried Chinese black mushrooms
4 teaspoons imported soy sauce
1½ teaspoons Chinese rice wine or dry Sherry
2½ teaspoons imported sesame oil
½ pound lean ground pork
2 tablespoons chicken broth
2 teaspoons peeled and finely chopped fresh ginger root
1½ teaspoons cornstarch
1 large garlic clove, very finely chopped
½ teaspoon sugar
½ teaspoon salt
4 tablespoons peanut oil or flavorless vegetable oil
6 ounces shrimp, shelled, deveined, and finely chopped
½ cup finely chopped scallions, including 2 inches of the green tops
2 recipes Short Crust Pastry (page 364), substituting vegetable shortening or lard for the butter, if desired
1 egg, well beaten

In a small bowl soak the mushrooms in hot water to cover about 15 minutes, or until they are soft. Drain the mushrooms, remove and discard the stems, and finely chop the caps. Reserve.

In a medium bowl combine 1 teaspoon of the soy sauce, ½ teaspoon of the rice wine or Sherry, and ½ teaspoon of the sesame oil. Add the pork, mix well, and set aside.

In a small bowl combine the chicken broth, the remaining 3 teaspoons soy sauce, 1 teaspoon rice wine or Sherry, and 2 teaspoons sesame oil, the ginger root, cornstarch, garlic, sugar, and salt. Set aside.

Heat a wok or heavy skillet over high heat until very hot. Add 2 tablespoons of the peanut oil or vegetable oil and heat until very hot. Add the pork mixture and sauté over medium-high heat, stirring constantly, 1 to 2 minutes or until it separates and changes color. Transfer it to a colander to drain. Add 1 tablespoon of the remaining peanut oil or vegetable oil to the pan and heat until very hot. Add the shrimp and sauté, stirring constantly, about 1 minute or until it turns pink. Transfer to the colander. Add the remaining 1 tablespoon peanut oil or vegetable oil to the pan and heat until very hot. Add the reserved mushrooms and sauté, stirring constantly, 30 seconds. Stir in the scallions and pork mixture. Stir the cornstarch mixture to recombine it and add

it to the pan. Cook, stirring, until the sauce is thickened. Transfer the contents of the pan to a bowl. Allow to cool to room temperature, then cover and chill 1 hour.

Divide the pastry dough into two equal parts. Roll out one part at a time on a lightly floured surface to ¹⁄₁₆-inch thickness. With a 3-inch cookie cutter cut out circles. Reroll the scraps and cut out additional rounds. Place 1 rounded teaspoon of the meat mixture in the center of one half of each circle. Moisten the edges of the circle with a finger dipped in cold water. Fold over the other half to make a half-moon shape and seal the edges by pressing them firmly with the tines of a fork. Arrange the turnovers ½ inch apart on a large ungreased baking sheet. Brush the tops with the beaten egg and prick them with the tines of a fork. Bake the turnovers in a preheated 400°F oven about 20 minutes or until golden brown. Serve hot. Makes about 36.

SHAO MAI
Steamed Dumplings

Dumplings have long figured importantly in Chinese cuisine.

Pork and Shrimp Filling (page 380), or Chicken and Shrimp Filling (page 380)
About 48 ready-made shao mai wrappers (available at Oriental groceries), thawed if frozen, or about 48 ready-made won ton wrappers (available at Oriental groceries and many supermarkets), thawed if frozen and cut into 3-inch circles

Prepare the filling of your choice.

Fill each dumpling as follows: Place a pastry wrapper in your hand and cup it loosely. Put about 1 tablespoon filling in the center. With the aid of your other hand, gather the sides of the wrapper around the filling, allowing the wrapper to pleat naturally and leaving the filling exposed on top. Gently squeeze the middle of the dumpling to give it a waist, being careful not to allow any of the filling to spill over the sides. Lightly tap the dumpling on your work surface to flatten its bottom so that it can stand upright. Smooth the top of the filling with the back of a spoon dipped in cold water.

Arrange a batch of the dumplings, not touching one another, on the tray of a Chinese steamer (refrigerate the remaining dumplings, covered with plastic wrap, until ready to use). Place the steamer over boiling water in a wok and cover tightly. Steam over medium-high heat about 20 minutes or until the pork is tender and the shrimp are opaque. If you do not have a steamer, use a heatproof plate set on a trivet above a shallow layer of water in a large, tightly covered roasting pan. The plate should be slightly smaller in diameter (about 2 inches) than the pan to allow the steam to rise and circulate freely. Do not allow the water to come within less than 1 inch of the plate. Have a kettle of boiling water at hand so that you can add more water to the wok or roasting pan to replace that lost by evaporation. With chopsticks, tongs, or a slotted spoon, transfer the cooked dumplings to a heated serving platter and place a domed cover over them to keep them warm while you steam the remaining dumplings. Serve at once. Makes about 48.

Note: If desired, garnish the tops of the dumplings with a little grated carrot, fresh coriander leaves, shelled peas, minced ham, or small whole shrimp.

PORK AND SHRIMP FILLING

1½ cups finely chopped celery cabbage
¾ teaspoon salt
1 pound finely ground lean pork
¼ pound shrimp, shelled, deveined, and finely diced
1 slice fresh ginger root (about 1 inch in diameter and ⅛ inch thick), peeled and very finely chopped
1 scallion, finely chopped, including 2 inches of the green top
2 tablespoons imported soy sauce
2 tablespoons dry Sherry
1 tablespoon imported sesame oil
1 tablespoon cornstarch dissolved in 3 tablespoons water
¼ teaspoon sugar
Few grindings pepper

In a small bowl sprinkle the cabbage with ½ teaspoon of the salt and let stand 5 minutes. Squeeze it dry lightly and combine it in a large bowl with the remaining ¼ teaspoon salt and the rest of the ingredients. Mix thoroughly.

CHICKEN AND SHRIMP FILLING

6 dried Chinese black mushrooms
1 cup skinned, boned, and finely chopped chicken breast
¼ pound shrimp, shelled, deveined, and finely chopped
12 water chestnuts, finely chopped
4 scallions, finely chopped, including 2 inches of the green tops
3 tablespoons imported soy sauce
1 tablespoon imported sesame oil
1 tablespoon dry Sherry
¾ teaspoon salt

In a small bowl soak the mushrooms in hot water to cover about 15 minutes, or until they are soft. Drain the mushrooms, remove and discard the stems, and finely chop the caps.

In a large bowl combine the mushroom caps with the remaining ingredients and mix well.

ARMENIAN NOODLE AND SPINACH-CHEESE SQUARES

Delicious hot, even better cold.

1 pound fresh spinach
3 tablespoons olive oil
1 medium onion, finely chopped
2 tablespoons breadcrumbs
2 eggs
½ pound feta cheese, freshly grated
¾ cup cottage cheese
2 tablespoons freshly grated imported
   Parmesan cheese
   Salt to taste
½ pound medium-wide egg noodles
4 tablespoons butter
   Garlic Yogurt Sauce (page 392) (optional)

Wash the spinach thoroughly under cold running water, discarding the tough stems and bruised leaves. Drain and dry the spinach leaves, chop them, and reserve.

In a medium-sized, heavy skillet heat the oil over moderate heat. Add the onion and sauté, stirring frequently, until soft but not browned. Add the spinach and simmer about 10 minutes or until soft, stirring frequently. Mix in the breadcrumbs, remove from the heat, and set aside.

In a medium mixing bowl beat the eggs lightly. Add the cheeses and spinach mixture and blend well. Taste and add salt if needed. Set aside.

Cook the noodles according to package directions. Drain well in a colander. Return to the hot pot in which they were cooked and toss gently but thoroughly with 2 tablespoons of the butter. Place half the noodles in a buttered 9 by 9 by 2-inch baking pan. Spread evenly with the spinach and cheese mixture. Cover with the remaining noodles and dot with the remaining 2 tablespoons butter. Bake in a preheated 375°F oven 30 minutes. Uncover and bake about 15 minutes or until golden brown. Remove from the oven and allow to cool 5 minutes, then cut into squares. Serve hot or chilled, accompanied with the Garlic Yogurt Sauce, if desired. Makes 6 servings.

PASTA WITH GORGONZOLA SAUCE

Whether you love or leave this first course will depend on your attitude toward Gorgonzola cheese. If you love it, you may hate to leave it.

¼ pound Gorgonzola cheese, crumbled
⅓ cup milk
3 tablespoons butter
⅓ cup heavy cream
1 pound spinach pasta, fettuccine, or
  spaghetti, cooked al dente and drained
  Freshly grated imported Parmesan
  cheese

In a large, enameled skillet combine the Gorgonzola cheese, milk, and butter. Cook over low heat, mashing the cheese with a wooden spoon and stirring to incorporate it into the milk and butter, until the mixture is smooth. Add the cream and stir until the sauce is hot and well blended. Add the hot pasta and ⅓ cup Parmesan cheese and toss lightly until the noodles are evenly coated with the sauce. Serve at once directly from the skillet, with a bowl of additional Parmesan on the side. Makes 6 to 8 servings.

GREEN FETTUCCINE WITH MUSHROOMS, PROSCIUTTO, AND PEAS

Unforgettably good.

¼ cup butter
6 ounces mushrooms, sliced
6 ounces prosciutto or other ham, cut into
  julienne strips
1 medium garlic clove, finely chopped
¾ cup heavy cream
1 cup shelled green peas, cooked until
  almost tender, or 1 cup frozen tiny green
  peas, thawed
¼ teaspoon freshly grated nutmeg
½ pound green fettuccine, cooked al dente
  and drained
  Freshly grated imported Parmesan
  cheese
  Salt and freshly ground white pepper to
  taste

In a large, heavy skillet melt the butter over moderate heat. Add the mushrooms, ham, and garlic and cook, stirring frequently, until the mushrooms are lightly browned. Add the cream and peas, bring to a boil, and cook, stirring constantly, until the cream is slightly thickened. Reduce the heat to low and stir in the nutmeg. Add the fettuccine and ½ cup Parmesan and toss lightly until the pasta is heated and evenly coated with the sauce. Season with salt and white pepper. Transfer to a warmed serving dish and serve at once with a bowl of additional cheese on the side. Makes 6 to 8 servings.

BEDOUIN FRIED STUFFED RICE BALLS

These will prove as intriguing to the palate as they look on paper.

6 cups water
2¼ teaspoons salt
1½ cups uncooked long-grain white rice
½ teaspoon grated lemon rind
1 tablespoon butter
¼ cup pine nuts
½ pound lean ground lamb or beef
1 small onion, finely chopped
1 medium garlic clove, finely chopped
¼ cup seedless raisins
2 tablespoons finely chopped parsley
½ teaspoon cinnamon
½ teaspoon allspice
¼ teaspoon cumin
    Flavorless vegetable oil for deep-frying

In a large, heavy saucepan bring the water and 1½ teaspoons of the salt to a boil over high heat. Stir in the rice and reduce the heat to low. Cover and boil gently about 40 minutes or until the water is absorbed and the rice is tender and sticky. Stir in the lemon rind, remove from heat, and let cool.

Meanwhile, in a small, heavy skillet melt the butter over moderate heat. Add the pine nuts and sauté, stirring constantly, until golden. With a slotted spoon transfer the nuts to a plate and set aside. Add the ground meat, onion, and garlic to the skillet and, breaking up the meat with a fork, cook until the meat is no longer pink. Drain off any excess fat from the skillet. Stir in the reserved pine nuts, raisins, parsley, the remaining ¾ teaspoon salt, cinnamon, allspice, and cumin. Taste and adjust the seasoning.

Prepare each rice ball as follows: Place about 2½ tablespoons cooked rice in the palm of your hand and flatten it into a thin, round cake. Place 2 to 3 teaspoons of the meat mixture in the center. Cup your hand to mold the rice around the filling. Top with additional rice, press together to cover the filling completely, and form the ball into an oval shape. If the rice is too sticky to handle easily, moisten your hands lightly with water.

In a deep-fryer or large, heavy saucepan

heat 2 inches oil to 450°F. With a slotted spoon lower 1 rice ball at a time into the hot oil. Fry 6 or 8 balls at a time, turning them frequently, about 4 minutes or until golden brown on all sides. As each batch is done, transfer the balls with the slotted spoon to a baking dish lined with paper towels and keep them warm in a preheated 200°F oven while you fry the remaining balls. Arrange the balls on a heated platter and serve at once. Makes about 24.

SUSHI

Widely appreciated in Japan as well as in Hawaii, sushi is gaining popularity in this country. To shape the rolls, use a bamboo mat or special reed mat called a sudaré *(available at stores that sell Oriental cooking equipment).*

> *Fish and Spinach Filling (page 385), or Shrimp Filling (page 385)*
> *2½ cups water*
> *½ cup rice vinegar*
> *1 tablespoon sugar*
> *1 teaspoon salt*
> *2 cups uncooked short-grain white rice*
> *2 sheets dried seaweed (nori, available in Oriental food markets)*
> *¾ cup Japanese soy sauce*
> *Thin slices of peeled fresh ginger root*

Prepare either of the fillings and set aside. In a medium-sized, heavy saucepan combine the water, vinegar, sugar, and salt. Bring to a boil over high heat. Add the rice, cover, reduce the heat to low, and simmer 12 minutes. Remove from the heat and let stand 10 minutes without lifting the lid.

Soften the sheets of seaweed in a bowl of warm water 3 minutes. Place a bamboo mat or *sudaré* on your work surface with the strands running crosswise. Have a bowl of cold water nearby for moistening your hands as you work with the rice. Lay 1 sheet of dried seaweed on the mat. Moisten your hands and spread half the rice over the surface of the seaweed, leaving a 1¼-inch border. Arrange half the filling in a horizontal row in the center of the rice. If using the Fish and Spinach Filling, place the scrambled eggs on the rice first, then the spinach on top of the eggs, and, finally, the fish on top of the spinach. Holding down the filling ingredients with your fingers, lift the mat with your thumbs and use it as a guide to roll up the seaweed, pulling away the mat as you roll and using a little pressure to tighten the roll. Press in any ingredients that protrude from the ends of the roll. Wrap the roll in plastic wrap and refrigerate. Repeat this procedure with the remaining sheet of dried seaweed, rice, and filling. Chill the rolls at least 1 hour before slicing.

Cut the rolls into ¾-inch-thick slices and arrange them on a serving platter. In a small bowl combine the soy sauce with the slices of ginger root and serve as a dipping sauce for the sushi. Makes 8 servings.

FISH AND SPINACH FILLING

2 eggs
4 teaspoons sake or dry Sherry
1 tablespoon sugar
½ teaspoon salt
¼ cup flavorless vegetable oil
1 3-ounce flounder fillet, cut lengthwise
   into ¼-inch-wide strips
   All-purpose flour
½ cup thoroughly drained cooked spinach

In a small bowl beat the eggs lightly. Stir in the *sake* or Sherry, sugar, and salt. In a small, heavy skillet heat 2 tablespoons of the oil over moderate heat. Add the egg mixture and reduce the heat to low. Cook, gently stirring the egg mixture, lifting it up and over from the bottom as it thickens. Remove the scrambled eggs from the heat and set aside.

Dredge the pieces of fish in flour, shaking off the excess. In another small, heavy skillet heat the remaining 2 tablespoons oil over moderate heat. Add the pieces of fish and sauté about 1½ minutes on each side or un-til the fish flakes. Remove from the heat and set aside with the spinach.

SHRIMP FILLING

2 eggs
6 large shrimp, shelled, deveined, and
   very finely chopped
2 tablespoons sake or dry Sherry
1 tablespoon sugar
¼ teaspoon salt
2 tablespoons flavorless vegetable oil

In a small bowl beat the eggs lightly. Stir in the shrimp, *sake* or Sherry, sugar, and salt. In a small, heavy skillet heat the oil over moderate heat. Add the shrimp mixture and reduce the heat to low. Cook about 4 minutes, gently stirring the mixture, lifting it up and over from the bottom as the eggs thicken. Remove from the heat and set aside.

SAUCES

It is said that cooks are judged by their sauces. A selection of savory sauces should be in every cook's repertoire. Not only can a sauce add splendor to the humblest of dishes; it can often provide the final touch of perfection to an aristocratic one. In many cases it is the sauce that makes the dish.

In this chapter you will find recipes for sauces that are called for in appetizers described elsewhere in this book. I am confident that you will also find them useful in enhancing many of your own creations as well.

———◇———

SAUCE VINAIGRETTE

2 tablespoons wine vinegar, or 1
　tablespoon each wine vinegar and freshly
　squeezed and strained lemon juice
½ teaspoon salt
　Freshly ground pepper to taste
½ teaspoon Dijon-style mustard (optional)
⅓ to ½ cup olive oil, or a combination of
　olive oil and corn oil

Combine the vinegar (or vinegar and lemon juice), salt, pepper, and mustard (if used) in a small bowl. Stir to dissolve the salt, then gradually beat in the oil. Makes about ½ cup.

VARIATIONS:

LEMON VINAIGRETTE

Substitute 3 tablespoons or more freshly squeezed and strained lemon juice for the vinegar or vinegar and lemon juice.

LIME VINAIGRETTE

Substitute 3 tablespoons or more freshly squeezed and strained lime juice for the vinegar or vinegar and lemon juice.

GARLIC VINAIGRETTE

To Sauce Vinaigrette add 1 medium garlic clove or to taste, crushed and finely chopped.

MAYONNAISE

An electric blender greatly simplifies the preparation of mayonnaise.

1 egg
2 tablespoons freshly squeezed and
　strained lemon juice or white wine
　vinegar, or 1 tablespoon each lemon
　juice and vinegar
½ teaspoon dry mustard
½ teaspoon salt
⅛ teaspoon freshly ground white pepper or
　to taste
1 cup olive oil, corn oil, or a combination
　of both

Put the egg, lemon juice and/or vinegar, mustard, salt, pepper, and ¼ cup of the oil in the container of an electric blender. Cover the container and turn the motor on high. Immediately remove the cover and add the remaining ¾ cup oil in a thin, steady stream. Turn off the motor as soon as all the oil has been added and the mixture is thickened. Use the mayonnaise at once, or transfer to a clean jar, cover tightly, and refrigerate. It will keep up to one week. Makes about 1¼ cups.

VARIATIONS:

HERB MAYONNAISE

Add 1 tablespoon each finely minced fresh parsley, chives, and tarragon or dill. Mix well. Taste and adjust the seasoning.

SAUCE VERTE (GREEN MAYONNAISE)

In the container of an electric blender combine 1 cup Mayonnaise, ⅔ cup coarsely chopped watercress leaves, 3 tablespoons minced parsley, 2 teaspoons minced scallion (include 2 inches of the green top), and 2 teaspoons minced fresh tarragon; the greens may be blanched before using. Cover and blend at high speed until the mixture is smooth and evenly colored. Taste and adjust the seasoning.

PESTO MAYONNAISE

Add ⅓ cup Pesto Sauce (page 393). Mix well. Taste and adjust the seasoning.

SHALLOT MAYONNAISE

In a small saucepan combine 2 shallots, minced, 3 tablespoons each tarragon wine vinegar and white wine, and 2 teaspoons minced fresh tarragon. Cook the mixture over medium-high heat until the liquid has completely evaporated. Remove from the heat and cool. Combine 1¼ cups Mayonnaise with the shallot mixture, 2 teaspoons capers, rinsed, drained, and minced, 2 tea-spoons each minced parsley and chives, and 1 teaspoon Dijon-style mustard. Mix well. Taste and adjust the seasoning.

TOMATO-COGNAC MAYONNAISE

Add 2 tablespoons tomato ketchup or thick homemade tomato purée and 2 tea-spoons Cognac. Mix well.

MUSTARD MAYONNAISE

In a bowl mix together ¾ cup Mayonnaise and 1½ tablespoons each Dijon-style mustard and freshly squeezed and strained lemon juice. Carefully fold in ⅓ cup heavy cream, whipped, and season with salt to taste.

CURRY MAYONNAISE

Add 1 teaspoon curry powder or to taste and ½ teaspoon freshly squeezed and strained lemon or lime juice. Mix well.

ALI-OLI
(Garlic Mayonnaise)

A favorite throughout the Mediterranean, where it exists in numerous versions, this sauce probably originated in ancient Egypt and was brought to southern Europe by the Romans over two thousand years ago. The name ali-oli, *by which it is known in Catalonia (a region in northeastern Spain), reflects its long history, deriving directly from the Latin for garlic* (allium) *and oil* (oleum). *A close relative is the Provençal* aïoli *of southeastern France.*

1 cup Mayonnaise (page 387)
2 large garlic cloves or to taste, crushed to a smooth purée

Combine the Mayonnaise and garlic in a small bowl and blend well. Cover and chill at least 1 hour before serving. Makes 1 cup.

VARIATION:
ALI-OLI WITH MUSTARD
Add 2 teaspoons Dijon-style mustard or to taste.

LOUIS DRESSING

½ cup Mayonnaise (page 387)
¼ cup heavy cream, whipped
2 tablespoons chili sauce
2 scallions, finely chopped, including 2 inches of the green tops
2 tablespoons finely chopped green pepper (optional)
2 teaspoons freshly squeezed and strained lemon juice
Few drops Tobasco sauce
Salt to taste

Combine all the ingredients in a small bowl and stir until well blended. Taste and adjust the seasoning. Cover and refrigerate. Makes about 1 cup.

HORSERADISH SAUCE

1 cup sour cream, or ½ cup each sour cream and Mayonnaise (page 387)
1 to 2 tablespoons freshly grated horseradish or to taste

Combine the ingredients in a small bowl and mix well. Cover and chill 2 hours before serving. Makes about 1 cup.

VARIATION:

Omit the Mayonnaise. Use 1 cup sour cream or ½ cup heavy cream, whipped, and add along with the horseradish 1 teaspoon freshly squeezed and strained lemon juice or white wine vinegar (or to taste), ¼ to ½ teaspoon sugar, if desired, and salt to taste.

EGG SAUCE

1 hard-cooked egg, or 1 hard-cooked egg yolk
⅔ cup sour cream
⅓ cup Mayonnaise (page 387)
1 teaspoon Dijon-style mustard or to taste
2 teaspoons finely chopped dill or to taste
Salt to taste

Sieve the egg or egg yolk into a small bowl. Add the remaining ingredients and blend thoroughly. Taste and adjust the seasoning. Cover and chill. Makes about 1¼ cups.

MUSTARD SAUCE

1 hard-cooked egg yolk
1 raw egg yolk
1½ teaspoons Dijon-style mustard
½ cup olive oil
1½ tablespoons white wine vinegar or to taste
Salt and freshly ground pepper to taste

In a small bowl mash the hard-cooked egg yolk with the raw egg yolk and mustard until smooth. Gradually whisk in the oil. Combine the vinegar, salt, and pepper, add to the oil mixture, and blend well. Taste and adjust the seasoning. Use at once, or cover and chill up to 1 hour before serving. Makes about ⅔ cup.

MUSTARD-DILL SAUCE

3 tablespoons fresh dill
¼ cup corn oil
2 tablespoons dry white wine
2 tablespoons Dijon-style mustard
2 tablespoons white wine vinegar
1 tablespoon sugar
1 tablespoon heavy cream
¾ teaspoon dry mustard

Combine all the ingredients in a food processor fitted with the steel blade or in an electric blender. Process until well blended and the dill is finely chopped. Transfer to a bowl, cover, and refrigerate until ready to use. Serve with Gravlax (page 188). Makes about ¾ cup.

SOUTH SEAS DRESSING

¼ cup Mayonnaise (page 387)
½ cup heavy cream, chilled
2 teaspoons grated lime or lemon rind
2 tablespoons freshly squeezed and
    strained lime or lemon juice
2 tablespoons freshly grated coconut
2 teaspoons honey
½ teaspoon peeled and finely grated fresh
    ginger root or to taste
    Salt to taste

Place the Mayonnaise in a bowl. Combine the remaining ingredients in a chilled bowl and beat until fluffy. Fold the mixture into the Mayonnaise until well blended. Taste and adjust the seasoning. Use at once, or cover and refrigerate up to 2 hours before serving. Makes about 1 cup.

CHUTNEY DRESSING

⅔ cup unflavored yogurt
½ cup sour cream
¼ cup fruit chutney, finely chopped
    Grated rind and freshly squeezed and
    strained juice of 1 lime
¼ teaspoon ginger or curry powder or to
    taste
    Salt to taste

Combine all the ingredients in a small bowl and stir until well blended. Taste and adjust the seasoning. Cover and chill. Makes about 1½ cups.

VARIATION:

Substitute ¼ cup Mayonnaise (page 387) for the sour cream and add 1 tablespoon chili sauce or ketchup.

SOUR CREAM AND AVOCADO SAUCE

1 large, ripe avocado
½ cup sour cream
1 tablespoon finely chopped scallion,
    including 2 inches of the green tops
1 teaspoon finely chopped fresh dill or to
    taste
    Salt to taste

Halve the avocado, remove the pit, and peel. Place the avocado flesh in a medium bowl and mash to a smooth purée. Add the remaining ingredients and mix well. Taste and adjust the seasoning. Cover and chill. Makes about 1½ cups.

GARLIC YOGURT SAUCE

1 cup unflavored yogurt
1 medium garlic clove or to taste
¼ teaspoon salt

Spoon the yogurt into a small bowl. Crush the garlic with the salt to a smooth paste. Mix with a few tablespoons of the yogurt, then add to the remaining yogurt in the bowl. Mix well. Taste and adjust the seasoning. Cover and chill. Makes 1 cup.

VARIATION:

HERB GARLIC YOGURT SAUCE
Stir in 1 to 2 tablespoons finely chopped mixed fresh herbs (parsley, chives, and mint, basil, or dill).

MINT OR CORIANDER LEAF CHUTNEY WITH YOGURT

1 cup firmly packed chopped fresh mint or coriander leaves
1 fresh hot green chili pepper, seeded, deribbed, and chopped (optional)
3 tablespoons cold water
1 cup unflavored yogurt
1 tablespoon freshly squeezed and strained lemon juice
½ teaspoon cumin or to taste
½ teaspoon salt or to taste
⅛ teaspoon freshly ground pepper

Put the mint or coriander leaves, chili pepper (if used), and water in the container of an electric blender. Cover and blend the mixture to a smooth paste.

In a medium bowl combine the yogurt, the paste from the blender, lemon juice, cumin, salt, and pepper. Mix well. Taste and adjust the seasoning. Cover and chill. Makes about 1½ cups.

VARIATION:
Omit the chili pepper. Add ⅛ teaspoon cayenne pepper or to taste along with the cumin.

PESTO SAUCE

Some cooks insist that this classic Genoese sauce is at its best only when prepared by hand in a marble mortar. Those who are not inclined toward laborious pounding, however, can still turn out excellent pesto with the aid of an electric blender, a fact that no doubt accounts in large part for the great increase in its popularity on this side of the Atlantic.

    2 cups coarsely chopped and firmly packed
       fresh basil leaves
       Olive oil
    ¼ to ½ cup pine nuts
    2 medium garlic cloves or to taste, finely
       chopped
    ¾ teaspoon salt or to taste
    ⅓ cup freshly grated imported Parmesan
       cheese
    2 tablespoons freshly grated Romano
       cheese

Put the basil, ½ cup olive oil, pine nuts, garlic, and salt in the container of an electric blender and blend at high speed until the ingredients are smooth. Transfer the mixture to a bowl and beat in the Parmesan and Romano cheeses by hand until thoroughly blended. Taste and adjust the seasoning. Transfer the pesto to a clean jar and cover the top with a thin film of olive oil. Seal the jar and refrigerate. Before using, spoon off the layer of oil. Makes about 1½ cups.

SKORDALIA
Greek Garlic and Potato Sauce with Pine Nuts

This pungent preparation, a relative of Ali-Oli (page 389), is one of the three major sauces of Hellenic cuisine. It makes an exciting dip for vegetables and seafood.

    2 medium baking potatoes
    4 medium garlic cloves or to taste
    ½ teaspoon salt or to taste
    ¼ cup pine nuts
    ¼ cup freshly squeezed and strained lemon
       juice (or more)
    ⅔ cup olive oil (approximately)
       Freshly ground pepper to taste
    1 very small egg

Drop the potatoes into lightly salted boiling water and cook briskly until tender. Drain the potatoes thoroughly, peel, and mash them to a smooth purée. Set aside.

With a large mortar and pestle crush the garlic and salt to a fine paste. Add the pine nuts and pound the mixture until a thick paste is formed. Add the nut paste to the mashed potatoes. Rinse the mortar with the lemon juice and pour the juice onto the potatoes. Mix the ingredients together, using an electric mixer or a wooden spoon. Stir in enough olive oil, a little at a time, to obtain a mixture the consistency of very thick mayonnaise. Add the pepper and beat in the egg. Taste and adjust the seasoning. Cover and chill. Serve as a dip for vegetables such as tiny cold cooked beets or Brussels sprouts, cucumber rounds, and cherry tomatoes, for fried, broiled, or boiled seafood, or for Keftedakia (page 254). Makes about 2 cups.

TARATOOR BI TAHINI
Middle Eastern Sesame Sauce

 1 to 2 garlic cloves or to taste
½ teaspoon salt or to taste
½ cup freshly squeezed and strained lemon
    juice
½ cup tahini (sesame seed paste, available
    at Middle Eastern groceries)
    Cold water as needed
½ teaspoon cumin
 2 tablespoons finely chopped parsley or
    paprika

In a deep bowl crush the garlic and ¼ teaspoon of the salt to a paste. Stir in a little of the lemon juice. Add the *tahini* and mix well. Gradually beat in the remaining lemon juice and enough cold water, a spoonful or so at a time, to obtain a thick, creamy, and smooth mixture. Add the remaining ¼ teaspoon salt and the cumin. Taste and adjust the seasoning. Transfer the sauce to a serving bowl and sprinkle with the parsley or paprika. Serve as a dip for Falafel (page 151) or warmed pita bread. Makes about 1 cup.

SINGAPORE-STYLE PEANUT SAUCE

½ cup salted Virginia peanuts
 1 small onion, cut into chunks
 1 medium garlic clove, chopped
 2 small dried hot chili peppers or to taste
 1 tablespoon peanut oil
 1 teaspoon coriander
½ teaspoon cumin
¾ cup Coconut Milk (page 395)
1½ tablespoons brown sugar
 1 tablespoon freshly squeezed and
    strained lemon or lime juice
 1 tablespoon imported soy sauce

Place the peanuts in the container of an electric blender. Cover and blend until finely ground. Transfer to a bowl and reserve.

Combine the onion, garlic, and chili peppers in the blender container. Cover and blend until the mixture is smooth. In a medium-sized, heavy skillet heat the oil over moderate heat. Add the onion mixture, coriander, and cumin and cook, stirring occasionally, 5 minutes. Reduce the heat to low and add the reserved ground peanuts, then gradually stir in the Coconut Milk, brown sugar, lemon or lime juice, and soy sauce. Cook, uncovered, over very low heat, stirring occasionally, about 15 minutes or until the sauce is thickened; do not let it boil. Transfer the sauce to a heatproof serving bowl. Serve hot or warm. Makes about 1¼ cups.

COCONUT MILK

Blender method: Combine 1 cup diced fresh coconut meat with 1 cup hot, but not boiling, water in the container of an electric blender. Cover and blend until the coconut is very finely grated, almost puréed, then squeeze it through a double thickness of dampened cheesecloth to extract all the liquid. Makes about 1 cup.

Hand method: Soak 1 cup freshly grated coconut meat in 1 cup hot, but not boiling, water 30 minutes, then squeeze through cheesecloth as above. Makes about 1 cup.

SAMBAL KACANG
Javanese Peanut Sauce

½ cup chunk-style peanut butter
¼ cup Kecap Manis (page 400)
2 tablespoons hot water
1 tablespoon freshly squeezed and strained lemon or lime juice
1 teaspoon sugar
1 teaspoon crushed fresh or dried hot red chili pepper
1 medium garlic clove, crushed

Combine all the ingredients in the container of an electric blender or a food processor and purée coarsely. Transfer to a small serving bowl. Cover and refrigerate. Bring to room temperature before serving. Makes about 1 cup.

CHINESE PLUM SAUCE I

Plum sauce, a traditional accompaniment to Chinese roast pork and egg rolls, is also known as duck sauce because it is one of the condiments served with the renowned Peking duck.

   1 pound tart red plums, halved and pitted
   1 pound apricots, halved and pitted
2¼ cups cider vinegar
   ¾ cup water
   1 cup firmly packed brown sugar
   1 cup granulated sugar
   ½ cup freshly squeezed and strained
      lemon juice
   3 tablespoons peeled and finely chopped
      fresh ginger root
   1 small onion, thinly sliced
   1 fresh hot green chili pepper, seeded,
      deribbed, and chopped
   1 medium garlic clove, thinly sliced
   1 stick cinnamon
   1 tablespoon mustard seed, toasted
   1 tablespoon salt
   1 jar (7 ounces) pimentos, rinsed and
      chopped

In an enameled saucepan combine the plums, apricots, 1¼ cups of the vinegar, and water. Cover and cook over moderate heat 5 minutes. Reduce the heat to low and simmer the mixture, uncovered, 15 minutes or until the fruits are soft.

In a large, heavy enameled kettle combine the remaining 1 cup vinegar, brown sugar, granulated sugar, and lemon juice. Bring to a boil over moderate heat, stirring constantly, and cook 10 minutes. Add the fruit mixture, ginger root, onion, chili pepper, garlic, cinnamon stick, toasted mustard seed, and salt and simmer over low heat 45 minutes. Add the pimentos and simmer, stirring frequently, 45 minutes. Remove and discard the cinnamon stick and put the contents of the kettle through the coarse disk of a food mill into a bowl. Return the mixture to the kettle and simmer, stirring frequently, until it is thickened. Remove the sauce from the heat, ladle it into sterilized jars (page 168), cap the jars loosely, and let the sauce cool. Tighten the caps and store in a dark area at least 2 weeks before serving. Makes 2 pints.

CHINESE PLUM SAUCE II

This is actually a simplified adaption of Chinese plum sauce.

1 cup plum preserves
½ cup mango chutney, finely chopped
1 tablespoon cider vinegar
1 tablespoon sugar
  Pinch five-spice powder (optional)

Combine all the ingredients in a small enameled or stainless steel saucepan. Cook over low heat, stirring constantly, until heated through. Serve hot or cold. Makes 1½ cups.

BÉCHAMEL SAUCE

2 tablespoons butter
2 tablespoons all-purpose flour
1 cup hot milk
  Salt and freshly ground white pepper to taste
  Pinch freshly grated nutmeg

In a small, heavy saucepan melt the butter over moderate heat. Add the flour and cook about 2 minutes without letting it brown, whisking constantly. Add the hot milk and cook, stirring, until the mixture comes to a boil and is thick and smooth. Add the salt, white pepper, and nutmeg, reduce the heat to low, and cook, stirring, 2 to 3 minutes. Taste and adjust the seasoning. Makes 1 cup.

VARIATIONS:

THICK BÉCHAMEL SAUCE
Use 3 tablespoons flour.

MORNAY SAUCE
Beat in ¼ cup freshly grated Swiss cheese or a combination of grated Swiss and freshly grated imported Parmesan cheese until it has melted and blended with the sauce. In a small bowl beat 1 egg yolk, then beat in a little of the sauce from the saucepan. Add the yolk mixture to the saucepan and cook, stirring constantly, 1 minute. Remove from the heat. Taste and adjust the seasoning.

CURRY SAUCE

2 tablespoons butter
1 medium onion, finely chopped
1 small garlic clove, finely chopped
1 tablespoon curry powder or to taste
¼ teaspoon ginger
2 tablespoons all-purpose flour
2 cups chicken or beef broth
  Salt and freshly ground pepper to taste
1 teaspoon freshly squeezed and strained
  lemon or lime juice

In a medium-sized, heavy saucepan melt the butter over moderate heat. Add the onion and garlic and sauté, stirring frequently, until the onion is lightly browned. Reduce the heat to low. Add the curry powder, ginger, and flour and cook about 2 minutes, stirring constantly. Gradually add the chicken or beef broth, salt, and pepper and cook, stirring, until the mixture is thickened. Reduce the heat to low and simmer gently about 5 minutes. Remove from the heat and stir in the lemon or lime juice. Taste and adjust the seasoning. Makes about 1¾ cups.

TOMATO SAUCE

3 tablespoons olive oil
1 large yellow onion, finely chopped
2 large garlic cloves, finely chopped
2 pounds ripe tomatoes (preferably Italian
  plum tomatoes), peeled, seeded, and
  chopped
3 tablespoons tomato paste
2 tablespoons finely chopped parsley
  (optional)
1 tablespoon finely chopped fresh basil, or
  1 teaspoon crushed dried basil
2 teaspoons crushed dried oregano
1 bay leaf
1 teaspoon salt or to taste
⅛ teaspoon freshly ground pepper or to
  taste

In a large, heavy saucepan heat the olive oil over moderate heat. Add the onion and sauté, stirring frequently, until soft but not browned. Add the garlic and cook, stirring constantly, about 2 minutes. Stir in the remaining ingredients and bring the mixture to a boil. Reduce the heat and simmer, partially covered, about 45 minutes or until the sauce is thickened and fairly smooth, stirring occasionally. Remove and discard the bay leaf. Taste and adjust the seasoning. If you wish the sauce to have a smoother consistency, purée it through a food mill, or rub it through a sieve with the back of a large wooden spoon. Makes about 2 cups.

SALSA CRUDA
Mexican Uncooked Tomato Sauce

2 medium-sized, ripe tomatoes, finely
    chopped
¼ cup finely chopped onion or scallions
    (include 2 inches of the green tops of the
    scallions)
2 fresh hot green chili peppers or canned
    serrano chilies, seeded and chopped (or
    to taste)
1 tablespoon finely chopped fresh
    coriander leaves or parsley
Pinch sugar (optional)
Salt to taste

Combine all the ingredients in a small bowl and mix well. Taste and adjust the seasoning. Makes about 1½ cups.

TERIYAKI SAUCE

½ cup Japanese soy sauce
¼ cup dry Sherry
3 tablespoons sugar
1 teaspoon peeled and finely chopped
    fresh ginger root
1 medium garlic clove, finely chopped

Combine all the ingredients in a bowl and stir until the sugar is dissolved. Makes about ¾ cup.

COLO COLO
Indonesian Sweet and Sour Sauce

2 tablespoons peeled, seeded, and
    chopped ripe tomato
2 tablespoons Kecap Manis (page 400)
2 tablespoons water
1 tablespoon freshly squeezed and strained
    lime juice
2 shallots, sliced
1 teaspoon sliced fresh hot red chili pepper
½ teaspoon sugar or to taste
½ teaspoon salt or to taste

Combine all the ingredients in the container of an electric blender or food processor. Mix until smooth. Transfer to a small serving bowl. Cover and refrigerate. Bring to room temperature before serving. Makes about ½ cup.

KECAP MANIS
Indonesian Sweet Soy Sauce

¾ cup sugar
1 cup Chinese soy sauce
¼ cup water
2 lemon grass stalks (about 5 1-inch pieces), or ½ teaspoon sliced stalks (available at Oriental food markets)
1 medium garlic clove, crushed
1 Chinese star anise

In a small enameled or stainless steel saucepan melt the sugar over low heat until it is dissolved and has attained a light caramel color. Gradually stir in the remaining ingredients, blending thoroughly. Cook the mixture over low heat about 10 minutes. Remove from the heat and let cool 1 hour. Strain the sauce through several layers of cheesecloth into a clean jar. Cover tightly and refrigerate until ready to use. Makes about 1½ cups.

SOME INTERNATIONAL APPETIZER BUFFETS

Although appetizers, strictly speaking, are intended to be no more than curtain raisers, tantalizing the taste buds without doing injury to one's enjoyment of the meal to follow, most of us have found them so enticing that we have often been tempted to make them the meal itself. And why not? The appetizers of the world, with their limitless variety of taste sensations and visual appeal, can easily provide en-

tire buffet meals that can more than match sit-down dinners in adventurousness, excitement, and satisfaction.

An appetizer buffet can be created from a wide choice of themes. One can, for example, assemble dishes that are entirely from one country or region: America, France, Italy, the Middle East, or the Orient, to name only some; or one can exercise some creative ingenuity by bringing together an imaginative selection of appetizers from various cuisines.

Both guests and cooks can profit from the advantages offered by an appetizer buffet. The format provides a warm, relaxed atmosphere for entertaining that is *suitable for such occasions as an open house or patio party. Guests can sample a wide variety of dishes in any order and amount, unlike the courses of a dinner, and return to their favorites as often as desired. The advantages to the cook are that many dishes can be prepared ahead and the staging is simpler than that of a formal dinner (though equally effective), allowing for more time with guests.*

On the following pages you will find information and recipe suggestions for seven appetizer buffets, each featuring a separate cuisine from a different region of the globe: antipasto from Italy, tapas from Spain, mezzeh from the Middle East, smörgåsbord from Scandinavia, zakuski from Russia, pupus from Hawaii, and appetizers from Latin America and the Caribbean. Decide upon the cuisine, choose from the list of suggested foods, and make your party as simple or elaborate as you wish.

ANTIPASTO

The well-deserved fame of *antipasto* has traveled far beyond Italy. Meaning "before the meal," this type of appetizer can be as modest or sumptuous as you like. As part of an Italian home meal it generally consists of just a few items, sometimes only one or two, unless there is a holiday or special occasion. In restaurants, however, antipasto is far more extensive, often displayed so as to capture a patron's attention immediately upon his arrival and swiftly overcome what willpower he may have.

Antipasto is a visual as well as a gastronomic experience that challenges a cook's artistic imagination and creativity; it is a poem of flavors, textures, and colors. Fish, meat, and vegetables form its foundation, although cheese and eggs are sometimes present. Fresh seasonal foods are artfully deployed along with an inviting array of sausages and canned, bottled, and pickled delicacies. There are alluring salads that make use of rice, pasta, and legumes and succulent melon or figs combined with slices of *prosciutto*, while standing close by are top-quality olive oil and wine vinegar and crusty, chewy Italian bread or crisp breadsticks. Not to be overlooked in cooler weather are hot dishes such as savory *crostini* and *fritto misto*.

The scope and variety of foods available for antipasto are almost overwhelming. With some judicious planning you will be able to assemble a stunning buffet chosen from a selection of both homemade and delicatessen fare, all without having to endure a long incarceration in your kitchen.

Italian black and green olives
Italian Black Olives with Anchovies (page 12)
Peperoncini (Italian-style pickled peppers)
Pickled hot green or red peppers
Roasted sweet green or red peppers
Tiny roasted eggplants
Marinated artichoke hearts
Marinated mushrooms
Giardiniera (page 167)

Bagna Cauda (page 26)

Fresh raw vegetables such as tomatoes, radishes, and fennel or celery hearts
Vegetable Antipasto (page 125)
Artichokes, Mushrooms, and Olives Sott'olio (page 131)
Caponata (page 138)
Sicilian Baked Stuffed Tomatoes (page 146)
Italian Stuffed Artichoke Bottoms (page 149)
Italian Stuffed Mushrooms (page 150)
Fried Artichoke Slices (page 150)
Eggplant Cannelloni (page 154)

Roasted Pepper Salad (page 106)
Tuscan White Bean and Tuna Salad (page 108)
Roman White Bean and Caviar Salad (page 109)
Panzanella Toscana (page 111)
Italian Pasta Salad with Pesto (page 115)
Italian Mozzarella and Tomato Salad (page 115)
Cappon Magro (page 116)

Provolone and fresh mozzarella cheese

Tuna-Stuffed Eggs (page 63)
Spinach-Stuffed Eggs (page 64)
Italian Spinach Timbales with Fonduta (page 74)

Canned anchovies, sardines, mussels, and tuna, all packed in olive oil
Italian Stuffed Clams (page 203)
Baked Oysters with Prosciutto and Mushrooms (page 206)

Assorted sliced Italian cold meats such as prosciutto, mortadella, capicolla, soppressata, and Genoa salami
Vitello Tonnato (page 230)
Prosciutto with Melon (page 233)
Prosciutto with Figs (page 234)
Polpette (page 255)

Crostini alla Toscana (page 289)
Italian-Style Spinach Toast (page 289)

Mozzarella in Carrozza (page 290)
Italian Clams on Toast (page 292)

Cocktail Cheese Puffs (page 363)
Cocktail Pizza Squares (page 369)
Pesto Pizza (page 371)

Fritto Misto (page 324)

Sliced Italian or French bread
Breadsticks *(grissini)*

Italian vermouth
Italian wines such as white Soave, Frascati,
  or Verdicchio or red Chianti or Bardolino

Although not traditional antipasti, the following dishes are Italian in spirit and could
be considered when planning an antipasto
buffet.

Green Olives Stuffed with Prosciutto Filling
  or Gorgonzola Cheese and Prosciutto
  Spread (page 11)
Miniature Frittatas (page 68), omitting the
  Garlic-Yogurt Sauce
Parmesan Chicken Wings (page 223)
Cherry Tomatoes Filled with Pesto Sauce
  (page 145)
Stuffed Italian Plum Tomatoes (page 146)
Shrimp Pizza Wedges (page 305)
Pepperoni and Green Pepper Pizza Wedges
  (page 307)
Miniature Italian-Style Crêpes (page 312)

Italian-Style Spinach-Cheese Crêpes (page
  316)
Parmesan Zucchini Fritters (page 332)
Ham and Cheese Fritters (page 338)

QUICK ANTIPASTO PLATTER

A delicious and varied antipasto can easily
be assembled with ingredients from a good
Italian grocery or delicatessen. It can be as
modest or sumptuous as you wish and need
not be restricted to being a preamble to an
Italian dinner. An antipasto platter can successfully precede a steak or roast.

On a large serving platter lined with lettuce leaves arrange an array of foods chosen
from those suggested below, using contrasting colors, textures, and flavors. Your
selection should include meat, seafood, raw
and cooked vegetables, olives, and eggs.
Serve the antipasto with accompanying
cruets of fine-quality olive oil and red wine
vinegar and with baskets of Italian bread
and Italian breadsticks *(grissini)*.

Cherry tomatoes or tomato slices or wedges
Radishes
Fennel or celery hearts
Scallions, trimmed

Green and black olives (preferably Italian)
Marinated mushrooms, drained
Pickled eggplant
Caponata
Roasted green and red peppers
Peperoncini (Italian-style pickled peppers), drained
Fried and stuffed peppers
Giardiniera (Italian pickled vegetables)
Cannellini beans
Artichoke hearts
Marinated garbanzo beans (chickpeas)

Hard-cooked eggs, quartered or sliced
Canned tuna (preferably Italian tuna packed in olive oil), drained
Anchovy fillets, rolled or flat, drained
Sardines in oil, drained

Thinly sliced Italian cold meats such as prosciutto, mortadella, capicolla, soppressata, and Genoa salami

Provolone cheese, sliced

TAPAS

Anyone who is fond of hors d'oeuvre would feel at home in Spain, where the serving of *tapas* is one of that country's most enjoyable culinary customs.

Spanish dining habits differ somewhat from ours. The main meal of the day, called the *comida*, is taken at about two in the afternoon, while dinner, or *cena*, is not eaten until around ten at night. Snacking, however, is a way of life in Spain, especially as evening approaches. At this time many Spaniards stop for some nibbling on tapas in bars called *tascas*, whose countertops invitingly display earthenware bowls containing an enormous variety of appetizers, which are accompanied with glasses of wine or Sherry. Often people amble from one tasca to another, sampling a little of this or that specialty, standing at the bar with one elbow on the counter while sipping their drinks. This pleasant habit can be part of a ritualized stroll known as the *paseo*, during which the citizenry takes the air, chatting with friends and acquaintances. In Madrid the practice of bar-hopping for tantalizing morsels is referred to as a *chateo*, named for *chatos*, the snub-nosed two-ounce glasses from which wine is drunk in the tascas.

Tapas are unique in that they are not eaten at home but are found only in tascas, where they are available from before lunch to late at night. Unlike American bars, these lively, family-oriented establishments cater to a clientele that is more interested in eating than in drinking, and their arrays of edibles tempt many people to skip dinner altogether in favor of making a meal of these luscious snacks.

The word tapa means "cover" or "lid," and the precursors of today's tapas were just that: pieces of bread used to cover wineglasses to keep out flies. There are two kinds of tapas: naturales, served as is, such as olives, cheeses, oysters, ham, and sausages; and *de cocina*, usually cooked, which are served hot or cold. These can be miniature portions of what are normally entrées as well as omelets, salads, various tidbits impaled on toothpicks or small skewers, tiny sandwiches, and many other dishes. Even though they do not form a part of traditional Spanish home cooking, tapas are ideal for American home entertaining, where a selection can make an exciting cocktail or appetizer buffet. Offer them with wine or Sherry or, in summer, with *sangría* (see Spanish Sangría, page 407) or some other cooling beverage. They will invariably be conversation pieces that will surprise and delight your guests.

Mediterranean Fried Almonds (page 1)
Spanish Toasted Hazelnuts (page 2)
Moorish Pine Nuts (page 3)

Black and green olives, plain or stuffed with anchovies, pimentos, onions, almonds, or lemon rind
Wine-Marinated Spanish Olives (page 12)
Dill gherkins
Pickled beets
Spanish Marinated Mushrooms and Onion (page 164)

Radishes
Moorish Pimentos (page 141)
Cooked artichoke hearts served with Mayonnaise (page 149)
Fried Artichoke Slices (page 150)
Spanish Mushrooms in Garlic Sauce (page 157)

Roasted Pepper Salad with Tomato and Onion (page 105)
Roasted Eggplant and Pepper Salad (page 106)
White Bean Salad (page 107)
Spanish Chickpea Salad (page 109)

Tuna-Stuffed Eggs (page 63)
Tortilla de Patata a la Española (page 68)

Pickled herring
Smoked salmon, trout, or eel
Oysters on the half shell with lemon juice

Mussels on the half shell with lemon juice

Cold boiled shrimp served with Ali-Oli (page 389)

Spanish Mussels in Almond Sauce (page 183)

Mussels with Sauce Vinaigrette (page 184)

Mussels with Tomato Sauce (page 184)

Shrimp in Garlic Sauce (page 195)

Shrimp in Green Sauce (page 196)

Changurro (page 201)

Spanish Clams a la Marinera (page 203)

Spanish Fried Clams (page 204)

Spanish Fried Mussels (page 204)

Galician Scallops (page 204)

Calamares a la Romana (page 209)

Frogs' Legs Valenciana (page 210)

Spanish Chicken Livers in Sherry (page 224)

Sliced cold meats such as serrano or other cured ham and Spanish sausages

Pinchos Morunos (page 244)

Catalonian Meatballs (page 256)

Fried green peppers and chorizo sausage

Spanish Chorizo Sausage in Red Wine (page 264)

Grilled slices of chorizo sausage on food picks

Spanish Kidneys in Sherry (page 266)

Anchovy and Pimento Canapés (page 273)

Empanadillas (page 350)

Spanish Chorizo Turnovers (page 350)

Tartaletas de Ensaladilla (page 365) and Variations

Spanish Cod and Potato Fritters (page 335)

Sliced crusty bread or rolls

Spanish Sangría (below)

Dry or medium-dry Sherry

Spanish red or white wine

SPANISH SANGRÍA

½ cup freshly squeezed and strained orange juice

⅓ cup freshly squeezed and strained lemon juice

⅓ cup superfine sugar or to taste

1 bottle (750 ml) dry red wine (preferably imported Spanish wine)

¼ cup Cognac

¼ cup orange-flavored liqueur (such as Triple Sec, Cointreau, or Curaçao)

1 orange, thinly sliced

1 lemon, thinly sliced

1 bottle (7 ounces) club soda, chilled Ice cubes

Combine the orange juice, lemon juice, and sugar in a large glass pitcher and stir with a long-handled spoon until the sugar is completely dissolved. Stir in the wine, Cognac, orange-flavored liqueur, and sliced fruits. Refrigerate at least 2 hours or until thoroughly chilled. Just before serving, stir in the club soda. Serve the *sangría* in 6-ounce goblets or tumblers filled with ice cubes. Makes 8 to 10 servings.

VARIATIONS:

Instead of using a pitcher, you can make and serve the sangría in a punch bowl.

Other fruits, such as sliced apple, peach, and nectarine and whole strawberries and raspberries, may be added.

MEZZEH

The many peoples of the Middle East and, to a considerable extent, the Balkans share a common cuisine of unusual brilliance and inspiration. Nowhere is its genius more creatively displayed than in the seemingly endless number and variety of its appetizers, of which the populace is passionately fond, savoring them daily at home and in restaurants. Although a number of words are used to mean "appetizers," one term with several variations is most frequently encountered throughout the region: *mezzeh* (or *meza*, *maza*, or *mezethakia*). The category of Middle Eastern food that most frequently turns foreigners into its ardent devotees, mezzeh can range from a simple assortment of raw and pickled vegetables, cheese, olives, and pita bread to a spectacular collection of up to a hundred different dishes.

Mezzeh and socializing are a traditional combination in Middle Eastern countries, where they are usually complemented by an indigenous aniseed-flavored apéritif known as *arak* in the Arab world, *ouzo* in Greece, and *raki* in Turkey. Beer is another popular accompaniment. Wine, although frequently served in Greece, is less common elsewhere in the Middle East. The most opulent mezzeh are featured in restaurants that specialize in their preparation. In my native Lebanon these were found both in the coastal cities and in the resort areas in the higher elevations. The very mention of hors d'oeuvre calls to my mind the vision of a seaside mezzeh table in the orange glow of the setting sun or a lunchtime feast set on a terrace in invigorating mountain air.

Whether offered as a prelude to a meal or with drinks at social occasions, mezzeh occupy an honored position in Middle Eastern life. Westerners can also successfully incorporate them into their entertaining, from a small selection with cocktails to a sumptuous array for a dazzling buffet.

Salted pistachio nuts
Mediterranean Fried Almonds (page 1)
Greek olives
Marinated Greek Olives (page 13)
Armenian Pickled Vegetables (page 169)

Labneh (page 57)

Skordalia (page 393)
Baba Ghannouj (page 18)
Hummus bi Tahini (page 19)
Taramosalata (page 22)

Roasted Pepper Salad (page 106)
Beet Salad with Yogurt (page 106)
White Bean Salad (page 107)
Tabbouli (page 114)

Greek Artichokes (page 130)
Armenian Stuffed Grape Leaves (page 133)
Stuffed Chard Leaves (page 134)
Zucchini Imam Bayildi (page 148)
Eggplant Imam Bayildi (page 149)
Falafel (page 151)
Bulgarian Fried Peppers Stuffed with
Cheese (page 159)

Omelet with Herbs, Walnuts, and Currants (page 70)

Midia Dolma (page 184)
Oyster Plaki (page 186)
Greek Skewered Shrimp (page 197)

Circassian Chicken (page 212)

Kibbeh Nayye (page 263)
Ground Meat and Egg Rolls (page 241)
Keftedakia (page 254)
Fried Stuffed Kibbeh (page 263)

Tiropetes (page 347)
Sanbusak (page 354)
Bedouin Fried Stuffed Rice Balls (page 383)

Pita bread
Lavash (Armenian cracker bread)

Arak, *ouzo*, or *raki*
Beer
Greek, Lebanese, or California wines

Although the following are not traditional mezzeh, they can make a welcome addition to a Middle Eastern appetizer buffet.

Moorish Pine Nuts (page 3)
Black Olives Stuffed with Serbian Herb Cheese Spread, Herb Yogurt Cheese, or Taramosalata (page 11)
Mushroom Dip (page 17)
Serbian Herb Cheese Spread (page 28) served with pita bread
Cucumber Cups Filled with Taramosalata, Serbian Herb Cheese Spread, or Herb Yogurt Cheese (page 136)
Cherry Tomatoes Filled with Hummus bi Tahini, Serbian Herb Cheese Spread, Herb Yogurt Cheese, Tabbouli, or Kibbeh (page 144)
Middle Eastern-Style Tortilla Pizza Wedges (page 306)

SMÖRGÅSBORD

Undoubtedly the best-known element of Scandinavian cookery is the Swedish *smörgåsbord*, an appetizer table that can encompass as many as sixty or more dishes. Although supposedly a premeal affair, it obviously possesses the capability of being a lavish buffet in itself and frequently is in some Swedish and Swedish-American restaurants. Possibly it evolved from rural get-togethers of former times, to which guests brought some of the food themselves. All of their contributions, in addition to those of the host, were arranged buffet-style on the main table.

Smörgåsbord translates as "bread and butter table," and no matter how extensive the selection of dishes may be, these two foods are invariably present. Nowadays the large type of smörgåsbord has been supplanted in homes and most restaurants by a small group of appetizers that are placed on the table or passed on a tray. Besides bread and butter, this scaled-down version, like its more opulent relative, always starts with fish, particularly herring, and ends with cheese. Even in its tiniest form, which contains but three items plus bread, the basic components of the smörgåsbord are still represented: herring, cheese, and butter *(sill, ost, och smör,* often abbreviated "SOS" on restaurant menus). This formula is likewise the cornerstone of other Scandinavian appetizer tables: the *kolde bord* of Denmark, *koldt bord* of Norway, and *voileipäpöytä* of Finland. In Norway and Denmark appetizers are often presented atop bread slices as inviting and artistically assembled open-face sandwiches.

The proper way to partake of a smörgåsbord is to make three or more trips to the table (more like five to do justice to the selection) in order to enjoy the full spectrum of offerings. To make only one trip is to do both oneself and the food a disservice; the resulting hodgepodge piled on a single plate is scarcely more purposeful or esthetic than an army recruit's tray after he has been herded through the line in a mess hall. Rather, begin by sampling the various kinds of seafood, to be eaten along with bread and butter. Choose first from among the herring preparations (including Jansson's Frestelse, even though it is a hot dish); follow that by helping yourself to the other seafood selections. Next, essay the eggs and cold meats and vegetables, then the hot dishes, and, finally, some cheese on rye crispbread or a fruit salad. For each trip remember always to take clean plates and silver, which should be provided at the end of the table. The traditional beverages for smörgåsbord are ice-cold aquavit and beer, a quick swallow of the first being followed by a quaff of the second.

A smörgåsbord is meant to provide visual as well as gustatory pleasure. If you take care to decorate and present each dish attractively and arrange the whole to create an overall effect of warmth and generosity, as the Scandinavians do, you will surely be rewarded with joyful smiles of satisfaction and toasts in your honor.

Assorted cans or jars of caviar, anchovies, sardines, pickled or smoked herring, and smoked salmon, eel, or other fish
Herring Platter (page 189)
Danish Marinated Herring in Sour Cream Sauce (page 189)
Scandinavian Herring Salad (page 119)
Jansson's Frestelse (page 208)

Smoked Salmon Cornets (page 187)
Gravlax (page 188)
West Coast Salad (page 117)

Anchovy- and Herb-Stuffed Eggs (page 62)
Stuffed Eggs with Asparagus (page 62)
Caviar-Stuffed Eggs (page 63)
Salmon-Stuffed Eggs (page 64)
Stuffed Eggs with Salmon and Caviar (page 64)

Radishes
Pickled Cucumber (page 164)
Danish Pickled Beets (page 166)

Swedish Seafood Pâté (page 78)
Scandinavian Liver Pâté (page 86)

Swedish Cheese Puffs (page 362)

Assorted sliced cold meats such as sausages, boiled or baked ham, tongue, veal loaf, head cheese, smoked reindeer meat, and smoked goose breast
Jellied Veal (page 231)
Tongue with Horseradish Sauce (page 337)

Boiled new potatoes with dill
Swedish brown beans
Omelet filled with creamed mushrooms, asparagus, sweetbreads, or lobster
Köttbullar (page 259, Variation)

Assorted Scandinavian cheeses such as Danish blue, Edam, Havarti, Kuminost, Gjetost, and Herrgård

Assorted thinly sliced Scandinavian breads such as dark caraway rye, Danish rye, dark pumpernickel, and Swedish *limpa*
Norwegian *lefse*
Scandinavian crisp bread *(knäckebröd)*
Butter (balls or other shapes)

Aquavit
Beer

In addition to the preceding dishes that usually appear on the smörgåsbord, here are some others that can be included on a Scandinavian appetizer buffet.

Norwegian Red Caviar Dip (page 23)
Swedish Cheese Spread (page 28)
Smoked Salmon Spread (page 30)
Cucumber Cups Filled with Caviar and Cream Cheese Filling, Anchovy and Cream Cheese Filling, or Smoked Salmon Spread (page 136)
Cucumber Boats Filled with Norwegian Red Caviar Dip or Swedish Cheese Spread (page 137)
Mushrooms filled with Swedish Cheese Spread (page 139)
Cherry Tomatoes Filled with Smoked Salmon Spread or Cream Cheese and Bacon Filling (page 144)
Ham Cornets with Asparagus (page 233)
Swedish Smoked Salmon and Asparagus Canapés (page 273)
Danish Caviar Canapés (page 274)
Finnish Sandwich Loaf (page 277)
Miniature Copenhagen-Style Crêpes (page 312)

ZAKUSKI

In Russia the hour before dinner is the time to enjoy the national institution of *zakuska*, an array of appetizers that in its most lavish form is seldom if ever surpassed by its counterparts in other cuisines.

The word *zakusits* means "to have a snack." *Zakuski*, or "small bites," are hot and cold appetizers set out on a table in an area separate from the dining room and eaten standing up. The custom is a very old one, probably originating among the aristocracy on their country estates. With bad roads and, during much of the year, bone-chilling cold, travel was long and arduous. Guests would arrive at any time of the day or night, often unanticipated and usually famished. Zakuski took the edge off their hunger while a meal could be prepared.

For the prosperous few in pre-Revolutionary Russia the zakuska table, by the middle of the nineteenth century, was indeed munificent, if not extravagant. It could contain up to a hundred different zakuski, all arranged and decorated to form an elaborate work of art composed with a careful eye toward esthetics as well as taste, the whole encompassing pâtés, aspics, galantines, cold cuts, stuffed vegetables, salads, pickles, relishes and condiments, and breads.

Fish, particularly herring, was offered in a multitude of guises, along with copious amounts of caviar. Other cold zakuski included a myriad of dishes made with meat, fowl, vegetables, eggs, and cheese. As if this were not enough, early in the twentieth century hot zakuski were added, among them savory pies, turnovers, and pancakes, seasoned meatballs, stews, and sausages and variety meats in a number of different sauces. Men washed all this down with plenty of well-chilled vodka, which was poured into small glasses that held less than half an ounce and then tossed back in one quick swallow. Some fifteen or twenty kinds, both clear and flavored (see page 415), stood available on the table. Women, however, usually drank Sherry instead. It is no wonder, then, that the zakuska table presented such a temptation to unsuspecting foreigners that they frequently overindulged and were unable to do justice to the meal that followed.

With the advent of the Revolution the formidable dining habits of the wealthy became a thing of the past, and today zakuski are no longer served with such prodigality. Under normal circumstances they consist of just a few appetizers, often served at table in an informal family meal, but at a party the assortment, while not as extensive as in the past, can still be quite stunning. For a small group of people a selection of five dishes, four cold and one hot, is considered adequate by modern Russian standards. For a full buffet dinner, however, offer an ample selection of zakuski. While vodka is the traditional accompaniment, other alcoholic beverages such as Champagne, cocktails, or Sherry can also be served.

Caviar (black, gray, and red)
Caviar with Crème Fraîche (page 191)
Russian Caviar Cheese Ball (page 58)

Herring (pickled, smoked, and marinated in wine)
Herring Platter (page 189)
Russian Herring in Mustard Sauce (page 190)

Canned anchovies and sardines
Smoked salmon, sturgeon, whitefish, and eel
Raw oysters
Cooked crayfish
Shrimp or lobster served with Mayonnaise (page 180)
Russian Fish in Aspic (page 193)

Fried smelts
Russian Fish Cakes (page 208)

Anchovy- and Herb-Stuffed Eggs (page 62)
Caviar-Stuffed Eggs (page 63)
Salmon Stuffed Eggs (page 64)

Stuffed Eggs with Salmon and Caviar (page 64)
Mushroom-Stuffed Eggs (page 65)

Black and green olives
Pickled beets, cucumbers, green tomatoes, pearl onions, mushrooms, and melon rind
Russian Pickled Mushrooms (page 165)

Baltic-Russian Cucumber and Sour Cream Salad (page 104)
White Bean Salad (page 107)
Salat Olivier (page 121)
Rossolye (page 122)

Stuffed Grape Leaves (page 133)
Russian Mushrooms in Sour Cream (page 158)

Eggplant Caviar (page 17)
Russian Liver Pâté (page 32)

Russian Chicken Livers in Sour Cream (page 225)

Assorted sliced cold meats such as sausages, boiled or baked ham, smoked tongue, smoked reindeer meat, and smoked turkey
Jellied Veal (page 231)
Tongue with Horseradish Sauce (page 237)

Ground Meat and Egg Rolls (page 241)
Meatballs Stroganov (page 260)
Russian Kidneys in Madeira (page 265)
Forshmak (page 267)

Pirozhki (page 356)
Blini (page 318)

Thinly sliced black bread, pumpernickel,
   and rye bread
White rolls
Butter curls

Clear vodka
Flavored vodkas (page 415)
Sherry
Champagne
Tea

FLAVORED VODKAS

In addition to the basic spirits, a wide variety of flavored vodkas have traditionally been
offered on the *zakuska* table. Their preparation is not difficult, as can be seen from the
sampling given below. Vodka can be seasoned either in the bottle or in a decanter and
the flavoring agent removed before serving,
if desired. Always chill vodka in the freezer.
Due to its high alcohol content the liquor will
not turn to ice but will be, appropriately, ice
cold.

LEMON-FLAVORED VODKA

Place 5 or 6 strips of lemon rind in 1 bottle (750 ml) vodka (use a vegetable peeler to
make the strips, taking care to avoid any
white pith). Cover and leave at room temperature 2 or 3 days. Chill the vodka in the
freezer before serving.

VARIATION:

ORANGE-FLAVORED VODKA

Substitute orange rind for the lemon rind.

CHERRY-FLAVORED VODKA

Place 20 halved, pitted dark sweet cherries or 10 dried cherries in 1 bottle (750 ml)
vodka. Cover and leave at room temperature
2 or 3 days. Chill the vodka in the freezer
before serving.

TEA-FLAVORED VODKA

Place 1 tea bag in 1 bottle (750 ml) vodka.
Cover and allow to steep at room temperature several hours. Chill the vodka in
the freezer before serving.

ANISE- OR CARAWAY-FLAVORED VODKA

Place 1 teaspoon aniseed or caraway seed
in 1 bottle (750 ml) vodka. Cover and leave
at room temperature at least 2 or 3 days.
Chill the vodka in the freezer before serving.

PERTSOVKA (PEPPER-FLAVORED VODKA)

Place 12 whole black peppercorns in 1 bottle (750 ml) vodka. Cover and leave at room temperature at least 24 hours. Chill the vodka in the freezer before serving. (Not for the faint of heart!)

PUPUS

Outstanding appetizers, as one can see from perusing this book, are by no means confined to the great cuisines of Europe and the Middle East. Oriental gastronomy has also developed a brilliant collection, a sampling of which is irresistibly displayed on the pupu trays of Hawaii.

Unlike their more Western counterparts, *pupu* trays feature a medley of international starters, most of them hot, that reflects the ethnic diversity of the Islands' population. Oriental delicacies from China, Japan, Korea, the Philippines, and Polynesia coexist with specialties from Spain, Portugal, and the Middle East as well as with mainland favorites.

The preparation of pupus is considered as much an art as pastry and sauce making. Although groups of pupus are arranged on trays for cocktail parties, for an appetizer buffet they can be placed together on a table. Offer the beverages of your choice; however, drinks made with rum and various tropical fruit juices (see Hawaiian Rum Punch, page 418) would be most appropriate. For real authenticity use Okolehao, a potent Hawaiian liquor distilled from the root of the ti plant. (Since Okolehao is difficult to obtain on the mainland, rum may be substituted in drinks calling for it.) While beverages flow freely, mainland-style, the emphasis, understandably with such an elegant and elaborate spread, is placed on the food.

Salted macadamia nuts
Hawaiian Coconut Chips (page 8)

Hawaiian Cream Cheese Balls with Ginger and Coconut (page 57)

Hawaiian Shrimp Kebabs (page 197)
Chinese Shrimp Balls (page 198)
Scallop, Water Chestnut, and Bacon Brochettes (page 205)
Scallop, Pineapple, and Bacon Brochettes (page 206)
Scallop, Green Pepper, Tomato, and Bacon Brochettes (page 206)

Chicken, Pepper, and Onion Kebabs (page 216)
Chicken, Pepper, and Pineapple Kebabs (page 216)
Cantonese Sesame-Nut Chicken (page 218)
Curried Sesame Chicken Wings (page 221)
Yakitori (page 222)

Ham with Papaya (page 234)
Ham and Mango Tidbits (page 234)
Ham and Fruit on Skewers (page 236)
Korean Steak Tartare (page 273)
Hawaiian Beef, Pineapple, and Mushroom Kebabs (page 243)

Chinese Barbecued Pork, Chicken Liver, and Scallion Rolls (page 245)
Chinese Roast Pork (page 246)
Chinese Barbecued Spareribs (page 247)
Spareribs South Pacific (page 249)
Rumaki (page 250) and Variations (250)
Honolulu Ham and Papaya Kebabs (page 251)
Hawaiian Meatball and Pineapple Kebabs (page 254)
Chinese Meatballs and Kumquats in Sweet and Sour Sauce (page 261)

Snow Peas Stuffed with Cream Cheese and Bacon Filling or Prosciutto Filling (page 140)
Lomi Lomi Cherry Tomatoes (page 145)
Chinese Stuffed Mushrooms (page 156)

Papaya with Lime (page 172)
Stuffed Kumquats (page 174)

Korean Steak Tartare Canapés (page 239)
Chinese Shrimp Toast (page 285)

Egg Rolls (page 374) or Spring Rolls (page 375)
Pork, Shrimp, and Mushroom Turnovers (page 374)
Filled Mandarin Pancakes (page 320)

Tempura (page 325)
Coconut Shrimp with Curry Sauce (page 332)

Chinese Stuffed Chicken Wings (page 336)

Hawaiian Rum Punch (page 418)
Chinese, Japanese, or domestic beer
Iced tea

For an Asian appetizer buffet that goes beyond even the eclectic largesse of pupus, you could include some of the following dishes:

Indian Cashews (page 3)
Cantonese Fried Walnuts (page 4)
Toasted Nuts Teriyaki (page 5)
Bombay Cocktail Mix (page 5)
Philippine Sweet Potato Chips (page 6)
Chinese Red-Cooked Eggs (page 66)
Ikan Bakr (page 207)
Apricot-Glazed Chicken Wings (page 220)
Singapore-Style Chicken Satay (page 222)
Singapore-Style Beef or Lamb Satay (page 222)
Vietnamese Pork Patties in Lettuce Leaves (page 252)
Pakistani Meatballs (page 253)
Tahu (page 162)
Japanese Marinated Mushrooms (page 166)
Samosas (page 357)
Lumpia (page 373)
Sushi (page 284)
Pakoras (page 328)
Indonesian Fish Fritters (page 335)
Tokyo-Style Crab Croquettes (page 339)
Tokyo-Style Chicken Croquettes (page 340)

HAWAIIAN RUM PUNCH

1 liter dark rum
½ liter light rum
¾ cup turbinado sugar
1 vanilla bean
½ ripe pineapple, peeled, cored, and cut into 2-inch pieces
1 mango, peeled, pitted, and cut into 2-inch pieces
1 papaya, peeled, seeded, and cut into 2-inch pieces
1 banana, peeled and cut into 2-inch pieces
1 orange, cut crosswise in half
1 lemon, cut crosswise in half
1 lime, cut crosswise in half
1 bottle (750 ml) dry white wine, chilled

Combine the rums, sugar, and vanilla bean in a large crock or widemouthed jar and stir until the sugar dissolves. Add the pineapple, mango, papaya, and banana. Squeeze the juice from the orange, lemon, and lime into the rum mixture and add the citrus rinds. Cover the crock or jar loosely with cheesecloth and a rubber band. Allow it to stand 3 days, stirring from time to time. Strain, reserving the fruits for another use. Pour the rum punch over ice in a punch bowl and stir in the chilled wine. Serve in punch glasses. Makes about 2½ quarts.

VARIATIONS:

For a milder drink, add freshly squeezed and strained orange juice to taste.

If desired, garnish the punch with sliced fresh fruit and float washed vanda orchids or fresh gardenias on top.

A LATIN AMERICAN AND CARIBBEAN APPETIZER BUFFET

Latin American cooking of former times did not encompass a large number of dishes that functioned specifically as appetizers. That of the present day, in contrast, has assimilated a wide spectrum of European and American hors d'oeuvre to go with a rich heritage of small foods taken from the traditional indigenous cuisine and adapted to serve as cocktail fare or starters. The category of appetizers is known under different names in different countries, for example *antojitos*, *picadas*, *entradas*, and *entremeses* (just to list a few) in Spanish-speaking areas, and *salgadinhos* in Portuguese-speaking Brazil. Popular items include a host of nibbles such as banana and plantain chips, many kinds of turnovers, and filled tortillas in countless guises. In the non-Latin countries of the region, especially those of the Caribbean, local foodstuffs have been combined with others brought by the many ethnic groups who have settled there over the centuries to fashion an intriguing and imaginative cuisine that includes a wealth of beguiling appetizers.

A Latin American and Caribbean appetizer buffet, with its exciting combination of tastes and textures, is certain to be a crowd-pleaser. Any number of beverages can make suitable accompaniments including cocktails, wine, *sangría* (see Mexican Sangría, page 421), beer, and iced tea.

Puerto Rican Plantain Chips (page 7)
Caribbean Banana Chips (page 7)

Black and green olives
Mexican Anchovy-Stuffed Olives (page 11)

Chile con Queso (page 16)
Mexican-Style Bean Dip (page 20)
Guacamole (page 21)

Caribbean Duck Pâté with Orange and Pistachios (page 84)

Stuffed Eggs with Lobster and Avocado (page 63)
Crab-Stuffed Eggs (page 63)
Chicken-Stuffed Eggs (page 64)
Ham-Stuffed Eggs (page 64)
Mexican Eggs with Green Chilies and Bacon (page 70)

Mexican Shrimp Cocktail (page 179)
Escabeche de Pescado (page 191)
Dominican Shrimp and Potato Balls (page 200)

Pollo en Escabeche (page 215)
Caribbean Chicken Rolls (page 217)

Assorted sliced cold meats such as Italian salami, mortadella, roast beef, corned beef, roast pork, and ham or turkey
Matambre (page 229)
Carne Fiambre (page 242)
Carnitas (page 245)
Latin American Meatballs (page 258)

Mexican Cauliflower Salad (page 107)
Mexican Shrimp Salad (page 118)
Cherry Tomatoes Filled with Guacamole (page 144)

Papaya with Lime (page 172)
Brazilian Stuffed Prunes (page 173)

Tomato Canapés with Guacamole and Bacon (page 271)
Avocado-Caviar Cups (page 271)

Chorizo-Cheese Tortilla Wedges (page 298)
Spicy Tortilla Tortes (page 299)
Miniature Picadillo Tostadas (page 300)
Sopes (page 301)
Fiesta Nachos (page 302)
Dominican Pickled Chicken in Sope Shells (page 304)

Empanadas (page 351)
Empanaditas (page 351)
Pastelillos (page 353)
Barquetas de Caviar (page 366)
Brazilian Seafood Barquettes (page 367)

Sliced crusty bread or rolls

Mexican Sangría (page 421)
Mexican or domestic beer
Red or white wine
Iced tea or coffee

Some of the following dishes are either
Latin American or Caribbean in inspiration;
all are compatible with an appetizer buffet
chosen from the above selection.

Avocado Dip with Bacon (page 22)
Tuna-Stuffed Eggs (page 63)
Ham Cornets with Asparagus (page 233)
Dominican Pickled Chicken in Pita (page
   304)
Mexican-Style Beef Pizza Wedges (page
   306)
Olive-Filled Cheese Balls (page 363)
Shellfish and Avocado Puffs (page 362)
Miniature Mexican-Style Crêpes (page 313)
Crab Fritters (page 334)
Ham Fritters (page 337)

MEXICAN SANGRÍA

*1 cup freshly squeezed and strained orange
   juice*
*½ cup freshly squeezed and strained lime
   or lemon juice*
¼ cup superfine sugar or to taste
*1 bottle (750 ml) dry red wine (preferably
   imported Spanish wine)*
Orange slices (optional)
Ice cubes

Combine the orange juice, lime or lemon
juice, and sugar in a large glass pitcher and
stir with a long-handled spoon until the
sugar is completely dissolved. Stir in the red
wine and orange slices (if used) and refrigerate at least 2 hours or until thoroughly
chilled. Serve the *sangría* in 6-ounce goblets
or tumblers filled with ice cubes. Makes 8 to
10 servings.

Hawaiian Shrimp Kebabs 197
Hawaiian Shrimp and Vegetable Kebabs 198
Scallop, Water Chestnut, and Bacon Brochettes 205
Scallop, Pineapple, and Bacon Brochettes 206
Chicken, Pepper, and Onion Kebabs 216
Chicken, Pepper, and Pineapple Kebabs 216
Curried Sesame Chicken Wings 221
Ham with Papaya 234
Ham with Mango 234
Ham and Mango Tidbits 235
Ham and Fruit on Skewers 236
Hawaiian Beef, Pineapple, and Mushroom Kebabs 243
Spareribs South Pacific 249
Rumaki 250
Honolulu Ham and Papaya Kebabs 251
Hawaiian Meatball and Pineapple Kebabs 254
Korean Steak Tartare Canapés 275
Coconut Shrimp with Curry Sauce 332
Hawaiian Rum Punch 418

INDONESIAN

Tahu (Indonesian Fried Soybean Cubes) 162
Ikan Bakr (Indonesian Barbecued Fish) 207
Indonesian Fish Fritters 335

PHILIPPINE

Philippine Sweet Potato Chips 6
Lumpia (Philippine Deep-Fried Pork, Shrimp, and Vegetable Rolls) 373

SINGAPORE

Singapore-Style Chicken Satay 222
Singapore-Style Beef or Lamb Satay 222

VIETNAMESE

Vietnamese Pork Patties in Lettuce Leaves 252

RUSSIAN (INCLUDING BALTIC AND CAUCASIAN)

Eggplant Caviar 17
Russian Liver Pâté 32
Russian Caviar Cheese Ball 58
Anchovy- and Herb-Stuffed Eggs 62
Caviar-Stuffed Eggs 63
Salmon-Stuffed Eggs 64
Stuffed Eggs with Salmon and Caviar 64
Mushroom-Stuffed Eggs 65
Baltic-Russian Cucumber and Sour Cream Salad 104
White Bean Salad 107
Salat Olivier 122
Rossolye (Estonian Meat, Herring, and Potato Salad) 122
Russian Mushrooms in Sour Cream 158
Russian Pickled Mushrooms 165
Herring Platter 189
Russian Herring in Mustard Sauce 190
Caviar with Crème Fraîche 191
Russian Fish in Aspic 193
Russian Fish Cakes 208
Russian Chicken Livers in Sour Cream 225
Jellied Veal 231
Tongue with Horseradish Sauce 237
Ground Meat and Egg Rolls 241
Meatballs Stroganov 260
Russian Kidneys in Madeira 265
Forshmak (Baked Herring, Meat, and Potato Appetizer) 267
Blini (Buckwheat Pancakes) 318
Pirozhki (Russian Turnovers) 356
Flavored Vodkas 415

SCANDINAVIAN

Norwegian Red Caviar Dip 23
Swedish Cheese Spread 28
Anchovy- and Herb-Stuffed Eggs 62
Stuffed Eggs with Asparagus 63
Caviar-Stuffed Eggs 63
Salmon-Stuffed Eggs 64
Stuffed Eggs with Salmon and Caviar 64
Swedish Seafood Pâté 79
Scandinavian Liver Paste 87
Scandinavian Herring Salad 120
Pickled Cucumber 164
Danish Pickled Beets 166
Danish Pickled Beets 166
Smoked Salmon Cornets 187
Gravlax (Swedish Dill-Cured Salmon) 188
Herring Platter 189
Danish Marinated Herring in Sour Cream Sauce 189
Jansson's Frestelse (Jansson's Temptation) 208
Jellied Veal 231
Tongue with Horseradish Sauce 237
Köttbullar (Swedish Meatballs) 259
Swedish Smoked Salmon and Asparagus Canapés 273
Danish Caviar Canapés 274
Finnish Sandwich Loaf 277
Opera Club Sandwiches 283
Miniature Copenhagen-Style Crêpes 312
Swedish Cheese Puffs 362

SPANISH/PORTUGUESE

SPANISH

Mediterranean Fried Almonds 1
Spanish Toasted Hazelnuts 2
Moorish Pine Nuts 3
Wine-Marinated Spanish Olives 12
Tuna-Stuffed Eggs 63
Tortilla de Patata a la Española (Spanish Potato Omelet) 68
Roasted Pepper Salad with Tomato and Onion 105
Roasted Eggplant and Pepper Salad 106
White Bean Salad 107
Spanish Chickpea Salad 109
Moorish Pimentos 141
Fried Artichoke Slices 150

Spanish Mushrooms in Garlic Sauce 157
Spanish Marinated Mushrooms and Onion 164
Spanish Mussels in Almond Sauce 183
Mussels with Sauce Vinaigrette 184
Mussels with Tomato Sauce 184
Shrimp in Garlic Sauce 195
Shrimp in Green Sauce 196
Changurro (Basque Crabmeat with Sherry and Brandy) 201
Spanish Clams a la Marinera 203
Spanish Fried Clams 204
Spanish Fried Mussels 204
Galician Scallops 204
Calamares a la Romana (Fried Squid, Roman Style) 209
Frogs' Legs Valenciana 210
Spanish Chicken Livers in Sherry 224
Pinchos Morunos (Moorish Brochettes) 244
Catalonian Meatballs 256
Spanish Chorizo Sausage in Red Wine 264
Spanish Kidneys in Sherry 266
Anchovy and Pimento Canapés 273
Spanish Cod and Potato Fritters 335
Empanadillas (Spanish Meat Turnovers) 350
Spanish Chorizo Turnovers 350
Tartaletas de Ensaladilla (Spanish Tuna and Vegetable Tartlets) 365
Shellfish and Vegetable Tartlets 366
Ham and Vegetable Tartlets 366
Anchovy and Egg Tartlets 366
Spanish Sangría 407

PORTUGUESE

Portuguese Tuna Pâté 30
Portuguese Clams with Sausage and Ham 202
Portuguese Linguiça Rolls 295

WEST AFRICAN

West African Filled Papaya Halves 173

COLD APPETIZERS

NUTS, SEEDS, AND CHIPS

Mediterranean Fried Almonds 1
Almonds with Apricots 2
Roman Almonds 2
Spanish Toasted Hazelnuts 2
Moorish Pine Nuts 3
Indian Cashews 3
Roquefort Walnuts or Pecans 3
Cantonese Fried Walnuts 4
Salted Mixed Nuts 4
Toasted Nuts Teriyaki 5
Bombay Cocktail Mix 5
Toasted Pumpkin Seeds 6
Philippine Sweet Potato Chips 6
Homemade Potato Chips 7
Homemade Tortilla Chips 298
Puerto Rican Plantain Chips 7
Caribbean Banana Chips 7
Hawaiian Coconut Chips 8
Crêpe Chips 8

OLIVES

Stuffed Green Olives 11
Stuffed Black Olives 11
Mexican Anchovy-Stuffed Olives 11
Italian Black Olives with Anchovies 12
Olive, Cheese, and Nut Hors d'Oeuvre 12
Wine-Marinated Spanish Olives 12
Marinated Greek Olives 13

DIPS

Blue Cheese Dip 17
Mushroom Dip 17
Eggplant Caviar 17

Baba Ghannouj (Middle Eastern Eggplant Dip) 18
Hummus bi Tahini (Middle Eastern Chickpea Dip) 19
Guacamole 21
Avocado Dip with Bacon 22
Avocado Dip with Caviar 22
Taramosalata (Greek Salted Fish Roe Dip) 22
Norwegian Red Caviar Dip 23
Sour Cream and Red Caviar Dip 23
Lobster Dip 23
Clam and Cream Cheese Dip 24
Smoked Salmon and Avocado Dip 24
Salmon Remoulade Dip 25
Tapénade (Provençal Hors d'Oeuvre of Olives, Anchovies, and Capers) 25

SPREADS

Roquefort Cheese Spread 27
Roquefort Cheese and Walnut Spread 27
Gorgonzola Cheese and Prosciutto Spread 27
Swedish Cheese Spread 28
Serbian Cheese Spread 28
Serbian Herb Cheese Spread 28
Shrimp Paste 29
Smoked Salmon Spread 30
Portuguese Tuna Pâté 30
Chicken and Almond Pâté 31
Chicken Liver Pâté 31
Chicken Liver Pâté in Aspic 32
Russian Liver Pâté 32
Liverwurst Pâté 32
Liverwurst Pâté with Mushrooms 33
Liverwurst Pâté with Bacon 34

CHEESE

Homemade Creamy Cheese 50
Herb Cheese 51
Liptauer 52

INDEX

INDEX

ABOUT THE AUTHOR

Sonia Uvezian was born and brought up in Beirut, Lebanon, the gastronomic capital of the Middle East. A concert pianist, she studied music in her native country and in New York City and has taught piano both privately and at the university level. She also worked for a number of years as a fashion model in New York. The author of five other highly successful cookbooks and a recipient of the prestigious R. T. French Tastemaker Award, Ms. Uvezian has contributed food articles and recipes to such magazines as *Vogue, House & Garden, Gourmet, Bon Appétit,* and *Family Circle* as well as to numerous newspapers and anthologies. Three of her previous books have been selections of the Book-of-the-Month Club, and three have been published in foreign editions. Sonia Uvezian is married to David Kaiserman, a concert pianist and university professor, and divides her time between the United States and Europe.

OTHER BOOKS BY SONIA UVEZIAN

THE CUISINE OF ARMENIA

THE BEST FOODS OF RUSSIA

THE BOOK OF SALADS

THE BOOK OF YOGURT

THE COMPLETE INTERNATIONAL
SANDWICH BOOK